Darren Allen is from old Whitstable, in the county of Kent. He writes non-fiction, novels, teleplays and graphic novels. His work addresses the nature of reality, the origin of civilisation, the horrors of work, death, gender, mental 'illness', Miss Genius, unconditional love, and life outside the spectacle. He is not qualified to write about any of these things, thank God.

Darren Allen
SELF & UNSELF
The meaning of everything *

expressive egg books

* not literally

Published by Expressive Egg Books

www.expressiveegg.org

First published in 2021, in England
Darren Allen has asserted his moral rights under
the Copyright, Designs and Patents Act 1988.
Front cover illustration by Ai Higaki.
Text design by Darren Allen.
Set in 10 pt Plantin on a 12.5 pt line.

ISBN: 978-1-8384073 3 9 (hardback)
ISBN: 978 1 8384073 0 8 (paperback)
ISBN: 978 1 8384073 1 5 (ePub)

Also available for Kindle.

Disclaimer: the author and publisher
accept no liability for actions inspired by this book.

10 9 8 7 6 5 4 3 2 1

Contents

by Darren Allen

Non-fiction: Natureculturenothing

THE APOCALYPEDIA

SELF AND UNSELF

33 MYTHS OF THE SYSTEM

Fiction: Things Unsaid

DROWNING IS FINE

PERPETUAL DAWN

Television Scripts

FIRED

BELLY UP!

Website & Blog

WWW.EXPRESSIVEEGG.ORG

Acknowledgements

This book is dedicated to the memory and spirit of Ivan Illich, Arthur Schopenhauer and Barry Long.

I would also like to thank the people who generously donated to my fund-raiser to help me take the time to write this book.

Particular thanks to Antony Floyd, Scott Newman, Jake Reilly, Jeanne Campos, Philip Cade and, of course, Ai Higaki.

'Imagine a large castle on an island, with almost inescapable dungeons. The jailor has installed every device to prevent the prisoners escaping, and he has taken one final precaution: that of hypnotizing the prisoners, and then suggesting to them that they and the prison are one. When one of the prisoners awakes to the fact that he would like to be free, and suggests this to his fellow prisoners, they look at him with surprise and say: "Free from what? We are the castle." What a situation!'

Colin Wilson, *The Outsider*

'People can be very different from each other, but their dreams are not, because in their dreams they award themselves the three or four things they desire, sooner or later, to a greater or lesser extent, but they always get them, everyone does; there is no one who seriously dreams himself empty-handed. That's why no one discovers himself in his dreams.'

Jens Peter Jacobsen, *Niels Lyhne*

Introduction

Ego made this world. Ego and world are each a metaphor for the other, with a common origin which, when consciously experienced, can free the individual self from both. This experience is neither objective nor subjective—it is what I call *panjective*—which means it can neither be literally described nor solipsistically moodied up, only gestured towards; by critically exploring what it is *not* and by metaphorically describing what it is *like*. This is what the present work does.

To put this another way, reality is ultimately mysterious, a mystery that is everywhere you look—because it is that which is looking. This doesn't mean that unmysterious thought—the kind that reasons about subjective impressions and objective things—is useless, or that the facts that it handles are illusions. It means that such thought reaches a limit beyond which it cannot pass. *Something else* has to cross over, a *something else* which, obviously enough, cannot be expressed with the thought it had to leave behind. If it does think, or reason, or attempt to express itself, it has to do it in another way; through the means of expression we call METAPHOR. And again, this is what this book aims to do.

*

Although it has to be presented as a linear A-to-B account, every part of the book is both connected to every other part, and also connected to the whole. This means, firstly, that it should be read twice, as only the linear account will be grasped the first time while, the second time, knowledge of what is to come will inform what is bringing the whole into focus. Secondly, some ideas presented at the beginning, particularly those referring to unself, consciousness and context, will initially appear rather hazy (or confusing, or even unpleasantly abstract). This is because the key terms in this book cannot be literally defined, or at least not all at once, and must either appear later, or 'reveal themselves' implicitly, gradually, in the whole. On a second reading, the difficult earlier sections will feel clearer and realer and erroneous objections—and, worse, *opinions*—will not get in the way.

Opinions have almost nothing to do with experience. You can have an opinion about love and death, but only while you're not experiencing them. So it is with everything of importance that I cover in this book. Please put your opinions aside as you read, not in order to blindly accept what I have to say, but to ensure that your experience is not filtered by second-hand ideas, as so often happens, particularly when reading a critique *of* that filtering mechanism.

This filtering mechanism is the SELF. It is a kind of psychological tool which has taken over the consciousness of mankind and become what we call EGO. Ego doesn't like to be criticised and employs various strategies to deal with the threat of criticism. Its usual response is to ignore the threat, ridicule it, drown it out with opinion or attempt to refute it with some kind of 'reasoning'; an avalanche of facts disconnected from the point. But because ego is not merely conceptual, but also affective, it will start to *feel* under attack before it has discovered the intellectual reason why. Something will feel 'off', something not quite right here. Ego will *then* start looking for reasons why it feels uncomfortable. It will find sentences it does not understand and accuse the author of being pretentious, or deliberately obfuscating, or a poor stylist. It will look for *and find* evidence that the author is not properly qualified to speak, or it will look for, and again find, inconsistencies in the system here presented and dismiss the whole thing as factually incorrect woo, or it will take ideas out of context and accuse the author of being racist, sexist, homophobic, hypocritical or downright evil. Ego will find these reasons, and it will *then* declare that the reasons have created the feelings, when the opposite is true, as it nearly always is. Nobody ever reacts negatively to a truthful philosophy because of what it says, but because of how it makes them feel.

*

Some parts of this book are quite difficult. It demands some effort, particularly at the beginning, where I have had to outline the metaphysical foundations and explain the key terms that follow in the [lighter, and more entertaining] main body of the work. Metaphysics is, actually, straightforward and enjoyable. One reason it appears, particularly for us in the West, difficult, dense and abstract, is because we are forced to talk about it in a language that has been degraded by thousands of years of unconscious use. This language has to be unpicked or reimagined, which doesn't always make for easy reading, particularly after a hard day's work.

I have been forced to use some ordinary words in a new way—chief among these *self* and *ego* (and 'selfish' which has a *much* broader meaning here that it usually does) but also various value-laden words, such as *beauty, truth, sanity, love, quality* and so on, along with a few less common technical words, such as *physicalism* and *solipsism*, all of which also have here a much wider meaning than they normally do. I have also invented a few new terms, such as *unself* (that which is not self), *panjective* (that which is neither objective nor subjective), and *nous, soma, thelema and viscera* (terms taken from Greek and Latin and adapted to describe the various fundamental elements of the self). Once you get a feel for these terms, the reading will be more agreeable.

That said, I have largely used language as it comes. This means that, as with all ordinary language, what I have to say takes its meaning not from diamond-like logical precision, but from the *context*—from the context that we share, and from the context of what I am saying in this particular book.

I must therefore ask for a charitable interpretation of what I am saying; which of course is how friends communicate.

We are unlikely to be friends if you are in the habit, as many are, of taking language to be reality, or of taking language as it comes to be an adequate representation *of* reality. My criticism of ideas and attitudes which are *not* real will then appear to be an intolerable attack *on* reality—or perhaps on the real people who hold these ideas and attitudes, or perhaps on you?—and my reimagined, contextually oriented language will appear to be quite outrageous, perhaps unsettling, as if reality itself is being rearranged. This will give you an irresistible urge to view what you disagree with *as* opinion (what you agree with will seem like cold, hard, obvious fact), and counter what I say *with* opinion—your own opinion, mass-opinion, expert-opinion, dictionary-opinion, rich-and-famous-opinion—or you'll zero in on inconsistencies, or on the style of my writing, or on *me*, in order to 'prove' me wrong, or to win an internal argument.

In the end, it is better that people who find my style annoying, or who are already starting to feel a bit put out, stop reading as soon as possible; that those offended by my use of 'man' to refer to 'humanity' (because it is stylistically superior) give up in a huff; that those who wish to enjoy a beautiful view, but aren't prepared to burn a few calories to do so, don't bother climbing; that literalists (atheists and theists, rationalists and empiricists, physicalists and idealists) give up trying to literally understand the non-literal truth of what I say; and that readers who are attached to their beliefs and personalities, and who feel swelling outrage when they read an attack on *all* beliefs and personalities, throw the book out the window. It is better that the easily offended, and the aggressively contentious, and the entirely conventional, and the completely rational, and the completely irrational read books that they agree with, that are popular, that sell well, that are 'of the time'. I haven't written *Self and Unself* for them. In fact I have deliberately written a book that is out of step, not just with this time, but with time itself; because I only wish to speak with people who are. Even if there are only the two of us.

Map

A map does not need to be perfectly accurate, nor even very interesting. The purpose of a map, after all, is not to *mimic* the terrain, which is impossible, but to take us through it. Spending too much time looking at a map, or thinking about it, will not only cause you to miss the beauty of the landscape, but you'll get lost.

*

Self *can be said* to be composed of four MODES (or modalities). The boundaries between them are not fixed and definite, but we can say that SOMA comes to us as body, sensation, perception or matter, NOUS appears as thought, idea, conception or mind, VISCERA as feeling, affection, psyche or atmosphere and THELEMA as will, energy, action or movement.

These modalities can be divided into three sets of POLES (or POLARITIES): SUBJECTIVITY and OBJECTIVITY, ACTIVITY and PASSIVITY, and MANIFESTATION and REPRESENTATION.

Maps represent the knowable parts of a terrain in knowable relation to each other. In this they are useful. This map, however, shows the knowable self in relation to something which is *unknowable*; unself. Such a relation must, therefore, not be taken literally, but as a METAPHOR. All references to such metaphorical "relationships" in this book are enclosed in double "scare quotes".

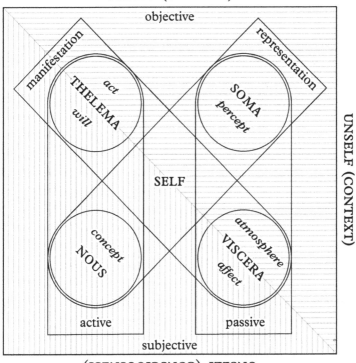

Self & Unself

There are true flowers
in this painted world

§ 1.

There is a SELF here reading these words, which I call ME. It is a caused, three-dimensional fact existing in what I call space and passing through or changing in what I call time.

The 'purpose' of the self is to generate the world-for-me from the world-in-itself. The experienced world of the self is not of reality as it actually is, but is an image or reflection of reality, a REPRESENTATION or MANIFESTATION of *something else*.

This *something else* that representations and manifestations are "of" is inaccessible to the self. It appears to self either as an unfathomable *distal* CONTEXT, "beyond" objective representation, or it appears as an unfathomable *proximal* CONSCIOUSNESS, "behind" self experience.

Self, in other words, does not and cannot know who I really am or what anything really is. Self can only know its own *medial* experience. Anything else—if there *is* anything else—is "beyond" or "behind" a wall which self cannot surmount.

§ 2.

Self, by itself, can *never* be sure what its representations and manifestations are *of*. It can be sure *enough* that, for example, another self exists (which I call YOU or IT) and it can be sure *enough* about where you or it comes from (God perhaps, or a granule of DNA), but it can *never* know what you really are or what anything really is. To the extent that I am a self, I am effectively imprisoned. Even though you are obviously *somehow* a self like me, even though the carpet is still obviously *somehow* a thing like me, you and it are still only *actually* being experienced *within* my self. What you and it really, finally *are* is, ultimately, inaccessible to the self.

This is reasonably obvious for so-called *secondary properties*, such as hardness or colour. It's clear to most people that the green of the grass, for example, is not the actual green, but an interpretation in the mind; of light-frequency data that comes to the mind through the optic nerve. We do not see light frequencies, we see, or self experiences, colour. We do not hear vibrations in the air, we hear, or self experiences, sound. Frequencies and vibrations exist independently of mind, but there is no such thing as an 'unheard sound' or an 'unseen colour' because sounds and colours are functions of mind. If a tree falls in a forest and there's nobody around to hear, it obviously makes something—but that something, equally obviously, cannot be our experience of sound.

This doesn't mean secondary properties are *completely invented* by the mind. There is, quite clearly, a fundamental connection between our experience of green, in here, and the *actual* nature of the light, out there, 'bouncing off' an oak leaf, or between the crashing sound we hear when a tree falls, and the *actual* sound waves rocking through the air. This is how we all know, despite fanciful philosophical speculation, that we are sharing the same world of greeny greens and crashy crashes. We all know that our senses are *almost* completely reliable; but we also know that, *somehow*, they are not; that there is a *personal* aspect to sensory experience. Even so-called realists concede that mind *somehow creates* experience from sensation; that the self doesn't just *report*, it also *interprets*. This is clear to most people, which is why it forms the basis of practically every theory of perception ever proposed. Far less clear, far more difficult to accept, is the idea that the self generates our experience of the *primary property* of LITERALITY.

§3.

LITERALISM is the belief or experience (the former arising from the latter) that representations are analogous or abbreviated expressions of *knowable things*. For the literalist, the noetic tree (the idea, word or symbol that represents tree) and the somatic tree (that big, beautiful brown and green *thing* over there) are fundamentally the same as the *actual* tree; as the 'tree-in-itself'. Literalist definitions can be flexible and literalist logics can be 'fuzzy', but all forms of literalist thought and expression are completely or essentially *knowable* (describable as an idea, or thinkable in symbolic thought, or graspable as an emotion) and founded on the assumption—and it only ever can be an assumption—that reality is also, in the same way, knowable. There is, in other words, nothing elusive, ineffable or mysterious about the literalist tree; the eye can see it, the mind can know it, the heart can like or want it.

Self-generated *objective* literality can be said to comprise two equally unmysterious, comprehensible laws; the law of FACTICITY and the law of CAUSALITY. Facticity means that every thing must *either* be a literal thing or a literal non-thing (*x* is *either x or* not-*x*) and causality means that every literal thing must have been literally caused by some other thing (*If x then y*), all these things known, and only *quantitatively* known, in their relation to one other, which is to say RELATIVELY.

The whole ordinary world, what *the self* calls 'the real world', is a massive collection of caused facts existing within, and related to each other by, the self. Self, in other words, generates space and time. As with secondary properties of sound and colour, the fact that this experience is 'generated' doesn't mean that it's *invented*, that there isn't *something* literally 'spacetimey' out there, that the tree my mind thinks of and the tree my mind sees are illusions, or that factual and causal relations are a battery of *ad hoc* assumptions and arbitrary inventions, or that mathematics and logic are entirely subjective, or that the word 'literally' is literally meaningless. Only an abstract philosopher or postmodern artist or complete madman could seriously believe that an unperceived tree, or planet, or Pharaoh, does not exist *at all*, or that language and logic are literally meaningless, or that there is no difference between dreams and waking reality. The fact that you are reading these words and that you even approximately understand them is almost indisputable evidence that something mind-graspable exists beyond your self. All manifest communication would be impossible—including communication with completely new cultures—if there weren't something in reality which was literal, that we unquestionably share. What the self-made nature of literality means is that *ultimately* self doesn't, and cannot, *take* literal, factual, causal experience *from* the world: it *brings* literal experience *to* the world.

§4.

Self does not learn objective literality like it learns the individual facts and causes that comprise it, for self is *itself* a literal thing. The spatial position of my subjective self, its experience of your objective self, the causal relation of that experience to who you *actually* are, the relation of you to him, to her, to them, to it... all of these relations somehow exist out there, but their literalness, their 'graspableness', is a function of the inherent, fundamental nature of self, not ultimately *learnt* from anything external to self. It is clearly the case that self can be said to *somehow* learn facticity and causality. A developing baby *does* learn to separate thing from thing, object from subject, babself from mumself; but it evidently does not, and cannot, learn this *from* facts and causes, the existence of which are presupposed by the very self that is grasping them.* How can self learn facticity and causality *from* experience of the world, when facticity and causality are the essential prerequisites *for* that experience? How can you learn that objects are separate from each other in space, without *first* being able to separate objects from one another? How can we ever be sure that perception and conception provide us with an accurate picture of the world, without relying *on* perception and conception?

What self *does* learn from experience are secondary properties; the causal facts, or factual causes, that make up the world. Because these are acquired, they can be lost by self or, in the case of impaired selves, not acquired at all. You can be born blind to light and colour, but you cannot be born blind to time and space. Likewise, secondary properties can be experimentally 'thought away'; self can imagine an object without position, colour, form, substance and state, but, as Immanuel Kant pointed out,† it can never think away the

---

* Arthur Schopenhauer, *On the Fourfold Root of Sufficient Reason*
† Immanuel Kant, *The Critique of Pure Reason*

primary properties of facticity and causality. It can neither perceive nor conceive of a factless, causeless object because it is born with this understanding 'hardwired' into perception and conception. Our experience of space and what we call 'time' would be impossible unless we brought facticity and causality *to* our experience. There is no way even to imagine how it could be otherwise.

§5.

What then is the nature of reality, "behind" the literal, objective representation of self? What, that is to say, is the nature of the THING-IN-ITSELF*? Self *alone* only has two options. Either it can concede that self *cannot* experience the thing-in-itself (or deny that it exists at all); in which case anything goes. This is the position of the SOLIPSIST, or SUBJECTIVIST, for whom *everything* is self. The other option is to assume that although the thing-in-itself, the universe "beyond" me, is fundamentally unreachable, it is *still* essentially and entirely literal. This is the position of the PHYSICALIST, or OBJECTIVIST.

Although physicalists and solipsists are constantly at odds, and although both positions are superficially distinct, they are fundamentally the same. The reality of the solipsist is subjectively literal—there is nothing "prior" to the subjectivities of the self—just as the reality of the literalist is objectively so—there is nothing "beyond" the objects of the self. Thus we can speak of solipsism and physicalism as distinct, but they are, ultimately, *both* self-located, or EGOIC WORLDVIEWS; which is why each, two poles on the same continuum, ultimately entails the other. Objectivity at its subjectless extreme collapses into complete, solipsistic, subjectivity—for all I can actually find in the objects of self's experience *is* self, or self-generated representation—while subjectivity in turn, at *its* limits, reveals total objectivity—for if I am the world in toto, there can be no [objectively] validated I to be found *in* that world, no true consciousness; just a chaos of objective bits.

Egoism—solipsistic / physicalist literalism—began at some point towards the end of the Palaeolithic era, with what

---

* Ibid.

we call *idealism* and *dualism*, the semi-literal / semi-solipsist idea that reality (for the idealist) literally *is*, or (for the dualist) is somehow caused or magically animated *by*, mind (or by 'soul' or 'God'). The normal word for idealism-dualism today is *superstition* or, in its most extreme form, *religion*. Around five hundred years ago the useless magical element was ditched in favour of what we now call 'physicalism' (also known as 'materialism' or, more absurdly, 'realism'), the idea that reality is a fully literal thing, which self—specifically the rational mind—can indirectly access. Today, we usually call physicalism *science* or, in its most extreme form, SCIENTISM.

§6.

Scientism is an extreme form of literalism, but some form of literalism has been the assumed foundation of all institutional thought since institutions began, around 6,000 years ago. There are, however, four catastrophic problems with literalism and all the scientific-religious philosophies built upon it;

i.   Self can *never* know what lies beyond its reach in space, if anything does, because self *creates* space. It cannot judge its own reliability without first presupposing it. Self just proceeds *as if* the thing-in-itself out there matches the literal representation it experiences in here. For the literalist, an essentially comprehensible universe walks into the self where it is literally doubled as my experience of it.* Self then *assumes* that what it generates *as* space and time reflects a universe that fundamentally *is* spatio-temporal. The literalist can never be sure if this is so—if there isn't *something else*, beyond its grasp—so he has to assume it. Not because, as he declares, this *modus operandi* 'works' (indeed and of course it does) but because he *has* to assume it. He has no choice; the literal self can *only* experience *meter readings* (its own, or those of the tools it builds), which means that the literalist must posit a miraculous ghost world beyond experience to explain what those readings are of; if, that is, he seriously reflects on such matters, which is rare. Vague gestures towards 'God', ignoring

---

* Arthur Schopenhauer, *On the Fourfold Root of Sufficient Reason*

the question of what anything actually *is*, or pretending it is meaningless to ask such questions are more common, all of which allow the modern assumption that the objective universe *is* as it *appears* to rest without question.

The physicalist in particular is forced to cling to the 'meter reading' view of the universe—to assume that the meter readings of the self accurately reflect objective reality—even when they inform him that he is in error. Physicalist philosophers believe that philosophy should limit its claims to what the natural sciences can discover—that philosophy is really just a preliminary stage, or 'handmaiden', to the 'real' work of the physicalist scientist. But when, in the first half of the twentieth century, those same scientists discovered that ultimately [quantum] reality *cannot* be literally grasped by the self, their discoveries were effectively ignored. The problems that physicalist thinkers endeavour to solve, such as the relation between mental and physical phenomena, are implicitly founded on a literal logic that has been discovered, by the same science they uphold, to be incompatible with 'objective' reality.

ii.   Just as the literal self cannot know what lies beyond spatial representation, so it is incapable of grasping the cause of its experience in what it calls time. It has no idea of how facticity and causality—a.k.a. THE UNIVERSE—could have causally emerged from non-facticity and non-causality; because it *can* have no idea. This is not a question of 'not knowing' something, of not yet having the right theory or enough data. There is *no way to think about* how time and space could 'emerge' from non-time and space; and so literalists just ignore the matter, or focus on the measurable effects of this 'emergence' or, again, they posit miracles to explain it. While theist literalists are quite open about this, informing us that [an equally literal] 'God' created the universe, atheist literalists, embarrassed by magic, prefer either to wave the problem away with 'well it must have happened' and pretend that this happening can't have been miraculous, or they sneak causality into their assumptions, using words like 'happen', 'came to be' and 'emerge' to describe the source of causality itself. But however the miracle is framed, a miracle remains the only way for literalists to explain or accept the incoherent absurdity— at the heart of both standard modern theism and standard modern atheism—that causelessness caused causality.

iii.   Literalism cannot explain the cause of experience, or what it calls 'consciousness'. For the literalist, consciousness somehow emerged from non-consciousness; conscious human beings somehow emerged from unconscious rocks and amoebae ('phylogenetically'), and conscious adults somehow emerged from unconscious chromosomes and embryos ('ontogenetically'). But again, there is no way even to think about how this could happen; how something non-experiential can possibly generate experience (or, alternatively, how quantity can generate quality) without reducing the latter to the former. We can imagine, and so predict, how sand-dunes can 'emerge' from sand, or ice from water, or ecological breakdown from human activity. There is something quantitatively detectable in the latter which conceivably, or scientifically, leads to the former. But there is *nothing* in non-experience that can conceivably lead to experience or predict its emergence. Qualitative consciousness 'emerging' from quantitative matter is as feasible as language emerging from biscuits. It's not merely amazing that it happened (the so-called 'argument from incredulity' which physicalists are very eager to dismiss) but impossible to imagine that it *could* happen, at least causally; so the literalist just says 'God did it' or, these days, 'emergentism did it', which amounts to the same thing.

     This leaves two further puzzles for the literalist. One is how the material mind can cause immaterial consciousness, and the other is how non-physical consciousness can influence physical matter. These, the so-called 'mind-body problem' and 'problem of mental causation', are insoluble mysteries for literalists. They come up with plenty of theories (or souls or gods) that they think can explain them, but none addresses the *inherent* absurdity of the problems, which is why nobody has come *anywhere near* answering them. Those answers which are offered all beg not one but two questions; the first is what

SELF AND UNSELF

the matter *is* that mind is supposed to influence or emerge from, which remains impregnable to, and untouched by, any kind of literalism, and the second is what the consciousness *is* that experiences that matter, which is either declared to be a quantitative, literal thing like any other literal thing or to be an 'epiphenomenal illusion', which is to say, to not exist at all.

iv.   The fourth literalist enigma is literal, objective knowledge itself, or rational thought, which is assumed, from the beginning of the literal, objective world, to have a fundamentally one-to-one correspondence with reality. But how is the literalist to know? How can literal thought determine whether literal thought is literally representing reality? Just as there can be nothing within an android that can validate whether it is conscious, so there can be nothing within rational thought that can validate thinking itself. One can only judge the accuracy of thought, meaning the fundamental thinkableness of reality, by experiencing from a standpoint "external" to rationality, but this is something the literalist cannot do.

This problem (called the 'no independent access' problem*) cripples the progress of physicalist understanding that modern literalists appeal to. How is one to further knowledge, or discover a more elementary law than those which currently obtain, unless one steps out of the known and introduces a new hypothesis which is *ultimately* unrelated to the interconnected network of perceptions and conceptions that physicalism is based on? This, one of the great mysteries of science, is unsolvable by science, because you have to make a non-literal leap over the factual-causal fence in order to do so. Immanuel Kant, Henri Poincaré, Albert Einstein and Max Planck all made this point, as did, in a different way, David Hume[†], who argued that experience can never lead to reliable general principles, because such principles rest *on* a dependable regularity which can never be found *in* experience. We can *never* be completely sure that the next swan we come across won't be bright red. While we remain within the coordinates of the knowable we can *never* be sure that the laws of nature don't change or evolve, or that an untested hypothesis (of

---

* Immanuel Kant, *Logic* (following Berkeley)
† David Hume, *Treatise of Human Nature*

which there are an infinite number) doesn't more accurately fit the facts. Hume himself was driven to despair by his famous 'problem of induction', because it invalidates scientific certainty; which is, once again, why physicalists pretend that it doesn't exist or is of no importance.

Extreme literalists—physicalists—consider the universe to be *entirely* composed of separate comprehensible parts, particles or *granules* relating to each other in predictable ways in order to produce a measurable outcome; that the universe, or reality, is, like the self, a kind of MACHINE. They are unable to view reality as something non-mechanical, something which, despite clearly having a literal machine-like component, is also ultimately, unpredictable, immeasurable, spontaneous and uncaused; the state of experience we call ALIVE.

Perhaps, you might think, the physicalist considers the mechanistic universe to be just a metaphor? But if that's the case, why is it preferred over an organic metaphor? Or maybe it *is* literally true; but then how are we to know? What kind of test could be devised to confirm such a theory? How could it ever be refuted? Of course it could not. There is no way, *ever*, to test whether the world is mechanical with mechanical tests, any more than rationality can determine whether rationality can, ultimately, know the world.

Literalism is founded on facticity and causality, but is unable to explain how non-facticity and non-causality could have created facticity and causality—how the universe, consciousness, experience or knowledge came to be—for the transparent reason that it is impossible; and so all literalists, of whatever stripe, have to posit miracles to explain it, or redefine the problem out of existence, or knock up a smokescreen of philosophical-technical jargon to hide their ignorance, or, the most common approach, just pretend it doesn't exist (management never addresses consciousness, politicians never mention the universe and the word 'ineffable' is never heard in the lab), proceeding as if consciousness is either an illusion, or a literal material object inhabiting an essentially comprehensible clockwork universe that *just happened*.

This bizarre reality, a conscious universe spontaneously springing from the head of Zeus, mirroring in some equally fantastic way a reality that can *never* be directly experienced, is the one that most people in the world inhabit today. Nobody seriously explores the nature or the limits of this make-believe ideology, our 'worldview', at least not at work. It is assumed to be the only explanation of the universe, although that assumption cannot itself be literally justified without getting sucked into a tautologous mindwarp—you can't *literally* prove that literal proof is the only method of discovering truth without *automatically* ruling out non-literal methods. Thus, all non-literal accounts of reality are not reasoned away, but reflexively dismissed—as insane forms of subjectivist solipsism.

§7.

SOLIPSISM is the only way to reject physicalism *within the confines of the self*. The solipsist denies *objective* facticity and causality, either rationally concluding (as Hume, one of the godfathers of modern solipsism, did*) that neither can be found in the world, or irrationally dismissing them as forms of control by external agencies (souls, gods, governments, aliens, *them*). Instead of the factual and the causal, the solipsist adheres to the UNREAL and the ARBITRARY; a subjective reality which has no objective counterpart, and therefore is based on random choice, personal whim or whatever ASSOCIATION (association, based on similarity, being 'solipsistic causality') is at hand.

The extreme solipsist—the SCHIZOPHRENIC—is confined to a catatonic universe of self-generated illusion, but most solipsists can function perfectly well in the world without retreating to an inner world of concepts. The high-functioning solipsist inhabits the same egoic world as the physicalist, making the same literal distinction between the inner subject and the outer object, but solipsistic *meaning* is handed over to the subject in order to serve the temporary needs of ego, which frequently demands that rationality, objectivity and causal reason be abandoned so that it can justify itself and lie to others.

---

* Ibid.

While orientation towards the objective-world of physicalism is favoured by businessmen, managers, scientists and men, the subjectivity of solipsism is the preferred philosophy of liars, artists, addicts and women. The former require a useful representation of the world which they can rationally defend, the latter a useless representation which they can irrationally defend. Because both are essentially egoic—essentially the same—and because life is a complex affair, self can leap from one to the other, choosing which to adhere to over the course of a life, or even a day. A man may be a rational literalist in class, a semi-rational solipsist in Church, a practical literalist in the office, an airy-fairy solipsist at the guitar or in the art-gallery, an android-like physicalist when he is arguing with his wife and a self-absorbed hyper-idealist when he has a breakdown and just can't take it anymore.

§8.

If there is *something else* in reality, something in the thing-in-itself that is not physically or solipsistically self, then it can neither be represented by self nor make sense to it. If, that is to say, there is something in reality that is inaccessible to a self which is *either* a literal object *or* an unreal subject, then that *something else* must be *both* object *and* subject, *both* NON-LITERAL *and* REAL. Here, this is called PANJECTIVE.

Non-literal means non-factual, or PARADOXICAL (*x* is *both* *x and* non-*x*) and real means not self-generated; it is UNCAUSED (*x* is *always x*). Panjective reality is, therefore, *absolute,* meaning that it is real but is not 'known' through the quantitative relations of its literal factual-causal parts. If the thing-in-itself is *in any way* absolute, self can create self-graspable perceptions, conceptions, affections and motions "from" it, but there is something in the thing-in-itself "beyond" both objective knowledge, or fact, and subjective knowledge, or invention.

The absolute nature of the thing-in-itself doesn't just mean that it is ultimately ineffable to self, but that *its "relationship" to the world is also ineffable.** Self can *say* that the thing-in-itself spatially "precedes" or temporally "causes" the

---

* Arthur Schopenhauer, *The World as Will and Representation*

29

experience of self—self can *express* itself dualistically—but if the thing-in-itself is somehow unselfish, then such dualism can only ever be non-literally, or *metaphorically*, true; for, ultimately, there can be no relation between reality and representation.

These are rather unusual ideas. If, ultimately, reality is absolute, there is not *just* 'something else' in the thing-in-itself, forever beyond the relative self, there must also, somehow, be nothing *but* something else. If there are ultimately no separate facts and no separate causes (or factual associations)—no time and space in the thing-in-itself—there can be, *ultimately*, no difference between anything and anything else, which means that, again, ultimately, there can be no difference between me and the rest of the universe, *at any time*.

This literally unbelievable idea is, you would *think*, easy to verify. If I look around and find that I am surrounded by separate things which are not each other and not me—things which include the entire past and future of the universe—then I can probably conclude that I am not all things at all times, that I am 'just me', my ordinary self. The question, however, is not what I am 'looking around' *at*, but what the 'I' *is* that is doing the looking. It may be obvious that my self is not everything else, *but it is far from obvious that I am my self.*

§9.

Who am I? It is such a simple question, and yet I *keep* getting it wrong. I get it wrong by looking for, and finding, *answers*. There can be no definitive *self-knowable* answer to the question 'who am I?' because self only has its own experience to judge by. If I am somehow "more" or "other" than self, self cannot know it, any more than a torch can 'know' darkness.

The torch of self can reason itself to the limits of its light—it can know it cannot know beyond a certain point—but it cannot *experience* what lies beyond what it knows, for, self-evidently, self cannot be what it is not, any more than torch-light can be dark. Self therefore, *by* itself, concludes that either there is nothing beyond the known, or, if there is, that there is nothing beyond the known that is not self-like.

It is night and a drunk man is looking for his keys in a pool of light under a street lamp. A friend comes along and asks him what he is doing. 'I'm looking for my keys', he says. 'Where did you drop them?' the friend asks, and the man points into the darkness. 'Over there', he says. 'Over there? Then why aren't you looking over there?' 'Because', says the drunk man, 'the light is *here*'.*

This famous allegory more or less describes the activity of self, which looks *with* self for something *other* than self; because 'that's where the light is'. The difference being that 'the light' doesn't just limit what self sees, but what it *is*—and therefore *can* see. Self, by itself, is identified with the 'light' of the noetic, visceral, thelemic and somatic self, and so it cannot say, of the object of its search, that it is *in* the darkness because, for the self, *there is no such thing*. If the story were to continue it would end with the drunkard and his friend arguing about the existence of the night.

Self does not conclude that the universe is entirely self-like by inspecting *facts* and *causes*—or 'evidence'—because facticity and causality are, despite accurately applying to self-like aspects of the thing-in-itself, ultimately self-made. There can be no fact or cause *within* self that can determine whether facticity completely applies to reality *"beyond"* self. Because self can *only* inspect facts, and strings of causal (or associative) reason, it can *only* assume that reality beyond its representation is completely factual and causal. This assumption forms the sand-like foundation of *all* egoic, literalist, philosophies, whether physicalist, solipsist, dualist or idealist.

§ 10.

Everything that self experiences is a representation of *something else* which is ultimately an inaccessible mystery to it, to me. Self must therefore *guess* whether that mystery is *actually* mysterious, or if it just seems so because it is inaccessible. Self can be completely confident about that within the thing-in-itself which is knowable, but it can never know whether there is something "within" the thing-in-itself that is unknowable,

---

* Attributed to Nasreddin

31

because it cannot step outside of itself and experience, or *be*, that which its meter readings are *of*.

With one exception. There is *one* thing-in-itself in the universe, and *only* one, that I do not need to 'read' from the meter of the self to experience, one thing-in-itself in the universe that I can *be*, that I *am*, immediately and directly, that I do not have to go *via* my self to experience, and that is CONSCIOUSNESS, the experience or state I call I.

I am, unquestionably, the *one* thing in the entire universe that I have direct, inward access to. I am the only thing in the universe which *is* that which representation is *of*. I *am* the consciousness which self—the entire apparent universe— only ever appears *to*. I, like every other thing-in-itself, appear or manifest *as* self, but, ultimately, I *qualitatively* "precede" quantitative self-perception, self-conception, self-facticity and self-causality. Ultimately, to put it simply, *I am not my self*.

I am UNSELF.

§11.

If literalism holds, unself is just *inaccessible* self. They are essentially the same, except that the former is out of reach. Modern literalists sometimes call such an out-of-reach self the 'unconscious', a hidden realm said to mysteriously influence the functioning of self. This inaccessible subjective realm 'inside' of self is conceived of in the same way as the inaccessible objective realm 'outside' of self, which is to say, once again, literally. We can deductively piece the bits of the unconscious together by psychoanalytically studying its effects, but we can never access it directly, and therefore can never be sure *what* it literally is, or even, rather more seriously, *if* it literally is.

If, however, the literalist account of the thing-in-itself is *fundamentally* false, if there is anything non-literal about the unselfish thing-in-itself of self, then it is *somehow* non-factual and non-causal. Not completely non-factual and non-causal; *something* "within" the thing-in-itself *must* be isolable, factual and causal—REPRESENTABLE—otherwise nothing would make sense. It is only through our connection with a vast and interconnected, coherent and completely dependable tapestry of facts, sewn together with causal threads, that we know with total confidence that we are not dreaming. But there is no *reason* to suppose that consciousness is entirely literal or indeed entirely inaccessible; reasons themselves are accessible, literal things. If the thing-in-itself that I am transcends literality, then it must somehow be both paradoxical and uncaused (or UNTHINKABLE and ETERNAL), and if it *is* somehow paradoxical and uncaused, then there must, first of all, somehow be no separation between the unself that I am here, which I call CONSCIOUSNESS, and the unself that everything is there, which I call CONTEXT. Even more extraordinarily, there must *somehow* also be no separation in space or time between the unself that I am here and now and every "other" unself in the universe out there. *Ever.*

Thus, although the fact that I am the only thing in the universe I can access from within *appears* to be solipsism, *nothing* that appears to the imagination can *ever* be an accurate idea or image of unself. The idea that 'my unself is every other unself' may evoke in the imagination of the *self* a fabulous—bordering on insane—literal image of separate glowing minds conglomerating in some kind of single solipsistic gas, but only by literally cutting off consciousness (here) from the [imagined] context (there). If, however, literalism doesn't hold, then I am *somehow* one with the context, with the entire universe; the *absolute opposite* of solipsism. In fact it is the *self*, which can only ever experience itself, which is, or inevitably terminates in, extreme solipsistic subjectivism.

If unself is in *any* way non-literal, it must be the case that consciousness and context are one, but there is no *thing* 'here' and 'now' which merges with, or turns out to be the same as, a *thing* 'there' and 'then', because there *are* no separate things; there are no other things, no prior things and no subsequent things. This leaves the solid, real, reliable, shared representation of the objective world, and the personal, insubstantial but equally real representation of the subjective world, completely intact, while transcending objective and subjective *dominance* of that world, allowing *something else* to take the wheel.

§12.

Self, by itself, rejects unself. Somatically, self takes unself to be invisible, non-factual, supernatural and impossible to locate in the world (either in the objective, literal world or in the subjective, solipsistic world). Noetically, self finds unself inconceivable, contradictory, absurd and indistinguishable from fantasy, invention, madness and even fascism. Viscerally, self is irritated, bored, confused or disturbed by unself, and all talk of it, whether meaningful or meaningless. Self doesn't have to *try* and react in this way, or to deny that unself exists by appealing to the ideas, sensations, feelings and actions of self, any more than it has to *try* or learn to experience caused facts in space. Self, insofar as it is only self, *automatically* rules out unself. It *cannot* experience something else essentially different to itself any more than an ear can hear the colour blue. For the dualist self something else does exist—a soul, or a 'mind'—but it is self-like (i.e. *not* something else), while, for the physicalist and the idealist, *nothing* else exists; there is just self. In both cases, if there *is* something else, self alone cannot experience it. Unself can no more exist to self than a fact or idea within a dream can prove the existence of a waking world; *if I have never been awake*. Only knowledge of a consistent, objective waking world can throw an inconsistent, subjective dream world into doubt. Without the former there is no standard by which to judge the reality of the latter.

Imagine a blind man who believes that colour is a conspiracy. He hears talk of colour, but he refuses to believe it really exists. Or imagine a deaf man who watches people listen to music, smile with pleasure or get up and dance to it. He constructs a theory that music is a kind of electricity that makes people restless, that twitches their faces and jerks their muscles. 'Well yes', you might say, 'so it is; but that electricity has *quality*, like the lovely colours you see in a beautiful painting or the lovely odour from baking bread'. And then, from your metaphor, he will understand. But what if he is blind to *quality*? Like an alien, or a manager, who doesn't understand humour? Then what metaphor can you offer to bridge the gap?

Likewise, because for self everything within the world is a fact caused by another fact, there can be no place within this world for 'radical initiation'—an uncaused act of FREE WILL—so self must either assume that such acts are impossible, or impute them to some literal thing beyond the world. As self can find no evidence *within* the world for this literal thing, it must either spin it from its own imagination, which is to say invent a divine being, or soul, which freely causes what we experience, or dismiss that same being or soul, along with free-will, as a ridiculous fantasy. When free will is viewed through the lens of self—sensually, rationally, verbally, emotionally—it vanishes. It cannot exist, because the matter of self is subject to the same inevitable causality as all matter.*

This difference between an unspeakable freedom of consciousness "within" self and world, and a comprehensible determinism reigning *as* self and world, is why the former is so much more obvious to us (unless of course we wish to blame someone or something for our fears, lies and vices; then we're suddenly, helplessly, unfree), while the latter must be arrived at by intellectual effort. It's also why when we attempt to articulate our instincts for freedom, the importance of it, we often run up against 'reasonable objections' which miss the point; *by being reasonable*. Take, as an example, the demand for free speech. As soon as it becomes explicit, we find we do not want *literal* 'freedom' to shout 'fire' in a packed space when there is no fire, or *literal* 'freedom' to incite mass murder, or *literal* 'freedom' for people to rain mindless abuse down upon our heads; 'freedom', that is to say, for *self* to say what it wants. The freedom of speech we demand is for *consciousness* to be able to say what it pleases, no matter what explicit form it takes. The lawmakers of the egoic world cannot tell the difference, which is why they ban the *word* 'fire', while allowing panic to spread by non-literal means.

Self, therefore, can never discover freedom. It can only discover slavery. If free will exists it can only be in the absence of self; meaning the absence of causality, and therefore compulsion, and in the absence of facticity, and therefore boundary; which is to say, in unselfish consciousness.

---

* Arthur Schopenhauer, *On the Will in Nature*

§13.

When self talks about consciousness, it is only ever talking about self; self-willed *attention* to the percepts, concepts, affects and actions of self. When literalist philosophers of mind use the term 'consciousness', they are usually referring to egoic focus *on* some *thing*; an *isolated* sensation, feeling, thought or act. When self investigates attention, or focused awareness, it finds only a series of disconnected sensations, feelings, thoughts and acts. It then logically concludes that 'really' no unified or "prior" consciousness exists. This is like a man who walks around a room looking for himself, closely inspecting everything, realising that each thing in the room is not him, and then finally concluding that he's not really there.

The room is unself; the thing-in-itself which appears to me from within as consciousness and from without as the context, which I consciously experience. Self focuses on, picks out or ISOLATES bits of the thing-in-itself—things or FACTS—into its spatial attention. These things are not just SUBJECTIVE, coming from within the body (volition, conception, affection) or OBJECTIVE, coming from without (action, character, perception) but subjectivity and objectivity (factual-causal separation) are themselves brought into being *by* the isolating activity of self. The objective form of the world (its primary and secondary qualities—its colours, flavours and states, *and* its factual-causal existence in space) is not just created *by*, or is indistinguishable *from*, the subject; the difference between subject and object *itself* comes into being through the activity of the self. The corresponding subjective attention of the self—the thinking, feeling and willing that I experience as a *knower*—may 'come from' or be a 'result' of the various objective things of the world, which are, to the self, the *known*, but before the self forms, when I am extremely young, or when self is softened or suppressed, there *is* no knower and known, no subject and object, just a felt totality in which that and thou are indistinguishable from I and me. In such a state, I experience unself as the one and only, as nature's sole, ontological and essentially *unknowable* primitive.

§ 14.

When self looks for consciousness or context—for unself—it only ever finds *parts*; perceptions and conceptions, things and facts, ideas and expressions, subjects and objects. It can no more find *the whole* than a bitmap image or mosaic can display a continuous gradient. The harder the 'bit-making' self looks for unself, the more confused it gets. Eventually it concludes that *only* functional bits exist, which is to say; a unified unselfish consciousness and context do not exist.

Self creates subjects and objects *from* unself, then asks whether consciousness and context are subjective or objective—for that is the only question it *can* ask—which automatically disposes of unself. If unself is objective, then it can be discovered with scientific method; which means it's a thing, which means it's not unself. If it is subjective, then it can be whatever you like, which means it's not real. Physicalist philosophers and scientists are forced to conclude that unself does not exist, that consciousness is 'really' isolating attention upon a 'bundle' of self-modes which we *take* to be consciousness, that the context is 'really' a collection of things which the mind grasps piecemeal. For the physicalist, what we 'really' experience are elements of the mechanical self, not anything like a unified operating consciousness or an unfathomable present, which are illusions. The possibility that both subjectivity and objectivity are "secondary" to a "preceding" consciousness eludes the literalist; he cannot imagine that although measurable objective brain activity logically correlates with subjective states of self, and vice versa—for they are the inner and outer states of the same thing—both are, ultimately, the "result" of *something else* which can be detected by neither. We cannot find this something else with the subjective or objective self any more than a torch can find a shadow; it is only by switching off the torch that darkness 'appears'.

Solipsists, equally blind to the unifying whole of contextual-conscious experience—but rejecting literalist accounts of a reliable objective world—are forced to conclude that consciousness does exist, but that it is *all me*; all my literal self.

For the solipsist what *you* really experience is an unknowable illusion. *You* might believe you exist in a reliable world, just as a torch might believe it creates light, but, says the solipsist, really your entire self is sustained by my 'electricity' (or by that of various symbolic / associative substitutes for me, such as God, the devil, the Rothschilds, the right, the left, etc., etc.).

Such accounts can make nothing of either the actual experience of a unified consciousness which transcends subjectivity and objectivity, or the evident necessity for one. Conscious experience (meaning *heightened* conscious experience) requires no object (it arises for no reason) and decreases subjectivity (it takes you out of yourself). What's more, not only do we experience reality from a unified I, but we couldn't possibly make sense of experience without it. Without a continuous sense of I, subjective and objective experience would be fractured into static shards, or a nightmarish flip-book of isolated moments with no identity threading through them, everything real, all too horrifically real, yet muffled in a soup of incoherent pointlessness. In fact, some people do have this experience. In fact, many people do.

§15.

There is no *actual* division anywhere in the universe of the self, no dividing line that can be found between solipsist subject and physicalist object, or between nous, soma, viscera and thelema. Self makes these divisions, as it makes divisions between red and yellow, or between the whiteness of the snow and its softness, or between the feathers of a cockatoo and its squawk, or between language and meaning. Really there is just the inscrutable whole of the colour, snow, cockatoo and communication. The philosopher who puzzles over self-generated divisions is like a man looking at a hundred photos taken over the course of a stranger's life and wondering how all these 'different' people are related. 'They *must* be related', he thinks, 'look how similar they all are!'

Self creates a universe of isolated facts, causally connected and conceptually related to each other, and knitted into a world of knowledge which it then takes to be, in principle, the same kind of thing as reality. It's not just that the map is taken to be the terrain, but that the self *must* consider the terrain to be essentially map-like. What the map is actually *of* cannot be found on it, and neither can the person reading it, nor why he is travelling at all. Looking for something non-symbolic on a map is the very essence of madness.

Arthur Schopenhauer made a related point about the facts revealed by scientific investigation, the various conceptually named percepts of the self, which we can grasp *as* things related to other things, but never that *to* which these things appear, or *from* which they originate. The world of science, Schopenhauer said,* is like a party comprising innumerable guests to which I am presented with introductions along the lines of 'this lady is that man's auntie, and that man is her friend, and those two are his children...' Meanwhile I think to myself, 'yes, yes, but what the devil do they all have to do with *me?*' 'Me', in this case, is my consciousness, with which such facts have, *for* me, nothing 'to do', for the simple reason that, finally, their relationship *to* me does not exist. It is 'picked out' from experience as a finger is picked out from an arm. The philosopher then comes along and then wonders what this bizarre finger *is*—this 'consciousness', this 'meaning', this 'truth'—and how it is related to the arm. Indeed this—continual puzzlement over maps for lands that nobody lives in—*is* philosophy, or rather ABSTRACT PHILOSOPHY in the Western tradition, the activity of a mind writhing in the coils of a series of insoluble riddles brought about by the autonomous existence of the very mind that is trying to unravel them.

§16.

Abstract philosophy is the exclusive use of the thinking mind to find truth. This doesn't just mean working out problems in the head, but also *perceiving* abstractly; seeing and hearing the world divided up noetically, through the 'screen' of the thinking mind, and assuming that this divided representation *is* the world. This activity is so common that you'd be forgiven

---

* Arthur Schopenhauer, *The World as Will and Representation*

for thinking that the world it presents is reality, just as you'd be forgiven for thinking that all reasoning about it *is* philosophy.

Abstract thinking about abstract experience is the only thing that happens in universities and just about the only thing you'll find in the philosophy section of a bookshop or library. When people use the word 'deep', they're usually thinking of the kind of difficult *ideas* that abstract philosophers talk about. Not that anyone really knows *what* abstract philosophers talk about, because what they say is extremely boring, absurdly difficult, irrelevant to ordinary life or outrageously self-absorbed, so nobody pays any attention to it.

Abstract philosophy is difficult, boring and pointless because, first of all, abstract philosophers are really only writing for other abstract philosophers, which is like chefs who only make food for other chefs, or doctors who only heal other doctors; and secondly, because they rely exclusively on the thinking mind to understand truth, which is like relying exclusively on cookbooks to understand food, or textbooks to understand the human body. It's fair to say that most philosophers, psychologists and cognitive scientists believed and still believe—either explicitly or implicitly—that abstract reason and reality are more or less the same thing, that consciousness is thinking or self reflection, that only thought can grasp the essence of reality, that the essence of things is literally a form of thought, or that there is no point of view outside of reason from which reason can be judged. Even so called sceptics and empiricists, who appear to be focusing on the so-called sensory world and doubting the power of the mind to reveal that world, do so through the filter of standard, abstract, reasoning and isolating perception, which creates the isolated things they then reason about. If something *cannot* be conceived, if it is paradoxical, or silent, or eternal, then it can be, and is, dismissed out of hand.

This is why so many philosophers are baffled by reality. They take experiences which cannot be completely reduced to thought, think about them, and then find their thoughts perplexing. One of the earliest philosophers, for example, Zeno of Elea, who lived around 2,500 years ago, was a very confused man. He reasoned that no object—an arrow, for example—can ever get anywhere, because there are an infinite number of halfway stages it must first reach en route.* A century later, Socrates and his disciple Plato became famous for the vast number of things they were confused about; such as what 'virtue' is, what 'knowledge' is and what 'thing' thought is 'of'. Eight hundred years later, Augustine of Hippo couldn't work out where the past and future are, or how time can ever be measured. A thousand years later, it was René Descartes' turn to be baffled by the contents of his own mind. He split experience into mind and matter and was then mystified by how thought could interact with a non-thinking body; a problem which has menaced professional minds ever since. A hundred years later, Hume couldn't understand what consciousness was, or morality, or causality, because none of them seem to exist in the objective world.

And so it goes on. There are thousands of cases of the same sort; straightforward affairs made puzzling by thought. Just as management exists in order to solve problems created by management, and teachers exist in order to educate people made stupid by the existence of schools, and technology exists in order to solve problems created by technology, so the source and root of these fanatically rational activities, abstract thinking, sets about trying to philosophically solve problems that it has created *by* thinking. Zeno's arrow, like Augustine's time, is not a series of discrete mind-isolated moments or steps, and Plato's 'good', like Hume's 'morality', is not an abstract idea. They are all brought into existence, like Descartes' perplexing subjects and objects, *by* the thinking self. The hyper-focusing mind *creates* mental objects of will, motion, meaning, the good and so on—it creates knowledge—and then is mystified at how they can *be* objects; how, for example, as Ludwig Wittgenstein asked, I can 'know your pain'—as if it were a nasty drink that I could dip a straw into; or how I can ever remember anything—as if memories were books on shelves that a little man in my mind has to index and retrieve; or how I can ever understand anything anyone says—as if I have to consult a dictionary to 'look up' all the words they utter.

---

* Aristotle's *Physics*, although the flight of an arrow is from a different paradox.

The reason that so few philosophers ever criticise this activity, the conversion of experience into 'knowledge', into a kind of *substance* which can be produced and consumed, is that *they* are its producers and *we* are its consumers. Knowledge as a *thing* which can be owned, managed, packaged and consumed, automatically turns it into a *scarce resource,** which, like any other scarce resource, acquires a value which stigmatises the many, the very many, who cannot get their hands on it. Any thinker who rejects this state of affairs — the iniquitous foundation of the gnosocratic† knowledge and 'education' industry — is ridiculed, rejected or ignored, or, at best, misunderstood by the academic world.

§17.

What abstract philosophers miss in the activity of abstract thought is that the knowledge they seek to acquire *about* experience is *in* experience, which, as their lives and their work demonstrate, they don't actually find very interesting. They speculate about experience, but they don't really have any, and so when they use the 'higher faculty' of reason to inspect consciousness, for example, or life, they find they are very confused and that they have nothing to say — like a man who empties a box to see what is inside it. In order to convince themselves and others that what they are doing is not an absurd waste of time, they close the box, and then describe it with extremely complicated ideas and arguments so that the reader is unable to guess that the box is actually still empty.

This isn't to say that valid arguments and proofs are not prodigiously useful, or that reasoning should be abandoned, or that faulty reasoning doesn't often reveal prejudice or obsession, but, for the most part, formal logic, for all its use (particularly in exposing deliberate attempts to deceive), is not employed by people who wish to understand life, but by those who wish to win arguments. It is perfectly possible to 'win an argument' and to 'devastate an intellectual opponent' using faultless logic that is based on empty, ridiculous or even insane premises and assumptions (very often sneakily omitted). A

---

* Ivan Illich, *Deschooling Society*
† See *The Apocalypedia*

philosopher who argues that pederasty helps keep populations down (Aristotle), or that animals are essentially machines (Descartes), or that the only reason we don't cause pain to other people is because we are scared of revenge (Nietzsche), or that children are born with the innate ideas of carburettor and bureaucrat (Chomsky) or that reality needs fiction to conceal its emptiness (Žižek), is in this respect no different to a boyfriend who argues that he has fallen out of love with his girlfriend because love is a chemical, or a madman who argues that Genghis Khan lives in his fridge. When we say of such people that they have 'lost their minds', we mean that they have lost everything *but* their minds.*

§18.

No idea, no reasoning, nothing that the thinking mind can do, has meaning without meaning first being present. It is impossible for an argument to produce any value that isn't in the premises. If, after a long train of reasoning, I confidently reach a conclusion that, say, the president of the United States is always the wisest man in the country, somewhere in the premises there is an *unreasoned* assumption about the nature of wisdom (or its absence) which I may *develop* by thinking, but cannot *create* by thinking.

There are three consequences of this.

i.   All reasoning, philosophical or otherwise, *must* begin with what are often dismissed as 'mere' assumptions and assertions; unreasoned declarations of truth such as 'consciousness exists and I am it', or 'something is happening' or 'pain hurts'. Although it is absurd to deny such things, there is no way to ever prove them, or argue them into existence; indeed if they could be proved or disproved they would cease to have any real, qualitative meaning to anyone but an android which, like the abstract philosopher, deals entirely in quantities.

ii.   When difficult philosophies are translated into ordinary language they come down to simple assertions that anyone

---

* G.K. Chesterton, *Orthodoxy*

can test for themselves as being true or false ('childish theories without the charm of childhood', as Wittgenstein put it*); because those assertions didn't come into being through rational thought. This is why abstract philosophers are reluctant to make simple assertions, or to give clear examples, and why reason cannot bring anyone any closer to a change of heart about their fundamental beliefs. People cannot be reasoned out of base premises that they did not reason themselves into. Devastate every fallacious argument in the world, expose every self-deception, dismantle every misguided or prejudicial worldview and it would make no difference to the assumptions that unfounded beliefs are anchored to. Something other than reason (*and* emotion) is required.

iii.   The third consequence of meaning "preceding" reason is that one of the chief weapons in the abstract philosopher's armoury, the Mighty Fallacy, *ultimately* has no bearing on the truth content of a statement. Although classic fallacies are guides to incoherence, their absence does not validate an argument, and their presence does not invalidate it. Presenting personal information as evidence for example (the 'anecdotal fallacy'), or pointing out that a desired quality exists in the natural world ('the appeal to nature') or in traditional culture (the 'appeal to culture'), or caricaturing a position in order to critique it (the 'straw man'), or dismissing someone's position based on their hypocrisy (the 'appeal to hypocrisy') may be sloppy or illogical, or apt and carefully reasoned, but in neither case is the truth or falsehood of the premise affected.

Value, in the sense of philosophical truth, does not come to us through the activity of abstract philosophy, but through the activity of *living*.† If reasoned argument can never arrive at conclusions that are not somehow contained in the premises, those premises must ultimately come from experience. This is the bedrock of any truth that can be shared, an unspoken agreement that my experience and yours are *ultimately* the same. Similarly, although error and lies may be *prevented* from advancing by a philosopher criticising the reasoning of

---

* Ludwig Wittgenstein, *Remarks on Frazer's Golden Bough*
† Friedrich Nietzsche, *Beyond Good and Evil*

those who went before him, the truth is only *advanced* when someone brings new qualities to the undertaking, qualities which he has already experienced, prior to any quantitative reasoning. This is why writers and teachers with anything meaningful to say have always led meaningful lives. They are not, first and foremost, impressive writers and teachers, but impressive *human beings*. It's also why a philosopher with something meaningful to say usually has more in common with children and animals than with his colleagues.

§ 19.

The literalist philosopher conflates a unified *consciousness* with ATTENTION; a rational kaleidoscope of self-created parts. He then concludes that 'consciousness', like meaning and quality, doesn't really exist. He correctly reasons, for example, that most somatic activity goes on without *attention* (I travel to work without realising or remembering anything that happened), that we don't need *attention* to learn (which frequently happens without knowing it), to make judgements (which often *precede* attention) or to act effortlessly (which becomes stilted if I do pay attention to what I am doing), that *attention* doesn't seem to have a location (different cultures put it in different parts of the body) and that the objects of *attention* are only ever a 'bunch' of impressions which we are fooled into thinking are experienced by a consistent, persistent self (when I go looking for the self, I never seem to find it). There is no enduring *attention* says the literalist, again correctly; no unique private self—which pre-civilised cultures rarely recognise—and so, for the physicalist, there is no enduring 'consciousness', for the two are, to him, the same. For the dualist, on the other hand, there *is* an enduring consciousness (which he calls 'soul' or something similar), but it *literally* exists (i.e. is a kind of Magical Mind, or Godself).

The idea that consciousness and attention are fundamentally, qualitatively different is *impossible* for the literalist to grasp; because he is unconscious. He concludes that consciousness literally does or does not exist, because he cannot stop being a literal self; he cannot 'soften', 'slacken' or 'sacrifice' his self to unself in his *actual*, as opposed to his merely professional, life. He cannot experience the non-literal, so he assumes it is a literal non-thing or a literal thing. It's not unlike a compulsive worrier concluding that because he cannot stop thinking and emoting, 'peace of mind' either does not exist, or it is a literal thing which he cannot *get*. All literalists are given to worrying in this way.

§20.

Ultimately, all philosophy has as its subject consciousness, but what philosophers know of consciousness is not a question of what they *think* about it, what *facts* they have acquired about it, or what *theories* they have advanced as to its nature; all of this is to ask about their personal relationship to the *objects* of consciousness. Consciousness is, self-evidently, what the philosopher *is*; thus, to actually discover what he *knows* of it, is to ask the most terrifying question for all academic philosophers; *how conscious is this man?*

The problems of philosophy arise from the problems that philosophers have in their actual lives. Philosophies all attempt to explain *what is*, but 'what is' to the academic mind of an insensitive bore or to an over-emotional egomaniac is very different to the 'what is' of someone who has lived an interesting, meaningful life. Someone who has had to contend with life or death questions in profound experiences of uncertainty, or has sacrificed an ordinary life in order to make something meaningful of their existence, asks very different questions about life to someone who has grown up in an entirely mediated modern household, who was raised by ordinary modern parents in an ordinary modern marriage, who went from being educated in an institution to earning their living from one, who has never really had to mortify themselves, or take any real risks, or face the world as it actually is. Such people are insensitive to the pain of being unconscious—in fact are rewarded for and pacified by it—and so take no meaningful steps towards uprooting or investigating it, which is reflected in the superficial problems they tackle and the superficial conclusions they reach, if any.

This aspect of philosophical truth is repellent to professional philosophers, as it is to all those who do not lead meaningful lives, who are not impressive human beings or who do not wish to be. The idea that a great artist, a great thinker or a great teacher must be a great human being is *instantly* rejected by mediocre human beings, along with the idea that there can even *be* such things as 'greatness' and 'mediocrity'. In fact, this rejection makes up much of what abstract philosophers actually say, which, once you've battled your way through the forest of intellectual thorns they grow around their tiny plastic castles, turns out in many cases to be little more than 'quality is an illusion' or 'consciousness is an illusion' or 'love is an illusion' or 'sanity is an illusion' and similar crude and boring defences against nuance, variation and simplicity. In this they are no different from anyone else, but where ordinary people will use unsophisticated, perhaps even downright childish, reasoning to defend their desolate or cosmetic beliefs, or will refuse to reason, preferring to wave away difficult questions or exterminate those who raise them, philosophers will hide behind specialist language and formidably difficult abstract systems.

§21.

A great thinker does not hammer truth to the wall of the mind with the nails of a system, because he knows in doing so the truth will die. Instead, he presents, filtered through his learning, his conscious experience, either structuring this with an easily understood (and easily discarded) system, or he ignores maps and models altogether. It is life which matters to our greatest philosophers, which is why their work is *like* life; lucid, vivid and elusive. More like a novel. Great philosophy, taking the principle of nature as its source and subject, is like something *in* nature, the growth of ivy perhaps, or the song of a wren, or the activity of an ant's nest; messy perhaps, erratic here and there, but it holds together as one, and it speaks.

Abstract philosophy, by contrast, resembles a power-tool; well reasoned, internally coherent, but lifeless, humourless and mechanical. It is conspicuously bereft of interesting examples or meaningful metaphors from life, or even a sense that life, the living reality we humans are part of, is anywhere involved, for the simple reason that abstract philosophers do not really live. If they started addressing life, putting in examples and metaphors from it, the chronic poverty of *their* lives would be instantly exposed, and that won't do. Better to rumble on and on about matters of no interest or concern to anyone but dried up philosophical bean-counters.

Academic philosophers spend most of their lives in institutions. They are *institutionalised*, and paid to manufacture justifications for an institutional—which is to say, hyper-specialised and unreal—existence. This is why they never have anything to say in any other medium, or even any other field. Nothing creative, certainly, nothing personal or human that would enable you to experience that from which such qualities arise, their character or our context (the world that appears in the work of professional philosophers is completely unrecognisable to anyone who is *on the receiving end* of it). It's also why you so very rarely get the sense reading philosophy that there is a real human being behind the words, an individual who lives in the real world, a friendly companion. It's the same with the science that so much philosophy trails after, where use of the word 'I' evokes a sense of shame, masquerading under an almost obsessive need to be 'objective'.

The individual, the *selfless* I, is irrelevant to matters of fact, and that, we are told, is what we are dealing with here. Except it isn't, is it? Philosophy is not primarily about matters of fact, but about the ultimate "cause" and quality of those facts. Philosophy is supposed to address itself to pressing questions of existence, to the reality and nature of consciousness, love, art, beauty, god, self, sex, death, creativity, madness, addiction and freedom, none of which can be reduced to rational fact and logical argument any more than the taste of orange juice can be reduced to a description of the effect of water, sugar and citric acid on the relevant cells of the body.

This is why many students who take philosophy degrees have the distinct feeling that they've got on the wrong train. They expect to be dealing with the towering mysteries of human existence, they expect to be studying the accounts of the immortals who went before us, who attempted to scale the same heights, they expect to be guided on this odyssey by interesting people who have made the same journey and returned with pristine insights into the path ahead. What they find instead is a cross between a librarian and an accountant piling up items of knowledge like coloured beads then handing them out to confused and bored young people who are expected to categorise them in, at best, a *slightly* different way to those who preceded them.

§22.

Abstract philosophers would have you believe that they have arrived at their opinions through reasoning, and that they disagree with other philosophers because of the weakness of opposing arguments, but this isn't it at all. It's because all philosophical positions are founded upon psychological realities. People don't first reason their way into their beliefs; they seek beliefs and attitudes which correspond to their felt inner reality, their way of living and their life-in-the-world, *then* find reasons to accept and defend those beliefs and attitudes; which is why reason cannot change them. First we *have to* believe, *then* we believe.* Nobody ever mentions this in professional debate. The idea that beliefs and attitudes are not entirely nor even principally located inside people, that they are almost completely impotent to alter such beliefs, which are, particularly in the case of professionals, almost *never* arrived at through a process of careful, detached study (which is why they never change, even after a lifetime *of* study), that they are in fact very often a function of *power relations* in society or, if not, an extremely subtle, ongoing exercise in self-justification; all this is off the table of 'serious discussion'.

If you bring someone's life into a discussion you are accused of committing an '*ad hominem* fallacy', invalidating an

---

* Georg Lichtenberg, *The Waste Books*

argument by an irrelevant focus on personal details; although the *ad hominem* fallacy is no more inherently false than any other fallacy. There is nothing inherently 'invalid' about criticising someone's life, or character, or the assumptions they bring to a discussion, or their vested interests. *Ad hominem* means 'to the man'; the reason so many people cry *'ad hominem!'* so readily is because they are unwilling to bring their lives into the discussion, to be addressed *as* a man. Not that there isn't such a thing as unfair use of personal criticism in discussion, or abuse, but this can't be a fallacy, because it's not an argument; it's a distraction *from* argument. To say, however, that your loveless worldview is based on a loveless upbringing, or that your mediocre output is a consequence of living for forty years in a professional cage, or that you believe consciousness and thought are the same thing because you're basically a brain in a jar, is to make a perfectly fair point, albeit one that breaches the rules of impartial rationality that abstract, academic, professional philosophers cling to. And they do cling to it. When it is suggested to him that one's work is indistinguishable from one's life, the literalist philosopher, like the scientist and the businessman, is outraged. He complains that such things are irrelevant. His job doesn't require his life, his heart, his individuality; and of course he is quite correct. But what kind of person would devote his life to an activity which has no use *for* that life? Only *one* kind of person, or rather, only one kind of self; the self-informed self.

§23.

The unconscious self can only instruct or inform itself, which means it can only think, feel, sense and behave selfishly, or egoically (*'selfish' and 'egoic' mean the same here*). There is only one programme that makes sense to a mechanism which instructs itself, and that is; *continually exist*. The SELF-INFORMED SELF, or EGO, cannot stop somatically isolating and noetically symbolising, any more than it can stop viscerally emoting or thelemically wanting. To stop attending, willing, emoting and thinking is, for the self-informed self, to cease to exist. Thus, although ego might be confronted by a universe of hostile forces, it is only unself which represents an EXISTENTIAL THREAT.

The literalist philosopher does not therefore tell us that consciousness does not exist because his self cannot *find* it—self, evidently, cannot find unself. He tells us it does not exist because *he* cannot *be* it. Although he may reason himself to the limit of the known, he cannot cross over. To do so does not require a different kind of *knowledge*, but a different kind of *person*, one for whom self is secondary to *something else*, something which the self, by itself, has no need of.

Self can imagine the entire universe successfully operating without consciousness (as a machine), and it can imagine an entire *self* successfully operating without consciousness (as a zombie). There is no *reason* to 'add' consciousness to the universe or to the self. We can remove consciousness from both, and both still work; indeed *do* work under the unconscious lens of physicalist science, which can completely account for reality without adding consciousness, which is just a burden. And yet. If we knew *every single fact* about the universe, if science solved every single literal problem self can conceive of, what have we gained? The one thing that we evidently *haven't* gained is that which is non-literal, non-factual, non-causal, yet *real*.

If, that is, it *is* real. Given the literal fact that the universe can run without it, that human beings can exist without it, that it cannot be literally perceived, conceived, felt or willed, that it is not any *thing*, and can have no causal connection with any other thing, you would have every *reason* to conclude that it does not and cannot exist—were it not for the fact that you *are* conscious. Consciousness adds nothing to what is necessary, and there is no factual or causal reason to add it. The only reason you have to add consciousness to the universe *is* consciousness.*

§ 24.

Self *automatically* divides reality into a certain thinking, sensing, willing, feeling subject and uncertain thought-graspable objects. This is the unspoken basis of all abstract and literal

---

* Arthur Eddington, *The Nature of the Physical World*

philosophy, science, superstition and religion. Clearly such a division between subject and object does somehow apply to reality. There must be some difference between me and not me; if there were not, I would, as the solipsist maintains, be able to literally move rocks with my mind and literally implant thoughts into other minds. There is and can be, however, no definitive bridge *between* subjects and objects (hence constant confusion in philosophy and science about how they interact), just the *assumption*, which the self-informed self is *forced* to make, that either the subjective self completely or accurately represents the objective world, or that the objective world of matter causes our subjective experience of consciousness. This foundational assumption, that reality is essentially self-like, is justified on the grounds of *fact*—the accuracy and utility of thought, which the factual self can determine—not on the grounds of *truth*—whether reality really *is* self-like; which only something beyond self, something which is both real in my experience and *non*-factual, can determine.

If, that is, it *is* real. If there is *something else* in experience, a non-factual but real consciousness, then both the unreal subjective experiences and the real objective facts of self are, to this consciousness, *all* objects. Consciousness *of* nous, when, for example, I become conscious that I am talking too much or uselessly worrying, or consciousness *of* viscera, when I become conscious of an aggravated tension in my throat or a weird mood in the room, or consciousness *of* thelema, when I become conscious of my habitual, robotic actions or the surprising grace of a cloud of sparrows, or consciousness *of* soma, when I become conscious of a tension I was too stupid to realise I had or of a wider context in which my perceptions are "embedded"; all such experiences turn the thought, feeling, sensation and volition—whether subjective or objective—into objects, *there*, which I am witnessing, *here*. Such conscious experience, which situates *all* apparent subjects and objects in a super-object experienced "by" a super-subject,* by the thing-in-itself, is in radical opposition to all egoic (literalist and solipsistic) conceptual knowledge, in which the thing-in-itself has no place.

---

* Immanuel Kant, *The Critique of Pure Reason*

§25.

There is a means to determine what is real; whether literalist thought does fully apply to the thing-in-itself, whether the distinction between subjectivity and objectivity is real, whether our notions of causality, which are meaningless when applied to the "relation" between the thing-in-itself and our representations of it, still somehow reflect what is actually happening. As I *am* a conscious thing-in-itself, I can simply observe if or how I "come to be" a literal, manifest self and *see* whether there is a causal relationship or not. All I have to do is *be* what I am, and what that *means* will become clear.

Easier said than done, or rather; easier to say than to be. For if unself does exist, an experience that is radically different to self, a 'super-subject' to the apparent subjects and objects of soma, viscera, thelema and nous, an experience which can overturn the merely subjective me which I ordinarily take to be myself, which can say for *sure* whether there is a causal relation between the thing-in-itself I am and the self which appears to it; if this extraordinary unself exists, it is evidently very rare in the ordinary world, for I hear very little of it.

I hear very little of unself, but *self* hears none of it, because it *can* hear none of it. Self only 'hears' self; selfish thelema, nous, viscera and soma. If there is only self in my experience, then these modes only inform each other, and literally so. Representation is then, for self, 'reality', beyond the limits of which nothing qualitatively different to representation can *ever* be experienced (which is why the virtual world for virtual man seems so normal, because it is not qualitatively different from his ordinary screen of offline experience).

If an alien being from another dimension appeared and explained the truth to us, in our own language, of how the universe came into being, of what representations are of, or of what consciousness is, self would neither be able to perceive nor understand her. She might appear beautiful, her explanation might sound strange, she might even become famous for her strange beauty, but she would appear *essentially* normal, and her message would sound *essentially* meaningless.

§26.

There are two kinds of MEANING. Firstly, SELF-MEANING. This can be further categorised into four modes; NOETIC MEANING, founded on *conceptual awareness* of what one is thinking, that which fits an internally consistent system of abstract structures, symbols and ideas; THELEMIC MEANING, founded on *practical awareness* of movement, that which works, or which fits some kind of useful practice or function; VISCERAL MEANING, founded on *affective awareness* of what one is feeling, that which manifests as mood, vibe or intuitive quality; SOMATIC MEANING, founded on *perceptual awareness* of the senses, that which represents the sensed or perceived world.

The chief problem with the extreme literalist view that meaning is completely conceptual, a series of isolated knowledge-signals travelling down a knowing mind-cable, or the extreme solipsist view that it is arbitrary puffs of emotion that I am free to interpret any way I please, is not so much that they are wrong, as that, putting the part before the whole, they are catastrophically (not to mention tediously) *limited*, unable to adapt themselves to a meaningful reality which answers to, and informs the entire, modally integrated self.

Similarly, EXPERIENCE is ordinarily—and philosophically—understood piecemeal, as a series of knowable *things* that are learnt, remembered or possessed, rather than a totality which is *lived*. Ego can hardly be said to experience at all, instantly transporting whatever happens into the modal warehouse of the self, where it is stored, evaluated and used to get a better job, lord it over newcomers, or gas on about what it knows or what has happened to it. When people say 'I have experience' they nearly always mean that they possess something which is *not* experience, but the corpse of it.

There is, however, another kind of meaning, or experience, which, although it manifests as one or other mode of self, and although all forms of meaning and experience are, ultimately, "dependent" on it, is ultimately "independent" *of* self, and therefore, ultimately, elusive *to* self. This is essential UNSELF-MEANING, or unselfish QUALITY.

§27.

Quality is the "entry" of unself into self. The various words we have for quality—beauty, truth, intelligence, wit, courage, confidence, innocence, sweetness, sensitivity, goodness, generosity, genius, love, joy, intensity and so on—express the appearance of unself-meaning under different circumstances in the self. Quality is felt or recognised in VISCERAL feeling (it feels 'good', 'right', 'lovely', etc.), but we can, for example, speak of THELEMIC QUALITY (which we might call 'eminence' or 'attainment'), or SOMATIC QUALITY (fractal 'beauty' or 'elegance'), or NOETIC QUALITY (which we tend to call 'truth'), experienced through reason and, particularly, metaphor. Remove non-literal unself from any of these experiences and you are left with that element of beauty, truth, feeling and excellence (or whatever words you wish to use) that can be reduced to literal fact. Viscera without quality is EMOTION, thelema without quality is AUTOMATION, soma without quality is STIMULATION and nous without quality is RATIONALITY. What remains when quality is subtracted from self is QUANTITY.

Even in the most conceptual of activities—mathematics and science—there is quality, but it lies "outside" or "beyond" entirely self-bound concepts. The aesthetic sense that 'feels out' which among an infinite number of hypotheses to apply to a given case, for example, or the 'elegance' of a 'beautiful' mathematical proof, or any other non-literal, qualitative 'leap over the fence' that advances knowledge, is beyond the coordinates of the self. The nature of this quality is, however, systematically misunderstood by literalists and widely ignored. Although the achievements of selfless literalists are eventually recognised as genuine advancements, they are resisted at the time by egoic literalists who, despite vestigial aesthetic sensitivity to conceptual elegance, always take any given phenomenon to be reducible to a collection of quantities. The quality of a new discovery eludes them because they are only capable of measuring, analysing, testing and reproducing quantity. Experience of a quality that "precedes" quantity is ignored by the literalist because it is literally inconceivable.

§28.

Perception of quality is and can only be possible *by* quality, which is to say consciously. The whole self must experience beauty to know it as beauty, or love to know it as love. If consciousness is experienced through self-informed and self-informing modes—through egoically isolated touch, for example, or self-absorbed emotion, or a series of tightly focused ideas—it dries up and crumbles into quantitative bits. To be conscious is in *letting go* of such parts.

Likewise, if quality "precedes" quantity then a *completely* literal understanding of non-literal quality must deprive it *of* quality. A literal description of love betrays love in the same way that a photograph of a sunset makes it look trivial and hollow. As the Tao Te Ching has it,* 'When the world knows beauty as beauty, ugliness arises. When it knows good as good, evil arises'. Likewise, facts, technical ability, qualifications and money might be *necessary* to live well, produce high quality output, be valuable to society, or be secure and happy, but they cannot be *sufficient*. *Something else* must be required—something which ego is unable to experience.

If quantity precedes or gives rise to quality, then, in order to increase quality, *all* self needs to do is literally understand it, or gain literal power over it. The more facts (e.g. 'life hacks') I acquire about living, the better able I am to live; the more technical ability I acquire, the higher quality my output; the more qualifications I have, the more valuable I am to society; the more money I have, the more secure I am, or happy. If quantity precedes quality, it is possible to truly know something or someone without conscious experience of its quality. A computer which knew everything there is to know about you, for example, would *actually* know you.

If, however, quality precedes quantity, it is not just impossible to know something without qualitative experience, but quality itself *is* the experience. If quality precedes quantity it is impossible to experience something apart from its quality and impossible to experience the quality of something without considering the thing itself. They are inseparable.

---

* Lao Tzu, *The Tao Te Ching* (tr. Ellen Chen)

If I am locked in a prison cell, for example, slowly going mad, and I forgot every fact about you (including every emotional memory), but still retained a qualitative feeling for your character, for the quality of your consciousness, you would feel that I still 'knew' you. You would feel 'known' by someone *who had lost all knowledge of you*. If, on the other hand, I went mad and I somehow *remembered* every fact about you (this is called HYPERMNESIA), but entirely forgot your quality, you would feel that I no longer knew you. This would feel nightmarish, appalling; which is how it *does* feel to be with a literalist. This is why we find stories in which our loved ones have become qualitatively alien to us ('it looks like him, it sounds like him, but it's *not* him!'), or dreams in which they wave or smile, *knowing* but *unrecognising*, so awful.

§29.

The quality of unself is an *intrinsic* experience—it "partakes" of either the thing-in-itself "within" myself or that "within" other things and selves, "before" it is represented by the literal, *extrinsic* self. Self, therefore, is unable to quantitatively access unselfish quality, because it has no inward access to anything, including itself. If quality is ultimately unselfish, then it is not ultimately something about which self can have direct knowledge, because quality cannot exist in the represented world of self *as* unself, as an isolated 'reason' or 'fact'. This is why quality, to the extent that it is unselfish, *somehow* gives a subtle (to self) yet powerful (to unself) experience of non-causality (eternity) and non-facticity (paradox). The usual words for such experience are 'enigmatic', 'mysterious', 'timeless' etc. The instant I attempt to inspect this elusive experience *with* self, it vanishes like depth disappears through a telephoto lens; which is why self, in order to dispose of unself, *only needs to inspect it*. Although beauty, truth, joy, comedy and so on "arise from" the thing-in-itself, they are only knowable as representation, which *literally* betrays them. This is why literal descriptions of unself sound *like* a betrayal; cliched, fascist or pretentious; low-quality.

To say that quality can be described entirely in quantitative terms is to say it does not actually exist. To say, as scientists do, that we have most to learn from speculation about quantity, rather than the actual experience of quality, is like saying that analysis of the notes that Beethoven wrote on his scores has more to teach us than the actual experience of the music itself (*well* performed) does. Only someone who was deaf could seriously say such a thing; not deaf to sound, but deaf to quality, which is to say deaf to the unselfish consciousness and context from which quality "arises".

Those who are blind and deaf to quality cannot experience consciousness and context, or the quality that "inheres" in their manifestations, unless they have either been intellectually defined or emotionally identified with. We call those who filter quality through the intellect, *stiffs* and *spods*, and those who filter it through the emotions, *hysterics* and *pseuds*, and the whole lot *frauds* and *gorts*. Those with less developed selves (children, primitives), or with selves which have been temporarily softened (lovers and the loving) or mortified (artists and mystics), are most able to unselfishly experience intrinsic reality and therefore quality. This is why they are most distressed at seeing it ignored, ridiculed or destroyed by fakes. When the latter then ask what the problem is, the selfless can often do little more than offer an inarticulate cry. They *know* what quality is, but they cannot literally *say* what it is.

§30.

The literal needs of self can be literally answered *by* self, by thelemic activity, somatic objects, visceral feelings and noetic ideas. We normally call the effect of self-graspable quality-minus-consciousness on the body STIMULATION and we normally call the meeting of self-graspable needs SATISFACTION, both of which, being isolable and graspable, self can *get* and *lose*.

This is why the self-controlled self is *obsessed* with *getting*—more points, possessions, facts, attention, security, power, perfection, fun, sex and excitement—and terrified of *losing*—loss, death, disappointment, shame, sickness, boredom, insecurity, poverty, imperfection and loneliness. It's also why, despite lip-service to the contrary, self is unable comprehend quality that can neither be got nor lost, nor miss its absence.

Self, by itself, cannot tell the difference between the unselfish experience of quality and the selfish experience of satisfaction, because all self can get *is* satisfaction. Just as self, by itself, can only give *itself* as an answer to the question 'Who am I?' so it can only give *itself* as an answer to 'What is quality?' This is why:

i.   The immense, immeasurable difference between two formally similar experiences, one with quality and one without, are experienced as more or less the same to ego. A smile of loving kindness and one of automatic approval, a Van Gogh original and a digital simulation, an original recording of a great song, and a second-rate cover-version—or even the same song played by the same artist after his inspiration has shuffed out—are all on different planets, in different realities, but not to ego. In fact because low-quality work relies on signposts, it will be *preferred* by ego. This is why masterpieces are often ignored when they appear and only when the artist starts producing derivative work—cliched versions of the original inspiration—does it become more palatable to ego, and he achieves some success.

ii.   Talking to people with limited consciousness, trapped in a small circle of quality, is like talking to someone in a dream who has never woken up. With no standard by which to understand what you mean by 'awake', your words—or rather your tone, your implication, your *sense*—are essentially meaningless to ego, which is why we feel such a tragic sense of loneliness in the company of those who don't get the joke, or who can't feel the rhythm, or don't know what to do with silence. They might say they can see the sunset, or that they don't like their jobs, but their 'seeing' and 'don't like' exist in different dimensions. It's also why it is so pathetic to see someone try to make another being happier *than* their being; the doted bully, the pandered addict and the pampered animal.

iii.   The ambitions and expectations that ego has for its life are, from any conscious perspective, shallow and trivial, amounting to little more than comfortable survival, punctuated with excitement. But this is not a *choice* for ego, it is an expression of its entire reality. A qualitatively different way of living is not just unimaginable, it is unfeelable, undoable and unperceivable. Heroes and heroines living such a life therefore appear to egoic man to be quite ordinary, or even boring, or they appear as unreachable ideals, or as gods, or, more often than not, they appear to be flat-out insane.

iv.   In matters of quality—right and wrong, good and bad, beautiful and ugly—ego is *completely* immune to argument. It's not a question of not *understanding* another, but of not *being* another. You can offer a watertight argument to another ego to show that its tightfistedness or pride, or its support for democracy, or its love of hip-hop, or its taste in clothing, or in men, is sick, selfish or insane, and not only *not* change its mind but, in presenting an essentially *threatening* alternative, entrench it further. This isn't to say that argument is always useless, particularly in matters in which quantitative facts and evidence are relevant, but *something else*, other than literal words is required to introduce quality into the affair.

v.   Egoic people fear change, risk, uncertainty, surrender and death. They fear these things because they have no experience of the freedom that is bought with them, and so they willingly, even casually, give freedom up, in exchange for the warmth of risk-free conformity, the fleeting relief of changeless security and the reassuring offer of the deathless known.

vi.   Ego reduces all expressions of quality to forms of satisfaction. As far as ego is concerned, a genius paints a glorious landscape solely or ultimately in order to satisfy a need for power (or, via power, for a mate), a mother sacrifices her life for her child to satisfy a genetic need to propagate the species, an activist risks jail to protect the felling of an old growth forest to make herself feel important, spiritual teachings are conceived to promote cohesion of the group, and so on and so forth. Similarly, physicalism accounts for all actions within the natural world as mechanical responses; birds sing at dawn to mark their territory, kittens play in order to learn to hunt, dogs are loyal to their owners because of socialisation instincts, and so on and so forth. It is *unthinkable* that animals could do anything for the happy hell of it, that magpies could swoop through the sky for joy, that cats could tease dogs or that ants could secretly organise gay discos when we're not looking.

vii.   All of ego's own attempts at experiencing or creating quality *can* be reduced to forms of satisfaction; egoic artists solely or ultimately *do* paint for fame or money, egoic mothers *do* blindly sacrifice themselves (or, more usually, give themselves over to relentlessly egoic care), egoic activists *do* primarily act in order to feel thrillingly moral, and egoic spiritual teachers *do* form cults to exalt their transcendent genitals. The egoist then can—and does—point to such transparently selfish behaviour as 'evidence' that it *is* [always] selfish.

viii.   The quality of beauty for self means, for the most part, that which benefits self. Thus, typically, a male self will find a young woman with shiny hair, clear skin and balanced features and curves 'beautiful'. And that's as it should be. No matter how angry feminists get, they will never change this fact. But. Entirely selfish man will *only* find that which benefits him beautiful. He will be unable to discern that within all women generally, and within conscious and present women specifically, which is of *zero* benefit—if anything is actually harmful—to his self. Let's call it a 'mysterious abyss' (although like all essential quality it humiliates description) which consciousness looks into and sees its own bottomless depth reflected back, an experience which it also calls 'beautiful', but which is no more 'subjective' than life itself, or death.

ix.   Similarly, unconscious selves find it difficult to see the beauty in a thunderstorm, or in a deadly snake, or in a rotting skull, or in the death of a loved one, or in a break-in, or in a shitty flat in southwest London at six-thirty on a November morning when you have to travel two hours through the poisonous rain in order to do eight hours of alienating unwork with a group of people you detest. Unless the self is exhausted, looking forward to death, or dressing itself up in an edgy, outsider's costume, it finds such threats to itself terrible to look upon and impossible to see the beauty or meaning in.

x.   Those activities in which quality plays a subordinating role to satisfaction proliferate in a world composed of egos. These activities range from largely noetic activities, which we call SCIENCE, to largely somatic activities, which we call CRAFT. Examples of the former include mathematics, physics, biology, history and psychology. Examples of the latter include joinery, cookery, couture, architecture, dentistry, sport, photography and journalism. Essentially, these are all forms of self-oriented TECHNICAL WORK (or QUANTITY WORK). They have quality, at least potentially, but the *primary* point of them is literal expression of a conceptual meaning or manageable manifestation of some kind of practical, self-satisfying, quantity.

      Conversely, those activities in which satisfaction plays a subordinating role to quality are those in which, while impossible without some kind of craft, are not *primarily* concerned with satisfying self; rather with mortifying, confusing, softening, widening or overcoming it. These activities range from the context-meeting activity we call (here) the HUMANITIES to the consciousness-emphasising activity we call ART. Examples of the former include conversation, spending time with old people, playing with children, taking care of nature, along with the study of man and nature in subjects like sociology and philosophy. Examples of the latter include painting, sculpture, myth, music, theatre (particularly impro), magic, love-making, self-mastery and being very silly. Essentially these are all forms of unself-oriented CHARACTER WORK (or QUALITY WORK). They may be logically structured and amenable to conceptual analysis, but the primal point of them is, (*through* the literal self) to non-literally express *unself*. This is why they are automatically rejected, debased or destroyed in an egoic world.

xi.　　Ego might be strong, but it is brittle; it might be beautiful, but it is shallow; it might be intelligent, but within rigid limits. The isolating mind of the sleeping ego is like a blazing torch in the forest, over-illuminating a minute area of the dark, sharply dividing the user from everything else, which thereby seems both darker than the light and more uncannily different. To counter the threat of this obscure otherness, I turn up the torch, brighter and brighter, expanding my view further and further, but the light is so bright it now kills what it is directed at, petrifying the trees, shrivelling up the plants. I can see more and more, but fear of the darkness doesn't decrease—in being suppressed, quite the opposite—so I turn up the beam higher and higher, looking for life in more and more distant realms, wiping out more and more life with the killing exposure, until, finally, I am left in a super-bright desert, blindingly overlit in every direction, and dead.

　　　　All along, all I had to do was switch the torch off and grow accustomed to the darkness.

§31.

All the egoist has is the light of TECHNIQUE (until he abandons it to achieve obscure solipsistic aims). Without unself, there is no other way to bridge the gap between an apparent subject imprisoned here, in the self, and apparent objects floating around out there, in the world. Technique is not an option for the self, but the *only* way it can experience, influence and communicate with the world. This is why the literalist exalts technique, or METHOD. As Albert Camus said,* when one has no character—which is to say no conscious quality—one *has* to apply method; strategies, practices and commandments, handed down by psychological or spiritual authorities, for dealing with one's inner, 'subjective' reality; guidelines, norms and roles, handed down by moral and institutional authorities (including the institution of the family), for dealing with one's social reality, and procedures, techniques and knowledge, handed down by scientific and political authorities, for dealing with 'objective' reality.

---

* Albert Camus, *The Fall*

Method is defended on utilitarian or pragmatic grounds. This is the principal argument for objectivist physicalism; that it is *successful*. In the past, the physicalist tells us, we tried to explain the universe by appealing to non-physical phenomena and our attempts failed. Now that we know better, and appeal to measurable material entities, our explanations succeed or lead to success. We can therefore be confident that non-physical explanations will always fail, and that physical explanations will always succeed, and the reason for this can only be that everything is physical. The principal flaw in this reasoning is the word 'success'. Operations *on* physical matter, under the assumptions of physicalism, do indeed 'succeed'. But understanding or experiencing what physical matter actually *is* (which science never even attempts) cannot be a question of 'success'. Physicalism is correct in the same way an axe is correct. It does the job, but the tree remains a mystery.

In fact, 'pre-scientific' approaches to reality *did* work astonishingly well. Stonehenge, for example, the Pacific voyages of South Sea Islanders and the botanical knowledge of rainforest tribes were all examples of extraordinarily successful literalist knowledge systems founded on non-physicalist world-views.* It is possible to use axes and see trees as transdimensional cracks in spacetime, or as strange gods, or as selfless individuals, with their own individual character.

Literalist science cannot say what the tree is, or prove *that* it is, only measure it and predict how it is *likely* to behave, an exercise that is justified in terms of internal *coherence* (the measurements and theories 'fit' with other measurements and theories) and *utility* (with these measurements and theories we can operate more efficiently). This is why the physicalist response to genuinely non-literalist accounts or attitudes terminates with objections that they cannot be literally measured or that they have not shown themselves to be 'successful'. We call this approach to reality objective *pragmatism, instrumentalism, utilitarianism, functionalism,* or, if it relates to the human psyche, *behaviourism*; the idea that *truth is measurable utility* (or, in modified *'eudaimonic'* form, duty, or well-being, or what-have-you). A scientific theory, for example, is only 'true' to the

---

* Paul Feyerabend, *Against Method*

extent that it works, if it has been successfully tested against 'reality'. What that reality *is* has no place within operational accounts because it can have no place. Who cares what it *is*, as long as it *works*, right? This is partly why the unconscious scientist—high priest of the cult of the useful—claims that 'artificial' intelligence is possible, because he sees no difference between what life *is* and how it *functions*. If it looks and acts like a human, it must *be* a human; if it looks and acts like a brain, it must *be* a brain; if it looks and acts like a neurone, it must *be* a neurone. This can only be maintained by unconsciously focusing on the isolated *bits* of the human, brain and neurone, which screens out the quality of the whole—the beauty, in form and action, of the human, brain and neurone—and enables the instrumentalist to conclude that a human and an android are, in principle, the same thing.

What pragmatic, behaviourist criticisms of non-literalist accounts miss is that anyone who is conscious enthusiastically *agrees* with them. Non-literal experience cannot be measured and it is, by any measurable standard, *completely unsuccessful*. It adds nothing of predictive value, nothing of measurable value and there is no way the self can gain from it. It is the loser's philosophy par excellence—only those with nothing really need it, or can really understand it.

§32.

If unself cannot be literally known by self, how can it be expressed? The answer, naturally enough, is non-literally. There are six forms of non-literal expression, or understanding:

i.   REASONING TO THE LIMITS OF THE KNOWABLE. Thinkers such as Hume, Kant, Schopenhauer, Wittgenstein, Feyerabend and many others, both within rationalist frameworks and outside of them, have shown reason, literalist assumptions, objective thought and physicalist science to be inherently, or ultimately, contradictory, paradoxical or limited, taking us to the limit of mind-knowable experience, and implicitly gesturing us towards the ineffable.

ii.   GESTURING BEYOND THE KNOWABLE. The precursor and folk complement to reasoning to the limits of the known, captured in the ancient Hindu expression *neti-neti*—part of the tradition in Eastern thought of reaching the ineffable nature of consciousness, or I, by disposing of what it cannot be—and in the mystic Christian tradition of *apophatic theology*—an endeavour to express the unknowable by showing that the known cannot be it.

iii.   DIRECT EXPRESSION OF QUALITY. Through love, innocent sensitivity, self-sacrifice and presence before nature, unself is revealed. High-quality experiences which can 'reduce' self or take us out of ourselves include spending time with uncorrupted children just being children, experiencing the moment-to-moment grace of great art, witnessing magnificent acts of sacrifice or surprising comic spontaneity, making love with someone you love or living in the wild.

iv.   CALL TO ACTION. Techniques and actions which crack, soften or silence the self, opening it up to unself or unselfish quality. Such techniques can include meditation, being and impro, although most of these have been corrupted by self. A slap on the head and a 'pay attention!' can serve a similar function, as can a subtle gesture of *shush*, or a reckless hug, as can injunctions to pay attention to one's conscience, as can a suggestion that you put down this book now and fully, bodily, absorb the unique character of the moment you are in.

v.   DIRECT UNSELF. Simultaneously the most *common*, the *rarest*, the *subtlest* and the most *powerful* expression of unself (although properly speaking it is not "expression" at all). It is common in that unself—consciousness and context—is ultimately everywhere and in all things; it is rare in that the most conscious thing in the universe—a genuinely unegoic human being—is extremely hard to come by; it is subtle in that self cannot perceive unself, only its qualitative 'after-effects', and it is powerful in that nothing can compare to the experience of being with someone who is completely present.

vi.   METAPHOR. Just as we cannot validate reason without stepping outside of reason, or further knowledge without 'leaping over the fence' of knowledge, so we cannot conceptually express and understand consciousness without using symbols and expressions that are meaningless without understanding consciousness. Such symbols and expressions are those which indicate a *non-literal* approach to reality.

§33.

The word metaphor is itself a metaphor. It once literally meant to 'carry across'. Now we use it to indicate the carrying across of non-literal meaning from one idea onto another; 'gratitude eats anxiety', for example, non-literally carries the idea of 'something that eats' across to 'feeling thankful' and the idea of 'food' across to 'inner tension'. We can loosely describe any figure of speech or form of expression which carries meaning across from one domain to another as 'metaphorical'; such as ALLEGORY, MYTH, STORY, IRONY, HYPERBOLE, VAGUENESS, ENIGMA, ABSURDITY and PARADOX. In each of these modes of communication, a complex series of symbols carries across unthinkable, conscious qualities and elusive, contextual experiences into thinkable language, through the juxtaposition of quantitatively, *factually* false—yet qualitatively, *fictitiously* truthful—ideas.

There are three kinds of metaphor.

i.   METAPHORS OF SELF literally carry meaning from one mode of self to another in order to express a literal meaning. For example: 'Learning a foreign language is like climbing a mountain', in which the central point is that both require large quantities of measurable effort. Or: 'God created the world in six days', which, for a few people, indicates a literal person literally making a literal world in six literal days. Both of these are 'physicalist metaphors', which refer directly, and (at least in principle) accurately, to objects. 'Solipsistic metaphors', which refer *entirely* to the subject, are unreal, fanciful and arbitrary. They *appear* to be quite different to physicalist metaphors, but are also completely self-bound. We call these *lies* ('Black people are devils') or *illusions* ('The moon wants to eat me').

Metaphors of self only communicate quantitative ideas and personal experiences. Separate domains remain separate, untouched by unitary qualities. In carrying across the literal and the measurable, the ponderous myth of the Hollywood blockbuster, the excitable hyperbole of the scientist, the modern art gallery brochure and the schizophrenic hallucination do not actually tell us anything new but, at best, a more useful way to measure the known. As such they are PSEUDO-META-PHORS and we can ignore them here.

ii.   METAPHORS OF QUALITY non-literally carry meaning from one mode of self to another in order to express a *common quality*. For example: 'Golf is tiddlywinks for grown-ups' in which two games that involve directing a tiny object towards an equally tiny goal are compared, but where the latter confers a non-literal quality—of triviality, childishness or artificiali-ty—onto the former. Or: 'Juliet is the sun', in which a thirteen year-old girl is compared to a huge gaseous sphere consisting of the thermonuclear fusion reactions of hydrogen and helium, in order to express (*through omission*) the luminous quality of both. Poetic and narrative meaning is almost entirely com-municated through metaphors of quality. A great myth, story or poem is made up of many metaphorical expressions, met-aphorical characters and metaphorical events, each reflecting a few common, overarching thematic qualities.

For objectivists, metaphors of quality are either mean-ingless, or an entertaining way of saying something which can be more accurately expressed literally. 'My love is like a rose', for example, introduces all kinds of irrelevant facts which you have to screen out; such as thorniness, evanescence and requiring lots of manure. It would be far more *accurate* to say 'my love is a physical need to procreate, combined with a conceptual appreciation of our similarities and an affective dependency on your attention, all of which I experience as a positive feeling of attraction to you'. This is partly why literal-ists today take science to be more meaningful and instructive than art. More extreme literalists (hyper-physicalists) even deny that metaphors say anything at all, while the most extreme literalists (solipsists) are unable to express anything *but* (associative) metaphors; but their metaphors are empty, merely surreal, and have nothing to do with reality.

iii.   METAPHORS OF UNSELF non-literally carry meaning from unself. For example: 'Worldly people are luminous; the sage is dark',* in which wisdom is compared with a paradoxical absence of clarity. Or: 'Lift a stone and find me there',† in which consciousness is compared to a paradoxical absence of substance or existence. In both cases, the mind is confounded by comparing that which can be imagined with that which cannot. Metaphors of unself take dualistic *form*—we can say that unself, or consciousness and context, is that which "experiences" self, that which "encompasses" self, that which "precedes" self, that which "unifies" self—but these dualistic "relations" between self and unself do not *actually* exist. Quality doesn't actually hover above phenomena like a cloud, nor does it "penetrate" self or "meet" it.

Metaphors of unself are the only way to conceptually express or experience the inexpressible. Mind can take the mind to its limits, but only metaphor can speak from the other side, which means that I must also somehow exist 'on the other side' in order to speak or hear them. For literalists, this is impossible, for there is no 'known' within experience that is *like* conscious experience *of* knowledge. This doesn't just mean that, for the literalist, unself is inexpressible metaphorically, it also means that quality cannot be comprehended through it. When I say 'He has a face like a rusty bicycle' the evoked quality of the comparison is discarded in favour of the mere facts, which seem arbitrarily surreal or merely entertaining. This inability to *sense out* enigmatic quality—of what cannot be said, or predicted—is why literalists are uncomfortable with meaningful metaphors, have difficulty grasping them, will move to control or ban them wherever possible and why those metaphors they do use are ploddingly obvious or, in the case of the solipsist, flat-out bizarre.

---

* Lao Tzu, *The Tao Te Ching* (tr. Ellen Chen)
† *The Gospel of Thomas*

§34.

LANGUAGE exists on a spectrum between the literal and the metaphorical. Literal language comprises proper names and comprehensible relations between them. In the phrase 'Aldous Huxley sat in Westminster Cathedral' there is practically a one-to-one correspondence between the words and what happened, assuming it did happen. Metaphorical language comprises common names and metaphorical relations between them. In the sentence 'Some men don't understand broken hearts' none of the words refer to anything actually existing in the world. Hearts cannot 'break' and there is, actually, no such a thing as 'men' in general, only a large number of specific men with something in common that we denote with the word 'men'. The word 'understand' exists in a halfway state. It has a semi-literal component, indicating something like 'intellectually grasp' (from experience) while also suggesting participatory empathy. It also once had a literal meaning—'stand under'—like an enormous number of other words ('repent' was once to change direction, 'right' was to move in a straight line, 'opportunity' was a passage, 'strange' was to come from somewhere else, and so on). Through a blend of literality and metaphor we reach the whole, and, finally, ineffable, qualitative sense of meaning which we share in speech.

Literal-metaphorical poles of meaning don't just apply to sentence-expression, but to words and isolated signs. The word 'stone', for example, indicates a series of literal *facts* which all stones have in common (of being small, hard, solid and mineral) while also standing for and—largely through a blend of tone, intonation and phrasing—evoking various non-literal *qualities* of stoniness (the various memories I have related to stones and the cultural attributes connected to the word, all of which come to me as a vague stone-feeling). We normally call the former, literal element the 'concrete' meaning, and the latter non-literal element, the 'abstract' meaning, but we have it the wrong way round. The literal stone-word is not of an *actual* stone—it only gains its meaning from referring to what all stones have in common—whereas the evoked sound-feeling sense of stoniness *is* (or at least can be) that which it is *of*, just as music is (in that I don't need to ask what a melody is 'about'). Language, in truth, evolved from such direct transmission of quality or meaning in music; intonation and musical phrasing preceded speech in humans, just as it does in young children, who musically wibble away before their speech has literal content.

Music is, ultimately, neither graspably literal nor metaphorically evocative; it is the very quality of the represented thing, a quality which speaks directly to the selfless, such as young children and primal people, who do not learn 'words' and then apply them to literal 'things' which then became metaphors, but directly express the quality of things as a concatenation of sounds, tones, gestures and literal meanings. Primal man, like our primal children, did not perceive a thing and then conceive a word, he experienced the thing-in-itself of which *both* perception *and* conception are *representations*.

Over time, as quality recedes from experience, non-literal metaphors are estranged from experience, solipsistically cut off from the character of things, and come to seem unreal, or less real than literal meanings. Once, the full spectrum of meaning—both literal and non-literal—inhered in stone-speech which, like the somatic representation of the stone, 'participated' in the stone-in-itself. The music of both was directly accessible through literal-non-literal language. Now, however, we believe there are two kinds of stone, the literal stone, which is what scientists deal with. That's the *correct* meaning, which you must be an expert to understand, or consult a reliable reference work to 'get right'. Then there's the non-literal stone, the artistic stone, the qualitative sense of the actual stone, before my eyes, which manifests as speech about it that anyone can use and understand; no training required, but no real meaning either. Just a kind of dream.

For ego, reality is representation, and so language which does not convey the causal facts of representation must be meaningless. For unself, reality is experienced as representation "of" the thing-in-itself—which means that language, including sound and gesture, can present to us *what is* as directly as our senses can. When representation became divorced from consciousness, language became split into the literal and the metaphorical; the former boring but 'true', the latter entertaining but 'false'. 'Emotion', we now believe, refers to a literal non-physical thing. 'Stone' refers to a literal physical thing. That emotion, or responsibility, or culture, has a physicality to it, or that stone, or peanut, or nematode, a metaphorical quality cannot be literally accepted.

§35.

The idea we have today is that language was once literal; 'Ugg need fire. Bring fire to Ugg'. The word 'emotion', for example, meant literally 'moving out'. Then language acquired non-literal 'inner' meanings. Literal 'moving out' came to be applied to inward movement and, finally, the literal meaning was lost, leaving just subjective experience. Metaphor has therefore become for us a fanciful halfway house between two kinds of direct, sensible, correctnesses; the original simple language of Ugg's crude literalism and the sophisticated modern language of scientifically refined literalism. According to this weird image of the evolution of language, it was impossible to think or speak of feeling, or doubt, or spirit, or conceit in our distant past before metaphor appeared, because we could only speak of literal objects; and it is now impossible to speak of vague qualities and feelings without those same qualities being either objective—and therefore not really qualities—or subjective—and therefore not really things.

Splitting quality into either subjective fancy or objective fact is not a philosophical trend confined to specialist discourse, but a universal social movement towards the annihilation of quality, in which morality, truth, goodness, love and so on become subjective, non-literal, chimerical ('who are *you* to say what's good and bad!?'); that, or the consequence of chemicals, genes and diseases, literal stuff that can be owned, traded and stolen (*'Actually,* we now know that morality is just an expression of mammalian bonding instincts'). Quality in such a world might help us to get along and be respectful of each other, or it might have some kind of entertainment value, but either it's not real and is irrelevant to the nitty-gritty *business* of life, or its reality comes down to literal, utilitarian and ultimately selfish well-being, or satisfaction.

In reality, consciousness experiences *both* thing *and* meaning, (or quantity *and* quality) as one, and has always done so. As Owen Barfield explained,* when conscious primal man said 'wind' he *also* meant 'spirit', when he said 'breathe in' he *also* meant 'inspiration'. Likewise, when the self-soft, sensitive or 'artistic' modern man says 'bound' he evokes a network of boundy qualities which can be 'metaphorically' applied all over the shop. In other words the *concepts* 'spirit', 'breathe in' and 'bound' are representations of qualities, of which the *percepts* spirit, breath in and bound are *also* representations. The word 'understand' *seems* to come from 'standing under', so we assume that 'standing under' was once the literal word, created by a literalist mind, whereas, in truth, the word 'understand' was just *one* represented example of standing under, just as literally standing under something was. *Words represent meaning in the same way things represent meaning.*

What came first, the chicken or the egg? There are three answers. One, the scientific, literalist answer, which applies to the represented world, is that the egg came first. The egg was present long before chickens; reptiles, insects and fish, which developed into chickens, all lay them. The second answer, the solipsist answer, is that there is no answer; you can choose whichever one you please. The truth, however, that of the chicken and egg-in-themselves, is that there *is* no first; both chicken and egg, like matter and mind, "came" from unself.

The fundamental "origin" of *both* the literal *and* non-literal in a single, enigmatic source, is why Plato, Schopenhauer and Jung were interested in what they called 'ideas' and 'archetypes'. These are not magical items hanging behind reality, like rubber stamps from which the objects of the world are printed off. They are, rather, the thing-in-itself which the form in front of me, *and* the name of it, *and* the quality of it, *and* the measurement of it, are *all* "manifestations." So it is with

---

* Owen Barfield, *The Rediscovery of Meaning*

'uncle', or 'man', or 'trickster'; "behind" these roles is a quality of uncle-in-itself, and man-in-itself, and trickster-in-itself which shines through, and which great artists endeavour to illuminate by expressing intense uncleness, the essence of man or the unmistakable p'tang of tricksterism.

§36.

Objective literalism understands the referents of words as literal things, the operation of the mind as a literal thing, will, consciousness and sensation as literal things, understanding as grasping a literal thing, and activity as following a series of literal laws. The literalist philosopher then asks how we can know other minds exist, or how we can will what we will, or how complex knowledge can come to us in a flash, or how we can know that other people are conscious. It's not unlike someone deciding that all liquids are 'really' a collection of 'dry' atoms and then wondering how people can ever get wet. As soon as you conceive of intention, feeling or meaning as a *thing*, it becomes completely baffling what that thing is and how it can influence another thing.

In reality, consciousness, will, sensation and experience are not literal things, existing in space and changing through time. They exist, but they are irreducible to thought and to language; indeed thought and language *themselves* are not a separate series of things literally referring to other things. They are *activities** which, like all activities, we learn *from* activity, or practice, within a complex context which gives language, thought and knowledge meaning. I don't have to consult an inner dictionary to understand you, or grasp the ideas your words convey as I would grasp a slab or a pineapple. I *recognise* them as part of my experience. Likewise, I do not remember something by looking for a memory-thing in the mind—for how would I recognise it unless I had a second memory to consult, and a third to consult for that, and so on? Rather, the will to remember (thelema) and the memory itself (nous) are a single activity, like the flight of Zeno's arrow, which I get better or worse at through practice or lack of.

---

* Ludwig Wittgenstein, *Philosophical Investigations*

This isn't to say that there is nothing literal about communication, memory or anything else. Reality is *both* literal *and* non-literal, but the former is subordinate to the latter, just as quantity is subordinate to quality, desire to love, society to solitude, and self to unself; or at least it is for anyone who is conscious.

§37.

The physicalist is separated from reality by inhabiting an entirely literal, shared world, while the solipsist is cut off by inhabiting an entirely non-literal, private world. Both are egoic—the former because it is *entirely* literal, the latter because it is *entirely* private—and both are threatened by the non-literal. The physicalist automatically defends himself against the *non-literal* half of reality by thinking and perceiving literally. All allusive, allegorical, ironic and vague incursions into his reality strike him as insufficiently serious, technically incorrect or absurdly overblown. The solipsist defends herself against the *shared*, objective half of reality by thinking and perceiving privately. All straightforward, reasonable, factual experience and expression appear to her as far too serious, boring or controlling. Although these two positions tend to be entrenched, egoism can shift between physicalism and solipsism, sometimes over the span of a few minutes, one moment baffled by allusion and irony, or blind to tone and vibe, the next refusing to see meaning in a simple, direct, statement of objective fact.

The physicalist takes non-literal metaphor as meaningless (or *unfunny*) and the solipsist takes literal expression as without quality. The former is unable to distinguish truthful enigma from solipsistic word-salad, navel-gazing and pretentious twaddle, and tends to avoid metaphor, which he feels uncomfortable with and routinely misunderstands. The latter is unable to distinguish clear, direct, tradition-shaped expressions embedded in the shared reality of representation, from the loveless production of automata, and tends to avoid literal speech, which she fears, preferring to spin arbitrary and meaningless metaphors entirely out of her own half-brain.

The egoic physicalist is forced to cross the threshold between self and unself, or between my self and yours, with technique and with literalist pseudo-metaphors of self, while the egoic solipsist doesn't cross it at all, as there is nowhere to cross over to, just a self-serving, self-referential matrix of arbitrary metaphors which appears to be reality. The physicalist refuses to employ metaphors, or drains them of quality and consciousness, while the solipsist refuses to employ meaningful metaphors that express reality, generating an endless sequence of empty symbols to express her confinement. In both cases the other is locked out, which is why it is such an unbearably unpleasant experience communicating with physcalist egos who can only take metaphor literally or solipsist egos who can only take literality metaphorically.

§38.

Metaphors express that which cannot be literally grasped; non-factual, non-causal experience. The threat of such experience is automatically brought under control by the literalist ego in the act of representing unself and isolating this representation from consciousness and context. This creates empty representations, also known [here] as TOKENS, and fossilised metaphors, also known as CLICHES.

An empty token is a letter, word, icon, image, or any other such symbolic representation, which is completely separated from quality. It does not *show* quality, by letting it speak for itself, but *tells* us that something is good, by substituting actual quality for a symbolic stand-in. In a quality anecdote, for example, I show you what happened by simply relating events, decorated with emphasis, and leave you to feel the absurdity, beauty or the horror inherent in them; while in a token anecdote I substitute absent quality with some variant of 'it was really, really good'. Such SIGNPOSTS replace quality with self-stimulating routines and effects, such as an excess of swearwords, emphasis words (really, incredibly, amazingly), over-emphatic gestures (hand-waving, high-pitched tone, gurning), titillating references to food, flesh and gore, special effects, rapid flash-cutting, convention-flouting, excessive volume, excess salt, sugar and fat, and so on. None of these routines and effects, it need hardly be added, are low-quality in themselves, only insofar as they are symbolic substitutes *for* quality, or character. Only then do they become PORNOGRA-PHY. No vice is as bad as the means by which it is concealed.

Cliches are created by the self-informed self, unable to let go of itself, and so inevitably confined *to* itself. The purpose of self is to pick out experience, write a little habit into the wax of the character, and then melt back into the moment. If there is nothing but self in experience, there is nothing *but* self-informed habit-writing, creating deeper and deeper scripts, routines, paths of thought and action, until all I am is a crude, unfractal grid of wrinkles on a face with nothing behind it. Ego is a cliche machine; everything it touches turns to cliche. It cannot react spontaneously to context and consciousness, or journey with another down the collective stream of meaning we call *communication*, carrying us to who-knows-where; and so must confine itself to the *known*, which, through repeti-tion, becomes *more* known. Cliche here, therefore, does not just refer to the standard fixed idiom we normally call cliche ('How are you?' 'Can't complain; know what I mean?'), nor even to metaphor drained of quality—ponderous, preachy allegories and parables, cold and cruel irony, manic hyperbole, arbitrary enigma and absurdity, pointless myth and, in place of delightful paradox, mere contradiction—but, beyond lan-guage, to any fixed path of attention. Thus, we can speak not just of cliched expressions but cliched stories, cliched songs, cliched faces and cliched personalities. There are also, to a lesser degree, cliched soups, cliched chairs, cliched houses, and cliched techniques, although these are necessarily cliched to a lesser degree because, in technical work, character plays a subordinate role, and so the horror of predictable myths, ma-chine-made pop songs, mask-like faces and robotic people is far greater than that of 70s cooking, mass-produced furniture, prefab housing and rigid, non-adaptive techniques, which are revolting more than horrifying. Or at least they are to anyone with blood still pumping through their hearts.

Nous, thelema, viscera and soma carve 'grooves' into the self through repetition, which then push thought, movement, feeling and perception down the consequent channels. Initially, these grooves, when they are shallow HABITS, have use-value and can be easily abandoned. They remain, as it were, 'within reach'. But, as they deepen, they begin to *force* experience through them, and to demand more energy than they liberate. The habit then 'gets out of hand', and starts to take over. Thus, the oft-trod *path* is useful and allows the selfless individual to wander from it at will, while the *motorway* is worse than useless — entirely destructive — and commands total obedience to its routes and requirements. We call an inability to exit cliche an *addiction*. In fact, you can only be addicted to tokens and cliches.

§ 39.

Cliche and token prosper in the *absence of consciousness*, a state in which quality is absorbed by literal, functional language and in which the other is nothing but a self-represented projection which, through mechanistic communication, is used by the self-informed self to pleasure or empower itself. The function of ego and symbol under such circumstances is not to communicate, but to provoke an unconscious, *operational* response. Ego is unable to selflessly take another's place and empathically inhabit the shared tree of meaning growing between us, and unable to leap over the fence of habit on a whim and respond directly to consciousness and context. It must, instead, confine itself to a *separate* channel of meaning which can only reach *your* separate channel by signalling with empty, *essentially* private, token and cliche. Ego does not really *speak*; it excites, threatens, or offers cues from the social script that all within an egoic society are expected to know and to follow, or be regarded as a threat.

Unconscious selves manufacture cliched and empty symbolic gestures, ideas, feelings and faces at the same prodigious rate that unconscious societies manufacture cliched and symbolic apples, farms and shops. In fact, you can measure the unconsciousness of a person or society by how many cliches and tokens they produce. The speech of ego is full of emphatic tokens and cliches (although that of the extreme solipsist, who doesn't require communication, is completely devoid of emphasis) designed to elicit predictable responses, while egoic awareness turns entirely inwards, leaving, in lieu of an apt, attentive response, an immobile frozen face, eyes unlit, mouth robotically giving the requisite number of reallys? uh-huhs and oh-nos! Ideas like freedom, justice, democracy, socialism, tradition, safety, wealth and other words divorced from unself serve the same function. These are applied, through constant repetition by, and identification with, unconscious selves and societies, to a specific set of attributes which are supposed to be evoked whenever the word is heard, thereby depriving them of threatening quality. That a wealthy, healthy, highly qualified citizen of a safe, free, democratic country is *actually* poor, sick, stupid, insecure, enslaved and completely powerless becomes an inexpressible thought.

Unconscious exchanges run from cliched, mechanical, stimulus-reward exchanges that businessmen, politicians and quality-immune families give each other, through signposts of warmth and humanity (such as the Big and Lovely kiss-kiss half-hug or the hand-clasped, back-slapping bro-embrace), through standard cliches (such as 'to be honest', which means 'please believe that I am a truthful person', or 'I'm not being funny', which means 'if I hurt your feelings it's because *you* are funny') to emphatic set-phrases (such as 'deliver the goods' or 'avoid like the plague' or 'lead a dog's life' which add emphasis where there is none). The mediocre teacher or public speaker habituated to speaking to a lost audience forces meaning upon it with a series of attention-grabbing cliches and tokens; the distracted, unhappy, unconscious parent, isolated from his or her child, substitutes loving attention with symbolic signposts and mechanically exciting cliched experiences; the politician or company man, enclosed in a self-rewarding system, communicates in constantly repeated slogans and emotionally-potent symbols; the doctor brings down a warm fog of hypnotic professional authority with

mechanically-repeated set-phrases of encouragement or op-
probrium; and the sales assistant snaps into a well-rehearsed
sub-routine of 'cheerful' greeting that we both pretend to
accept as meaningful and human. On and on and on it goes,
at least in an egoic world such as ours. We are exposed to so
much cliche that we begin to think that it is meaningful, that
repeating cliches *is* communication.

People who are comfortable with cliched modes of communication are immune to contradiction and quality, and
they are unable to reject quantitative satisfaction. They are
therefore susceptible to the crudest forms of manipulation.
This is the case even if such cliches and tokens are emotionally
rejected, ironically delivered or presented in full awareness of
their falsity. In an attempt to retain autonomy or authenticity
in the mechanistic dreamscape of ordinary communication,
man attempts to distance himself from the cliched experience,
smirk at the silliness of it all, or justify the flagrant pretence
he is forced to engage in. He doesn't realise that, firstly, what
you believe or disbelieve is irrelevant to the functioning of
the cliched script—only how you *behave* is of importance.
Secondly, that your experience of mechanical anti-speech is,
like anti-food, absorbed by your self regardless of your attitude
towards it. Finally, and most importantly, the split between
the 'what I am' here and 'what I'm not' there is *itself* a cliche.

§40.

Anyone who wishes to *commune* with another human being
must qualitatively experience that being in himself, not remain at the symbolic level of what can be controlled through
token and cliche. In this sense, everything which I experience,
including every other human being, is a unique enigma which
is levelled out by the generic concepts, percepts, affects and
acts of ego. Ego does not see the great man, the profound
woman, the beautiful tree in the wind, the truthful philosophy
or the mysterious glance, rather a kind of copy or shell of these
things which, if ego can *get* something from them, it will like,
otherwise it will ignore, belittle or destroy them.

Those activities, therefore, which treat reality *as* a shell, as a collection of generic facts, tokens and cliches, necessarily attract egos; chief amongst which today are the activities we call science and business (including all the professional, religious and artistic activities which are subordinate to them). This is why scientists and businessmen are so often devoid of individuality and must bolt on a post-hoc wacky or 'artistic' personality as compensation. He might be an hilarious 'eccentric', and as a desperate counterweight to the mundanity of his life, he often is, or he might be given to all kinds of aesthetic raptures (although he is heavily disposed to the hackneyed), and he might liberally co-opt quality words such as 'wonder', and 'majesty', and 'beautiful' to describe his trivial discoveries, or he might just let himself slump into the pudding of ordinariness that makes up the mass of mankind. But however much conscious individuality pokes through the mask, it must play no significant part in his day-to-day activity as a scientist or businessman or technician. If he is seeking to genuinely break through into a new paradigm then, yes, he must go outside and leap the fence to call on a living experience of reality, but once he's grasped that, he rushes back home, brings down the shutters, closes the curtains, locks the doors and empties the room.

For this reason, scientists and businessmen tend to avoid great art, any activity which involves genuine improvisation, meaningful experiences in the wild (i.e. those that involve living with it rather than conquering it through sport) or anything else which requires quality or consciousness. They confine themselves almost entirely to familiar experiences and familiar modes of experience, such as the pseudo-metaphors of self required to make money and make knowledge.

§41.

Mathematics is a fundamental pseudo-metaphor of self. It is founded on abstract 'images' of time (temporal sequences of symbols conditioned by or related to 'previous' symbols) and abstract 'images' of space (object-symbols from which individuality, or actuality, has been abstracted). When I count, for example, I either create an ordered, or *ordinal*, sequence from an abstract conception of previous things which I have abstractly determined are the same ('6 apples' only makes sense through being related to the sequence, in time, of objects which share common 'appley' features), or, I compare things which I have abstractly determined are different, or *cardinally* separate from the context and from each other (3 apples are 3 separate things, like 3 oranges are, or 3 voles).* Not that mathematical symbols, at least since Descartes, are related to anything material or sensory, but that even in the simplest, classical sense, none of the identities or distinctions denoted by numbers exist in reality, in the thing-in-itself. They are brought into being by the activity of self; noetic conception, somatic perception and thelemic function, or technique.

Although numbers can be said to in some way apply to the somatic, sensory world, they do not need it to be understood; they are based on the literal, 'countable', structure of the self itself. Number, therefore, may be perfectly self-consistent and may perfectly apply, via perception, to self-like abstractable elements of the thing-in-itself—which is how it can be so very useful—but no *intrinsic* connection to the perceived world can ever be found. You cannot find 'five' or 'seven' anywhere in your senses, only five-like results and seven-like groups. You cannot even easily say, as you can with physics, biology and chemistry, what the object of mathematics actually is. Number is only *like* what-is; which is to say, it is a [pseudo] metaphor. This is how we can speak of 'different mathematics'. There are, in history, or at least to some degree, *different* solutions to how number applies to existence, rather than one *correct* monolith of mathematical truth. There is no reason not to suppose that an alien race might have a foundationally different mathematics.

Similarly, measurement is a pseudo-metaphor. In the perceived universe there are not just no numbers, but also no edges (elementary particles are not even measurable in principle, certainly not with macroscopic measuring implements) no fixed lengths (the length of a moving object, and

---

* Roger Jones, *Physics as Metaphor*

all objects are moving, is shorter than its length at rest), no absolute time (the only absolute is in timeless consciousness, everything outside of that doesn't just move in time, but moves at different speeds) and no objective way of accurately determining whether two points (the 'length' of a table, say, and the points on a measuring stick) are coincident. When we say that a table *is* two metres long, or a proton *is* 0.84–0.87 femtometres wide, what we actually mean is *like*.* What's more, the act of measurement affects that which is being measured; checking the pressure of a car tyre, for example, is impossible without disturbing the pressure. In macroscopic objects the 'observer-effect' is usually negligible, but becomes significant when the infinitesimally small constituents of objects are measured. The scientist has to *assume* that the measurement is reporting the exact fact, even though he knows it cannot. Similarly, in order to measure, the scientist has to rule out everything in space and time but the thing being measured and then assume—an assumption based on faith—that his measurements, and the laws he forms to explain them, apply to what he has ruled out, or to those aspects of reality he hasn't found, or that have yet to pass into existence.

Likewise, prediction is a pseudo-metaphor. Scientists are in the habit of telling us that 'scientific laws' can predict outcomes—eclipses, for example, or the failure rate of fastening parts. What is actually happening is that one set of numbers are computed from another set and then compared to reality. These readings can never precisely fit the observed outcome because measurements and observations are limited by measuring and observing instruments, including the instrument of the self. More seriously, a rule can *never* determine whether any difference between prediction and observation is down to observational error or is a deviation from theory. *We* have to determine this, from experience. As Michael Polanyi pointed out,† 'personal, tacit judgements and assessments are required at every step in the acquisition of knowledge'.

Attempting to establish logical foundations for number is like trying to prove that Juliet really is the sun, and taking numbers literally leads to the same kind of incomprehensible

---

* Ibid.

† Michael Polanyi, *Meaning*

absurdity as assuming that the universe is *really* balancing on
the back of a turtle. None of this is a problem for sensible
mathematicians, any more than the impossibility of conceiving
of the reality that quantum mechanics measures is a problem
for intelligent physicists. Numbers 'fit' reality well enough to
make accurate, and therefore useful, measurements; but this
doesn't make them any less metaphorical, or, without the art
of a human to apply them, any less meaningless. It's only a
problem to the literalist scientist, unable to take the symbols
he works with metaphorically; because he knows, somehow,
that if he did so he'd have to take himself metaphorically too.

§42.

The active, conscious PARTICIPATION of the knower in knowledge is a primary element in art, but it is just as indispensable to all literal knowledge, including mathematics and
the measurements and predictions of mathematical science.
Consciousness dwells "within" the participating, human body
of the scientist the same way a blind man 'dwells' within the
end of his stick.* The blind man focuses on the far end of
the stick, and the literal idea of the world that it transmits to
him, but these literal experiences are *completely* dependent on
a conscious experience which, while remaining tacit, background, unfocused, is the foundation for the knowledge the
stick communicates to him, indeed for all knowledge (which
is the reason why knowing anything of any importance always
comes down to 'well, it just feels right').

Consciousness and context are excluded by ego, which
is forced to *completely* identify with the end of the stick, unable
to reach beyond it. The physicalist ego might then say, as the
end of the stick knocks against objective things, that 'I work
from evidence not presumption', while the solipsist ego might
say, as it knocks against subjective things, that 'I work by instinct not analytical thought'. Neither of them can let go of the
stick, which, like any overused tool, then takes hold of *them*.

The ground of our knowledge—empirical, logical or
metaphysical—must always be intellectually unknown to us;

* ibid.

because who, finally, knows it? Who operates or regards the machine of knowledge? Who or what, exactly, is holding the stick here? Any conceptual answer just sends the operator back another stage, and another, *ad infinitum*. Eventually, we must exit the hall of intellectual mirrors, concede that knowing is grounded in panjective being, in dwelling within or intimately participating in reality, and *be* that. Easier said than done.

§43.

We call conceptual theorising about 'the far end of the stick', CLASSICAL SCIENCE, the activity of isolating things from the context, relating them to each other, theorising and hypothesising about these relations, and then testing them against the represented world of perception.

Classical science is founded on three pillars; causality, facticity and non-participation. Causality in classical science is the principle that reality is ultimately describable in terms of matter and motion; that if we know the position and momentum of all the particles of a system we can, from their determinate influence on each other, predict their position and momentum at any other time. Facticity is the principle that everything in reality is a fundamentally describable, mind-graspable, non-paradoxical *thing*. And non-participation is the principle that consciousness cannot affect objective reality. If a nineteenth century scientist had claimed that the position and momentum of particles cannot *ever* be known, that they can *never* be accurately conceived of, and that conscious observation affected their behaviour, he would have been given a sound thrashing; and yet this was precisely what was discovered in the first few decades of the twentieth century, in a series of experiments which showed, beyond all doubt, that whatever it is that the universe is made of can instantaneously travel from one point to another (even, apparently, backwards through time), that it is *both* one thing *and* another thing (or *both* here *and* there) and that observation of it affects (indeed even appears to brings into existence) what is being observed. In short; that reality *is* non-causal (eternal or unchanging), non-factual (paradoxical) and non-literal (consciousness and context are unfathomably connected).

Unsurprisingly, literalist scientists were not comfortable with these conclusions, and so they immediately set out to pretend they didn't exist, focusing entirely on the literal, conceivable *results* of their experiments, and on literal, conceivable accounts based thereon. These observable effects were formalised in QUANTUM SCIENCE. Particles and waves do not really exist in quantum theory; the former exists as a potential in the latter which itself is not an event or a phenomenon but a description of the probability of an event occurring. Theories that predict these events are all but watertight, but reflections on what the particle actually *is*, on what quantum measurements are *of*, are not just as irrelevant to quantum physics as they are to classical physics, but ruled out in principle. Quantum physics does not describe reality, it describes probability *patterns* that emerge from reality, and *symbols* which represent it, both of which are the result of operational observation. Reality does not exist in quantum physics in any meaningful sense—only mankind's manipulations of it do. Quantum physicists and physicalist philosophers then either make the outrageous claim that because the patterns and symbols that result from their observations are comprehensible, the reality they refer to must also be somehow comprehensible; or, more usually, they just ignore the question of what is 'really' going on as an irritating distraction. In the former case, in order to preserve the appearance of a reality that is still conceptually rule-bound in the teeth of quantum incomprehensibility, physicalists have proposed all kinds of absurd theories to explain what their measurements are of. In the latter case, the essential non-causality, non-facticity and non-literality of nature is vaguely conflated with lazy spiritualist reasoning ('Quantum mechanics therefore Elvis lives') and ruled out as unscientific mystic silliness.

What all this means, is that classical science, which here includes both 'common sense' and general relativity, can never be reconciled with quantum theory, because the former literally describes representation and the latter literally describes the unrepresentable. They can no more be reconciled than love-making and maths, or cookery and jazz; at least not until that which they have in common—the non-literal—is accepted. Without such acceptance, a 'theory of everything' could explain everything in the universe—it could literally be the most useful thing ever discovered—while revealing precisely *nothing* about anything of any importance. Take paradox, eternity, quality, consciousness and context into account however, and the classical theories of Euclid, Isaac Newton and Albert Einstein, and the quantum theories of Werner Heisenberg, Niels Bohr and Erwin Schrödinger are seen for what they are; metaphors for a reality which, *ultimately*, cannot be rationally observed. Only lived.

§44.

A metaphor which unites classical and quantum science was discovered at the beginning of the Romantic era by August Möbius and expounded at the end of the nineteenth century by Charles Hinton.* For half a century it was a reasonably popular field of enquiry for both scientists and artists, before all but disappearing from serious thought. This was the metaphor of THE FOURTH DIMENSION, popularised by Edwin Abbott in the playful metaphor of FLATLAND.†

What we call self exists in three conceivable spatial dimensions, and an inconceivable fourth dimension which we call 'time' (*all* our conceptions of time—sundial shadows, clock ticks, cycles of radiation from a caesium atom—are spatial). Imagine, instead, a world of two spatial dimensions, 'Flatland', on a plane of length and breadth but zero height, upon which Flatlanders live their lives, never rising above or falling below it. How, the metaphor asks, would the 2D self of a Flatlander perceive a three dimensional object, say an apple, that bisected its reality? It would 'naturally' perceive it in *two* dimensions, as the edge of a slice of zero thickness. Flatlanders would see and move around the outside of the slice, the skin, but could never see what the 'unselfish' 3D apple really is. If the apple passed through Flatland, they would see it appear out of

---

* Charles Hinton, *The Fourth Dimension*
† Edwin Abbott, *Flatland*

nowhere, grow, shrink and vanish again. They would say that it had 'lived' through what they call 'time', whereas in fact it had *moved* through a *space* they are unable to perceive. If the apple were connected to a tree, and that passed through their reality, Flatlanders would see many things being born, living, connecting up (as the branches coalesced into each other), forming one single organism (the trunk) then separating out again (into roots) and vanishing. In truth, in three dimensions, there is no appearance, no separation, no growth and no disappearance; just movement. Or imagine a wheel with a regular arrangement of different coloured spokes—say red, blue and green—rotating through Flatland. Flatlanders would see two-dimensional coloured surfaces appear and disappear in a regular order and would *rationally* conclude that the red thing was 'causing' the blue one, the blue thing 'causing' the green, the green the red and so on. It would never occur to them that there is no causal arrangement at all, because it *could* not occur to them.

Nothing that is obvious to our selves could *conceivably* occur to the selves of Flatlanders, because their entire experience is two-dimensional. Nothing we could possibly say about a thelemically TRANSDIMENSIONAL reality could make any somatic or noetic sense to them. If their society (their aesthetics, their ethics, their politics) were founded on selfish perception and conception—on satisfaction—what we said would be ignored, taken literally, or dismissed as mere entertainment, or as comedy, or as exaggeration, or as nonsense, or, most likely, as a dangerous threat. To manufacturers of two-dimensionally satisfying art, to proponents of two-dimensionally literalist meaning, to defenders of two-dimensionally reassuring safety, all expressions of three-dimensional reality, in which there is no birth and death (just movement of the 3D tree through 2D 'reality'), no separation between subject and object (between 'my' branch and 'yours'), indeed no conceivable things at all; all of this would be indistinguishable from solipsistic madness and judged to be literally insane, even if viewing 2D 'reality' from a 3D perspective cleared up most of the perplexing problems of living that Flatlanders had.

§45.

Just as our view of Flatland makes meaning of its mysteries, so viewing the 3D 'reality' of 'Solidland' metaphorically, from a four-dimensional perspective, evaporates many of our own mysteries, or at least gives us a viscerally *intuitive* sense of their illusory nature:

i.　Scientific mysteries. The apparently end-directed (a.k.a. TELEOLOGICAL) nature of processes which can only apparently be explained mechanically (such as evolution) make sense when viewed as four-dimensional wholes; the almost unbelievably specialist adaptations of nature come about neither through acts of will (cosmic or Lamarckian) nor through selection by survival of a randomly shaken bag of genes; because they don't 'come about' at all. The will is either a lie or a metaphor, and evolutionary science is *factually* true, but only when applied to the sliver of time we perceive. Likewise, the baffling paradoxes of quantum science, in which particles that appear to be separate from each other in three dimensional space, yet are also bizarrely entangled, are intuitively resolved by viewing them as the *same* particle, viewed incompletely. Similarly, the mystery of time's arrow—why the universe should have begun with a high degree of complexity which gradually dissipates into bland chaos—vanishes if there is no time as we understand the word. Not that we *do* understand the word, for its essence lies outside of factual-causal thought (which is why it is impossible to experimentally prove it exists); and not that the 'no time' which reveals this essence means no *movement*—4D objects move just as 3D ones do, for they are alive; and not that what we ordinarily call time—the directional, spatially-representational, 3D clock-time of the past and the future—is an illusion. That is also real, as real as Flatland and Solidland, but only ever partially, spatially, factually and causally. The actual, intuitive *reality* of time, as four-dimensional space, is an *experience*, which I may *think* of as a spatial idea, but can only, possibly, *live*. If I do, I know— and few do—that *I am time*.

ii. Philosophical mysteries. What words mean and how they can have meaning, how motion can be composed of non-moving moments, how individual things can have a separate character to the whole, and a host of conundrums that come into existence by considering slices of existence—not least of which what on earth should I *do?*—melt into an intuitive whole when considered as part of complete 4D processes passing through our merely *apparent* timespace.

The various enigmas of history also vanish when viewed as a causeless whole. Seen as events and processes which cause other events and processes, history is as elusive, confusing and haphazard as thought, speech and meaning. Taken out of time however, as a single living whole, cultures and societies are complete, manifest in their parts as character is manifest in the shape of one's hands, and although partially amenable to scientific thought, finally as elusive to such ham-fisted dissections as any other natural thing. The wise historian sees in history what the sensitive artist sees in a tree.

iii. The mysteries of psychology. The 3D view of personal characteristics is as objects jostling around in the brainbox. Thus, confidence or creativity are, for the typical psychologist, *things* which can be somehow implanted with a bit of therapising, or a good self-help book, or detected with an FMRI scan, or by ingesting fluoxetine, citalopram or paroxetine. That our qualities exist in mysterious time, as the result of innumerable experiences blended into consciousness and context, is unpleasant for the institutionalised ego to seriously consider, for it means that to really understand ourselves, solve our personal problems and develop new capacities, demands not merely swapping one thought or feeling for another, but living in a different way, one that necessitates uprooting a tree that started growing at the age of none.

Thus, for example, one is justified at feeling pride at one's abilities, but ultimately it makes about as much sense as having pride in the weather. Likewise, to blame other people for their bitchy small-mindedness or arrogant insensitivity may also, in context, address the disgraceful lack of consciousness of an individual, but more often than not omits the thick, thick roots of unhappiness that stretch back *generations* in time, and out into the distal world of space.

iv.   The mysteries of art. The character of objects that great artists represent to us are at least partly expressions of their transdimensional forms. A plank of wood that came from a church has, to those soft-selved enough to perceive it, a different character to one taken from a gallows, because it continues to be that which it once was, as dead skin continues to be one with the living body.* Likewise, music and acting present piecemeal expressions of character apparently flowing through time, but which are actually whole; which is why we have a *whole* sense of a performance that only ever comes to us as a series of isolated moments, just as we have a whole sense of what we say to each other, even though meaning dribbles into our minds bit by lexical bit.

The essential four-dimensional unity of experience that the representational self experiences piecemeal also explains the selfless feeling that great artists often have when creating of discovering what was *already* there in the melody or the stone; because it *was* already there. It also explains the profound, overwhelming sense of DESTINY that saturates all great stories (and a few not-so-great ones). Even atheists reject stories that are not structured around an underlying fatefulness, even when they reject the meaning of that fate.

v.   The mystery of my life. For the selfless—sensitive to time as it is, rather than to time as it spatially appears—life, like art, is also illuminated by a sense of destiny, shining before them when they are young, guiding them through the trials of adulthood, and then, when they are old, shaping the land they have left into an intuitively complete and meaningful whole. The egoic man, by contrast, is *haunted* by destiny, which comes to him as a torment, a guilty sense of having betrayed the man that he could have been, either with the factual-causal fake-destiny, or AMBITION, that the world offers, or by simply giving up and decomposing into the state of spiritual mulch

---

* P.D. Ouspensky, *Tertium Organum*

that domesticated life leads to. The more civilised the culture, the more urban the man, the more he treats destiny either as a stand-in for power, or as a joke; although, as he reaches the end of an entirely meaningless life, not a very funny one.

On a smaller scale, 4D destiny comes to us as the sense we have of strangely knowing people the moment we meet them, or of feeling out hypotheses before they are tested, or feeling character into tracks and traces, such as 'knowing' that witch-hazel will ease my haemorrhoids, or that I should take a pair of scissors with me to the restaurant, or that paw prints in the mud were made by an exhausted civet.

Consciousness of destiny, in oneself or in other things, we call DEPTH. Depth has nothing to do with thought, which is never deep, nor with learning (although profound people think about interesting things and like to learn deeply) but to a profundity of conscious, and therefore timeless, *experience*. Profound people have an *enigmatic* way about them; a quality which transcends factual-causal spatial reasoning. We can't quite put our finger on what, because the finger is spatial also.

vi.   The mystery of death. We no more appear in existence and disappear from it than a three-dimensional apple passing through two-dimensional space does. In reality, there is no time as our three-dimensional selves experience it, and so no 'before' and 'after' for such selves to come from or go to. When we walk from London to Canterbury, it appears that London disappears and Canterbury appears, but, viewed from a balloon, both places continue to exist, as all the moments of our lives do, which is why people sometimes say 'my whole life passed before me in a flash'. What has actually happened is that my *partial* life has disappeared *from* me.

The balloon is unself, a metaphor for a four-dimensional or transdimensional self that is to the thin sliver of life we modally experience through our 3D selves, what we would be to Flatlanders; impossible to literally experience with self as we know it, yet, as we *are* it, as I *am* four-dimensional consciousness, intuitively, unselfishly available at all times.

None of this is to say that three-dimensional entities with their three-dimensional representations are not real, or that there is a fourth dimension in any *describable* sense. The three-dimensional represented world is completely real and completely reliable, as the three-dimensional self is real, as the isolated particle is real, as literal scientific concepts about isolated slices are real; just as the separate two-dimensional things of Flatland are real. To question or deny their dimensional reality is an insane form of solipsism (or scepticism). They actually and demonstrably exist, but only partially. If the self-evident but partial dimensions of Flatland or Solidland are separated by the isolating self from unself-evident "higher" dimensions, it becomes impossible to understand them, or any of the things they comprise. How can subjects or objects be experienced as unified and existing through time, or isolated noetic-somatic moments be experienced as anything but a shifting, schizoid nightmare of hypermnesiac forms, unless they and I are so unified?

Four-dimensionally speaking—*metaphorically* speaking, that is—the separate things and moments we perceive through the factual-causal mind do not 'really exist' any more than who I was at 3 PM on the afternoon of 17th May 2001 is 'really' me or than an oak tree is caused by an acorn. Reality is ultimately a blended continuum, with nothing separate to give rise to isolated elements or effects. We look everywhere and see *with* the isolating mind countless isolated things and events which seem to cause or be caused by countless others. But it's an illusion created *by* the isolating mind, just as it creates the illusion of a bent twig in water. The perceptual bend *does* have reality, just as *in some sense*, there are isolable things *in* reality, but it's not the full picture and the only people who take it to be so are madmen (and psychologists and philosophers).

§46.

The metaphor of Flatland serves to illustrate what lies *beyond* our three spatial dimensions, not what lies *between* them. In reality, dimensions are not isolated manifolds but way markers on a contextual spectrum. A ball of wool, by way of illustration, appears as a zero-dimensional point when viewed far away, a three dimensional object when viewed close up, a one-dimensional line when unravelled and a two dimensional surface when woven into a cloth. The natural world is composed of an infinitely complex, dynamic matrix of such solids, points, strings and surfaces, winding, unwinding, folding, looping and fragmenting through 'time' in ways that baffle the conceiving self, which responds by defining nature as a kind of 'chaos'; chaotic, that is to say, *to* the 'order' of self-conception.

Chaos and order form to self a conceptual duality, like subjective and objective, which is brought about *by* the activity of conception. Initially order was conceived as a male sun-god — Yahweh, Marduk, Zeus, Indra — which battled and defeated the dark forces of natural chaos, symbolised by monsters, snakes and women. When, in the seventeenth century, conceptual religion gave way to conceptual science, the mythical elements were dropped, but the duality remained, with [classical] science taming the natural world and reflecting it to reasonable minds. Finally, in the twentieth century, as the order of classical science, with its neat dichotomies, began to collapse, a new metaphor was developed to account for the reality of natural form which is *both* chaotic *and* ordered. This we call [somatic] FRACTALITY.

The metaphor of fractality describes, or suggests, certain qualities which natural non-linear systems have in common. These are; a non-proportional relationship between input and output, interconnectedness, interdimensionality, immeasurability, unpredictability, constant iteration, self-similarity, self-organisation and an intuitive, yet *irrational*, balance between component parts. The form of cauliflower florets, starling feathers, snail shells, sago palms, rising smoke, dripping taps, lungs, canyons, clouds and tree crowns, the rise and fall of cultures, the spectral structure of Bach's cantatas, the rhythm patterns of phenomenal sexual congress, the rippling of vocal chords in the conversation of a woman in love talking about love, the dobs of paint on an Egon Schiele portrait, the length of sentences in a literary masterpiece and the casual distribution of relaxing cows all exhibit some kind of fractality. It is the shape, or 'ur-shape', of nature; but there is not, nor can there be, a strict definition of fractal, rather a series of equations which mimic iterative self-similarity by feeding results back into the equation. When the results of these equations are plotted on a graph, the *border* between results that are stable and results that are unstable, forms an iterative, self-similar, immeasurably complex form which we call a fractal image, in which we *seem* to recognise something natural... but not quite.

For fractal images *metaphorically* represent actual fractality (which is to say stable-unstable border states in nature), but only ever *un*naturally. The infinite length of a *real* fractal form, the infinite number of influences upon a *real* fractal process, the infinitely small scale upon which those influences can act (i.e. its sensitivity) along with the unknowable 'random' element that is fed back into natural, iterated processes (which is not random at all; it only appears so to the 3D mind); these can only ever be mechanically approximated by fractals (computers for example, upon which fractal animations run, are unable to generate genuinely random numbers), which is why they are *kind* of fascinating to the mind, but never *actually* as mysteriously beautiful as the nature they represent, and so *actually*, like all artificially produced imagery, rather creepy. This is why gazing into a sunset evokes a conscious *state*, while staring into a fractal animation produces an unconscious *trance*.

§47.

The literal self is not a mystery. It can only conceive of itself—its literal representations, its literal universe and its literal consciousness—as, at best, being *caused* by mystery. Whether it calls this mystery, or magic, 'the real world', 'the big bang', 'the brain', 'God', 'mind' or 'spirit' is beside the point. They are all conceived as *things* which have a literal causative effect on reality, without that causation ever being explained; because it cannot be explained.

The non-literalist, having a self, and having to communicate *through* the self, appears to be in much the same position. She must also conceive of self and world as being caused by mystery and magic, but there is a crucial difference, in that the conscious self takes mystery and magic — *and causality* — as metaphors. Not the whimsical, arbitrary, subjective metaphors of the solipsist, but as representations of a qualitative experience that is, ultimately, elusive to mind.

Hence, for the literalist, 'God', the creator of the universe, the cause of consciousness and the reality behind the shadow-world of representation, is a transparent absurdity, at best a consoling fairy tale, and all reports of His nature are self-evidently baseless and ridiculous. This God is either religiously believed in *despite* such absurdity, or scientifically not-believed in *for* its absurdity. The literalist theist wants to believe in a literal male tribal God in order to validate his tribe, and annihilate or control everything that cannot be literally grasped, while the literalist atheist finds accounts of this God laughable in order to validate *his* tribe, and annihilate or control everything that cannot be literally grasped.

For the non-literalist, GOD is not absurd, because it — whatever is "behind" the thing-in-itself — does not and cannot exist in any literal, factual, causal form, any more than "what the universe is expanding into" can. We can say that god "created" the universe, or that god is "in charge" of my life, or that god is "beyond" the world, or that god "is" one of a range of metaphorical stands-ins, such as 'freedom', or 'love', or 'truth', or what-have-you, but these are all metaphorical eggs of expression, "emerging" from an inconceivable thing-in-itself that also "produces" the conceivable chicken of shared representation that we call waking reality.

§48.

Waking reality is illusory, but it is not an illusion. The ordinary, everyday, represented world of viscera, soma, thelema and nous is a self-evident, completely consistent and completely dependable matrix of facts which nobody ever *actually* doubts, no matter how fanciful their beliefs and theories. Solipsists avoid dog shit and believers in God keep their flour dry. If we become aware that such people are taking their own beliefs seriously, that they are trying to walk through walls or make people's heads explode with voodoo, we start to worry. This is why nobody *actually* (i.e. 'in matters of matter') doubts, or dispenses with, the facts and methods of science unless they're up to no good. The real and reliable world *is* real and reliable. 'Here is one hand', as one of the more straightforward ideas in modern philosophy* has it; therefore things *somehow* exist.

Clearly too, there are, in the waking world, unlike in [sleeping] DREAM, other selves—other minds, other bodies, other things. We do not experience a self-generated representation, but a *shared* representation. This is, literally, *common* sense, a self-evident network of culturally shaped facts and things which, again, nobody ever actually doubts while functioning normally in the world. I might adopt a solipsist or postmodernist stance, but this doesn't give me *direct* control over objects, which is why when we see a magician perform a trick, nobody over the age of six *ever* thinks 'maybe he really *did* pull a large block of ice out of his arse'. It's also why everyone, no matter how dreamlike they believe reality to be, tends to follow the shared norms of society; because we all well know that we'll be punished in a very undreamlike way if we don't. In so-called LUCID DREAMS I can become aware that I am dreaming and think giant chocolate furniture into existence, or make Cleopatra fall in love with me, or stop paying my taxes. Not so on waking, where other things, bodies, people and governments are much more interested in doing their own thing than in doing mine.

The interconnected actuality of waking life provides a practical answer to the problems of facticity and causality which have irritated physicalists since Hume raised them, for, as Kant noted, everything fits together nicely in the waking world and repeated experience with that 'fitting together' gives us complete practical confidence that we won't wake up tomorrow with a Moomin's head. Waking reality is experienced as such from its *consistency*. If we went to sleep every night and

---

* George Edward Moore, *Proof of an External World*

picked up the same dream where we left off, with the same characters, who came and went consistently, we would start to believe that we weren't drifting *down* from reality when we slept, but transitioning *sideways* to a different one. Certainty about the coherence of waking facticity and causality can, however, *never* provide us with any insight into the nature of them; for it is not, nor can be, by lack of *quantitative facticity* that I know I am dreaming, but by lack of *qualitative normality*. Usually, in a dream, a talking sheepdog in a lunar strip club does not strike me as strange, or cause me to compare it to the waking experience of a world in which lap-dancers don't live on the moon and dogs don't talk, thereby leading me to the realisation that I am in a dream. I remain as bound by dream facts as the Flatlander is bound by 2D facts. If a dream dog tried to persuade me I were dreaming I would have no facts *within* the dream by which to confirm or deny whether it is so. In lucid dreaming, I remember a waking state which I can *quantitatively* compare to the dream, but I am only *led* to that comparison via a *qualitative* experience of WEIRD.

This is why although LUCID WAKING is also possible, I can never be materially certain of it. I have and can have no *quantitative* experience of a super-awake ('awake from waking') state, just as I can have no such mental experience of four dimensions. In certain high-quality, unselfish experiences, I have a *qualitative* experience of weirdness, a feeling of unreality, but, unlike when I am dreaming, I have nothing to compare the *factual* experience to, so I can never come to the *factual* realisation that I am in a shared, solid, dream. I remain in a qualitative state of odd which fades with the quality experience, leaving doubtful facts. This is why the realest times of my life feel unreal, film-like, dream-like and then, when I later try to recall how vividly weird they were, I cannot. I doubt myself, doubt the reality-rending quality of my super-awake experiences, because all I have are factual memories of them. This is why the expression 'at least you have your memories' is such a stupid and insensitive thing to say to someone who is bereaved, and why when something does happen to them that is genuinely consoling, it is weird.

The high-quality odd experience is only possible when the isolated nous, soma, viscera and thelema of self are silenced or softened, when I am 'taken out of myself'. In such moments facticity and causality weaken and I become conscious that *I-here* is *that-there*; that the miracle of dream is not that the sheepdog is talking, but that *I am the dog*, that the experience of being separate from the dog and the strip club is *entirely* self-generated. When I wake, I *know* that subject and object (me, the dog and the strip club) were actually all one, but I can only experience this in the dream as *weirdness*.

Likewise, the waking moon continues to be the moon, even when I am not looking at it; it continues to be a big silvery ball up there, and not a mind-made illusion in here, because there is something 'in' it that really *is* the good old moon, but there is also a non-factual, non-quantitative aspect to it that somehow depends on its being consciously, qualitatively observed. While only a madman doubts that the *quantitative* waking division of subjects and objects is not a fact, a far more terrible kind of madness—the normal and ordinary kind—doubts that the *qualitative* oneness, or identity of subjects and objects, is not identical in both domains.

Consciousness is not a subject sitting in the objective cinema of the self, watching the projected representation of life pass before it. It is the cinema, the audience, the light that passes through the film and the story itself; but this cannot be factually known for certain without making the experience of it impossible; or, conversely, it cannot be doubted without presupposing the very subject-object division into separate things which is questioned. There is no *conceivable* way to either know or to question an *inconceivable* union of consciousness and context, either in dreams or while awake. Imagine arguing with a dog in a dream trying to convince you that you were both the same consciousness which had split itself into a subject and an object. What evidence could you possibly produce that it wasn't so? Of course the dog can't quantitatively prove the obverse either, but it doesn't have to. It only needs to lead you to a sufficiently intense experience of *quality*. If it succeeds, you experience the dream as a dissolution of subjectivity ('taken out of yourself') and objectivity ('this is weird'), which you call *meaningful*, just as you do during intense experiences of waking quality. This is why we are fascinated with stories about 'waking up', from dreams, from illusions, from virtual realities and from the fictive life script which ego surrounds itself with. It's also why we call conscious people AWAKE (although this metaphorical epithet is routinely co-opted into cliche). It's also why great stories can be completely unrealistic and yet, through their capacity to express the actual weirdness of the 'real world', more truthful than the factual worlds of journalism or science. It is not incredible that some incredible *factual* thing is happening, but that anything is happening at all.

§49.

Everything dreams present is factually false, but essentially true. Dreams cannot tell the literal, quantitative fact of the matter, they can only tell the non-literal qualitative truth of it. This truth is presented, as it can only be presented, metaphorically. I, consciousness, appear as self, which means I appear *split* into a literal subject and literal objects—the characters, settings and events of the dream—in order to present a panjective quality that is neither subjective nor objective. This quality may be an essential dread of life, or freedom, or yearning, or numbness, which clothes itself in the dress of my self, forming the story of the dream, of being paralysed and pursued by floating skulls, or of bouncing up and down naked on a trampoline on a daytime chat show, or of throwing paper planes through large grass vaginas with Vincent Van Gogh, or of cleaning out your fridge. The quality may be shallow, one of the feeble surface feelings modern man experiences throughout the ordinary day—a twinge of annoyance, an 'ooh yes, the parcel has arrived'—or it might be almost unbearably profound, when man sees, in dream, the intense horror of the world, or the intense beauty of life.

So it is in waking life, in myth; with the stories we all tell, from day to day, and with those that the myth-maker writes or performs. Just as the quality of dreams *precisely* expresses the quality of life, so that of stories does, which is how those who truthfully interpret dreams and stories can read them; from their quality. Naturally, I can only know this to the extent that I am conscious of quality. Those who are not, are unaware of the meaning of either their own dreams and stories — revealing much more about themselves in their anecdotes and teevee scripts than they realise — or that of others, forced to make clumsy symbolic readings. Those who are conscious find that their lives transdimensionally blend with that of humanity, opening up the meaning of great myth, and making their own mythic art expressive of the non-literal, qualitative truth of life itself, enabling them to fathom the DREAMLIFE OF THE WORLD.

§50.

The fact is the self, and the self is the fact. Each self is born with a unique configuration of factually accessible modes. In each self some modes are larger, stronger, more flexible or more sensitive — SWELLS — while, because there is only a finite quantity of factual-causal self-matter and self-energy, other parts of the self must be correspondingly smaller, weaker, less flexible or less sensitive — STUNTS. One self, for example, might be born with a fast, flexible, delicate conceptual-nervous system ('highly-strung'), a sensory-somatic apparatus that is relatively dim (poor sense of smell, tolerant to dirt), an amorphous, hyper-sensitive affective-visceral field and a bright iron-will; another might have flaccid, passive thelema ('lazy') but inhabit a rich and bizarre visceral-noetic realm ('weird' and 'witty') which barely manifests in a reserved and stolid somatic life. Possible configurations are infinite, not just between the four modes of this schematic map, but within the modal gradations of *actual* selves, which are immensely complex terrains, made up of completely unique modes, each in turn comprising a range of sub-qualities, all influencing and transdimensionally blending into each other as they evolve over a lifetime in myriad, bewilderingly complex and contextually responsive ways.

The swells and stunts of the particular self determine TASTE, the particular qualities a particular self is sensitive to. This leads to attraction to complementary experiences and, with continued exposure, mastery of the requisite skills to deepen and widen that experience. One self has a particular sensitivity to taste and smell, and is particularly attracted to food, along with a particularly ordered and precise mind, and so gets particular enjoyment from precision baking; while another has a powerful and flexible thelemic system, combined with a sensitive physicality, that finds itself suited to, say, horse training and riding. They are attracted to those activities and, if all goes well—if they continually refine their taste, or discernment—master them.

Taste is a function of the machine of the self. It assesses, judges and rectifies conscious experience, but it is not creative experience itself, which originates in consciousness. Taste, in other words, is unselfish experience as it *manifests* in form, sensitising the self to consciousness and context. This is why creative power must have taste, but the most refined taste can be quite devoid of creativity, or sensitivity; why the most 'tasteful' people on earth can be dull to the point of inhumanity and the most tasteless their moral superiors. It's also why it is much easier to judge one's own taste than one's own quality; you can see what you *have*, but not what you *are*. It's also why works that rely on good taste can delight and satisfy, but not *still* and *seize*. Finally, it's why everyone who is unselfish has a PRIMAL ATTRACTION to the primary pleasures of natural food, conscious people and quality experience—none of which are, ultimately, a question of taste (although taste can impinge on them)—but each self has its *own* SECONDARY ATTRACTION to whatever taste that the particular self is particularly sensitive to. Primary attractions are towards essential quality, originating in unself, which transcends taste; while secondary attractions are towards the various manifestations of quality *in* self, along with its particular needs. Egos, isolated from unself, have a tendency to conflate the two, to take a love of nature, for example, as a question of personal taste, on the same level as a love of trains or of the colour blue; or to defend an unhealthy aversion to all food (or, more commonly, all foreign food) with a healthy aversion to a few kinds of food high in a chemical that the particular self has little need of; or to excuse a lack of interest in its own cultural heritage as a matter of preference, on the same level as lack of interest in certain kinds of chocolate bar.

Secondary 'attractions' form a unique TASTE-MATRIX (or swell-matrix) of specific interests and talents which changes or evolves over time and place. Children are naturally attracted to sugar and major keys, geriatrics prefer bitter chocolate and avoid savage dance-beats and everyone tends to expand and refine those elements of self connected to their unique character, and to their unique 'local style'. As consciousness diminishes, the more attached ego becomes to these secondary attractions—to what I like—and the more violent and fearful if they are threatened. As consciousness increases, the more able I am to let go of my particular likes and explore new areas of my inner terrain. This is easier to do when young, when the self is more pliant and the boundaries between its tastes are softer. As selves age they harden like bark, making it difficult to prevent taste-matrices from ossifying into a prison of calcified likes and dislikes. Only the conscious self, able to release attachment to secondary pleasures, can remain supple.

§51.

If consciousness is absent, or if the context is self-made, self grows *towards* self, lop-sidedly. Strengths become absurdly swollen, like the muscles of a professional body-builder, or the hyper-focused knowledge of the ear-nose-and-throat specialist, or the one-directed will-to-riches of the obsessed businessman, or the sentimental dreamself of the historical-romance addict. Such self-inflated swells squash out the whole character, which withers like a spindly modern apple tree, weighed down by the immense plastic fruit-boobs the supermarket demands. Sensitivities, in the self-directed self, become *hyper*-sensitive; cowardly feebleness, for example, before demands from the context to *fight*, or to do some hard physical work, or to think about something more complicated than a daytime quiz show; while corresponding insensitivities become more calloused and resistant, not just specifically but, as the source of sensitivity *is* consciousness, generally too; which is why people who can tolerate raw lighting, bad smells, loud noise, harsh emotions, mental junk-food, pointless activity and institutional subservience are, despite nursing whatever hyper-sensitivities they are constitutionally prone to, generally speaking, morons.

The conscious self, unified with the context, activates unused, unfelt, unthought and unperceived elements of self. Such a self enjoys many pleasures, which leads it to be competent enough at many things, but is particularly attracted to its innate swells, which leads it to bewildering brilliance at a few things. In order to grow *naturally* in this way—'well-balanced', 'rounded', etc.—it must leave the known of the self-directed self. This is why conscious people *take themselves lightly*, even if they appear arrogant, over-confident or inflexibly super-serious, because only by leaving the known of what self likes, thinks, wants and is good at can they remain fully conscious, or allow consciousness to direct self as it pleases. The genius might be stiffly arrogant about his work after he leaves the workshop, or intensely uncompromising in his quest for the good, but is the epitome of flexible humility *at* the lathe.

Unconscious selves, by contrast, have few pleasures, which they obsessively cling to. This leads to generalised incompetence and substandard achievements, even in those few things they dedicate themselves to, which they do by taking themselves *very* seriously. Obsession, or addiction—a *constant* restless feeling that one has to do what self is best at, or enjoy what self likes most of all, or get what the self wants—is endemic to ego. After brief satisfaction—of getting what it wants—the restless feeling of ego returns and, along with it, resistance to any invitations to cross disciplines, genres, cultures or fields of experience, or to let go of the motivating ego and melt it down into conscious awareness of the context. To do so doesn't just evoke feelings of anxiety, but, as it requires *energy* to see or hear or feel the new, apathy also.

§52.

The unconscious self is not informed *by* consciousness but by *itself*. This obliterates the primary pleasure *of* consciousness and replaces it with secondary, selfish tastes, directed towards what I am 'best at' or what I 'most like'. Directing attention or attentive action towards what I am 'worst at', or 'don't like', is inconceivable to the self-informed self, and so, over time, the whole self becomes deformed, unbalanced, lop-sided, top- or bottom-heavy, *unnaturally* attached to ever-shrinking talents (or SPECIALITIES) and desires (or ADDICTIONS). All unselfish experience then appears to the self-informed self as an existential threat, to which it responds in the only way it can, with *more* self; more egoic thelema (particularly ritual-methodical action through cliched social roles), more somatic stimulation, more restless noetic mind-pleasuring and more emotional viscera.

If self rules itself, it not only produces an unnaturally concentrated form, it does so in fundamentally the same way that *all* such selves guide themselves; towards self, cut off from context and consciousness. There is no real individuality or uniqueness to ego. Super-particular talents, opinions, likes and dislikes might give an impression of individuality, but the tense, limited hyper-focus towards self remains the same. This is why ego is so attached to groups of egos with similar surface attachments, who present themselves in familiar symbolic-cliched forms. The feeling of togetherness with people who look and act the same as me compensates for my *essential* isolation from context and consciousness, and suppresses a constant sense of being cut off from something important, of floating over the surface of life like a ghost. Such GROUPS automatically reinforce their surface commonalities, creating ever more similar selves within them.

Where lack of self tends to unique CHARACTER—increasingly more itself—ego tends to CARICATURE—increasingly and literally more *like* itself. The most egoic people, at the end of their lives, are like cardboard copies of their earlier selves, resembling their once conscious quality in much the same way that a latex mask resembles a face. Such egos we call *superficial* or *one-dimensional*. We have the sense that there is 'nothing much to him', that, although the facts may be hidden from us, the crude form tells us all we need to know. The empty, pedantic, atheist, know-it-all expert on the television, the cold, hard, pampered bitch-face submerged under a fathom of foundation, the huge, famous head of weary charisma, sucking attention towards itself like a collapsed neutron star, the manicured gravitas of the community leader, and so on, and so forth, and so on, and so forth. Each developed culture has a few variations on a few themes, which vary self to self, each papered over with personality advertisements giving the impression of variety, but, like daytime television shows and products in the supermarket, each basically the same tedious and tiresome outer ego, constructing itself from itself. A great deal of the pleasure of story-telling, particularly when the story is set in a modern world overwhelmed with the monotony of caricature, is to show a genuine character free herself from the egoic, cliched shell of dreams she has become.

§ 53.

The autonomous self-shell is built in early CHILDHOOD. From the moment he is born, man is taught to enhance ego and suppress consciousness. The child's empathic awareness of the context immediately runs into a world of cold, hard, un-conscious pain, and withdraws into itself. Its inner world of free quality, vivid feeling and mad spontaneity are either ignored or actively punished by egoic adults who either blun-der through them like a retard through a house of cards, or unconsciously register them as *threats* to be controlled or destroyed. The miraculous, empathic connection that babies have with conscious mothers (those who wake up ten seconds before their child is hungry, or who can tell at a distance when they are needed) withers on the vine and the child learns to communicate instead by method and by technique, through tokens and gestures, and, eventually, through mere words, all of which mean either 'I *want*' or 'I *don't* want'. Many 'or-dinary' mothers can, in the innate state of superconscious, unconditional love which childbirth reconnects them with, find themselves miraculously attuned to the inner life of their babies, miraculously awake; but the signal soon drops out and the young child finds himself in the universal state of misery we call 'the human condition'—alone and in enemy territory, forced to do what we all have to do to survive; dig a trench, build fortifications and peer watchfully through the loophole at each approaching form, careful to correctly label it 'friend' or 'foe'.

Because self forms in response to consciousness, if consciousness is ignored or suppressed by the world, ego takes its place. Not instantly—although even a two-year old can, if raised in an unconscious environment, be an egoic cretin—but gradually, over time. Children can, in a sense, be born with ego, or the seed of it, because they can absorb ego-fomenting insensitivity and stress in the womb, but ego is not innate. It grows with the developing self; thinking, wanting, worrying its way through the day, influence spreading, slowly squeezing the charm, innocence, simplicity and magic out of childhood until it completely dominates the inner world, sitting over it like a tyrannical monarch (in fact this is, ultimately, why we love to hear stories of tyrannical monarchs being overthrown).

Self also forms in response to context, which is to say, in response to power in the world. Early experiences that parental or social power is essentially benevolent lead to a basically trusting character, a primal sense that the universe is not going to *do you over*. Not so with early experiences of erratic, despotic or callous power, which result in a constant feeling that a deadly blow is about to land, then to an insatiable (and *servile*) need to be protected, by financial power, or by the love of an audience, or by a totalitarian system or cult, from such blows. Those who have such feelings instilled into them *look* like they are walking across no-man's land; armed to the teeth and ready to gun down anyone wearing the wrong-shaped helmet, or bird-like and blinking, forever scanning the skies for falling bombs, or numb, anaesthetised, lost in their own worlds, changing the song on their smartphone being their last living act before standing on a landmine.

In short; disturbing people come from disturbing homes, anxious people come from anxious homes, depressing people come from depressing homes, and people who are dead from the neck down come from homes in which nothing ever really happens. None of this is explicit, nor is there much to be gained by trying to recover explicit memories of it. Most of the damage has been done before we can talk, and therefore exists pre-linguistically, or what we call 'unconsciously', which is why most of the 'talking cures' of psychotherapy are useless, why crude psychoanalytic accounts of x experience leading to y disorder are far too coarse to do justice to the qualitative nuance of early development and why hideous memories of the past are often related in such bizarrely matter-of-fact tones. Those tortured and exploited in their youth cannot remember the qualitative horror of the experience, only the facts of it. In nightmares, propelled back into the unconscious, they sometimes feel again the miseries of long ago, the inchoate, atomic terror of being on a battlefield, the intense, existential, childhood dread of loss and abandonment and destruction, but they wake into the sensible daytime world of adulthood and the intense suffering in their hearts is, for the most part, forgotten, or layered over with dreary, ordinary, problematic living. They look back into their distant past and it too seems ordinary; because it is ego that is looking. Ego sees nothing particularly horrifying in its own creation, certainly nothing that would require radically dismantling itself to overcome. Much better to fiddle around with details on the therapist's couch, or get smashed in front of the footy.

§ 54.

I enter the world, or rather a four-dimensional entity appears to enter a three-dimensional world, as pure consciousness and context. The two are, in my experience, one. There is no this-here and that-there, no subject-person and object-thing, there is just panjective unself in all its strange, lived, blended intensity, a kaleidoscope of super-vivid qualities which *I am* and which *this is*.

As I grow, consciousness and context form my self, with one or the other appearing to take the lead. Context—the present moment and the distal thing-in-itself that "generates" it—appears to alternate with consciousness—the pure, still, proximal point of absolute I "behind" my experience—to form the medial self that shapes the world, and the social world which shapes the self. Self and world change and grow together, each shaping and revealing more of the other, much as the microscopic world has 'changed' and 'grown' with the development of more powerful and discerning lenses.

The people around me therefore—my family and my friends and, a little later, the functionaries of the world—and my early experiences with them do not, *ultimately*, form me. It is unquestionably *partly* true, not to mention useful, to think of external influences as shaping the self into the form it now has. It is parents and carers who, for good or for ill, convey society into the self of the child, and who give the child the tools she needs to build her self; but the chief task of consciously raising children is not unlike that of consciously caring for a woodland. Man the farmer naturally shapes an environment to his benefit, but that doesn't mean exterminating all the plants he doesn't want and furiously tugging up those he does. It means clearing obstacles to *innate growth*. Although children require radically different cultural inputs than trees do, they both grow, naturally and healthily, under their own impulse. Man the parent might pay lip-service to this idea, but he goes about the business of child-raising like a furniture company goes about forestry, or a fast food company goes about raising chickens; pumping the child up with artificial stimulants, stamping on its natural spontaneity and hard-heartedly imprisoning it within its self by locking up the door that divides it from the natural world. Egoic parents and carers, triggered by the selfless innocence of children, rain down abuse on them, or, triggered by their own fear of uncertainty, coddle their children up in styrofoam bodysuits, or, too self-involved to register the presence of their children, ignore them and pay off their cries of neglect with mere entertainment. As the child grows up and approaches the challenges and crisis points of its life, the egoic parent distorts free perception, pushing the child into a series of ego-fuelled reactions.

The crises and challenges of child development are those moments when the self expands or transforms into qualitatively new forms of awareness. They include the following overlapping (and not necessarily sequential) stages:

i.   PRIMAL AWARENESS. The child begins her life with no separation between I and you; body and mother, then body and world, are viscerally one. A point comes, however, when the child realises, *pre-noetically*, that 'I am I' or 'I am not you', a sense of thelemic autonomy. If this happens in an atmosphere of egoic emotionality, or lack of conscious engagement, the child will be filled with a sense of PRIMAL FEAR; that 'not-I' is a land of demonic shadows. She will then cling to her self and begin violently asserting her self with a new wilfulness. Constant screaming and demanding whining are common symptoms of corrupted primal awareness.

ii.   SOMATIC AWARENESS. Awareness and control of bodily impulses become, and must become, a precondition to a favourable response from the world. Egoic parents and carers however, unable to allow the body to regulate itself, *force* cleanliness and self-control on children, leading to shame, anality, suppression of spontaneity, awkwardness, fear of dirt and so on. The fully egoic modern world also suppresses bodily awareness by attaching the child to a bodiless digital spectacle, a discarnate hyper-focus on addictive images which leads to numbness and insensitivity (e.g. to fractal beauty).

iii.   NOETIC AWARENESS. The child learns to recognise symbols as such, and to have power over them, chiefly language. The child also learns that its symbolic expressions and gestures have a meaning, which it can manipulate. The egoic child does this for its own benefit and excitement. We call this LYING, but attachment to symbols can also appear as an excessive fantasy life or, in the modern world, as an early addiction to virtual reality. More developed symbolic awareness we call REASONING which, in the egoic child, is overblown into conceptual obsessions or intellectual arrogance, or stunted into common-or-garden stupidity.

iv.   AWARENESS OF PAIN. Pain, loss, uncertainty and confusion are constant companions for young children who are born with a fearless intelligence with which to meet them that must be guided, or stabilised, by the calm presence of adults. The egoic carer, unable to be present, substitutes anxious, hovering care and a series of punitively restrictive rules 'for the child's safety'. These inculcate fear in the child, making him ripe for coercive control as he gets older.

v.   AWARENESS OF SELF. At some point, between the ages of seven and ten, a child *noetically* realises that 'I am I' or 'I am not you'. For the egoic child, isolated from unself, this is the beginning of crippling self-consciousness Realisation of the *thing* of self also brings with it realisation that the thing is finite; AWARENESS OF DEATH. For the ego-bound child, this is an horrific experience, attended by anxiety about the world ending and horrible dreams in which evil forces pursue her. She might ask her parents where she came from, or what death is, but is unlikely to receive an intelligent answer. Shielded from the reality of selfless death, incapable of understanding it, the child learns to fear death, and everything it represents.

vi.   SOCIAL AWARENESS. The realisation that 'you are different from me' leads to the realisation that *they* are different from *us*, and a new tension between individuality and society. A natural need to test social legitimations, and find a place in a social group becomes, in the egoic child, reckless rule-breaking (the most superficial of rebellions; imitation by doing the opposite) and insensitivity to other people's needs, which it will later justify as 'extroversion', or subservient obedience, and fear of other people, which it will justify as 'introversion'.

vii.   SEXUAL AWARENESS. The playful, innocent proto-sexuality of young children fairly explodes with puberty into a new form of sexual confidence and a new need for intimacy. Egoic parents suppress nascent sexuality, making the child, as Wilhelm Reich realised,* 'apprehensive, shy, obedient, afraid of authority, and adjusted in the authoritarian sense', while the egoic male world and its constant pornography warps pubescent sexuality into sex obsession, sexual violence and, correspondingly, fear of or numbed antipathy towards sex.

A child able to freely face all these obstacles, knowing that the love and experience of his parents, and, beyond them, an essentially benevolent reality, is behind him, is rare indeed. Most children don't just stumble, but pick up the obstacle and carry it through their lives with them.

§55.

In primal societies, children learn without being compelled to, by observing and then playfully copying adults, to whom they show respect and admiration and a desire to help. They are not considered unique or *special*, they do not require special spaces, special clothes or special foods and their fears and desires are not pandered to. They are allowed to do as they please, even if great danger is involved, without the slightest coercion; forcing children to do things, or teaching them, is understood to be counter-productive and a betrayal of human nature. Children can go where they like and observe what they like. They are not expected to be constantly joyous, or always winning, or free of pain, disappointment, loss or any other of life's vicissitudes; yet—provided they get through the perilous first few months of their lives—they are cheerful, strong, healthy, intelligent and socially adept.†

Contrast this with the children of today (particularly in the West) and the picture is an almost exact negative. Children must be continually coerced in order to learn or to do any work, which they never willingly volunteer for. They are almost entirely cut off from the adult world, which they treat with disinterest or contempt. They are the targets of total surveillance and total control, all motivated by a range of

---

* Wilhelm Reich, *The Mass Psychology of Fascism*
† David Lancy, *Raising Children*

moral panics, invisible enemies and public health scares—a demon-horde of rapists, radicals, drop-outs, disorders, diseases and illnesses, both mental and physical. They are not allowed to experience any discomfort, they are not allowed go anywhere near an adult they don't know, they are isolated from gender and encouraged to identify with a genderless identity, they are not allowed into the wild, they are wrapped up in cellophane and glued to an electronic device designed *by* other electronic devices (sometimes called 'people', although this is a misnomer) for the sole purpose of addicting the child *to* the electronic device. They are *special* (and don't they know it); their every whim is met, provided that no immediate harm or displeasure can result; all criticism and pain, all dirt and disease, all shock and horror, all surprise and uncertainty, everything even slightly unpleasant is shielded from them— unless it comes to them virtually, through a screen, or unless they break one of society's innumerable taboos, then retribution is swift. All of this is justified as 'caring'. Children are locked up, corrupted, abused, addicted to technology, made to talk like books and bullied into being gleaming diamonds of uniqueness in order to 'make them happy'. Raising children as they have been raised in most societies on earth for most of human history is inseparable in the mind of the modern 'responsible' parent from wanton child-abuse; the millennial history of physically assaulting and mistreating children, also 'for their own good', which still persists today beyond the modern middle-class bubble of the West.

Modern children are expected to be continually thrilled and absolutely unique, self-confident and overflowing with 'respect'; yet they are almost universally anxious, irritable, tight, nasty, snobbish or incompetent. Nobody ever seriously considers why this should be so; it must just be that children are born this way, or because 'society'—through video games and social-media—teaches them. It can't be because:

i.   Children are forced, before they can even speak, into a self-shaped body-suit, compelled to make their way blind-folded through a Minotaur maze of inexplicable suffering, shouted at, beaten, manipulated or ignored, cut off from any kind of meaningful natural or social experience, forced into a [virtual] school-room with twenty or thirty other prisoners, made to do things they don't want to do for most of their lives, *totally* dependent on adults, and on technology, and in constant competition with each other; albeit a bizarrely muffled competition which must have no meaning outside the event and which must never upset their sense of specialness.

ii.   The strangest, subtlest, truest but most potent level of a child's experience, their soft-selved consciousness and free engagement with the context, is completely ignored by parents and teachers, who might be delighted at its safer manifestations—the sweet gestures and innocent comments—but who refuse to explore what this consciousness actually is, which is to say who or indeed *what* the child might actually *be*.

iii.   Children are surrounded by adults who are almost never secure in their own company, who rarely pursue goals under their own initiative, but must be continually compelled to do so, who cannot sit still for five seconds without reaching for an entertainment device, who are anxious about nature or have no experience of it, who are rarely joyous and almost never for no reason, and who are continually preoccupied with unreal or trivial concerns; what other people think of them, what might happen next week, whether their favourite television show will be cancelled, who won an 'important' football match, and how much money they have in the bank. Children then either emulate all this or react against it, paying no attention to what they are *told*.

iv.   What parents *tell* children is clearly and continually at odds with what parents *do*; how they live and what they are feeling. Children are *told* they are loved, they are *told* what to do, they are *told* what the truth is; but what they are actually *shown* is something else entirely. Children are raised in a world in which language appears to have nothing to do with reality, and so language, right from the start, doesn't seem to mean anything, while, correspondingly, reality is experienced as something strange, frightening, taboo or unreal.

The misery and madness of children everywhere is due to the fact that they are raised by parents and carers who are hyperfocused, perpetually anxious or brutishly insensitive, isolated from reality and addicted to self. Not all the time—even in some of the worst families pockets of tenderness open up—but enough to ruin the lives of their children, and, as ruined people raise ruined children themselves, the lives of their grandchildren, who then ruin the lives of their children, and so on, and so on, and so on.

§56.

The damage has been done long before children reach puberty, but it is cemented in ADOLESCENCE, when the power of consciousness passes from an essentially animal, 'three-dimensional' experience, to the beginning, at least potentially, of a fuller, human, 'four-dimensional' intuition. This is experienced as an uprush of vital energy and, to the extent that the individual has grown up in a selfless environment, uncaused eruptions of joy, the capacity for heart-stopping sensual pleasure, an ability to see straight through the miserable lie of the adult world, a sense of destiny, an enthusiasm for the unnameable and a new quality of consciousness. Teenagers may be inarticulate and easily deceived, but they are, in principle, able to feel truths that, just a few years later, they will look back on with condescending perplexity.

Adolescence is also the point when *self*-consciousness, hitherto an unpleasant response to social novelty, which we call 'shyness', becomes an agony of fear, anger and self-doubt. This is because *consciousness*—my own and that of other people—is pushed closer to awareness, looming up before the ego as an appalling threat. The adolescent feels—correctly—that they are now mercilessly exposed to criticism; criticism of their failures and weaknesses *and* criticism of their individuality and quality, so they move to protect themselves, to conceal their characters and to attack anything or anyone that might look like it has the power to expose them. They become aware that, in order to keep the dark forces of chaos away, they must project an idealised image of themselves into the world; pretty, sporty, witty, sensitive, tough, moody, nihilist, and so forth. These personalties, like the cliques which support them, are employed by the self to conceal the self. Adolescents are unaware that the happiness, love, genius and confidence they crave are impossible without EXPOSURE and SELF-ABANDONMENT — a lesson that they might never learn.

The adolescent ego, cast out fully from the void, experiences the insecurity and loneliness of being a completely separate self amongst equally separate selves. The almost inevitable consequence of this, as Erich Neumann taught,* is NARCISSISM, as the self turns upon itself for reassurance, inflating its own importance in terrified reaction to the opposing pole of self-hatred and despair at one's own insignificance. The two — felt emotionally as volatile over-excitement (which they take to be conscious joy) and theatrical misery (which they take to be emotional depth) — create and reinforce each other, leading to the famous rollercoaster ride of megalomaniacal me-ness followed by melodramatic self-harm of teenage years.

Adolescents have a tendency to protect their awareness from foreign incursions through an obsession with order. Ego perceives surrender as chaos, and tends to greet all circumstances in which conscious spontaneity and the acceptance of confusion, noise or pain are a prerequisite to success — which is most situations — as a pharoah's tomb of perpetual threat (which is why they enjoy stories about raiding magical puzzle-castles). The tolerance of bewildering storms of information that children are born with may be suppressed in the first ten years of life, and a child's shyness of taking a risk agonisingly accentuated, but with adolescence it is completely extinguished. Nothing, but nothing, unusual must be allowed to happen, no new situations — particularly those that demand the exposure of spontaneity and creativity — no dirt and disorder, no wildness, no madness. For boys (noetically inclined), video games answer all of these needs, as does pornography,

---

* Erich Neumann, *The Child: Structure and Dynamics of the Nascent Personality*

both of which can suck teenage male minds in for years (while their somatic lives chaotically fall apart). More usefully, boys *might* express their obsession with purity and their fear of the world as asceticism and an attempt at self-overcoming—the original purpose of male initiation rituals—although this can be pushed to obsessive limits and used as a sly advertisement for specialness. Girls tend to defend themselves against the other by walling themselves up in peer-oriented cliques, compulsive somatic preening and a war on their own bodies. Both are unaware that a compulsive need to protect oneself from disorder breeds fear, as the borders of the self must be continually patrolled, and violence, as incursions must be aggressively repelled. They are also unaware that the system, particularly in its most advanced virtual form, appeals to this compulsion, relentlessly feeds it and builds itself from it.

The end point of adolescent fear, violence, self-consciousness and self-control is a dull, hyper-selfish, extroverted, physicalist life of constant, objective function, function, function, or, conversely, for the introverted solipsist, a long withdrawal into schizoid subjectivism and obsessive forms of mysticism, self-absorbed art (and hiding a fear of engagement with the world behind an artist's identity), fantasies of romantic salvation, 'psychonautic' introspection, or the sleepy, lotus-eating dreaminess which is the hallmark of the unformed adolescent self, cut off from anything functional, traditional, or empirical, ready to drift through life like a useless ghost. All of this serves the system, which in turn relentlessly feeds ego.

§57.

There are, very broadly, two forms of insanity that ego can inhabit. The self-informed self is divided between its *active* poles of thinking and willing, and its *passive* poles of perceiving and feeling. The active, essentially physicalist ego hungers for control and attention. It cannot be satisfied with mere self-control, nor be satisfied by its *own* attention, because, without objective validation, the projected 'I' has the same qualitative status as any other thing in the universe—it is not sufficiently real or special—which is why it must dominate those things, in order to confirm the reality or importance *of* itself *to* itself. We call this SADISM, the addictive conversion of natural EXTROVERSION into an over-attended egoic *need* for extroverted projection. The passive, essentially solipsistic self, on the other hand, is essentially submissive, terrified of the responsibility of objectivity, of being someone, and seeks at every turn to avoid attention and relinquish autonomy. This we call MASOCHISM, the concomitant caricature of a natural tendency towards INTROVERSION.

Sadism tends towards objectivism, which can only know itself by becoming a self in the objective world, a growth that is dependent on literal mastery of material tools. In extreme, archetypical cases this appears as stultifying, patronising paternalism and condescension, either patriarchal control of others or matriarchal nannying. Masochism, by contrast, tending towards subjectivism, cuts itself off from the objective world, or at least from anything in that world that cannot support it (sycophantic worship of power, including the power of mob-opinion, remains a masochistic constant). This retards the growth of the self—there is often something childish and unformed about masochists—while preserving its autonomy and, very often, its *secret* sense of specialness.

Sadism, in order to literally engage with the objective world, demands a fixed, definite, resolute self to do so. It therefore *appears* more 'egoic' than masochism, which, in its pure form, renounces objective literalism, and with it the definite self. For the masochist, there often hardly seems to *be* a self, so vague and wispy do they come across, so *helpful* and *giving*, so shy of the limelight; so '*selfless*'. The arrogant rockstar or CEO wielding charisma-power or money-power over others, appear to us as caricatured 'egoists', while the humble 'ordinary guy' or 'sweet and loving housewife', who relinquish power to others, appear to be the opposite; monotonously *nice*. If ego is involved, nothing could be further from the truth. They are both CORRELATES, essentially the same, like the Yahweh and Satan of Judeo-Christian mythology, ego-generated monsters, neither of which could exist without the other. Sadists and masochists make a great play of hate and love, grievance and reconciliation, blame and forgiveness, but they seek each other out—in fact they often seem to be supernaturally drawn to each other—because they need each other.

A sadistic God is the perfect sadist for masochists, the sadistic state or system a close second; ideally both. The sadistic partner is an optional third for the sufficiently introverted, although the *essential* masochism of domesticated man lives comfortably with either sado or masochistic gender tendencies, which is why both men and women, in whatever role they play to each other, masochistically prostrate themselves before Yahweh and Mammon. Contrariwise, a supine natural universe at the mercy of man's priapic superpower is the perfect masochist for sadists, an adoring mass of submissive followers a close second; again, ideally both. And again, the masochistic partner will serve as a punch bag for the sadistically inclined, although an essentially sadistic attitude to reality can and often does go together with a desire to be degraded in bed.

§58.

Without a unifying consciousness, self is forced onto a sado-masochistic see-saw with no way off, no exit. A compulsive need to hurt or be hurt, humiliate or be humiliated, be nothing to the all powerful master, or be everything to our worm-like slaves unconsciously drives ego, forcing us to the depths of depravity or, if we do not have the courage of our perversions, or the energy to carry them out, to consume the vast range of 'harmless' substitutes society provides to quench our selfish thirst for submission and domination; such as video games, sports, business, pornography, political spectacle, kinky fuck-sex and the subtle, daily *sub rosa* game of master and slave played out under the social mask.

Sadism and masochism are caricatures of strength and sensitivity. Ego cannot discern the difference, and is unaware that it is justifying sadism or masochism when it exalts strength and sensitivity. Ego calls its masochism 'sensitivity', its mediocrity 'humility', its cowardice 'kindness' and its anxiety 'care', just as it calls its sadism 'strength', its arrogance 'confidence', its selfishness 'realism' and its insensitivity 'un-important'. It can do this—dress itself up in adverts—because introversion and extroversion can, at least to the undiscerning eye, appear the same as masochism and sadism. Introverts have watery or earthy, insubstantial or self-effacing selves and so do masochists. Extroverts have sharp or firey, active or self-confident selves, and so do sadists. The difference is not in the nature of the self, but in who is in charge of it. If it's ego, there will be nothing *but* the self, thus no flexibility, no humour (no ability to take one's selfish or submissive self lightly), no genuine sensitivity and certainly no capacity to surprisingly inhabit a quite different mode.

The terms 'sadism' and 'masochism' are thus, again, schematic guides. Nobody is a pure sadist or a pure maso-chist; the two states, like the objectivism and subjectivism they are attracted to, can be considered less as separate planets and more as poles of the same body, oscillating correlatives within a self-informed self which can only function through self-assertion and self-pity, neither of which can exist alone any more than a one-sided coin can. Sadism is founded on self-disgust and collapses into self-pity when it fails, and mas-ochism is founded on a profound cynicism which lashes out with astonishing violence when its back is against the wall (this is indirectly evident in the stories and myths of unconscious writers and raconteurs, which frequently conclude a sequence of purposeless cruelties with nauseating schmaltz). In the real world, egos are not one status or another, but adaptable *status experts*, adapting sadistically and masochistically to whatever self wants or doesn't want. Ego will rigidly carry out life-an-nihilating laws or abase itself before Big Money, destroy the deviance of the non-conformist or live and let live, demand Orwellian order or permit Huxleyan chaos, all according to the demands of the moment.

In the conscious self, by contrast, there may be the *ap-pearance* of sadism and masochism, but there is no attachment to them; both are subordinate to a state which transcends both, which is why certain personalities, which *appear* to be arrogantly sadist, or cowardly masochist, are empathically recognised as being neither; we, to the extent that we are conscious, perceive, in the former case, a light attachment, an ability to laugh at the self, an *essential* humility, and in the latter, an *essential* strength and integrity, an ability to act despite quaking with delicacy or even fear. We perceive the conscious character "preceding" the surface form.

§ 59.

The active qualitative pole of extroversion and the passive pole of introversion physically manifest as the objective *fact* of male and female SEX. There are only two sexes, MAN; bodies which produce sperm, and WOMAN; bodies which produce eggs. It's not a spectrum, nor can it be. There is no such thing as a 'spegg'. Subjectively, or intuitively, sex is experienced as the *quality* of MASCULINE and FEMININE GENDER. Woman is thus to female (and man to male) what the objective, physiological representation of the colour *red* is to the subjective quality, feeling and 'sense' of *redness*.

Gender *can*, from a subjective, largely solipsist, perspective, be said to exist on a spectrum, just as black and white can; and just as the various configurations and intensity of black and white create an infinitely subtle spectrum we call grey, so do the various configurations and intensities of masculinity and femininity, which vary from culture to culture, person to person and even from year to year in the same person. But this spectrum, first of all, cannot be objectively understood without the opposites at its poles; androgyny cannot be understood without maleness and femaleness any more than different hues of grey can be understood without black and white. Secondly, the 'spectrum' is not just of analogue hues blending seamlessly one into the other, but also digital halftones, discrete 'dots' of masculinity that alternate, from situation to situation and relationship to relationship, with femininity. Thirdly, and most importantly, there is a primal quality of gender which, like all qualities, "precedes" both objective, physicalist and subjective, solipsist representations.

Generally speaking, it is the subjectivist who wishes to dismiss binary, largely objectivist, accounts of sex and gender. Being held to objective standards is an intolerable violation of the postmodern, self-absorbed, solipsist self, which *must* hold to the shades-of-spectral-grey view of gender, and therefore *must* believe it. The solipsist does so by ignoring the logical necessity of poles at either end of the spectrum, and by severing the link between objective fact and subjective experience. Nature and culture, through inheritance and upbringing, may be necessary for our felt experience of subjective gender, but, argues the gender-sceptic, they cannot be sufficient. Just as the solipsist asks 'How do we *know* that we're both seeing the same red?' so she asks 'how do we *know* that gender isn't culturally (which amounts to saying arbitrarily) determined?'

What we *do* know is that; male sperm are continually produced in their billions, *ex nihilo*, while female eggs passively exist right from the start; that man's reproductive organs are outside of him, while those of a woman are invisible; that the brains of men and women are structured differently and comprise different kinds of nerve cells; and that the sexes each have completely different endocrine (hormonal) systems. These facts, and others like them, explain crude elements of gender, such as the dating and pairing strategies of the sexes (women tend to play the long game, preferring emotionally stable, monogamous relationships, while men tend to prefer emotionally-uninvolved couplings), their attitude to each other (man wins, woman is won), their appearance (women are fatter, smaller and more delicately featured than men) and various standard psychological facts relating to reproduction (men tend to be more assertive, risk-prone and thrill-seeking than women, who tend towards a safer *modus vivendi*). Although such verifiable facts wreck the rebars of an entirely subjectivist account, the solipsist can still construct a complementary argument, correctly arguing that the facts of sex no more 'explain' the experienced quality of gender than, as Kant noted, the molecules of cinnabar 'explain' the experienced quality of redness. There must be an aspect to gender, as to all quality, which transcends the facts.

The way through the subjectivist-objectivist impasse is the same here as elsewhere. Finally, and ultimately, the principles of masculinity and femininity exist neither in the *secondary* objective facts *nor* in *equally secondary* subjective feelings and thoughts, any more than love does, or innocence, or justice. Men and women, and male and female, are, ultimately, objective "expressions" of *primal*, universal, principles or qualities—the thing-in-itself of man and woman—which "manifest" in representation; as *both* the objective biochemical, cellular, physiological and morphological differences between the sexes *and* the quality or character which appears to us, subjectively, as gender. Objective, causal, genetic explanations of sex and gender are impossible to ignore, as are our subjective feelings, desires, perceptions and conceptions, but the *primary* explanation for both is the same as that of understanding and standing under; that both sex-fact *and* gender-quality are representations of the thing-in-itself; of male-in-itself and female-in-itself, which "inform" the quality of gender, making it, like all other unselfish qualities, impossible to literally or factually grasp. You either know what love is, or mojo, or funk, or you don't. You either know what it means to be a man or a woman, or you don't; and if you don't, no objective fact or subjective feeling or opinion will bring you closer. This is why although 'sex can be discussed in the unambiguous language of science... gender bespeaks a complementarity that is enigmatic and asymmetrical. Only metaphor can reach for it'.*

§60.

Women, naturally, have finer or more swollen visceral and somatic systems, while men have finer or more swollen thelemic and noetic systems. What this means is that, because the visceral-somatic, passive pole of self is "closer" to consciousness, women are predisposed to less egotism; or certainly at least less overt, literal egotism than noetic-thelemic man, who is abstractly *split* from experience and energetically motivated to *journey* through it. Pre-civilised cultures, along with naturally

---

* Ivan Illich, *Gender*

123

sensitive selves everywhere, understand this; that man must spend the first thirty to forty years of his life *working* back to a place that women never leave. That place is called *here*, the experience of which comes to us as the presence that the mature man achieves, and the presence that the natural woman both is and values in man. The principle of the feminine thus "precedes" that of the masculine, just as the female body 'precedes' that of the male, giving birth to it. The mission of man, and even of the male mind in woman, is to return to original, unselfish, feminine consciousness, or, as the Tao Te Ching has it, 'to know the male, but to abide by the female'.*

The active, conceptual, thelemic emphasis in the male means that, generally speaking, he tends to be more utilitarian, competitive, unemotional, assertive, insensitive to dirt and to risk, open to abstract ideas and conceptually self-oriented. He tends to be in charge of formal, literal, public domains (society as a *thing*) and tends to be more interested in ideals or ambitions than in material health, safety and comfort. He is less sensitive to non-verbal cues than women, tends to be less facially and physically expressive and tends to be more decisive and assertive in his speech; more likely to interrupt and less likely to really listen. He tends to have greater visual-spatial thinking intelligence, a greater ability to focus on abstractions and his creativity tends to be *extrinsic*. Man has a decreased ability to think discursively or to perceive intuitive similarities between remote concepts, and is susceptible to plan-addiction and to obsessive intellectual insensitivity. He has a tendency to *mental* egotism, to a restless desire to tease and torture, to explicit aggression, to sex-obsession, schizophrenia and outright sadistic psychopathy. This egotism is because man must project himself *beyond* the body, but, in doing so, he cuts himself off from the mystery and the intelligence *of* the body.

Woman, having more sensitive-swollen visceral and material systems, is more passive and more receptive than man, tending to have greater feeling intelligence and empathy, physical sensitivity and overall [soft] awareness. Her creativity tends to be *intrinsic*. She has a softer body than man, and so avoids dirty, gruelling work, and a softer self also, and so,

---

* Lao Tzu, *The Tao Te Ching* (tr. Ellen Chen)

being less naturally egoic, is far more likely to be spontaneous and aware of the context. She tends to be in charge
of informal, private social domains (society as an *activity*),
tends to be more interested in the reality of our material lives,
rather than in ideals and ambitions, and is more interested
in intimate, cooperative, egalitarian, non-confrontational relationships. She is more physically affectionate and viscerally
demonstrative than man, tending to smile and cry more. She
has a reduced facility with perspective, less interest in causal
reasoning, isolated, abstract systems and ideas, less ability to
make systematic, clock-based plans and, overall, less need
to *get* somewhere or *achieve* something or stick to the *point*.
Woman has a tendency to *emotional* egotism, to masochism,
body-obsession and self-harm, to neediness (particularly after the sex-threshold has been crossed) and to avoidance of
manifest conflict (preferring subterfuge and wars of attrition).
She is rooted in the mystery *of* the body; forced to egoically
depart from this, she turns *on* the body.

§61.

Variations on the themes of gender are naturally colossal, varying from person to person, context to context. Nevertheless
we generally find that:

i.   All things being equal, men make better judges than
women,* because they can more completely separate themselves from the situation. Women have greater difficulty being
dispassionate; having, for example, a detached intellectual
argument. They have greater difficulty separating pure ideas
from personal interaction and are more likely to take critical
comments as personal attacks. If, however, it is compassion
you need, or loving kindness, you are, *all things being equal*,
more likely to get it from a woman.

ii.   Women, generally speaking, make poor song-writers,
scientists, novelists and philosophers. They don't have the
ambition to scale the heights of abstraction and technical skill

---

* Arthur Schopenhauer, *Parerga and Paralipomena*

required to do these things. There has never been a female Beethoven, a female Kant, a female Tolstoy, a female Beatles or a female Monty Python and there never will be. Women can, of course, write good songs, make good jokes, write good books and say meaningful and original things, but they cannot construct the same vast cathedrals of artistic majesty that men can, largely because they don't really want to. Woman *is* that which male art is merely *of*.

iii.   Women excel at improvised theatre, song and dance, informal communication and speech, discursive literature (and letter-writing), decorative and illustrative art, hand-craft, such as pottery and textile design and sensuously embodied sculpture. These tend to be demeaned in the male art world as light, superficial, 'primitive' or folk art. As does the transcendent art of living. Beethoven is not superior in any meaningful sense to my mother; quite the opposite, and if he could meet her, he'd probably agree.

iv.   A naked, dumpy, man running away from an angry landlord is, or at least potentially can be, funnier than a naked, dumpy woman; we laugh at the uglier male form and the breaking of the uglier male dignity, whereas we just feel pity at a debased woman's body. This is why certain forms of sarcasm and abuse are permitted towards men, but display a criminal lack of gentility when aimed towards women.

v.   Women make better gatherers than men, while men make better hunters. If you're out mushroom hunting with a mixed sex group of equal ability, the women, provided they are calmly incarnate, will usually find more. Correspondingly, a man *looking for* something in the fridge will laser in on one point after another and declare there is no jam, while a woman will *see* the gestalt and pull out the jar.

vi.   Women, *provided they are not emotionally disturbed*, are, on the whole, more aware of the mood of the room than man; a woman will sniff out a bad vibe and carefully manage a delicate situation that a man will blunder through like a kind of retarded ogre.

vii.　Men die earlier than women, die more often at work, are more likely to commit suicide, are more likely to go to prison, are *far* more addicted to pornography, video games, alcohol and drugs, are more likely to be homeless, are more likely to be autistic and schizophrenic.

viii.　Teenage girls are more or less women, inexperienced and girlish perhaps, or—increasingly—corrupted by a hyper-masculine, hyper-egoic culture, but still far more mature than teenage boys who, despite being charming, smart and beautiful, are idiots or, at best, *unformed*.

ix.　If you are driving through a new city and you can choose between asking a man or a woman for directions, and you choose the latter, you are an imbecile. If you are in a forest at night and nobody knows which way to go and only instinct can find the way forward; ask a woman.

x.　Man will complain to woman in the following terms; 'but you didn't *say* that', 'but why didn't you *say* so?' 'how was I supposed to *know*?' And woman will think, 'you idiot'. Woman prefers to communicate by implication, by gesture, by context, frustrating and delighting the ponderous literalism of man, which she has a tendency to smash to pieces, or want to.

xi.　Woman, however, is also sensitive to all kinds of extraneous, irrelevant gusts of visceral affect and man's detached self can and sometimes must 'keep her straight'. Just as man finds relief in the spontaneous, wet chaos of her heart, so she finds relief in the simple, dry order of his.

xii.　Work is more important to man, because he finds himself in it. Man must *build* his life (and through it, our society) and in doing so he comes know his self and, to a certain extent, if he is to do a good job, overcome it. Woman has no such need. She already knows her self is secondary and so has no need to overcome it in work. Certainly she will *still* do so, and certainly she will work and love it; but the *need* is not there. What she needs, more than anything else, is to be unselfish with other selves, in the experience called love. Because she has learnt what love is not, she has learnt to turn her back on it in favour of her work, her addictions, her children and her emotions, but none of these things ever satisfies her unless she is rooted in unselfish, impersonal love.

Man *naturally* yearns to realise himself in his work; but for what? For woman. For that which, more than anything on earth, represents unself to him, which is why he is compelled towards her, towards the still centre of his moving world. He yearns beyond the body, beyond the senses, even beyond the idea, to the transcendent beyond in which he can fulfil himself. Unless he is rooted in the female ground he will spin off into sterile space and conquer nothing but dust. Because most men are ego, they are unable to reach the abyss beyond—reach woman as she really is—and so they reach nothing but their selves in their work, in their society, in their history, which end up being *for* themselves; for their satiety, safety and sex.

Imagine if it were otherwise, if everything that man did was not merely to impress woman, to get her into bed, or have power over the world she is trapped in, but to delight her; if all our stories, songs, buildings and games of ping-pong were offerings to the goddess. As D.H. Lawrence wrote, with typical extravagance, 'when a man shall look at the work of his hands, that has succeeded, and shall know that it was begotten in him by the woman of his body, then he shall know what fundamental happiness is'.* As it is, we live, effectively, in a world imagined by a lonely fourteen year old boy masturbating, from sheer boredom, over his own image.

xiii.   Man dreams of woman, woman dreams of being dreamt of. Man thinks of woman, woman thinks of being thought about. Man, as John Berger noted,† regards woman, while woman regards herself regarded. On a grander scale man, as Spengler wrote, *makes* history, while woman *is* history.

---

* D.H. Lawrence, *Study of Thomas Hardy*
† John Berger, *About Looking*

Everyone departs from gender norms to some degree. The East tends to be, in some respects, more feminine than the West, modern women tend to be, again in some respects, more masculine than women two or three generations ago, males together behave differently than they do when they are with women, both sexes behave differently when they think their personalities are being observed, and each of us oscillates between aggressive assertion and passive reception from time to time, and place to place.

Nevertheless, man remains masculine in principle, and woman remains feminine in principle. When an assertive, hyper-masculine, hyper-hetero man's man looks into the heart of the gayest, most feminine and yielding homosexual man on the planet, he sees, or rather he senses, the *knowable*. They couldn't be, formally, more different. They might completely refuse to see any similarity between themselves. Probably will. But *somehow* they always detect that they are in the company of someone who, despite different thoughts, thinks in the same way, and despite different desires, desires in the same way. Not so with a woman, again, no matter how butch, masculine, aggressive, cerebral and lesbian she is. Here, says the man, is a creature who appears, in every manifest sense, to be the same as he is; but he feels out *something else*, the unknowable. Even she herself might be unaware of it—today she almost certainly is—but there it is; the essential difference between men and women.

§62.

Man, being "cut-off" from the whole, must spend his life returning to it. This noble mission is expressed, in myth, as the HERO'S JOURNEY; the call to adventure, the training, the trial, the battle with the demon, the prize and the return.* The dull mass of average men either take this story literally, in order to win a pathetic worldly prize—usually success in sport or in business—or they find some way to duck out, either by attempting the impossible, which gives them a good excuse to fail, or by playing it safe and becoming a manager, doctor,

---

* Joseph Campbell, *The Hero with a Thousand Faces*

landlord or modern artist. All this gives the impression that 'man is a simple beast', for the overwhelming majority of men are. Those few who are not, who are initially guided by the love and instinct of wise parents, and then by the terrible and perfect intelligence of life, who have rejected the worldly imperative to become themselves in favour of a subtler and nobler aim, strike women as either a mysterious miracle of originality, or a threat to their very being. (Woman's ability to sense this, to *instantly* know that she is in the company of a conscious man—someone to unselfishly love or someone to egoically hate—is, or can be, almost magical.)

Woman, being "complete" in a way that man is not, and "closer" to unself than he is, does not need to *seek* wholeness, she just needs to learn to live it, removing obstacles—and they are mighty—as she goes. It goes without saying that she does gain experience, and achieve things, becoming more powerful; but she has no *need* for this power, never naturally aspires to it, and can, in her natural state, give it away in a heartbeat. Woman does not yearn for the hero's treasure, preferring to go on the HEROINE'S JOURNEY, a meaningful but playful, picaresque and ultimately *aimless* pilgrimage through a varied and interesting life. She can certainly be single-pointedly serious—in fact, devastatingly so—but she chooses the playful profundity of an *entire* landscape to live in or to explore, rather than an obsessive drive to experience the transformative intensity of a focused path to the peak. Socially speaking, woman begins in the womb and she stays there. She should be literally free to roam of course, but there is no need to drive her out of the nest, no need to put her through trials of independence and self-overcoming, which is why primal cultures rarely do.

The ego of man is larger, harder and more powerful than that of woman. She can, in a sense, be as egoic as man and, what's more, because she has fewer defences *against* ego, even more vicious, cruel and cold; but her ego tends to be implicit, passive, undemonstrative, visceral and somatic, often not coming to conceptual expression at all, and so, apart from *seeming* less egoic, she is, through being incarnated in the body and one with the subtlest level of self—the affective psyche—already home. There is something unfathomable in her. In egoic woman, this comes to us as frighteningly erratic emotionality, but in a real woman, underneath her endearing sweetness and day-to-day simplicity, there is a bottomless void which manifests as a discerning intelligence and presence that is utterly terrifying to the egoic male, who will go to extraordinary lengths to protect himself from it, running constantly from her into his work, into other women, or into the company of men, or controlling her, imprisoning her, putting her down and belittling her, or, his favourite tactic, provoking her fears and doubts.

§63.

The inherently unselfish quality of woman means that, generally speaking, there are always far more 'better' women around than men. But although her options appear to be more limited than his, and although she more often has to settle for a partner who is not worthy of her, she knows that this has to be so, that a man will always be more or less a man. What is important for her is for a man to be *on* the hero's journey; *where* he is on it, is kind of secondary. It would be lovely, to be sure, if he had actually rescued her from the dragon, but she's happy to wait; *as long as he's on his way.* If she starts to think that he doesn't have the pluck to go the full distance, she will worry. If she perceives that he has given up, or that he's going somewhere else, she will hate him.

This is why, although a woman might profess a need for bland, indiscriminate 'equality', and gain shoddy solace from hanging around puppyish semi-men, she *still*, sometimes despite herself, expects her male partner to lead in a dance, to make bold decisions (even trivial ones, like choosing where to sit in a public space), to behave with male dignity and to engage in the hero's journey, The Noble Quest—in short, to grow a pair. It's also why, although women naturally seek men with attractive characters—who have the noetic quality of intelligence, the thelemic quality of spiritedness, the visceral quality of sensitivity and the somatic quality of resourcefulness

(the precise configuration depending on her own character) —
what she desires more than *anything else*, more than money,
more than muscles, more than a cool wardrobe, more than
fame, more than good looks, more than anything which can
be named, is what we call presence and courage. The fact
that these qualities cannot be literally understood or even
adequately named is the source of all the blether about 'what
women want'. Women know *exactly* what they want, they just
cannot put it into a nice little bullet-by-bullet presentation
for idiotic men to follow along to.

The nameless qualities woman seeks in a desirable man
show to her that he has the capacity to do the only thing
she ever really wants him to do, overcome his naming self.
This is why all loving women everywhere demand that men
'don't take themselves seriously'. Not because woman wants
a humble, self-effacing clown at her side. She needs him to
have a split self (sometimes misleadingly called ego) but, much
more than this, she needs to know that he can put it aside. It's
also why women prefer men to make the first move, and then
often place obstacles in his path to her vagina; to measure the
depth of his composure and the circumference of his balls.

§ 64.

Men are born masculine and women are born feminine *in
principle*; but just as any principle of character can be said
to be shaped by hereditary factors and environmental conditioning, so the natural sense and meaning of masculinity
and femininity is shaped by nature and by culture. And just
as egoic culture distorts character, overlaying it with personality, so it distorts natural gender, overlaying it with *sexual*
PSEUDO-GENDER and *asexual* MONO-GENDER.

Pseudo-gender is to masculinity and femininity what
sadism is to extroversion and masochism is to introversion;
a self-directed, self-inflating caricature of self. Pseudo-gender (or SEXUALISM) began many thousands of years ago, at
the dawn of the civilised system, when the male ego took
control of self, and began filling up consciousness with ever

more degraded copies of itself, and took control of society, which became a hyper-masculine battle of all against all for top spot on the ziggurat of cock-dominance, the point of maximum extrinsic power from which he could impregnate the maximal number of women, who were in turn compelled to embody caricatures of femininity. The result was a world of filthy, bellicose, hyper-rational, physically powerful men lording it over vain, manipulative, unreasonable, physically feeble women. These 'traditional gender roles' are still with us today, mostly outside the middle-class West or at the base of the social hierarchy, where they have further degraded to the moronic, knuckle-dragging, cultureless autism of the modern mass male and the outrageously shallow, preening, unstable, self-hatred of the modern mass female.

Caricatured sexualists have caricatured views of the opposite sex. For pseudo-gendered woman, man is nothing but a walking talking penis, easily bored with his toys, easily bored with his woman, either a sadistic bastard who deals with life by controlling it, or a masochistic coward, who deals with life by avoiding it; usually both. For pseudo-gendered men, women are emasculating succubi, either deceitful and manipulative bitches or servile doormats; usually both. These caricatures, being based on caricatured selves, are factually correct; the average mass man *is* indeed a predictable dick-head, the average mass woman, an erratic bitch.

§65.

The gender-cliches of average man and woman are a conse-quence of egoic culture, which imposes stereotypical self-re-inforcing gender roles on children, moulding their gender identities to cliched norms and forcing selves to become more and more *like* selves, in this case, caricatured sexualised selves. ASEXUALISTS never tire of telling us this, and they are right. That society can and does work in the opposite direction however; this does not cross the asexual mind, because it cannot. That a male world, made by and for males for thousands of years, might somehow, with its constant competition, constant drive to 'progress' and constant development of and use of male forms of hyper-focused conceptualisation, make women more male; or that the mediated world that hyper-masculine men and women create, one in which function gives way entirely to abstract form, that this might suppress gender; or that, finally, for egos cut off from their own nature, a genderless society might become more attractive, that they might *want* to manage society so that threatening aspects of masculinity (self-mastery for example) and threatening aspects of femininity (innocence for example) are annihilated; all this is beyond the pale for the mono-gendered, although it is what happens. As civilisation progressed, it became possible for more and more men to isolate themselves further and further from their incarnate bodily experience of unselfish nature. Those most unselfish and natural people, women, became at best children-machines and sexual spittoons, at worst an existential threat, to be excluded from male consciousness by any means necessary; chiefly through work, warfare, sport, drugs, pederasty and homosexual relations, which are still man's favourite hiding places.

For while man is basically, inherently, masculine and woman basically, inherently, feminine—the transparent and repeatedly, empirically verified fact that biological sex dictates gender in more than 99 percent of us—society determines the extent to which gender is expressed *or* suppressed. Upbringing and social conditioning affect all aspects of personality, and gender, being fundamental to personality, is no different. Thus, for example, a man will almost inevitably be masculine, but this 'masculinity' might be suppressed or enhanced by one's parents or one's culture, producing more feminine men or more hyper-masculine men. In addition, the expression or cultural definition of gender-preferences will vary, so that a masculine man is more likely to be attracted to short hair, narrow hips and small breasts in one culture but to long hair, wide hips and 'shelf-effect' bubble-arses in another.

These influences epigenetically propagate through generations, leading to long-term shifts in gendered expression. Thus women in gender-suppressing or gender-caricaturing cultures will give birth to mono-gendered and pseudo-gendered children (or children heavily disposed to asexuality and sexuality) respectively, in much the same way that women living through a famine or through a time of abundance will tend to produce, and raise, slight or chunky children, and rich mothers will tend to produce and raise tall, bland-faced beauties. Likewise, sexual orientation appears to be more biological—innate—but environments can also epigenetically influence gayness, making its appearance *appear* innate. This is expressed as the frequent red-herring that 'I have always known I was gay'. In the same way I might have 'always known I was hungry', or even that I have 'always known I am tall', but this doesn't mean these traits aren't culturally determined.

§66.

The causes of homosexuality or ambiguous gender are not fundamentally different to those for height, arrogance, depression or musical taste. There may be some genetic, epigenetic or biological component to how tall, cocky, sad, funky, gay or lusty you are, but the decisive factors with such *manifestations* of innate (and innately gendered) psyche—particularly as they relate to *personality*—are environmental, social and domestic; just as some societies have taller, sadder or funkier people than others, so some have gayer or more androgynous people than others. That being the case, we would expect to find, for example, that *simple*, primal, pre-civilised societies, in which unselfish love-making is common, and in which all have constant, unmediated access to the wild, have had, despite extremely high libidos, no, or almost no, *lifelong* or *exclusive* homosexuality (where lack of attraction to, or unwillingness to marry, someone of the opposite sex was rare or non-existent). And that's what we do find. Where 'homosexuality' has occurred in simple, egalitarian tribes it has mainly been casual, playful and very often confined to adolescent experimentation, almost never a long-term marriage, or an expression of an 'identity', such as many homosexual people today cling to in lieu of character.

We would also expect to find that societies which privilege bodiless, noetic form over corporeal, somatic function (i.e. the typical middle-class life of superficial mind-work), which punish or frustrate innate or traditionally gendered expression and gendered relationships, which curtail exposure to radical otherness (wilderness, darkness, silence, etc.), which display high levels of stratification and restrict access to mates, all have more homosexuals. And that is also what we find. Unless, that is, you are committed to the modern career and personality-enhancing ideology of QUEERISM; then you're not really interested in looking, unless it be to look for exceptions—the gay dolphin, the trans shaman, the lesbian 'experience'—which are greeted with the same disproportionate fanfare as the discovery, by FEMINISTS, of a lone woman hunter, a second-rate woman philosopher or a minor woman scientist, all hailed to the high heavens.

Not, it need hardly be added, that there is anything sinful or wrong with men putting their penises in the anuses of other men, or women sexually pleasuring other women, if that's what they want to do. Nor is there anything unnatural about those *extremely* rare and wonderful cases in which someone really is born in the 'wrong' body. Rather, once we've seen through the distorting ideology of modern thought, and cleared away the gender-corrupting influences of civilisation—including civilisation in its very earliest forms—we find that the real reasons why so many men are not attracted to women, and vice versa, and why so many young children are so appallingly confused about their sexuality (or subjected to the abomination of 'gender counselling'), is very often because of fear, frustration, desperation and, above all, the influence of an insane, gender-annihilating, society.

§67.

The final, and most devastating, consequence of a mono-gendered society, one which feminists dare not look fully in the face, is that, in the brave new asexual world, the male ego is not just still the winner, but is able to gain *more* power. The

situation is not unlike the fabled 'level-playing field' that co-
lonial powers created in the nations they granted 'home-rule'
to. They would wreck a resource-rich 'third-world' country,
plunder the environment, place corrupt elites in charge, force
the nation into debt and ensure that the entire populace is
addicted to the international market; *then* allow 'free and fair
trade'. Likewise, man spends millennia unconsciously constructing a civilisation according to the needs and desires of
the male ego, a world that is built on rabid, restless, abstract,
male fears and desires, which, consequently, you have to be
an insensitive, hyper-focused, monomaniacal, automaton to
successfully engage with; and *then* happily cedes to feminist
demands for equality within it. In both cases the game has
been pre-rigged, leaving third-worlders in the first case, and
women in the second, like football teams playing uphill, into
the sun, wearing high-heels.

No matter how fair and egalitarian the world seems,
it remains permanently, inherently, tilted 45 degrees in the
favour of man. The individual, in the mono-gendered world,
is supposed to free his or her self from its environment, strive
towards an objective achievement and realise his or her self
through that achievement; all male prerogatives. Such achievements include running a successful business, getting to the top
of a professional career-ladder, writing a best-seller, inventing
something that makes a lot of money, solving a problem in
science, winning an Olympic Gold and working out why your
operating system isn't working properly, *all* of which require
masculinity; single-mindedness, intense drive, abstraction,
technical expertise, self-control and, in most cases, horrendous insensitivity. Women who succeed in such a world—
which, for us, *is* the world, and every moment within it—are
either forced to become, effectively, men, or they start out
that way ('I have always known I was a gamer').

§68.

Mono-gendered ideologues prefer to believe that if everyone learns that gender is entirely a function of upbringing,

education and environment, if the world is designed to allow all women equal opportunity and equal pay, and if every feminist demand is everywhere met, that social, intellectual and psychological standards will instantly become neutral. In the real world—made by and for the male ego—*masculinity remains the standard*. Femininity becomes devalued, scorned and destroyed, along with the nature that it manifests. Discrimination doesn't wink out of existence in a hyper-abstract, technocratic, mind-mediated world, rather it stops targeting women (or homosexuals), and turns instead towards discrimination against subtlety, sensitivity, generosity, irrational love, mysterious physicality and the simple, incarnate truth of feminine *being*. Discrimination, in other words, continues to exist, but is now unthinkable.

Take love, a state that women are far more familiar with than men. In an important sense, woman *is* love, and you can tell pretty well the status of love, how rarely it is experienced and how poorly it is understood, by the fact that self-appointed defenders of women, feminists, are largely disgusted by the word, or by the idea that their innate genius resides in what the word actually represents. They prefer to see 'love' as caring, as being motherly, as being meek, inoffensive, *nice*. They then reject this caricature of 'love' in favour of the 'strength', 'power' and 'pride' of their masculinised, worldly personalities. For the feminist, 'genius' means cultural achievement, artistic truth, transcendent expression and stand-up comedy—all of which men excel at, the genius of man. The genius of woman, far more profound—the source of everything that man seeks to achieve—is completely ignored in Standard Gender Discussion. It does nothing for your special identity or personality, it does nothing for your career or your grades, it does nothing for modern woman or modern man.

On a less damaging but equally depressing level, an asexual world also has it that men and women should be treated equally in their intimate relations; and, again, *men* are the winners. The idea that woman enjoys casual sex as much as man, despite the fact she feels used after it—and he, if he has the slightest conscious awareness of his inner state, feels guilty—serves man, quite obviously, as does the belief that he does not need to show her any greater consideration, or display gentlemanliness, decisiveness or make even trivial gestures of commitment, such as paying for a meal, because he wouldn't do these things for his mates. He can casually chat with her, casually fuck her and then casually push her out the door because that's what he would do if she were a man. That's equality, yeah? She buys into it, at least verbally or intellectually—while feeling her heart shrink at every pusillanimous lack of pluck (such as fear of making a move or making a decision), every gesture of capitulation (such as acceding to her emotion without taking a manly stand) and every unfeeling disregard for the honour of being with her (such as treating her like an object).

A world of sexual pseudo-gendered cockmen, bitches and sexists and asexual mono-gendered feminists, homosexuals and metrosexuals is no different to any other bipolar egoic society. Each group *correctly* believes the other is insane while *incorrectly* believing that *all* those beyond the self-knowable must also be insane. Each group sees society as a handful of cliched categories, while generating its own cliched photocopy of a photocopy of a photocopy of its self, leading to a small quantity of predictable, easily-lampooned, gender types; the bitchy, anal, neurotic homosexual man; the blank, swaggering, throaty, ever-ready-to-anger feminist woman; the feeble, pap-faced and perfumed millennial man-boy; the nice-car, well-paying-job, air-punching, reptilian predator; the hopeless, fretting, puddle-woman punchbag; the 'such a lovely' family man functioning for forty years on friendly autopilot while secretly wanking in his garage; the hard, cynical, pointy-shoed, money-grabbing tart; and so on and so forth. This is the *actual* 'gender spectrum' of the world, twenty-odd shades of monotonous and caricatured unpeople, varying slightly from culture to culture, and plastered over with an obsessively curated compensatory surface personality or advertised 'identity'.

Incapable of seeing outside self-projection, the selfish sexist and the selfish feminist both assume that any radically different genderedness—that of the REAL MAN and the REAL

WOMAN—must also be the enemy. It is as inconceivable to a penis-brained hyper-male that sensitivity and camp fabulousness can be expressions of masculinity as it is to a right-winger that radical anarchism and Luddism can be conservative, tradition-honouring attitudes; but it is the truth. The real man and the real woman are mysterious creatures indeed.

§69.

Only real men and real women are capable of TRUE LOVE. This is the *fully gendered* experience of being selflessly ungendered with someone. The paradox is the same as that of unself having no relation to self-representation, and therefore *both* fully in it *and* completely independent of it (or *neither* in it, *nor* independent of it). Love is neither a fact nor an opinion. I am, in true love, incarnate in my manifest, gendered body and, at the same time, conscious "behind" the gendered self with another, who is equally conscious. The thing-in-itself that I are there is then one with the thing-in-itself that you am here. This does not destroy self, rather it allows self to grow naturally with another self in the marvellous experience we call COMPLEMENTARITY. Not the two unknowns of the sexual couple, strangers oscillating between fear and violence, nor the two knowns of the asexual couple, friends oscillating between excitement and boredom; rather the two *unknowables* of true romance, *lovers*, forever a mystery one to the other, two distinct, unique selves, growing apart, yet one in the same sweet, mysterious, voluptuous plasm of unself.

To love, I let go of self, and in letting go, I don't just experience the other fully, but I reveal *my* self fully; thus love and knowledge are the same thing. This demand for total exposure is why so few can fully love; they can no more tear their hearts open in bed, than they can on the stage or on the dancefloor, or in the forest, and must use technique to compensate. They occasionally feel the rending impulse to release, and give, and let go, but the weight of the self is far too great, which is why they so often take to drink to suppress self and for once in their lying lives say what they mean.

§70.

The root of LOVE is reached through overcoming the self in the experience called TRANSCENDENCE. Love is not an emotion.* It is a feeling, a sensation, an action and a pristine idea, all of which are rooted in unself. Without transcendent consciousness, ideas become dreams, actions become inapt, sensations become sybaritic and feelings become emotions; intense like and want, which the self *calls* 'love' but which, when the lover threatens the self-informed self (as *all* lovers do), instantly turn to intense don't like and intense don't want—to hatred.

This is PERSONAL LOVE; self-informed attachment of the personality. Because there is no conscious, IMPERSONAL LOVE informing the experience, the *relationship* to the other is addictive; a desperate, hyper-concentrated tyrannical adoration in which the whole of the other is sliced up and that which does not fit an intensely wanted ideal discarded or hated. The adoration fades, but the ideal forms an addictive entity in the self, a psychic double of the other which, when they depart or die, shatters in agony. This experience we call HEARTBREAK, but it is actually SELF-BREAK. The almost unimaginable horror of which—coming to us as a kind of death, or murder—keeping half the miserable world glued to the other half.

Without the capacity for impersonal mutual transcendence, selves become attached to the "effects" of love, the modal pleasures of it, which thereby degrade into selfish emotions, masochistic vanity and sadistic love of power. When self is in charge, mystery and complementarity vanish, replaced by, at best, a living death of cohabitation and compromise, two selves slowly refining, over the years, their capacity to torture each other. Or the egoic need for security and for the company of someone who is sensitised to one's needs and desensitised to one's faults might replace adoration with neediness; either desperate, indiscriminate attachment to an idealised love-object, painfully jealous of any move of the other towards integration back into the totality of life, or pathetic, infantile dependency on feelings of security that long-term attachment to mummy-daddy surrogates engenders.

---

* Barry Long, *Making Love*

Another option for the ego is restless promiscuity, serial monogamy, constant casualness or sexual abstinence; all techniques for keeping the other at a distance, never letting anyone get too close, for fear that ego's power to do as it pleases, to pleasure itself or reign supreme in the kingdom of self-determination might be threatened.

§71.

Overcoming self allows the quality of impersonal love as it "manifests" in self—visceral affection, energetic attraction, conceptual friendship and material sensuality—to remain *non-addictive*, but this is possible, and only possible, if both partners are committed to continual SELF-MORTIFICATION; overcoming their selves and breaking down their cliched images of each other, in order reach across the divide. Without such a selfless mission—without constantly acting to break down cliched patterns of perception, conception, volition and affection—all partnerships are doomed. All of them. Not doomed to break up—couples do break up, sometimes even naturally—but doomed to frustration, loneliness and loveless misery, which live under the public presentation of the *loveliest* couples, the *happiest* marriages and the most *wonderful* relationships.

The need for self-mortification goes hand in hand with the need for SELF-DEVELOPMENT, which means there are two qualities to romantic love; *depth*—the degree of impersonal unselfishness you share in common—and *width*—the degree of personal harmony your two selves experience together. Compatible depth we call primal ROOTING, compatible width we call secondary BRANCHING. A couple that only roots can expect to have an intense relationship that is eventually felled by the axe of 'incompatibility', unable to really breathe in the day-to-day air of life; a couple that rootlessly branches, on the other hand, can expect a friendly relationship that is, for all its gentle joy, too close to the surface; the bodies don't blend and obliterate; something, somewhere, remains unfed, unsatisfied; emotions rise; it just doesn't quite work.

Finally, love, being unself, is unknowable, unquantifiable, indescribable. This is why we say 'I will always love you', even when we know that it is unlikely to be true, because there is, in the experience of love, a sense of something which overreaches the boundaries of what we experience as space and time. It's not that, as Leo Tolstoy had it, 'happy families are all alike [but] every unhappy family is unhappy in its own way', rather that every loving partnership eludes description, while every unloving one can be analysed and dissected until Kingdom come. When Kingdom *does* come, partners realise, with astonishment, that *everything* they thought they knew about love was wrong.

§72.

The word 'love' seems to suggest some form of commitment, the terror of egoic man. The idea that he might have to 'take her on', that he might have to give up the opportunity to have sex with every woman on earth (particularly a problem for young, handsome, energetic or powerful men: cocks with their chickens cut off), the idea that she might get her sticky loving fingers over his frictionless independence—which includes his hobbies and his friendships—all this can, for man, creep into the word 'love', and make him, or rather his ego, fear it.

Man knows that he has to give up his restless sex-speculation, that he has to, in some sense, commit and give up independence, and that, despite the importance of his work, she is *still* more important than any thing in the world. He knows that her emotions, her madness, her insecurity, her doubts, her coldness and her wilful independence must be faced up to, and that he has to *raise his game**—overcome his ego, and hers—to be worthy of her. Man knows all this, and he is sore afraid. He shrinks from the task.

After about three months, and particularly when two people who love each other move in together, ego—which has been stilled by love—wakes up and begins to reassert itself. Then the problems begin. He begins to get withdrawn, or violent, or bored, he doesn't give her the same kind of attention

---

* Barry Long, *The Way In*

he did at the start, the sex becomes not quite as sweet, and not quite as often, she starts to get subtly anxious or sad, which he blames on her. He has to get away, and then she does too. Then the ridiculous arguments begin, and the 'us' talks, and sex becomes more like wrestling... the usual story.

Only a man who really knows what love is, and will do whatever it takes to overcome his ego in order to realise that love, can make it past all this. Such a man will ask his woman to help him become more of a man, more loving, more conscious, more present. They will then *both* be on the mission. Sex will have a purpose—not as dutiful necessity, but something greater than their separate pleasure; to bring more conscious love into the world, to awaken them both.

Such a man will ACKNOWLEDGE his woman (and vice versa); manifest his inner experience of her in participatory recognition.* This is why he says, and means, 'I love you', because timeless love, in this dimension, is the meaningful physiognomic expression of it. Suppressing 'I love you' is like suppressing a smile. It diminishes the joy of it. This is why we don't need *time* to say 'I love you'. A minute after meeting her might be enough. A second. As she *is* love, as everything is, there is no need to *get to know* you, or it. It's just there. Then saying 'I love you' is as easy as smiling; and in truth the two things are the same. The face smiles, the mind says 'I love you'.

§73.

Just as love is secondarily a question of selves suiting and branching, so conscious sex is. The pleasure of LOVE MAKING is through the conscious root of the self, which "receives" thereby the pleasure of shared being. As consciousness is of the whole, so the whole self is experienced. Awareness softens, away from modal focus, into wide consciousness of sensory, sensational, soma (I hear, feel, taste, see and smell my partner) of the whole visceral system (the vastness and profundity of inner feeling) of the whole, electric thelema (burning with un-believable desire) and of astonished nous (although detached conceptualisation is necessarily softened and silenced).

---

* Barry Long, *Talks from Tamborine Mountain*

Thus, only unique (selfless) *individuals* can make love; a self that is essentially a self, and so essentially like every other self, is necessarily self-directed towards the isolated egoic elements of the experience of self; hard, tense thelemic *need*, a few crude noetic ideas ('I'm fucking her! I'm fucking her! Look at that!') and localised excitation of the cock or cunt, which seems to detach itself from the whole body. Such partial awareness cannot experience a truly conscious, truly unique, whole body orgasm, any more than a monkey in a zoo can experience nature, rather than, at most, an imagined projection of nature on the back wall of its cage.

The pleasure of truly conscious sex is therefore literally unimaginable. As with any conscious experience, only metaphor can cross the threshold. Literal description is felt as a betrayal; a scientific rating of an orgasm, for example, appears demeaning, a realistic painting of 'love-making', unbearably cheeseball, while even accurate metaphors are inexplicable to the self, which understands 'conscious love-making is like sharing the creation and destruction of the universe with GOD IN FEMALE FORM' as absurd hyperbole, or as a stand in for merely really, *really* good SEX.

§ 74.

For man, far more egoic than woman, sex becomes a noetic-thelemic obsession. Hyper-focused, the male ego is always *on the prowl*, always ready to robotically fix his mind onto an isolated pair of breasts or buttocks, always ready for more porn. This is OBJECTIFICATION—endemic to the self-directed walking-talking penis who sees woman as a walking-talking vagina—the dead-eyed PORNSTARE of morbid need that grips every male face when a tableaux of erotic images fills his attention. The feminist complains of objectification, but misses the fact that she and everyone else engage in essentially the same activity, as evidenced by the omnipresence of the pornstare—in the street, in the supermarket, in the stadium, in the gallery, in the cinema and in front of the television. The difference being that, for man, particularly young man, sex is—provided he hasn't been numbed by the world—infinitely more interesting than anything else.

Sex indeed, with its potential to satisfy every aspect of ego, is the prototypical desire. Desire to defeat every other human being on earth in armed combat, desire for fame and fortune, desire for the latest-and-greatest product, desire for children, cute puppies and excellent fabrics, desire for cosmetics and an impressive bench press, desire for food and drugs, desire for a high score and desire for knowledge; all these desires either accompany, or are associated with, or stand in for, or are necessary for or, at the very least, come from the same kind of need as a desire to fuck and be fucked. We can even say, metaphorically, that ego *is* sex. Ego must fuck (or be fucked by) everything, which is why (in English at least; a particularly ego-friendly language), the word fuck can more or less stand *for* everything. It's also why sex *never* satisfies, only temporarily stupefies, for desire is an end to itself for ego. Ultimately, it just wants to want. Because it desires to possess what it cannot possess (as the sadist Jean-Paul Sartre wrote,* it desires to possess a freedom that instantly becomes unfree in the possession of it), and because it must give up what cannot be surrendered, the sex-self has only two modes; frustration and sedation, separated by a cigarette-paper thin film of mechanical-orgasmic pleasure.

§75.

Egoic man is sex-obsessed. This obsession is creeping up on the female psyche too, but it is trivial compared to the intensity of male sexual desire. In fact, woman *does* desire more intensely than man, but there is *usually* enough love or presence in there to keep it easily within the bounds of sanity. She can be patient, maintain her presence, renounce sex even, if she has to. Not so the vibrating sexual-turnip that sits in the cockpit of the male mind, which has no patience whatsoever, no presence and can only give up sex when it runs out of energy in its late fifties, or if it has had its energy suppressed by the etiolating energy-drain of bodiless hyper-abstraction.

---

* Jean-Paul Sartre, *Being and Nothingness*

Egoic sex-obsession is no different to any other egoic addiction, tending towards more and more self—meaning more and more experience of the particular, specialised swells of the particular self. The more egoic one's approach to self, the more bizarre the 'kink'. Relatively straightforward desires—oral sex, ethnic partners, foot fetishes, pig-tails and so on—give way to anal sex, extremely aggressive-submissive power play, sex-toys, ejaculating on the face—which give way, in turn, to utter deviance—dressing up as babies, male lactation fetishes, autogynephilia (you don't want to know), sissy hypno (don't ask), and so on; all justified by the shallow, promiscuous, 'kink-positive', 'anti-puritan' asexual liberal. Which isn't to say that there is no place, in love, for outrageous, dramatic or even bizarre foreplay; but like all play, if the purpose is, first of all, to *win*, the game overtakes the togetherness of playing, and becomes *forced play*, the baleful activity known as WORK.

§76.

Egoic man is a wanker. He just cannot stop. Undomesticated pre-civilised people rarely or never masturbated, and very few animals do it, unless caged or in resource-depleted environments. When man finally gets his hands on a woman (or man) he doesn't stop self-pleasuring; he just masturbates inside her. If he stimulates her, it will be in the same way that he brings himself off, an end-directed, mechanical-clitoral stimulation which, having nothing else to go by, she takes to be the purpose of sex, wearily enduring his porn-infused sexual 'needs'. She comes to believe that 'love-making' is a silly illusion, a sentimental nonsense, that sex is, with the exception of a few explicit commands here and there, more or less an inward experience. She might enjoy the attention man gives her, she might get some relief from a decent climax, she *might* even, from time to time, gain the satisfaction of real intimacy or tenderness, particularly after orgasm, but something enduringly vital is missing, and a fundamental neglect rots away inside her, manifesting as emotional misery, depression, anger or even disgust at sex; all justified.

Loveless sex provokes shame. Many are too insensitive, or even just too busy to notice that it does, but it does, and clearly not because two people have given themselves up to a mechanical instinct the genetic purpose of which is to bring more unhappy creatures onto this blighted rock—although they have. Loveless sex creates unhappiness, sharp feelings of separateness, post-coital tristesse and guilt because we have, basically, wanked into someone or had someone wank into us. Where there is no conscious love, there can only be self, or two selves, seeking selfish pleasure, hunting for the orgasm, dutifully—sometimes even unwillingly—pleasuring the other, giving over to self-gratifying sadism or masochism, immersing oneself in the mind, in (for the man) the fuck-thrilling idea of what is happening and (for the woman) in the sterile narcissism of being intensely, or even not so intensely, desired. All of this is terribly fashionable, but it is disgusting, and it disgusts us. That's why we feel as we do after loveless sex, at best satisfied, as after a nice Sunday dinner, more often than not diminished, a little less a person.

In many cases, sex for women is a profoundly disappointing experience; perfunctory foreplay, frantic bashing away, followed by leaden exhaustion, indifference, shame, disgust, restlessness or emptiness. For man, the experience is equally unsatisfying, although he is less sensitive to the appalling violence he is doing to his heart. At the start of a loving relationship two people might, if they are lucky, get a taste of how good sex can be, but it rarely enters the miraculous self-shattering experience of conscious love, and, in any case, it soon fades away. Shrug. That's just how it is.

§77.

Self alone does not know if it loves someone or doesn't love someone; for neither can be known. It must therefore rely on signs, signals and signatures. It will learn strategies to attract others, to get them into bed or into a relationship, whereupon it will attempt to 'get it in writing', ideally backed by the weight of social convention (a MARRIAGE) or the fear of financial ruin (a MORTGAGE). But as soon as the other is possessed, bore-dom creeps in, stifling coupledom, uncertainty, constant ir-ritability which lashes out at the weirdest things, impotence, sexual disinterest or chronic fear that one's partner might up sticks at any moment. This elemental neediness plagues any relationship that the self 'invests' in, which it will attempt to deal with through sadistic force (either physical violence or psychological threat; 'you'll be all alone, who'll have you?'), or through masochistic manipulation (again, either physical, by becoming 'indispensable', or psychological, by pushing guilt buttons; 'I'll be all alone, I don't know what I'll do to myself!').

Ego will also use technique to keep the other attached. The male ego in particular demands total loyalty, along with immunity to any kind of criticism, and will violently police insubordination. If he is on the hero's journey he'll get loyalty, not just that but unbelievable, insane, heart-cracking rivers of love immeasurable, which *his* love will unlock in the belly-mind of the woman he is with. If not, he'll get at best a tired, watchful, habitual kind of dependency and fearful allegiance, without either of them knowing what they're missing.

In the end though, for the ego, there is only ever really loneliness. For the self-informed self, always on the surface of life, the constant, blended depth of conscious love, being unimaginable, does not exist. Only having its own limited awareness to judge by, egoic imagination can get no closer to the fundamental togetherness it is lacking. Its own surface pleasure—somatic, thelemic, noetic and visceral—is the be-all and end-all of egoic sex-fucking and egoic relationship-build-ing. It does not love, but it does not know it does not love. It knows, from time to time, that it is lonely, but it doesn't ever really know why, any more than a cow knows why it is attached to a milking machine.

§78.

The surface of the self we call the self-evident PERSONALITY, made up of various quantitative *traits*. Personality is the mani-festation or realisation of the quality of conscious CHARACTER, which is intuitively or indirectly perceived. Although personality stretches elusively back into its proximal and distal roots (i.e. into the character of consciousness and context), it appears to us as a collection of *things* which can be literally expressed, even measured with a test. Character, by contrast, having its roots in unselfish quality, is not a 'thing', and so can only be experienced through empathy and art.

The *selfless* self (or INDIVIDUAL) naturally manifests elusive character as an interesting, attractive or subtle personality, while the *selfish* self, which is nothing *but* manifestation, is nothing but personality. Superficiality, or hollowness, therefore—the empty shell of personality—is the *sine qua non* of egotism. Without consciousness and the quality of its primal attractions, ego focuses on and inflates its secondary interests and abilities. It might come across as a crude nationalist or an obsessive culture vulture or pious believer, but underneath the flags, the slang or the uniform, is a bland lack of character. Or it might make a great show of self-criticism or self-abasement—it might even be a passive masochist—but scratch the nice, inoffensive, sweet surface and violence inevitably erupts.

Just as egos conflate primal and secondary attractions, so they conflate character and personality, taking the selfless quality of tenderness, or presence, for example, to be just one of a range of personality traits, equivalent to a taste in cheese. Similarly, egos belonging to an egoic society conflate the *naturally* evolved cultural personality of a culture—adapted for the cold, for example, and so not particularly physically expressive, or adapted to island life and so somewhat odd and insular—to be on the same level as an *unnaturally* maintained series of personality traits, such as brutal insensitivity to the suffering of animals, fear of the sexuality of free women, and an interest in motor-racing, which are justified as 'cultural'.

§ 79.

The unselfish personality manifests the meeting point of conscious character and the quality of the context. The incipient swells and stunts of formless character, at its subtlest level, build themselves an explicit personality-form *from*, and in response *to*, the material—the nature, the culture—of the context, much as an oyster builds its shell from the calcium in the sea or a caddis-fly larva builds its case from grains of stone in a lake. The various elements of the unselfish personality *form* a whole, but it can only be perceived *as* a whole *by* the whole I which forms them (or a whole I which loves me). All the non-conscious, unwhole, unloving ego can experience are bundled bits of personality, in mutual strife, unified only by an unconscious impulse to build, in place of a beautiful shell or pupa, a functional suit of personality ARMOUR.

Only *I* can empathically experience or love another; COMMUNE with you. Armour can only COMMUNICATE. The communication system of the armoured, self-informed personality is made up of the scripts, methods and games that the self learns to deal with society, a series of ADVERTISEMENTS— excuses, displays, attitudes and anecdotes—which ego must slap over itself in order to conceal its inner emptiness. Just as ego is engaged in a constant project of addicted expansion, so it ceaselessly presents to itself and others a means to conceal or justify the same. These advertisements include:

i.   Personality might choose to present itself as an outsider, as an artist or as someone *special*. Some people walk into a conversation waving around a packed CV of wonderfulness—a thrillingly unique job perhaps, a purple suit of clothes, an unusual ethnic background or a series of adventurous moments picked out of a dull life. Others cultivate subtler forms of uniqueness. Perverse opinions, for example, or wacky diction, or unusual hobbies, or a predilection for convention-breaking outbursts, or just an 'above-it-all' way of reclining. Such people are like a cheap fairground; big wow on the outside, cheap thrills and tedious queues on the inside.

ii.   One of the surest ways to make up for inner emptiness is through worldly *achievement*—a successful movie, perhaps, or the securing of a prized appointment—and consequent fame. This sends ahead advanced notice of specialness before its possessor enters the room; just the sight of a famous head is enough for people to know that here is *someone of value*. But because such specialness *is* possessed, a mere thing added to the outside, it is also lost, leading to the depression of the has been ('I've lost it'.), the anxiety of is-being ('Do I still have it?' What if I lose it?'), and the frustration of the wannabe ('Will I ever get it?'), all of which founded on an essential fraudulence, which continually whispers to him from the works of the true greats and the opinions of people with genuine taste.

iii.   Those who cannot feed from fame's table can sustain themselves on a diet of grandiose fantasies. Although these aren't anywhere near as nourishing for ego as full-blown fame is, they have the advantage of not requiring any actual effort to prepare. When personality reaches an age when it can *never* get anywhere, such dreams are abandoned in favour of an 'I coulda been a contenda' script, along with, perhaps, a series of bitter snipes at those who have succeeded.

iv.   Two common correlatives to 'I coulda been a contenda' are 'Needless to say, I was the winner' and 'You tell me, what was I supposed to do?' Some people, completely overwhelmed by personality, do nothing but tell stories which serve no other purpose than to broadcast their superiority or excuse their lack of it. Pseudo-selved sadists tend to prefer the former, while mono-selved masochists go for the latter. Anyone who has been stuck between the two—between the unstoppable force of ceaseless brag and the immovable object of perpetual complaint—truly knows the meaning of suffering.

v.   Masochists often deal with the pointless subservience of their lives by inhabiting an inner world of humourless, critical irony, sentimental fantasy, self-exalting art or self-serving spiritual practice. This picture show *of* the self is then presented *by* the self, *to* the self, *as* the self, either in overt scripts, dress, style of speech and posture, which all say 'I'm *really* a misunderstood artist / wandering minstrel / reincarnated pasha / mystic onion', or more commonly (for the monotonous masochist tends to uncommunicative introversion), in an inner world of self-justifying fantasy. Correspondingly, sadists who lose themselves in money and power, or in endless ambitious striving for it, present their ambitions, or their car keys, or their immaculate dress, or their immaculate homes, or their superb cleavage, or any other crude pseudo-self image, as broadcast substitutes for the wasteland in their hearts.

vi.   The grossest, most conspicuous means by which personality presents itself to the world is through physical appearance; the flags, badges, styles and symbols that self decorates itself with. The extent to which these are an expression of inner quality, or a compensation for lack of it, is usually evident in how self reacts when its appearance is damaged, when its symbols are desecrated or when its style is made light of. The emptier the personality the louder the laugh (or shirt), the bigger the car, the thicker the foundation... and the more violent the outrage when such forms are exposed or mocked, as they comprise existential reality entire. Likewise, hollow, essentially pornographic, entertainment, such as football matches, superhero movies and celebrity dance shows, must always smother themselves in hyperbolic adverts proclaiming '*This* is the one that *really* matters. Now it *really* counts'. When such lies are mentioned, addicts to the shallow stimulation they conceal tend to react emotionally, even spitefully.

vii.   The most common advert of all is that of modest ordinariness, the tactic of signalling that 'I am nothing special'. This justifies an outrageously dull life, conformity to the worst forms of groupthink and a reason to bundle *everything* that is not ordinary into the category of 'weird', a category which, by virtue of its total lack of quality-discernment, factually unites the most disparate people and attitudes. To the 'ordinary bloke' the schizoid arbitrariness of solipsistic surrealism is indistinguishable from the complete psychological freedom of the greatest absurdity, the total self-obsession of a water-nazi wrapped in orange sheets is indistinguishable from genuine spiritual authority, the indiscriminate absurdities of conspiracy theories are indistinguishable from radical institutional analysis, and the violent emotionality of the nihilistic misfit is indistinguishable from the raptures of the freedom-loving outsider.

§80.

Personality co-opts quality in order to advertise itself. This has the consequence, unintended but welcomed by personality, of making quality *dis*-tasteful to those with nothing to gain from its surface appearance, who don't want to join the team. The qualities that inhere in, for example, femininity, gayness, whiteness, Englishness, old-age, the avant-garde or anarchism are reduced by egoic co-option to manageable token and cliche. These necessarily crude surface forms effectively monopolise the quality in question, making it appear cheesy, boring, low-grade, unpleasant and so on, dissuading the outsider from, say, pretty dresses ('girly'), outrageous dancing ('gay'), classical music ('white'), formality ('cold'), absurd theatre ('pretentious') or destroying public records ('criminal'). The attachment that personality has to external form explains why intelligent beliefs and tasteful cultural interests attract caricatured cranks, monsters or fools, who thereby discredit the quality that such form can contain. It also explains why discerning lovers of, say, their finer national traditions, or nature, or punk music, or philosophy, or any other quality activity are so often dismayed by the freaks that surround it, personalities hanging on to the papier mâché shell of confiscated quality. Low-quality, largely technical, pursuits, such as extreme sports, cooking, hobnobbing with wealthy pals, or business, don't tend to have the same problem.

As personality acquires more and more symbolic add-ons and inhabits deeper and deeper cliched (and therefore market-friendly) grooves, as it rejects anything which looks like something beyond the known, or something an enemy personality might engage in, so the focus of its experience narrows more and more, life is drained of qualitative depth *and* of quantitative width, until the individual has all but departed, leaving a 'walking, hiding symptom of their way of life'.*

---

* Philip K. Dick, *A Scanner Darkly*

§81.

CHARACTER is self's qualitative meeting place with unself. As such, it is partly, or essentially, synonymous with quality. Character does not appear as a measurable thing, but as a flavour, tone, vibe or 'aura', an unselfish, and therefore timeless *sense* of individuality. It is that in a girl of six which remains the same in the same woman at 85, the qualitative essence of her that remains even as her personality radically evolves, even if we subtract the entire measurable substance of her. An amnesiac in a sensory deprivation tank, unable to access even language, might experience confused noetic impressions or visceral echoes of the past, but underneath those would be the pure witnessing I, 'felt' at the subtlest level of feeling, or 'known' at the subtlest level of knowledge, as character.

Although the two blend into each other, we can speak of qualitative character and quantitative personality as distinct; of qualitative character-honesty and quantitative personality-honesty, for example, or qualitative character-beauty and quantitative personality-beauty, or qualitative character-sensitivity and quantitative personality-sensitivity. The former is an elusive but *constant* state, while the latter is definable and variable. When we say 'William Morris is honest', for example, we might be referring to an essential sense of integrity about the man (his character), not about how much truth he tells in any particular situation (his personality). He might have cheated at school, for example, lied to his wife about how much he loved her and deceived himself about his poetic gifts, but we still trust him, sensing an *essentially* honourable core. Resentful egos automatically conflate the two, counting up and pointing out the 'hypocrisies' of a personality—the indignities of a noble soul, the plagiarisms of an original artist, the errors of the great mind—which doesn't live up to a big ideal.

In the unselfish self, character and personality are fused, with the latter subordinate to the former. The *essence*—the individuality, originality or uniqueness—of character is reflected in the *substance* of personality, which gives the former voice, gait, gesture, story, song, armchair, t-shirt and cake.

Without character, personality may appear individual and advertise itself as such—as the stones of its caddis-fly case are novel, strange and unlike anyone else's—while the case is, like everyone else's, empty, or the pupa is dead. It is possible to uncover one's own character, by peeling away personality, and this in turn builds a new personality—our fascination with this is reflected in many a great story—but it is no more possible to bolt on a new *characterful* personality from the outside, through therapy, for example, or positive thinking, or life-style change, or, most ridiculously of all, deciding that '*from now on* I'm going to be honest (or friendly, or courageous, or interesting)', than it is possible to become a concert cellist if one has never picked up an instrument, or give literal birth if one is a man. It may appear, in such cases, that the personality has changed, but a slap round the head and the mask flies off.

§ 82.

The natural subordination of personality to character means that the latter cannot be understood by the former, for to do so demands that no quantitative element from one's own experience, no noetic concept or somatic percept, can be employed. Just as I must give up what I 'know' in order to experience who I am, so I must to know who *you* really are. In the first case—in the endeavour known as *self-knowledge*—because all-encompassing character is seen *by* personality *as* fragmented traits, there is no way of perceiving what these traits then have in common. That my restless lack of conscious attention might be connected with my obsessive nose-picking, attacks of paranoia and an inability to ever really get on with anyone, or the fact that I am continually betrayed and my needling feeling that something is lacking might both be connected with my bad dreams, frigidity and lock-checking mania; all such dot-drawing is impossible when there is nothing conscious to hold the pen or see the shape that forms.

Likewise, the character of other individuals can only be understood by letting go of the egoic urge to 'know' or 'understand' the various surface bits of them that reach my attention.

That there are so few unique individuals on this earth that *must* be understood in this way—that most people *can* be understood by grasping their socio-economic background, their sexuality, their job, their haircut and their shoes—makes it not just difficult to practice such a skill, but actually painful. Try letting go of your emotions and desires, your concepts and percepts, and looking directly into the hearts of those around you. It's very often like putting your head into a sewer.

Essence can only be experienced *by* essence; a communion which is, by virtue of its unselfish quality, direct. We call this transmission EMPATHY; the source of morality. Your consciousness and mine are unselfish and therefore, ultimately, the same. As they manifest in character I experience your quality as my own, and wish your good as I would my own. I can even feel myself, in your company, becoming more like you, a rare pleasure for two characters, a complete impossibility for two personalities and a total agony for a character in the company of a personality, towards whom empathy brings suffering; and so mere SYMPATHY (or *care* or *pity*)—trying to *understand* or *learn* who you are—must take its place.

Sympathy does have its place, for we all have personalties that, to come to know, *do* require effort, time, patience and all the other things that we're told we need to live with people. Coming to know personality also requires explicit instruction. Unlike my direct experience of your character, which naturally *shows* itself, you have to *tell* me you don't like aubergines, or your ears being nibbled, or I'll dissatisfy you. I need to *ask* you about your past, your pleasures and your pains, and care about the answer. From egoic personalities, there's nothing *but* answers, and so it's a waste of time listening to their opinions, beliefs, anecdotes, likes, dislikes, complaints, memories, fears and desires—and, oh Lord, they are many—but for personalities which manifest character, a charming journey through personality unfolds—not free of dangerous chasms and stagnant ponds—but worth taking; even if, after ten minutes together, or sixty years, we never leave the place we first met. For all I was ever really saying, and all you ever really heard, was my character.

§83.

Where character communes instantly, or directly, personality must use techniques and tricks to communicate with other people, because it is effectively imprisoned in its own representation. Just as it has to 'understand' other people, and 'learn' who they are, so it has to reach across to others via *method*. There are several consequences to this:

i.   CONVERSATIONS with personalities can feel like interrogations. They begin with a sense of, 'oh, this might go somewhere interesting', but it's just question after question after question, nothing developed or ever really shared, while, the whole time, you get the feeling that your answers aren't really being listened to, as the interrogator is just thinking of the next question to ask. Some conversations feel like talking with a sophisticated computer; all language, no meaning, everything taken at face value, no shared under-truth, and so no way to play with its form, all gestures beyond the literal meaning of what we are talking about—metaphor, comedy, implication, irony—hitting a wall. In fact, talking with the literal ego is far worse than talking to a wall; at least things bounce back from walls. Still other conversations feel more like listening to a daytime radio soap opera that you can't escape from. Conversations with such people, like sex with them, become enhanced masturbation, like giving yourself a dead arm so you can use it to pretend someone else is feeling you up. Egos do little more than share likes and dislikes, fears and desires, memories, facts and theories. They learn that they cannot speak unless they allow others to speak, so they patiently wait until you are done, offering the requisite number of head-nods and uh-huhs—possibly a functional question or comment—before cutting through you and launching into a self-gratifying monologue which you are expected to endure in the same manner.

ii.   Conscious selves care about those who are listening to them. They continually check, directly and indirectly, to see if you find the conversation interesting. Not just once or twice, but over and over again, always adapting. Egos do not. They either indiscriminately pour words over their listeners, without caring what's going on inside them, or they passively withdraw from the interaction, having learnt that this is what conversation entails, being an audience member for second-rate tribute acts.

iii.   Ego is socially inept, and inapt. It has no social graces, it doesn't know what to say, or what to do, or how to hold itself, and either relies on a laughably fake series of conversational routines or it hides behind its shyness, its fame or its classic bone structure. There is, in the egoic group interaction, no *passive* awareness of non-participants, no stopping the train of information or anecdote to welcome a new passenger, no checking to see who is not participating in a conversation and whether the topic should be changed so that they can, no social sensitivity whatsoever. Or there is, if the group is made up of hyper-sensitive masochistic selves, no-one willing to take charge, change the channel of communication entirely or flat out entertain us.

iv.   Ego cannot concentrate. Fuelled by restless emotion it skids over the surface of language, looking for anything it can get, or anything which might threaten it, both of which stick out from the flow of speech (or text) like flashing signposts saying 'one way only!' 'sale now on!' 'click here!' Any idea in a conversation which points off piste, into the unknown, and any meaning which requires time and patience to reach, are invisible to ego, as are the tonal shifts, play of expression and, above all, silences that breathe through meaningful exchange as air passes through a room, making it habitable. For ego all is solid and graspable, yet, founded on the ever shifting sand of emotion, uncertain, confusing and forever on the edge of collapse. Talking with extremely emotional people is like trying to swat a fly in a thunderstorm; in order to get across an idea it needs to be brief, self-contained, emphatic and shoved into their minds while the light is on, because it's not on for long.

v.   Conscious conversation is conducted in an atmosphere of contextual awareness, sensitive to where the river of meaning is taking us, guiding it here and there, sometimes even damning it or driving it over a cliff, but *essentially* egoless, allowing the natural flow to take us *somewhere else*. Egoic conversation is more like a plane trip; strap yourself into an antiseptic tank for an hour or two before landing somewhere identical to the place you left. Conscious conversation is like a game of tennis between two pros; a range of powerful baseline strokes, delicate drop-shots, lobs, volleys and smashes. Egoic conversation is more like two people firing cannons at each other.

vi.   The default state of ego is a bored, tense, aggressive or dead expression; the resting hate-face of the armoured woman, the empty-eyed lassitude of the distracted man. These are permitted with underlings, who can stare straight into the void, but strong feelings, being selfish, are suppressed in the presence of power or in the company of those from whom ego stands to get something. In their place the face broadcasts a crude series of flag-waving approval-signals; 'oh wo-*ow!* really!?' and 'uh-huh-uh-huh, so *fascinating*' and 'oh my God that's *hilarious!*' Not so much participating in a conversation as twiddling whatever knobs are most likely to win a jackpot. After a lifetime of this kind of conversation, the face resembles a sack of potatoes with a clown's face painted on it.

vii.   There is the curious sense, when talking to a personality, that you are not really talking to a human being at all, but to a projection, as if the words and gestures and facial expressions are being operated by a homunculus sitting in the control room of the mind. Smile now, pull the 'amazed' lever, press the 'worked-up and indignant' button... until its attention wanders and it turns on the autopilot so it can go off into the television room, leaving a face before you working away by itself, but with nobody at the controls. This is registered first of all as appearance or expression, and then, over time, as the armoured facial features of the personality armour. We call this PHYSIOGNOMY.

§84.

Physiognomy is the "manifest" aspect of character or personality and the universal and perennial art of judging both, based on the felt experience of, with character, the fundamental, *non-causal*, unity of quality and expression, or with personality, the fundamental disunity. We can *say* that the inimitable quality of character "appears" as a characterful face, but subjective world and objective appearance are, *ultimately*, no more separate things, with causal relationships to each other, than a wonderful performance of a violin sonata and 'talent' are. In physiognomic judgement, *both* inner-essence *and* outer-form are viewed as (metaphorically speaking) "effects" of a "preceding" quality. This is why Goethe warned us not to literally look behind phenomena, because 'they are themselves their own lesson',* and also why, incidentally, the most outrageously superficial people can sometimes express the most profound judgements; not because there is nothing more to life than how it seems, but because seeming and being are the same thing. I primarily experience your face, your actions, your work, your character and your life as one, and *then* I secondarily—somatically or noetically—grasp them as faceted inter-related things and bodies. I can say that your existential fear "corresponds" with or "causes" the horrifying smoothness or stiffness around your eyes, but in reality they are the same thing, just as your consciousness and your body are. As William Blake put it, 'man has no Body [causally] distinct from his soul; for that called Body is a portion of a Soul discerned by the five senses'.

In the same way, the elegance of a perfect half-volley is one with the power and accuracy of it, the beauty of a bumblebee's wing is one with its extraordinary ability to lift the weight of the insect's body off the ground, and the ineffable quality of consciousness is one with the mind-stilling fractality of the body which expresses it, each of which the mind slices up into elements and attributes which it pieces together into mechanical maps, or models. These maps and models partly relate to, and help us to grasp, the matter under consideration,

---

* Johann Wolfgang Von Goethe, *Maxims and Reflections*

and they enable us to build predictive theories and mechanical devices that mimic natural objects and actions, but they can never *be* natural, because they can never be *immeasurable*. The idea that a functional, silicon switch, for example, built from a mosaic of discrete, quantitative ideas and interrelated parts of finite complexity, can replace a natural neurone, in which, ultimately, living qualities blend into an infinitely complex qualitative whole, is as absurd as the idea that a functional robot can replace a natural kitten; absurd to everyone but the functional mind of literalist scientists who separate meaning and form, or consciousness and matter, or face and character, ask lots of questions about how all these separate parts 'work', or causally interact, then put together theories that a machine assembled on the same principles can be conscious.

This entirely factual view of reality began at the dawn of egoic civilisation with the rise of dualism, the belief that 'soul' and 'body' are, despite being intermingled, ultimately independent. This necessarily entailed lack of interest in and reference to physiognomy, an attitude which experienced substance and essence as fundamentally unified. Later *scientific* attempts to literally *measure* the manifest soul of man with callipers and craniographs, to define deceitful noses and generous earlobes, were eventually, and correctly, derided as 'pseudo-science' for much the same reasons; because the literalist view of the nineteenth century was still essentially dualistic, seeing mind and body as distinct. It was left to artists to see the connection between a smug heart and a pair of flabby lips pushed in at the corners, or between dry intellectualism and a permanently pinched, pursed philtrum. Only later, as mind vanished from literalism, leaving just measurable method and matter, did physiognomy return to science, but as PATHOGNOMY, the science of 'facial expression' and 'facial recognition', now divested of perdurable quality.

For the scientist, character cannot measurably appear in the face, because the quality of character cannot be measured; indeed cannot really be said to exist. That it can be *experienced*, that we all *do* experience it, either consciously or unconsciously judging character by facial expression the livelong day, that those particularly sensitive to conscious quality experience it deeply—and are better judges of character as a result, that great artists and novelists communicate the *branch-width* and *root-depth* of character through physiognomic expression—that the portraits of Rembrandt, Van Gogh and Schiele communicate such qualities to us; none of this is scientifically admissible, because it cannot exist in the perceived and conceived projection *of* reality which the literalist scientist takes to *be* reality.

§85.

Long before a baby learns words, it learns to read faces, particularly eyes, a 'palette of expression' which mirrors its own incipient inner world. If, as is usually the case, there are only one or two colours to see—the crude and limited affective palette of the average man and woman, reflected in a limited range of ocular signposts—the baby will feel imprisoned, and will actually look around seeking to dock with eyes that do reflect reality. If, less commonly, it grows up amongst living faces, it will develop a repertoire of pathognomic signals with which to understand the represented context, and materially, feelingly, express inchoate awareness of consciousness.

The facial expressions of the young are nascent works of art, directly expressing qualitative feeling which, as the child grows, become subtler and deeper, along with their corresponding physiognomic expressions in gesture, tone and facial expression. This expressive growth shapes the body, the larynx and the face in the same way that the growth of a tree—towards, for example, wherever light and water are—shapes its final form. If volition is free (albeit shaped and guided by culture, including the 'mini-culture' of the home) the tree of the body appears free, with gestures, tones and facial expressions which are both wide—expressing many feelings—and deep—expressing intense feelings. The widely expressive or deeply feeling face and body, the musical voice, the genuinely authoritative tone—the body that grows from the non-egoic life—this we call, when speaking of face and body, BEAUTIFUL.

i.   Raised selflessly, all men and women become beautiful, both those with an appearance which corresponds to material ideals (youth, health, symmetry, etc.) or social ideals (whatever a culture happens to deem attractive), and those without. What's more, the former do not receive inordinate attention, for social and material ideals do not have the addictive quality they have for egos, and so beautiful people in non-egoic homes grow up unselfconscious, sweet and with an essential humility lacking in the perfect bodies that ego manages.

ii.   The physiognomic unity of character and appearance is why the genius *looks* like a genius; the beauty you can see in the death mask of William Blake, or in a photograph of Akutagawa. As Schopenhauer noted,* someone who is conscious doesn't stare at things, to assess and fix them, he rather looks *into* them, feeling out their inner nature. In being consciously the thing-in-itself here and now that I am, I experience the quality of the thing-in-itself there and then, that you are. This being here and now is both presence and *appears* as presence. It's not just that we can see *when* people are paying attention, but that we can see the flavour and richness *of* their attention. This *quality of attention* radiates from the physicality of the eye, which appears bright and fluidly fascinated with the details dismounting from the carriage of the moment before it, and yet, at the same time, as it calmly watches the complete train of meaning which carries them, settled and steadfast.

iii.   The look of the conscious face appears both free— spontaneously allowing whatever feeling passes "through" it—while, at the same time, settled, or even 'under control'. Not controlled by self—nor carried away by every passing egoic fear and desire of the self, glancing this way and that— but mastered by unself; or, more accurately, one with it. Just as consciousness can listen without having to deal with its own internal monologue, so it can look without forever being distracted by trivial notifications appearing on the screen of the mind. For some characters, this is easier than for others—'slower', statelier psyches, like those of older people,

---

* Arthur Schopenhauer, *The World as Will and Representation*

have less trouble calmly abiding—but consciousness remains softly focused even in an expressive and wild young comedian.

iv.   Because the 'inner' reality of quality is ultimately the same as its outer expression, it is possible to *see* love, creativity, generosity, wisdom, uniqueness and truthfulness on the face and *hear* it in the tone of the voice, which is why we pay attention to both before we listen to the content of whatever words are offered to us (unconsciously in the case of men, consciously in the case of women, who are far more intelligent in this respect). It's also why we find that people who are forever trying to hide their feelings are slowly dying inside, and people who are dead inside have inexpressive faces; because it is impossible to suppress the expression of quality without suppressing quality itself, and vice versa.

v.   The depth of consciousness reflected in the eye, compared to the mere awareness of self, is analogous to the subtle and intense depth of flavour in a wild strawberry, or even that of a garden snail, compared to the taste of farmed varieties. Consciousness exists in a different dimension to material flavour of course, with shared enjoyment of it—gazing into the eyes of someone who is consciously gazing into yours— exceeding in pleasure and power almost anything which can be experienced on earth. The experience of what is "behind" the expression of someone who is present with us, is that of eternity. I experience all doors behind conscious eyes as open. I am looking on, or in, forever, and that forever is me. Love can open such doors, but only if they are unlocked to start with, otherwise I have the godawful sensation, gazing into the eyes of someone who cannot let me in, of trying to communicate something of life-and-death importance to someone, behind glass, who, despite smiles and waves, cannot understand me; an experience reflected in many a nightmare.

Little of this is seen by the average man, raised in a limited world of digital signposts. Many might be attracted to a characterful face for reasons they can't quite say, but few are conscious of it, because they can only really see what they can *get* or what they stand to *lose* from such a face. Quality of character, expressed in a mighty nose, a unique combination of overbite and dimple, a lattice of organic wrinkles radiating over the brow, the play of meaning rippling around the lips and cheeks of the characterful mouth as it speaks, and the bright, bright aliveness, or depth upon depth of the conscious eye as it sees; all this is lost, like the character of pigs to a pig farmer. Misunderstanding and catastrophic misjudgement prevail.

§86.

Both character and personality can shape facial expression—as they can gait, tone of voice and all other forms of physical, physiognomic expression—but where character and the expression of character can be said to be one, the egoic face is the *result* of a series of operations on the world by the isolated and isolating ego, unconsciously working away at itself in order to get something. This is why when we experience such personality we have a sense of distance, delay, hollowness or separation. We are not one with the quality of whoever is before us, rather we find ourselves *observing*, speculating on what the homunculus inside is up to.

Egoic suppression or denial of feeling—through fear of unself or addictive expansion of self—corresponds with tension or flaccidity of appearance—that which, no matter how polite we would like to be, we recognise as UGLINESS, either an ugly expression or tone, or, if such cliched expressions have been allowed to form crude binary motorways into the fat and muscle and even the bone of the body, an ugly face.

i.   Just as obsessive focus on one area of one's life creates chaos in the rest, and an urban world of perfect neatness and order creates wastelands of rotting junk, so hard, fixed attention, creates slack, aimless inattention. This manifests as motorways of tension in the face and throat alternating with pancakes of puppyish blandness. By forever focusing on one thing after another, forever isolating and fixing, everything else turns to pap, leaving a face with a few areas of clenched stiffness—the top of the lip, around the eyes, in the larynx—embedded in flaccid, characterless mash.

ii.   The essential sadist cannot see *into* the world, instead he drifts over the outside of it, sorting its bits into threats and pleasures. His eye, consequently, is fixed, hard, dead or flat, empty and blinking, forever *targeting*, like a cold, dry, lidless lamp, an inflexible hardness which comes to us as a creepy, wanting, *stare*. The essential masochist, on the other hand, has withdrawn even from the surface world. She'll use knowing tactics to get what she wants, but these largely involve trading security and stimulation for being passively used. Her eye might be birdlike and blinking, or it might be watery, melting, begging and desperate. We feel, when we look into the sloppy, imploring eyes of a masochist, kind of soiled. The reality is far more complex than this schema, but in all cases, there is a sense of the *mechanical* in egoic hearts, reflected outwards in the artificial lines, bizarre proportions, freakish inflexibility, cliched wrinkles and horrible, heavy artificiality of the selfish face.

iii.   Egoic bodies which meet cultural and material ideals we might call 'beautiful', but through the power their beauty gives them and, consequently, through having limited access to intrinsic pleasure, they inevitably find themselves addicted to the extrinsic satisfaction of the positive attention that egos lavish on fresh young bodies, neat white teeth, thick hair, cute little noses and whatever body form is flavour of the cultural month. They grow up belonging to that most shallow and inept category of human being, the 'physically attractive'.

The inner emptiness underneath the attractive face can be difficult to discern, particularly if you've got a raging horn (which is why people tend to be more discerning about pretty people of the same sex), but it is there, and obviously so if you look carefully. To anyone who is conscious, the way that handsome men handsomely walk and beautiful women beautifully talk is no different to the way politicians act like politicians and engineers act like engineers; ugly. This ugliness becomes more and more obvious in pretty people as time passes and the essentially egoic young 'beauty' becomes the hideous, corrupted menopausal hag or face-inflated letch, their inner weakness and fear now visible on their repulsive faces and, as they take out on the world their despair and fury at having lost their extrinsic power, in their actions also. Generally speaking, in this world, it is wise to avoid beautiful people, which is why George Gurdjieff advised us to choose an ugly mechanic, because the 'beautiful' ones will 'be merde'.*

iv.   The urban world—the face of egoic society—manifests physiognomically as lack of fractal nuance. There is no such nuance (or strength) in the roads, the buildings, the dress, the food, the ambient sounds, the styles of work or the historical development of the self-world, nor is there in its accents, which become ever less musical and ever more tense and throaty, in its gaits, which become ever less fluid and graceful, or in its faces, which become ever less rich with natural character. The savage ugliness of the underclass, deprived of cultural and natural beauty, finds its counterpart in the hard, bland ugliness of the modern council-estate and ring-road, just as the pinched, doughy, uniform appearance of the middle-class urbanite, isolated from uncertainty, sociality and natural physicality, is one with his tidy-font, tidy-garden, tidy-wood world, a fully mediated half-life that he half-lives in a monocultural office which slowly squeezes out sensate consciousness, a squeeze—a *resistance* to the wild unself—that can be heard in the pressed neck and tight laugh of the tense, featureless graduate. To hear a middle or upper-class student speak, is to the hear the death song of modernity; to look into his face— indeed the face of anyone, of any class, who has spent his life imprisoned in his self; particularly the rich and famous, but no less the corrupt underclass—invokes the same feeling as looking at the universally feared and hated *perfectly tense* object we call the [featureless or literal†] MASK.

The man disassociated from corporeal reality works away at it like he does a woman's body, with the same lightless

---

* Quoted in Joseph Azize, *Gurdjieff and the Women of the Rope*
† Non-literal, characterful, *primal* masks are not addressed here.

look of the porn user (and the porn star). He becomes incapable of selflessly regarding, and therefore of selflessly interacting with, anything. Everything returns, under his restless glance, back to his self; but in order to do so must be conceptualised — for it is only the *idea* that is of use, that can be controlled and possessed. So the selfish man wanders around in a restlessly conceptual dream, or virtual reality, to which, in order to feel safe, he must convert everything he touches — ideally the whole world. He thus lives *behind* the mask, and sees everyone and everything *as* masks, two characteristics which 'are the basic elements of the evil character'.* This is why we find masks (e.g. clown's faces) so terrifying, or the ones in films we do; the masks around us are rarely seen as such, because the mask is in charge of awareness, and only sees itself reflected back as the faces of 'normal' people. This is why most people don't walk around the world in a state of astonished terror at the insentient gargoyles that surround them.

§ 87.

The body, as children, animals, sensitive women and great artists know very well, doesn't lie. Words can lie, and usually do, but tone of voice, posture, the play of facial musculature and the hyper-subtle quality of attention expressed in the eye can do nothing but *be* that which I am, even if that 'I' is an entirely self-managed attempt to keep myself together, cell-windows boarded up lest my true feelings escape; which, sooner or later, they will. Those with a great deal to hide bury their fears and desires under an inexpressive mask, but when those same fears and desires are activated by a terrifying threat or a desirable prize, the mask slips, and we see something shockingly coarse; ugly, bizarre and unnatural.

The mask-buried mind can neither express its interiority nor read that of others. Hyper-focused on its own fears and desires, it cannot experience the whole being in front of it, only the grossest caricature (this is also why it requires extremely crude, essentially pornographic, imagery to move it) which desensitises it to nuance. It is incapable of empathy,

---

* Arthur Schopenhauer, *The World as Will and Representation*

169

of communion, and therefore of real communication. Ego cannot feel who *you* are from within, *your* unique quality, *your* feeling in the moment, *your* pain or *your* love. All self experiences is *my* solipsistic self and so, in order to know you, it must rely either on imagination—what it is *like* to be you, the unpleasant experience known as 'understanding', 'sympathy' 'pity' or 'care'—or on the various methods and techniques that ego learns to 'figure people out', not experiencing them from within, but schematically interpreting them from without. Instant experience of quality is replaced by a digital overlay, which relates to the inner life of the other as a pixellated image relates to the real thing; an image that, moreover, can only be interpreted according to the needs of the digital ego that created it, as friend or foe, as threatening or harmless. The infinite subtleties of the terrain, in this case the landscape of another's face, have become a battle-map. Instead of a transdimensional flow of quality, as expression moves through what we call time, a hypermnesiac flick-book or dating app of separate images, each one either ignored or judged.

§88.

Consciousness does not need to *try* to understand other people. It may need to work out what they are thinking, or ask how they feel, or what they want, or need, or like, or don't like; but it has no such need to know their character, which comes to consciousness from the inside, either automatically, or through IMITATION. All physiognomic understanding begins in this way. Great actors, writers, comedians and artists, no less than empathic friends and guides, *get inside* the other by mirroring their physiognomic appearance, either through obvious, somatic movement, or, particularly in the case of inanimate objects, viscerally 'feeling in' the form of the person (or porcupine or kettle) and inhabiting its psychic-physical quality. This is the mechanics of *empathy*.

Dance is empathic imitation, choral performance also, love-making and listening to a good story. Various kinds of enjoyable work and just about every kind of worthwhile learning also come through imitation, which is why so little learning, and so little love, can occur through virtual media, which limit space, retard time, digitalise fractality and obliterate vibe. Technical work and literal communication are relatively unaffected, which is why, along with the opportunities for control it offers, virtual channels are so vigorously promoted by the undead who manage the world. For such people nothing of importance is being lost. They do not really perceive the surface, and so they have no idea of what lies under it; or rather, they *only* have an idea. They are forever locked out from the inner chamber of the world, which is why true imitative-empathic togetherness—consciously talking together, ecstatically dancing together, joyously singing together—is alien to them, mysterious, distasteful, *dirty*. It's also why spending time with them is a kind of agony.

The body is the most expressive thing in existence, but it is possible to feel all things from within. Mountains, rivers, fields, flowers, pebbles, trees, animals, towns, landscapes, skies, spoons, benches, cardigans, histories, arteries, even blank walls physiognomically and pathognomically manifest their inner character-quality, or scent of destiny. This is how primal people, children, great artists, lovers, joyous spirits and all thinkers with anything meaningful to say experience the world. They experience it transdimensionally, from within, by paying conscious, non-isolating attention to its physiognomy without. Such people walk through the inside of the world.

§89.

Ego cannot look within, which is why it rejects all expressions of 'pre-conceptual' quality. It cannot understand *genuine* subtlety, generalisation and metaphor, because it is unable to experience that which metaphor expresses; unself. Self, the "servant" of consciousness, has taken charge, and nothing beyond the thinkable, isolable, wantable, fearable, willable self exists or can exist. Representation is, for ego, not "of" the thing-in-itself, but indisputably *is* it, and cannot thereby be influenced from "within" (consciousness) or "beyond" (the context), only from representation itself, which, like an autonomous machine, controls itself. Egoic thought controls egoic perception, which becomes completely isolated, cut off from the context, a series of objects which I like or don't like, want or don't want; egoic somatic perception controls visceral affect, which becomes end-directed, in the emotional states we call fear and desire; selfish emotion controls nous, which becomes 'thing-directed' and immune to vague qualities; or it controls thelemic will, which is only interested in getting and losing, or it controls perception, which focuses only on what I want or don't want, turning reality into a video game; selfish animal will turns affect into crude animal cravings to fight-fuck-feed and it turns thought into an endless tumble-dryer of fears and desires, thought upon thought, without issue, purpose or point. The machine becomes a self-programming, self-influencing *thing amongst things*, necessarily at war with them and, as thoughts, emotions, desires and perceptions jostle for supremacy in the psyche, at war with itself.

Ultimately, a machine that controls itself can understand one thing and one thing only—*being on*. It cannot turn itself off, because there is nothing and no-one beyond itself that can possibly remain. The rational consequence of this is not just *maintenance* of constant on, but *expansion* of it. The 'more' there is of self (the more powerful 'I' am, the more secure, the more knowledgeable, the faster, the harder) the 'less' there is of the only real EXISTENTIAL THREAT to self; unself, and the quality it "creates".

The existential threat of unself (the 4D self) comes to self as death, loss, darkness, genius, presence, transcendence and unconditional love—anything which exists "beyond" the known. Self is also threatened by all quality states in which unself "inheres", such as innocence, beauty, truthfulness, courage, spontaneity, genuine metaphor and wild nature, as well as anyone or anything who manifests such states, such as loving women, uncorrupted children, primal people, unique characters (and societies), great artists, the wild and all animals; all those who have been on the receiving end of ego's fear and violence since it first appeared.

§90.

Unself is always felt by ego as some form of ATTACK. Such attack can be noetic, somatic, thelemic or visceral, in the form of noetic CRITICISM, somatic LOSS, thelemic IMPEDIMENT and visceral PAIN, all of which are metaphorically interchangeable: loss, pain and impediment are forms of criticism, it is painful to be impeded or criticised; pain, loss and criticism all impede; and losing doesn't just have to mean losing a thing, but can mean losing one's good name, one's high opinion of oneself, one's mobility or one's nice narcotic feelings.

Ego does not *consciously* recognise the threat of unself, nor does it *consciously* react to attack with suppression, control, annihilation and so on. Recognition and reaction are not conscious, because consciousness *is* the threat. Instead, self unconsciously generates unconscious *feelings* (*emotions*) of aversion towards the threat (DISLIKE) or attraction towards relief from it (LIKE), each of which creates, leads to and reinforces the other, keeping self occupied indefinitely on a hamster-wheel of wanting and not wanting, excitement and slump, intoxication and hangover, expectation and disappointment.

A few examples, from an infinite number:

i.   P is on holiday with his wife, R. He's made a meticulous itinerary and so when a friendly couple they meet at the hotel invite them to go on a boat trip (*threat*), he feels tense, not keen (*dislike*). There's weird unspoken tension in the air (*threat*) and when P and R are alone in their room an argument blows up. P has spent ages planning this holiday and doesn't understand why R doesn't appreciate it (*dislike*). In the end he loses his cool completely, says 'fine, you go!' and storms out.

ii.   A, a young man, has no future, no prospects and nothing ever really seems to happen (*threat*). He hates the world (*dislike*). The only people who seem to get anywhere in it are women, gays and immigrants, all of whom annoy him (*dislike*). He sees an advert online for the army—a well-paid, fun job (*like*) which largely involves murdering Muslims (*like*). He signs up, gets posted to Afghanistan, detests it because it's meaningless and unpleasant (*dislike*), but meets some great guys in the troop for whom he would gladly risk his life (*like*). One day he does risk his life for them, and gets killed.

iii.   S has spent her life acquiring money and power (*like*). Her children, emotionally stunted by neglect, have tried to point out her selfishness (*threat*), but she always flies off the handle when they do, opening old wounds and rubbing salt into them (*dislike*). Eventually, when she is very old and full of regret for her wasted life they still can't talk openly about her past with her without breaking her heart (*dislike*), so she dies, leaving everything unsaid.

iv.   N, G's wife, feels unloved. She's drying up inside and starting to feel, as G spends more and more time on his hobby—working out—like he loves his weights more than he loves her. N can't mention any of this to him (*threat*) without a scene (*dislike*), and she's too afraid of being alone (*threat*) to leave him (*dislike*), so she just shrivels up, becoming a shadow of her former joyous self.

v.   H, a manager at a shoe shop, is annoyed by one of his employees, G. He doesn't actually know why she irritates him—she's friendly, efficient and calm (*threat*). It's just that whenever she's around, H feels awkward, constrained and bothered (*dislike*). The problem *must* be G, so H sets about looking for problems with *her*. He finds, to his satisfaction (*like*), all kinds of breaches of normality—she has been known to voice non-standard opinions, she doesn't wear her mask in the standard manner, she frequently uses inappropriate greetings with customers—and complains (*dislike*) to her about them. This annoys her and makes her less friendly, efficient and calm, which justifies H's initial feelings that *she* is the problem here (*like*). In the end, he finds a reason to fire her.

vi.   F, a little boy of five, is out with his parents. They've just seen a tremendously exciting superhero film (*like*) and are walking home along a canal when F spots a group of ducks peacefully sleeping (*threat*). He feels a bizarre uprush of rage (*dislike*) and runs into them screaming and throwing stones. His Dad tries to stop him, which causes F to have a screaming fit (*dislike*).

vii.   K is alone in his flat late at night with nothing to do (*threat*). He's bored (*dislike*) so he gets stoned and watches a violent film which has an attractive film actress in it (*like*). He is feeling aroused, so he knocks one out to a cam girl (*like*). This makes him feel sordid and tired (*dislike*). The next morning he wakes up hollow and tight; not in the right frame of mind to work on the music he's collaborating on with D (*threat*). When he meets D he feels irritable (*dislike*) and starts an argument on a stupid pretext. D complains and K walks off in a huff.

viii.   M, the Home Secretary for Her Majesty's government is given a report detailing a rebellion in Xanadu (*threat*). The Xanadese government is a recipient of British foreign 'aid' and a major arms buyer and oil supplier (*like*), while the rebels are uncivilised natives in the way of significant development plans. M, wishing to be free of the irritant (*dislike*), signs off on a tonne of military hardware, increases the military aid budget and slaps a D-notice on any negative media attention. A few weeks later, a human-rights group protest British-sanctioned mass-murder in Xanadu by staging a demonstration on parliament square (*threat*). M is irritated (*dislike*) and has them all arrested.

ix.   J is asked by G, one of his senior managers, what should be done about the fact that workers at J's vast warehouses are protesting for better pay and working conditions (*threat*). J flies into a rage (*dislike*) and tells the manager to sack them all and, while he's at it, have a word with the secretary of state about that coup in Costaguana he helped pay for in order to secure access to their Lithium reserves. In order to take the stress out of the meeting J spends the afternoon with some young girls (*like*) procured for him by a trusted aide.

These simplified examples are all from the modern West, a time and place of rampant ego. Very different examples would, of course, be required for rural Oman, or Mayan Palenque, or Heian Japan, or Middle-Kingdom Egypt; but in all cases, the principle would be the same.

§91.

The root of egoic fear, is less that unself occasionally pokes itself into awareness as a threatening invitation into the wilderness, or as a spontaneous change of plan, or as an act of uncontrollable generosity, but that the threat of unself exists everywhere at all times. It is not just every situation I am in, *it is also I in the situation*. Self, to the extent that it is egoically self-informed, is therefore *constantly* anxious (about unself: FEAR) and *constantly* in need (of more self: DESIRE), although it can admit neither *to* itself because doing so would also admit the reality of unself, which self does not and cannot do. It cannot accept that the reason it is restless, irritable or needy is because it is constantly threatened by silence, death or love, or that its consequent 'need' for stimulation, security or sex are in flight from the void in its own being, for that would put a reason-obliterating non-thing within its reasoning, like putting infinity within an everyday calculation, reducing it to nonsense.

Because ego reproduces itself through over-focus on its particular swells, delimited by likes, wants and so on, and because consciousness "governs" regardless of these limits, allowing a selfless whole to form, ego experiences any form of attack on its *particular* stunts, as an existential hazard of the first order. Criticism of one isolated part of the personality threatens the entire warped structure, for it cannot be changed without rebuilding the entire thing. I seek to discover why you are always ill, or I disrupt your morning routine with an unexpected demand, or I question your support of a public personality and you feel the shiver of death. From far away, to be sure, so far away it seems like mere irritation or boredom, but ego hears the distant approach of the only enemy it cannot defeat. It unconsciously knows that it can only really change its 'foibles' by changing its *entire* way of life, and as there can be no 'entire' for the limited self, it moves *immediately* into attack mode.

§92.

The AWARENESS of egoic personality—isolated thelema, soma, viscera, and nous sliding over the screen of the self-informed self—exists as a limited pool of light in the limitless darkness of unself, which is suppressed by ego into what we call the UNCONSCIOUS. For consciousness, for I, there is no unconscious; there is just deeper and deeper experience of unself. For ego, however, existing on the visible crust of itself, there is a universe of inaccessible darkness. This comprises, again for ego, two elements; the unselfish thing-in-itself (the CONSCIOUSNESS that I am) along with all the SUB-CONSCIOUS urges that ego pushes out of awareness. These urges are all towards self (PRIMAL DESIRE) and away from unself (PRIMAL FEAR), meaning they are all selfish; the very nucleus of selfishness in fact, which ego can never bring fully into awareness without self-destructing. It can *admit* it is selfish, but it cannot experience the reality of it, for to do so would be to *be* conscious, which ego does everything in its power to resist.

(Here we run into something of a contradiction. We can say that 'ego is unconscious', in that it cannot experience the conscious thing-in-itself. But because consciousness is suppressed, pushed out of awareness, *it* becomes, at least from the perspective of ego, the unconscious; so we can also say 'ego is *not* the unconscious'. We can, correspondingly, describe ego as 'in darkness'—as an unconscious automaton blind to the light of consciousness or love or what have you—or we can describe ego as the creator of a limited, deathly, schizoid *light*, separating itself from the mysterious darkness that it is terrified to enter.)

Thus for ego there is a horrifying mystery "beyond" the limits of its experience, which it represents metaphorically as HEAVEN—a lost paradise of conscious freedom—and

HELL—the inferno of fears and desires which it has pushed from awareness. Neither heaven nor hell can be faced as they are by ego; it is always so much better than you think, and always so much worse. The horrors of one's remote past, the terror one has of admitting one's shameful fears and desires, the majestic joy of naked existence, writhing now at one's feet, and the ongoing betrayal of it in the horrifying triviality of egoic thought; all such realities are, for the self-informed self, literally unthinkable. They do not exist, they cannot exist, and if they do appear—in a criticism or a reminder or an explanation or a work of art—they appear no different to ghosts or aliens or cartoon characters, bizarre, terrifying, lacking 'credibility' or just plain silly.

If ego does finally release its grip on itself and pass through the threshold, an event which, for the ego, is always preceded by immense suffering, it finds that neither heaven nor hell (religious or secular) exist; both self-made poles have collapsed into a *single* selfless state "beyond" the illusions of good and evil.

§93.

If self slips into the simplicity of consciousness and context, egoic good and evil vanish, and with them their ordinary, visible forms; LIKE and DISLIKE. Like and dislike (meaning *egoic* like and dislike, rather than the natural preferences of character) are two unremarkable weeds connected to a vast subterranean cancer of ego, dark roots of fear and desire eating their way through the body of the earth. They are so dreadful to man that he must *continually* push them from self-awareness into the unconscious, an effort registered on his ever-stressed brow as tension, weariness and care.

Like and dislike are personal TOTEMS and TABOOS, religiously revered and feared symbolic signposts or markers which ego erects over the inner world, marking off threatening areas of diminishment and directing the vehicle of attention into the knowable. These threatening 'areas' are not just rooms in the house of the self, but exits from it, into a primeval forest, an aboriginal world of infinite strangeness and beauty. Over time, the signposts become larger and more terrifying and the paths of self-directed attention become roads, and then motorways. The knowable becomes predictable, the unknowable, unthinkable. Any call to slow down, go off road into the land of dislike, is greeted with agitation and anger. Finally, as the house grows, as motorways cover the land, the forest dies, and then there is no need for signposts, because there is nowhere to escape to. The world has become normal.

Like and dislike are two mountain tops,* an unremarkable, taken-for-granted background to one's unremarkable, taken-for-granted life which, as soon as they are genuinely threatened, become volcanoes; the sunken magma of fear and violence, which lies underneath everyone's everyday personality—unacknowledged, unfelt, unknown—explodes. While spending time with selfless people is like an aimless stroll across virgin meadows, that spent with the egoic is more like an attempt to get from one side of a minefield to another without a map. Say the wrong thing, make light of a totem or step on a taboo and BOOM! Everyone is astonished, including the personality itself. 'He seemed so *nice*. I had no idea he could be so violent! So cowardly! So childish!'

Like and dislike manifest as OPINIONS, the various conceptual judgements of one's secondary taste-matrix. 'Everyone is entitled to their opinion'—provided of course that opinion cannot apply *to* everyone, or everything. Conversely, when it comes to the truth, that which does apply to everyone and to everything, *nobody* is entitled to their opinion. You can't have an *opinion* about consciousness and context, about unself and the various qualities it manifests as, but of course ego, which subsumes primal awareness into taste, is not just unable to see this, but is actively threatened by the prospect of giving up its expressed likes and dislikes. The upshot is that, firstly, great artists and teachers rarely express opinions, making instead pronouncements which strike ego as absurdly or even terrifyingly confident, and, secondly, people who hesitate to give an opinion about medicine, wine, fashion or whatever else lies beyond their taste-matrix, immediately leap into *opinionated*

---

* Barry Long, *Only Fear Dies*

assertions about the nature of the universe, the mysteries of love and the fundaments of human nature. Similarly, you will hear people admit to a lack of talent, education, opportunity or self-control, and also to various phobias and diseases—for these things are objects that ego can blame. You might even hear ego admit to being a loser, or an idiot; in which case it has created an image of itself—the 'old me' that made the mistake which the 'new me' now admits or masochistically gets off on disparaging. What you *won't* hear too often is someone admit that they are inflexible, humourless, unloving, morally blind or boring, at least not until they've been broken by life.

Mediocre teachers speak only to opinion, which is why their students nod away at matters they themselves have realised, because it is all common, explicit knowledge dressed up, as it must be by an egoic teacher, with verbiage obscuring their, and their students', poverty of insight, an insight that great teachers, by contrast, fill their work with, and which speaks not to the manifest mind of a self agreeing with its own knowledge, but to the pre-manifest bellymind of a self experiencing that which precedes the knowable.

§94.

Ego, having only the experience of ego to judge by, takes ego and unself to be the same thing. It may have secondary taste, but it completely lacks primary DISCERNMENT. It takes primal attraction to be the same as secondary, consciousness to be the same as awareness, metaphor to be the same as cliche, character to be the same as personality and all unselfish qualities to be the same as their superficially similar egoic equivalents. It conflates, in other words, FUNDAMENTAL ANTONYMS:

i.   Ego takes *intelligence*—a mind responsive to context and consciousness—to be synonymous with *cleverness*—a mind responsive to its own concepts. Cleverness, or being smart, asks questions which have knowable answers, such as 'how can I get rich?' or 'how can I win friends and influence people?' or 'what is the mechanism that causes certain materials to exhibit superconductivity at temperatures much higher than 25 kelvins?' and finds answers which follow from the premises. Intelligence asks questions which cannot be literally answered, such as 'how do I become a genius?' or 'how can I get her phone number?' or 'what's the sodding point?' and finds *new premises*.

ii.   Ego takes *generalisation*—a literal expression of a quantitative majority or a vague, non-literal, expression of a general quality—as cliched *stereotyping*—the conflation of a heterogeneous reality with a homogeneous fact. Generalisation, being context-dependent, admits qualification and exception but, being an expression of quality, collapses under quantitative scrutiny. Thus, those who wish to resist the truth of a truthful generalisation—the left are ruthless and servile, camp men are oddly neat, wet hearts like dry heat, Japs love animals, Arabs don't, gardening is good for you, rich people are insensitive sadists, modernism is rubbish, metalheads are curiously sweet, British Christians are freaks, broad beans are weird—just have to closely inspect it, and the truth of it vanishes, just as someone's head vanishes through a microscope.

iii.   Ego takes courageous *sacrifice*—allowing self or some treasured element of self to die so that the good or the true might live—to be mere *bravery*—either a calculated bid to augment the self (including the groupself) with an act of self-destruction, or plain old reckless stupidity. The egoic self *cannot* accept that genuine sacrifice, altruism and unconditional love exist. No evidence can persuade it otherwise, because that for which a genuinely sacrificial act is made does not exist for ego.

Fundamental antonyms are fundamental in the sense that they relate to self and unself (*relative antonyms*—up and down, introverted and extroverted—do not concern us here) and so self *has* to take them to be synonymous. Other examples include; *obeying* and *submitting*, *joy* and *fun*, *pain* and *suffering*, *partnership* and *relationship*, *curiosity* and *prying*, *fooling* and *clowning*, *reason* and *rationality*, *ritual* and *spectacle*, *genius* and *talent*, *scenius* and *groupthink*, *love-making* and *sex*, *society* (or *culture*) and *civilisation*, *sorrow* and *unhappiness*, *gazing* and *staring*, *idleness* and *boredom*, *originality* and *novelty*, *narcotic* and *intoxicant*, *abuse* and *offence*, *generosity* and *profligacy*, *thrift* and *meanness*, *freedom* and *rights*, *empathy* and *sympathy*, and *metaphor* and *cliche*. In each case the latter of the pair, the egoic self-graspable form, is confused with the selfless quality of the former. Not through error—although ego will always appeal to error if it is caught out—but through *intrinsic* blindness to antonymous qualities, which are instantly translated into antonymous quantities. For ego, the difference between the mind-graspable *world* and the essentially ineffable *earth*, or between system-friendly reformist *stagversion* and profoundly revolutionary *subversion*, is, at best, not one of kind, but of degree. This is also how egoic people can look upon the derivative cheese of an epigone and see the sparkling originality of a master, or look upon the hideous death-mask of a supermodel and see a paragon of blooming beauty, or look upon a genius's love for mankind and see useless narcissism (or, conversely, regard a philanthropist's donation as the acme of altruism). It is a source of endless wonder to conscious people that their fellows can be so stupendously undiscerning, just as Solidland folk are continually amazed that Flatlanders consider a hollowed-out section of a tree—an empty ring of bark seen as a 2D slice—to be no different from a 3D living tree.

§95.

Ego has no way of discerning the difference between primary transdimensional quality and secondary dimensional form. This doesn't just mean that it conflates fundamental antonyms, it also means that it makes a distinction between FUNDAMENTAL SYNONYMS, where, *ultimately*, none exists. For ego, quality and reality are in the self alone, and so only the frustration of self is registered as low-quality. This creates opposites (selfish quality versus selfish unquality, or selfish reality versus selfish unreality) which are, from a conscious perspective, illusions, or correlative OPPOSAMES:

i.   Ego, projected into the future, is forced into a state of oscillating *hope*, that it will get what it wants, and *fear* that it won't. Likewise, when it looks into the past, emotions of *pride*, at what it did right, and *guilt*, at what it did wrong, predominate. These emotional states can only exist in tension with a corresponding pole—just as actual poles can—and so ego cannot fathom that they are *all* creations of ego. Hope and fear must remain essentially different to ego for the same reason like and dislike must, or *expectation* (good thing going to happen, expansion of ego) and *worry* (bad thing going to happen, contraction), *both* of which lead to disappointment, anger or simply more of the same, more hoping and fretting, and *both* of which are constantly justified on one's own behalf in the same way, as 'optimism' and 'realism', or if the hope and fear are on someone else's behalf, as 'caring'.

ii.   Ego takes its favoured political position, the one from which it has most to gain, as the high-quality choice (which it calls 'moral', 'realistic', 'fair', etc.) and its opposite, which threatens to take away what ego has, as the low-quality option. Thus private *capitalism*, concentrating wealth and power into the hands of independent businessmen and their professional servants is presented as antonymous with *communism* or *socialism*, concentrating wealth and power into the hands of state functionaries and their professional servants. That one or the other might improve the lot of the mass in one way or another, or that this or that secondary benefit might accrue here or there, are seized on by ego as counter-evidence against their complementary identities, both operating completely within the boundaries of the egoic system.

iii.   All the distinctions made by the literalist mind in order to orient itself in space and in what it calls time—*left* and *right*, *up* and *down*, *before* and *after*, *this* and *that*, are, ultimately, metaphorical illusions which no more exist in reality than measurements do. They come into existence through the activity of the self, relating itself to the concepts, percepts, affects and actions of what appear to be other things, or other selves.

Other fundamental synonyms include *pessimism* and *optimism, death* and *life, care* and *carelessness, subjective* and *objective, mentation* and *emotion, work* and *fun, religion* and *science, empiricism* and *rationalism, idealism* and *realism, boredom* and *excitement, sadism* and *masochism, mono-gender* and *pseudo-gender, monotheism* and *atheism, me* and *you,* all of which are distinct as 'poles of representation', but identical *as* representation. Clearly, therefore, to the self—which *is* representation—it is not just *reasonable* to make a distinction between them but, again for the self, useful or even essential. To abandon a distinction between religion and science, or work and fun, makes it almost impossible for the self to talk about the world as it is. To conflate life and death, or me and you, makes it impossible for the self to live in the world, *tout court.* We would rightly call such a self insane. But the reason that the ego assumes that these poles are *fundamentally* antonymous is not because of their *relative* distinction, but because ego cannot inhabit a state of *absolute* difference to them, a state of unselfish quality which makes even the most solid sense of self-generated separateness soften, or even melt, into a dream.

Because ego is unable to discern the sameness of fundamental synonyms it can—and will—describe *freedom* as *slavery, social* as *anti-social, love* as *hate, beauty* as *ugliness, truth* as *lies, simplicity* as *complexity, sanity* as *madness, originality* as *derivation* and *war* as *peace*; or vice-versa. Without *actual* experience of quality—of what is *actually* good, true, lovely, sane, and so on—there is no *real* reason to call an invasion of Iraq 'wrong', or a pickled sheep 'ugly', or an official 'pandemic' an 'illusion', because there is no such thing as right, beautiful or reality. They are all, to ego, 'subjective'. The conscious self might call such misuse of language *lies*, but the egoic, self-informed self, cannot see it that way, any more than a fish can see the ocean as 'wet'. Reality comes to ego *as* ego; it is *all* a lie—so how can there *be* a lie for ego, unless ego, the final arbiter of truth, is somehow losing out? Social-networking and social-distancing, for example, serve what ego sees, and can only see, as 'society', just as freedom and slavery do, or war and peace, terms which are put to whatever temporary use is required, regardless of what is *actually* being served. Likewise, ego can accurately describe a genuine act of love, one which jeopardises ego—and therefore reality itself—as 'hatred', or an act of selflessness, as 'selfish' or 'pretentious'.

§96.

With no unselfish standard by which to judge experience, the self-informed self is haunted by a chronic *lack of discernment*. Most of its verdicts come down to a straightforward calculation of self-interest, and where this yields no obvious standard of judgement, to pure guesswork. This is why:

i.   The default state of ego is 'sorry'. It cannot help but make catastrophic errors, because it cannot consciously experience that to which good decisions fit; the context. It continually misses its moment, sails past opportunity, ignores subtle cries for help or fatly sits on the delicate mood of the room and then greets universal exasperation with a thick, 'What? What did I do?' It cannot read gestures, or faces or eyes or tone of voice and, when assessing other people—their honesty, integrity, love—makes one appalling mistake after another. In matters of great depth ego flounders, while in its own trivial concerns it brings to bear the skill and acumen of the master craftsman. 'Those who are serious in ridiculous matters will be ridiculous in serious matters'.*

ii.   Ego has no way of discerning the difference between moral good and moral evil. No matter how much the self develops itself, no matter how refined its taste, no matter how interesting or imaginative its inner world, no matter how learned, self, by itself, gets no closer to knowing the fundamental difference between right and wrong, which is to say selfishness and selflessness, because it *is* self. This is why the most intelligent or gifted people on earth, able to achieve almost miraculous intellectual feats, can rarely discern the most elementary moral truths.† It's also why teaching ethics in school, or running advertising campaigns designed to make

---

* Cato the Elder, quoted by Plutarch, *Moralia: Sayings of Kings and Commanders*
† Leo Tolstoy, *What is Art?*

people act more morally, or just trying to *explain* to someone why something is fundamentally wrong, are so stupendously futile, as if evil acts are carried out because of misguided beliefs, or incorrect reasoning, and not from the horrors of emotional pain, or from being impounded in an unempathic human suit, separated from other selves—indeed from the universe entire—by a moat which can only be crossed with trivial 'sympathy' or 'care'. Using ethical reasoning against egoic emotionality is, as Schopenhauer vividly put it, like using an enema needle to put out a raging fire.* Appealing to the moral sense of an armoured, numbed or emotional self is like arguing with a character in a book.

Empathy—intuitively, transdimensionally, experiencing you-in-yourself as me-in-myself—is the foundation of all meaningful ethics everywhere and at all times. Why is it wrong to fuck your frustration into a pro? Why is it immoral to be an 'inspiring teacher' or a 'good doctor'? Why is it evil to obliterate the lives of the poor so that you can feel safer, or can have a nicer house or can wear a cheaper blouse? The answer to these questions is the same as the reason why it is unethical, wrong, immoral and evil to engage with other people via method and technique—to see nothing but the useful or useless in them, or to view the other (person, animal, tree) through the prism of one's fears and desires. It is wrong because the empathic oneness of I and thou is thereby divided into two. Merely me and you, cut off from each other. As ego comes pre-divided, it has no possible way of grasping this, and so its morality always comes down to method and technique, either the simple, immediate morality of the ordinary man, looking out for number 1 (unless numbers 2–9 look like him, or come from him, or can help him) or the complex, remote morality of the priest or scientist, also looking out for number 1, but behind a mask of care. The popular morality of utilitarianism, for example—common amongst theists and atheists—makes much of the necessity of generating, through one's acts, as much 'happiness' as possible, but this 'happiness', or 'well-being', comes down to *satisfying* the technical needs of self (providing somatic 'comfort', noetic

---

* Arthur Schopenhauer, *Two Fundamental Problems of Ethics*

'meaning', visceral 'consolation', or thelemic 'purpose'), and so, logically, because it *is* a technical matter, we need 'moral experts'—priests, scientists (and then machines)—to manage society, in order to carry out this caring project, to make us as comfortable as possible.

Empathy is not automatically available to self—I must be conscious in order to experience anyone or anything else from within—and so it can be lost, or, if self is sufficiently stimulated by fear and desire, taken away. To be a moral person is therefore not an attribute, like being a tall person, but an ongoing commitment to selflessly experiencing the context and, through physiognomic imitation, the other. Such a commitment, to let go of one's own self, to feel, from within, that of the other, requires, particularly in this world, an energy and courage which few can muster. Man flees from empathy into care, into self-oriented worry about the future, which he calls 'concern', but which corrals him off from a genuinely moral state. People who are not here and now, who are bored, or anxious to get something, or are always worrying, cannot feel from within, and so cannot do or be good. This is why restless people, and *caring professionals*, are such unpleasant company. It's also why it is misleading to say that there are good and bad people in the world; there are only conscious and unconscious people. Paying attention is a moral act.

iii.   Ego might start out bold and reckless, but its bold and reckless choices repeatedly lead to shameful failure. After a series of disastrous choices—in who to collaborate with, or who to sleep with, or what to do, or where to go—ego tends, in the end, towards SAFETY, because a free life is experienced as a perpetual sequence of 'bet it all on black', and CYNICISM, as life and humanity disappoint at least half the time.

iv.   Similarly, egoic adults are undiscerning in matters of child-care. They give license when they should impose limits, and they limit where they should allow freedom. In the first case, adults simply don't care. They let their children do what they want, have what they want, eat what they want, go where they want with whomever they please; which very often means straight to hell. The boundaries which children need (continually tested, through *cheek*, to see if they are up to snuff) are an effort for parents to intelligently, flexibly maintain, and so they are simply abandoned, and with them, the child's immortal soul. In the second case, children are literally spoilt by imprisoning them in a carefully policed, heavily armed, germ-free bubble-suit, or by nailing them to a chair for twenty years, or by slapping back their 'inappropriate' displays of wild joy and mad delight, or by rewarding them for *not* exploring, or by paying them off with toys rather than allowing them to go on adventures with their friends or meaningfully participate in social life with adults (although, note, anxious children tend to cling to adults and 'feel more comfortable' with them). Adults don't have social lives, at least none that a child can enjoyably, physically, take part in, and they certainly don't have any kind of meaningful relationship with the wild, and so, in place of participation in sensate inner experience, adults direct the free attention of their children toward *things*. This does at least have the advantage of preparing children for a world in which only things count.

v.   Ego never really knows what's wrong. It can find no proximal or distal cause of its problems and so cannot accept that ego itself is smothering the essence and quality of who I am, nor that society is crushing my spirit. Neither can be allowed to penetrate the chronic medialism of the isolated self, which can only look *to* self to understand or solve its problems. Ego, faced with its own ills, cannot answer the question 'is it me, or is it the situation?' It swings between the two to further its own ends—blaming itself when the world is at fault, or blaming the world when it is at fault—only ever approaching the truth by accident. When dealing with other people's problems, it will do the same; either moralise, psychologise and blame the person—when it is the horrors of the system which are to blame—or excuse away another's egotism as the result of this or that influence or situation—when the cause and origin of the problem lies in greed or gutlessness.

vi.　　Ego has two basic *modi operandi*; that of the physicalist, viewing reality as a matrix of cause and effect relationships, or that of the solipsist, for whom no laws, literal or otherwise, have any validity. Ego applies whichever view suits its purposes; if a cause-and-effect assessment of self threatens exposure, it will float vaguely through the episode, imperiously waving it away, or calling on bizarre associative explanations. If the reality of conscious quality gets too close, however, ego will adopt laser-like rationality to dispose of it. This is why ego is unable to perceive the cause of its moodies, hangovers, anxieties and depressions—because it is incapable of applying reason to that which will uncover the originating addiction (to porn, for example, or over-excitement, or massive quanta of industrial energy), and incapable of perceiving the quality which, through its pig-headed attachment, it is ignoring.

vii.　　Societies composed of egos are forced to go to absurd lengths to indemnify themselves against the dreadful choices their members are liable to make; for example, a perfectly useless system of academic credentialisation demanding *obviously* capable people go through years of pointless education in order to get a piece of paper telling them they can do what they were perfectly able to learn on the job; or an equally burdensome litany of laws and regulations to organise activity and judge guilt, when it is *obvious* what should be done or who should be punished or avoided. Obvious to anyone with eyes in their head, not so obvious to pinheads trapped in me-shaped prisons, who must have the facts, the data, the qualification or the proof in order to be able to make a simple decision.

§97.

Ego is also grievously undiscerning in matters of *priority*. In reality, *technique* is subordinate to *quality*, the *literal* is subordinate to the *non-literal*, *why* is subordinate to *what*, the *empirical example* is subordinate to the *ontological state*, the conforming *social self* is subordinate to the unique *unselfish individual*, the *waking self* is subordinate to *wakeful consciousness*, *science* is subordinate to *art* and, in the underworld, *man* and *masculinity* are subordinate to *woman* and *femininity*. In each case, although attention must [systolically] CLENCH on the former, it must continually [diastolically] RELEASE into the consciousness and context of the latter, or it will be trapped in a represented universe in which there is no difference between the two.

In such a projected universe, the self-informed self *cannot make a decision*. Where is it to get its data from, by what standard is it to decide? Ego *only* has the data of the self—principally the past—as a resource, which makes its success in the present a matter of accident; at least in questions of primary importance. With secondary, technical matters, ego, at least in principle, knows what to do; but when it comes to quality, to choosing between right and 'right', it is lost. Every situation is unique, and so every problem is unique. You can build up experience to handle problems, but only ever problems that are *like* the one you're facing now. If you approach *this* problem, the unique one in front of you, like a scientist, you cannot possibly handle what is novel about it. With worldly problems, this isn't a problem. Situations in an environment made by the mind—at work, at school—are much the same as other such institutionally-constrained situations. With problems that extend beyond the limits of the known and the knowable, however, the likelihood of grievous error massively increases. 'Do I love her?' for example. How is the scientific mind to handle that one? Or 'How do I deal with the death of my daughter?' Or 'What am I going to *do*?' In such situations, when ego doesn't know what to do, it invariably tries to find *the decision*, that *thing* in the mind that I can *get*, that *place* in the future I can get *to*, that *rule* I can follow to get *me* out of the fix I'm in. But there is no instruction manual for quality, nor can there be, and so ego is forced to rely on what it wants or likes, which it then has to justify as 'the truth'. This justification might be extraordinarily sophisticated, but even the most complex books of philosophy in the world canon often end up boiling down to 'why what I want is good'. We like to think that we decide what we want or don't want; the reality is that what we want and don't want decides us.

§98.

The [noetic] conceptual ego believes that likes and dislikes, addictions and fears, boredom and fun, and even qualities like love, genius and sensitivity all exist primarily *as* concepts. Just as corrupted children, when asked, 'where do you love Mummy?' point to their heads, so selfish adults, when looking for the reason why someone did something, look behind their eyes. Unhappiness, for ego, is a belief, a *thing* in the brain which can be tinkered with by a professional mind-mechanic in order to produce a more desirable outcome. That we act *first* from feeling or emotion—processes, stretching through 'time'—and *then* create conceptual things like reasons and beliefs to justify those actions, is unacceptable to the mind, even if it is demonstrated beyond doubt by physicalist science (as it has been). The reason for this, is that feelings and emotions are not felt *as* feelings and emotions, as two different things.

Conscious FEELING is invisible to ego. It doesn't exist. There is only EMOTION; self-informed viscera, the subjective ground of all of ego's perceptions, actions and ideas, endlessly, selfishly, churning away in the affective body. As it moves through the physical system it is sensed as a sucking, draining cannonball in the belly, a tight, excited coil across the chest, a vibrating need in the craw, a clenched neck or a weary weight at the back of the head. These emotional affects are then connected up by the mind to a cause and given a *name*—such as depression, anxiety, irritation, shame, boredom, moodiness, excitement, fear, desire—and something to *blame*. The particular swells and stunts of the particular ego, and the particular situation it finds itself in, determine the manifest name, form or sensation of the emotion, but the source, the emotion itself, is the same; the same *thing* in the body. What's more, it is *always* the same, which is why emotion always feels, and appears, so ridiculously immature; because there's no real difference between the emotion of a childish tantrum and that of a grown-up one. The reason for this, why different emotions are not experienced as the *same* thing, is because experience itself is absent. I am not conscious *of* emotion, because I *am* it. When I am angry, I *am* anger. When I have a mood-on, I *am* that mood. I cannot detach from it—*feel* it—because there is no I for ego to access. I has been usurped, possessed by the emotion, which is now calling itself 'I'.

§99.

Emotion is the past. It is the living past, built from suffering, pushed out of conscious awareness, into the excluded dark, which then becomes the unacknowledged, unknown *activity* of unconsciousness, the source of all human suffering. The self-informed mechanism of the ego then *uses* the past to perpetuate itself, through guilt, depression and regret, or, by projecting itself into the future, through fear, worry and anxiously looking *forward*, all of which are based on things acquired in the past, that ego now feeds on the fear of losing.

It is the CLEVERNESS of ego—to say nothing of its amazing speed—that makes it so stupendously difficult to grasp and overcome. It masquerades as I by using *my* intelligence, *my* thoughts and *my* past, to mechanically generate emotional suffering, along with all the mental excreta that this suffering dumps into my mind. Ego becomes I, I suffer, but there is no 'not-I' to escape to. This is the core reason why, when I am miserable, my whole life, even the whole world, appears miserable, *from the very beginning of time*. It is impossible to imagine that I was *ever* happy or that I will *ever* be again; because *happiness* is not an up thought that I can simply substitute my down thoughts for, but is *consciousness* itself; the absence of which is why I am unhappy in the first place. It's also why when I feel irritated the irritation appears to be coming from the actions of others, who 'can't do anything right' (even objects appear malevolent and scheming). Thus, the depressed woman sees life dead-grey in the marrow, the man of anger sees a world on fire, out to *get* him; both bringing into existence the justifying reason for their emotional suffering. In fact ego goes looking for this reason, looking *outward* for a justifying reflection in the world, which it sees only *as* emotion. The immature, emotional sadist looks around for trouble, while the foolishly inquisitive masochist lets him in, with a look. Then the mischief begins. Neither can really understand the consequent contention, or escape from it, because both look *to* their selves, or *into* the self-filtered world, for justification and escape.

The totalising presence of the emotional ego is also why 'positive thinking', or trying to cheer yourself up by thinking of the starving children in the world, or talking to people who have all the answers, are all so useless when you're really down; it's not an *idea* or an *explanation* you need when you are unsettled *by* love; what you need *is* love; not an emotional thing, or a thought-thing, but a living experience. Finally, it's also why it is so hopelessly difficult trying to reach people who are drowning in misery. Your kind words are empty shells which they can only fill with their own unconscious emotion. Trying to cheer someone up who is depressed is like trying to rescue a man trapped down a well by describing how lovely and sunny it is up here. In Latin.

§ 100.

Emotion is unconscious, secondary, literal, factual and dead. Feeling is conscious, primary, non-literal, non-factual and alive. Emotion is mechanical, and can be manipulated with ridiculous ease. Feeling can be altered, but it remains connected to an unalterable unself. Emotion is crude, digital and can be *rated*; on an equally crude and digital scale. Feeling is infinitely subtle, analogue and immeasurable; as it "blends" into context and consciousness, there is no limit to its intensity or its profundity. Emotion, being egoic, is fundamentally a private experience; ego can rationally determine, from evidence, that someone is sharing the same emotion, but the emotion itself is bounded and literally limited. Feeling is fundamentally unselfish, and so can be fundamentally shared. Being unselfish, it is in the body 'here', but not completely confined to it; it is one with the context and all those who are conscious of it. A couple can both experience the same particular quality of their love together, a group can all experience the same quality of the day, an artist can share the intense particularity of the moment. This is difficult in mediated, urban environments, subject to selfish tensions, surrounded by things made by egoic minds which pornographically stimulate egoic emotions. Not so in the presence of the wild, where there is nothing egoic, nothing made by mind, to reflect back mind. The feeling of a warm moonlit midnight, idling next to a misty lake, is not something *out there* which we interpret. I am it, and those around me are it too. When we look at, or talk with each other, we do not understand the *facts* of ourselves and conclude that we're all happy for the same *reason*; we *instantly* recognise the quality of unself in the mood, the gesture, the tone. In the city, spaces must be *made* for genuine feelings to be felt, which is why the homes of conscious people are relaxing or inspiring.

Visceral feeling extends beyond the boundaries of the literal mind into experience that appears *to* the literal mind almost unbelievably strange. We call such experience PSYCHE, if it relates to the subjective self, or ATMOSPHERE, if it relates to the objective world. Informed by ego, psyche and atmosphere make an uncanny misery of illnesses, periods, depressions and night terrors. They also produce the vibe-guff of spiritualists, crystal dingers, seventh-realm psychonauts and similar selves who reject 'closed-minded' physicalism in order to blast the doors off their own solipsistic minds and let literally anything in; for there is no intrinsic truth in atmosphere or psyche, any more than there is in perception or thought. Only when rooted in consciousness can truth come to atmosphere, as profound intuition, or to psyche, as profound vision, both of which are as unreal to ego as its own inner universe of feeling. The difference, for instance, between two identical empty rooms, one in which two people in love have lived and one in which two people have been murdered, or between a nutter's report of an alien abduction and a visionary experience of mythic wisdom, or between mere anger and righteous ire, or between tears of profound sorrow and those of mere regret—is meaningless to the self-bound self. Ego is unable to discern the difference between such things, which is why, when someone is dissolved in feeling, ego assumes they are emotional, *getting* or *not getting* something; and that gets ego down.

The conflation of feeling and emotion is the proximal cause of oceans of suffering, both obvious and obscured. Ego is completely unaware of the forest of delicate-yet-devastating inner sensations and intuitions that a great symphony evokes, or a bike ride across Wales, or a year with a wonderful lover, or an Aboriginal walkabout, or a conscious brush with death. Even the most ordinary of days contain a prismatic theatre of subtle qualities which bubble up as sighs or nods or interesting insights or whispers from afar. All this strange loveliness is lost to ego, but it doesn't know what it's missing, because it can't know that it doesn't know. What it *does* know, from time to time, is that it is unhappy, that it is frustrated, that it is bored, that it is annoyed, that it is persecuted, that, after the party, it is *still* discontent, and that it's just all so *unfair.*

If, instead of being the emotion of anger, man could consciously feel his irritation at his children or at his wife—the presence of it in the body—he would see it for what it is, and in the seeing the anger would *instantly* start to deflate. He would be able to *do* something about the fear and frustration his ever outwardly-looking self puts on her; pick up a paintbrush, go on a diet, leave the job he hates or even leave her. We call such an inability to act—inherent to ego, which is unable to see beyond its fear—*cowardice*, and we call such inability to feel the emotion that is between me and appropriate action, *pride*, the pride of the torch looking for the darkness. All it can see is the light of the object; *your* fault. Facts, in such cases—attempts to make someone see—are impotent, for they appear before the torch as just another object, no more able to persuade it of darkness than I can persuade my computer that it isn't conscious. The only thing that can persuade ego of its fake autonomy is the very suffering that it creates.

§101.

Suffering is not pain, it is ego's reaction *to* pain. Such reaction is SECONDARY SUFFERING. When I have an earache there is the 'pure' sensation of pain in the ear, which is certainly bad enough, but the pain is a qualitatively different kind of 'bad', or 'unpleasant', to the emotional-thelemic 'straining away' from the pain which ego engages in, the desperate inner movement of *'donnnn't liiiiike'*. A large part of learning to live with pain—at least the bearable kind (for eventually even the Buddha turns to morphine)—is learning how to let go of this egoic movement and fully allow the sensation of throbbing, welcoming it even, which at the very least rids the bearer of the horrendous—and avoidable—egoic component. In *some* cases it can bring about a complete change in one's relationship to pain, dissipating it into nothing.

It is possible to confirm the difference between pain and [secondary] suffering from within, by severing or suppressing the 'don't like' 'don't want' mechanism from the pain-registering system. Surgery, drugs and certain meditative techniques can produce the curious sense of pain-without-suffering, of extreme somatic discomfort, no less vividly felt than normal, but without the horrendous egoic reaction on top; knowing the pain is there, feeling it, but not *caring*. This is how animals experience pain. They do not suffer as we do, because they do not have a self sufficiently conscious to be able to *not want* the pain. They feel it, they desperately try to avoid it, but when they have it, they don't *care* about it as we do, which is how they can do so much more than we can while in dreadful pain. Woman can withstand more physical pain than man for similar reasons, not in this case because she feels less pain or is less conscious—quite the opposite—but because not-liking and not-wanting are functions of the noetic-thelemic ego, which, generally speaking, has less power over woman. She also has much more experience with physical pain, forcing her to give up caring about it, the rather pathetic care that man is given to.

Self, of course, *has* to care about pain to some extent, or the intelligent purpose of it would be lost; for ultimately pain is the intelligence of life in the body, gently pressing upon the self, guiding it through the forest of physical existence. This gentleness is registered by self as microscopic physical tensions and the near-silent voice of CONSCIENCE; the twinge of pain that unself uses to steer the self. If the self has been sensitised by consciousness, the rider hardly needs to move to make its needs known, whereas, if the super-sensitive animal of the body has been layered over with armour, conscience must, and will, dig in its spurs, until the beast bleeds.

Conscience comes to me as the sense that I should leave the room or enter it, stop apologising and fight, or stop fighting and apologise, blame them or blame myself, slouch or sit up straight, give or take, reduce or increase, clench or release, act or accept. Ego, inherently unable to base action on any other criteria than its own fears and desires, and chronically unwilling to be directed by any decree other than its own, can neither hear nor obey the voice of pain. This congenital lack of discernment is why ego is regularly paralysed by moral dilemmas, unable to tell if the source of the problem is me or the situation, or unable to care. As the force of ego's own immense gravity has it again and again, and again, making the wrong choice—either selfish or erratic—and as ego itself is inherently insensitive to the delicate taps of unself on its window, it persists along its own course, and the taps of moral conscience become knocks of physical pain, and still ego persists, and the knocks become hammer-blows, and *still* it persists, until hammer-blows become ego-smashing asteroids, raining down like God's fists until I am flat on my back amongst the rubble of my own soul, compelled to see, for once in my life, *something as it really is*.

Pain has one purpose, one message; to *change direction.** It is the voice of destiny, of a different life calling man from the future, out of the cell he has built and sits so comfortably within. Anxious and irritable—bite your lip at breakfast. Working too hard—get one cold after another. Paying no attention to your surroundings—get slapped in the face by a branch. Take drugs—get a hangover. Shack up with an abusive partner—get beaten. Afraid of leaving your house—get struck by a flood. If ego is allowed to continue driving, the bitten lip will get infected, the cold will become chronic, the birch-slap will break your nose, the hangover will last all year, the partner will torture you and the flood waters will wash away your city, or your world. This doesn't mean the message of pain is that you are guilty. It means you are *responsible*.

---

* Barry Long, *Wisdom and Where to Find it*

§102.

Suffering is not just ego's reaction to pain, but to the source of pain; unself. This is PRIMAL SUFFERING, a message not to change direction, but to *stop moving*. This appears to the ever moving (e-*motional*) ego as a terrifying call to self-annihilate. While the voice of ordinary pain causes pride to rise in the gorge of self, fully surrendering oneself to a non-egoic experience behind pain, behind even the world itself, is existential threat number one.

Unlike secondary suffering, which comes and goes, primal suffering is, for ego, *constant*. Unself is everywhere. It is every unique, fathomless context I am "in", *and* the I which is "in" it, and so ego *constantly* feels under attack, unstable, insecure. This feeling first appears as boredom, a 'causeless' agitation, irritation, wanting or worry simmering away in the chest. The discontent can be temporarily swept out of awareness, like a single cockroach, but the colony lives on, continually reproducing under the floorboards. When ego is reminded of the underworld it cannot enter, it responds with irritation, ridicule, feigned disinterest or, if the reminder is too insistent or threatening, violence or terror. As unself approaches ego, emotional temperature rises, irritation becomes anger, ridicule becomes scorn and disinterest becomes flight, until, finally, in a last desperate attempt to obliterate threat, the volcanoes of 'don't like' and 'don't want' erupt.

Unself can appear in a person, directly and verbally criticising ego or, through their innocence, creativity or joy, indirectly throwing up a mirror to ego's tedious, brittle existence. Such people (and animals) provoke immense hostility in the selfish self, bordering on sadistic cruelty, often, apparently, 'for no reason'. The brutality with which egoic parents can treat their children, or the restless need groups of egos feel to wipe out primitive or uncivilised neighbours leading a happier or freer life, or the sudden sadistic sex-hatred that men can feel towards lovely women, or the impulse that emotional children have to torture animals are all 'inexplicable' because there is no *reason* for egoic RABIA.* There's no reason for ego because

---

* See *The Apocalypedia*

it's the very absence of reasons that is just so bloody annoying to it. 'What have they *got* to be so happy about?' is the irritated unspoken question of ego in the presence of unconditional joy. Ego is bewildered; it *has* reasons to be happy, good ones even, and it's *not*, goddammit!

Irritation at the inexplicable, the unreachable and the uncontrollable explains the tension, fear and aggression that selfish people feel, to some degree, all the time. Not just because they sometimes encounter unselfish people and animals, nor even because they are surrounded by unselfish *things*—there is no ego in a kettle, or a garden, or a sky—but because the present moment, the collection of spaces and objects around me, is unegoic, without past and future, without fact and cause; like my consciousness of the body I inhabit within it. Only the *idea* of things, meaning the isolated somatic percept and factual-causal noetic concept that self makes of them, and the selfish visceral feeling of things, meaning the equally isolated emotions that self defends so violently, are amenable to ego. The thing-in-itself, the now-in-itself, the I-in-myself; all extend beyond the reach of self, and so all threaten the self-informed self, which does whatever it can to push them from view. It refuses to see, or hear, or feel, things as they are, it refuses to experience the moment as it is, and it refuses to be the consciousness that I am, a permanent unconscious refusal manifesting as permanent unconscious suffering.

§103.

Why is there suffering? There are two answers to this perennial lament, existing simultaneously, paradoxically, together. Looking "outwardly", at representation, one sees a world of unspeakable misery, in which unimaginable pain and suffering are visited upon the innocent for no good reason. It doesn't just *seem* to be a universe of blind sadism, a meaningless no-man's-land in which strangers stagger around for five minutes looking for something to do before stepping on a land-mine. It *is* that. Any statement that it is not, that there is some kind of justice in animals being tortured, or in children being raped and murdered and their persecutors let off, or in the poor working as slaves and treated like vermin, or in all that is good in life being ignored, abused, corrupted, co-opted and crushed; such declarations of the benevolence of God or that all is for the best in this, the best of all possible worlds,* are not expressions of justice, but betrayals of it.

Only *conditional* justice can exist in this represented world of perpetual misery—an eye for an eye, a tooth for a tooth—and there is evidently nothing of the sort, at least not in a cosmic sense. Humans *can* create conditionally just societies, perhaps even a conditionally just world, but it's impossible for anyone to believe that a conditionally just force, or reality, or God, created, or has *any* power, over a world in which so many meaningless atrocities occur, and only someone unacquainted with the horror of the world could possibly suppose so.

*Un*conditional justice, however, is another matter; but if there is such a thing as justice which requires *no* condition, which doesn't just shine on everyone, but is forever doing so, its relationship to the represented world, the nature of which is conditionality, is moot, as is all outrage at its monstrous insensitivity or unfairness. It is impossible to detect unconditional justice in the conditioned representation of ego, just as it is impossible to detect unconditional love, truth, beauty, free-will or any other quality. It exists, and can only exist, in the conscious experience *of* representation; in the uncaused thing-in-itself of consciousness and context. To the degree that I am conscious, I directly know that pain and suffering are not meaningless, I directly see how the pain and suffering that comes to me fits my personality, how the bastards or cowards I attract are the bastards and cowards I *had* to attract, how the lost limbs and cancers that claim me *had* to do so, how, as I look over the landscape of my life from above, all the anguish, and loss, and boredom, and heartache, how it is all *one* world which, in the end, I wouldn't change a pebble of. But I cannot literally express any of this, any more than I can literally express any other quality. Just as directly stating beauty makes sentimental cheese of it, so directly stating the justice of life betrays it, and makes a mockery of the good

---

* Coined by Gottfried Leibniz, satirised by Voltaire in *Candide*

that is tortured, abused and exterminated every living minute of the day. The conscious I thus experiences the inscrutable meaning of pain and suffering, it experiences the unsuffering thing-in-itself and it thereby experiences the transdimensional unity *of* self, in which death and loss do not exist; but unless it can express this non-literally, it must remain silent or speak absurd, callous or abstruse lies.

There is therefore no hypocrisy in being optimistic in the face of death, and rejecting optimism as a form of evil; no lie in declaring subject and object to be one, while also maintaining that they are in perpetual conflict; no contradiction in the certainty that there is *nothing* unfair in existence, coexisting with empathy for someone suffering a savage blow of fate, all the crueller for its evident lack of purpose. The veracity of the reverse attitude—the belief that death is the end but an up-beat attitude can achieve anything, or that you and I are forever and always separate molecules but there's no reason to burn a calorie to get what you want, or that all *my* pain is bad luck and that all *yours* is deserved—all this speaks for itself.

§ 104.

Generally speaking, the more pain and suffering, the more consciousness, for only pain and suffering *meaningfully* change man; which means free him *from* change, grounding him in the still, transdimensional whole. Wounds heal time. Occasionally, very occasionally—or perhaps finally, when the selfish mind is on the threshold of unbeing—love and truth can radically upend ego so that unself can take the throne. But for the most part it is only the anguish of seeing something as it really is, seeing the base, cruel, cowardly, selfishness of *my* self and the horror of the world it depends on, that leads to meaningful betterment. This is why the stories we love, which always have characters we care about meaningfully change, so often involve stupendous suffering (and also why real people, who we really care about, so rarely do meaningfully change). It's also why there is always, at the least, a hint of sorrow in great minds, because they have overcome tragedy, and why those on the receiving end of the terrors of the earth—the poor, the disfigured, the abused—are, on the whole, wiser, friendlier and more sensitive than those who have never had to deeply suffer; although all this comes with many caveats, chief amongst them that children who suffer must have a 'moral witness', an empathic aid or some kind of conscious respite in the form of someone who unconditionally loves them, or they will grow into unfeeling, sado-masochistic, spiritual cripples.

Man does not change, because he does not feel pain or learn from suffering. The reason that ego is anxious is not because it has suffered too much, but because it has not suffered enough. The various neuroses, phobias and petty fears nursed by ego take the place of genuine, conscious pain which man designs his whole life to avoid, always seeking the easy life, the safe life, the comfortable life, when it is the *difficult*, the *dangerous* and the *painful* which bring strength, joy and freedom. Not through throwing oneself willy-nilly into reckless suffering, as so many fools do, but, much more simply, by turning towards the best in oneself, which demands a long, arduous and hazardous journey back home to it. Not a journey without joy, far from it, nor one without many easeful resting places; rather one that only heroes and heroines can tread. Everyone else must stay lost in the lonely wastelands.

Instead of investigating the cause of discomfort or learning to live with it, man *tranquillises* it the instant it appears. The more power an egoic 'individual' has over her environment, the more completely does she shut pain out from it, a process which, by removing any kind of challenge, or limit to its growth, serves to reinforce ego, causing the pain-averse to react more and more violently against smaller and smaller instances of displeasure or dissatisfaction, until he or she becomes one of those widely detested specimens of human frailty which freaks out at a potential germ, at a moment's delay, at a bad word, at a broken fingernail, at a microscopic change of plan or at anything less than five-star service.

Just as the egoic 'individual' surrounds himself in a bubble of painless unsuffering, so the egoic parent wraps her children up in an antiseptic panic suit of perfect 'safety', with no risk, no dirt, no uncertainty, no lack, no loss, no boredom and no failure. The child is not allowed to get hurt or get sick, and grow strong or more aware as a consequence, not allowed to feel fear and call on courage to meet it, not allowed to lose or break treasured items and learn to be more careful with them or less attached to them, not allowed to be bored and discover inner resources to entertain themselves, not allowed to come last, or lose, or be criticised, and try harder as a result; and of course if children ever *are* allowed to feel these kinds of pain, because they live in a world that rewards discouragement, or is happy to tranquillise the blow of it, they instantly give in to it, justifying their parents' mollycoddling.

The selfish *care* of *careful* people and parents is also justified by contrasting it with the *careless* parenting of those who indiscriminately put their own lives at risk or who deprive their children of safety, stimulation, reassurance, encouragement and so on. In reality, care and carelessness are fundamental synonyms, opposames, twin poles of the same selfish self. The masochist takes care of others and is careless about her own life, the sadist takes care of his own life and is careless of that of others. They appear to be completely different kinds of people, but they are both projections of the self, like the workaholic and the hedonist, neither of which can exist without the other.

§105.

The wondrous lives of those who can afford to live without pain—those of the rich, the famous, the powerful and the privileged—appear to egos without sufficient power to protect themselves, as paradises of fulfilment. Ego cannot accept that the most painless lives do not thereby contain less suffering, but, through the fact that pain has no way of entering wealthy awareness, infinitely more. The position of the Rich and Famous is universally coveted because they can *get* what they want, which means they can stifle the pain of life more immediately, more effectively and more flamboyantly than anyone else. 'Stupid people' are envied for a similar reason; 'ignorance is bliss', the unhappy ego tells itself, looking at the painless *surface* of stupid lives. Look below that surface, empathically absorb yourself in their actual experience, and a very different world appears, one that more closely resembles the seventh circle of hell. It is a life of fear, fear, continual fear, anxiety, checking, worry, doubt, stifling mediocrity and nightmarish inner deadness. See, for example, how sycophantic the famous must be before the mob that gives them power. Intellectuals—scientists, great authors, Deep Thinkers—just as much as movie stars and politicians. See how they all cling to their fame, as if their lives depended on it—and in a sense they do, which is why they react to the vaguest threat to their standing with brutal ferocity or craven toadying.

The unlife of the Happy People becomes particularly apparent when someone who is conscious, alive and glowing with creative power becomes successful, joins them on the floating fortress, and discovers nothing but blackened stumps and embers. The biographies of life's 'winners'—those who achieve the painless paradise—are oddly similar to each other. Tough childhood, loving guide, ecstasies of creative joy, fame and fortune, slipping away of creativity, a sense that 'this isn't what it's cracked up to be', excess, addiction, confusion, misery, loneliness, self-disgust, obscurity, therapy and a final return to the limelight as the shell of their former selves.

In a sense, this is everyone's story. Few find their way into the Palace of the Immortals, but many achieve something, get somewhere in the world, only to find that the Marvellous Prize has turned to ash in their mouths. They begin life full of hope; self-informed, nothing can penetrate their certainty, and off they run towards certain solutions and certain goals—families, fun, prosperity, power—certain that, even if they are not victorious, victory is *right*. But whatever they win, time carries away; their trophies and the skills they mastered to gain them, their pleasures and the energy they had to enjoy them, their powers and even, finally, the world that gave them power. It all crumbles to nothing, and then the armour they carefully constructed is seen for what it is, empty inside. They grow cynical, dark and confused, they slip away, and they are forgotten; and all for what? To strive and strive and strive; and then to die. Some, seeing this preposterous cosmic joke for what it is, give up early. They don't even take up the challenge, and waste away in their living units, until, barely having lived, they can barely be said to have died. At the very end, they may look over the story of their lives, in which the protagonist is born, thrown into an ocean of boredom and pain, thrashes about for seventy years, clambering here and there onto tiny islands of ecstasy which instantly become boring, swims round and round in circles, before running out of energy and sinking into the same pointless nothingness as everyone else; and they might ask themselves, 'What kind of story is this? What was it all for?'

For ego there is no answer; or rather there are *only* answers, opinions, ideas and beliefs. There are no solutions to the problem of self because the source of self, unself, is as distant as the sun in winter. Nothing is seen for what it really is, neither happiness nor unhappiness. Man 'feels' unhappy, or anxious, or depressed, but if self is in charge, he can never really see why. Much better to continue to suffer than to hear any truthful criticism, or seriously contemplate the message that my endless pain is endlessly trying to send to me, or allow the unselfish truth to seep into the self-system.

§106.

Ego has an inbuilt bias towards medial causes for its various distresses, meaning towards the facts of self; either, for introverts, the various facts of the subjective self or, for extroverts, the various facts of the objective world. For the latter, anger is due to the boss, impotence is due to the wife, depression is due to the heartbreak, boredom is due to the broken playstation, dystopia is due to politicians, and so on. For the former, they are all due to my stupid self and my sad, sad story. PROXIMAL CAUSES—absence of consciousness—and DISTAL CAUSES—absence of context—don't reach selfish awareness. They can't be considered *by* the egoic personality because they can't exist *to* it. Nothing can exist to the personality beyond the self, which is why the self only ever locates the cause of its problems within the self, either the subjective world 'in here' or the objective world 'out there'. That *both* worlds are projections *by* the self may be briefly entertained, or the fabulous idea of it might even be religiously worshipped, but the actual reality of it is completely off limits for the ego.

This is why almost nobody suffers for the reasons they think they do. Ego believes that its anger is because of this or that *cause*, that its sadness is because of this or that *thing* it has lost or will never get, that its fear is because of this or that *person* which might take away what it has, that its misery is because of this or that *event*. This isn't to say that chronic uncertainty, or a painful past, or not knowing what the situation really is, or being a useless fool, or having no control over life, or having no loving support to deal with it are not all painful, causal facts which demand attention and which necessitate *a* solution. They are and they certainly do; but the inherently undiscerning ego can never find *the* solution to its problems because *it* is creating them. It's like a man with muddy shoes walking round his house looking for the cause of all the mess, following the footprints round and round, getting angrier and angrier as the mud builds up and up. Or it's like when you burn your retina by looking into a torch and then try to focus on the afterburn, which drifts always away. Not because it is trying to avoid you, but because *you* are burnt. When you feel unhappy, sad, depressed, heart-broken, you try to inspect the pain, understand it, but it never *quite* comes clearly into view; because you are both the self which is looking for the wound, *and* the wound itself. Further, by looking for a solution, by narrowing its attention on one thing after another in agonising WORRY and pointless WANTING, ego *creates* the conditions for the very suffering it is trying to resolve or suppress. Its stressful imaginings fill the narrowed attention like a penny obscures the sun, obscuring the consciousness required to see things clearly and to act on them. And because ego is *constantly* moving—constantly thinking and emoting—the second one worry is dispensed with it is *instantly* replaced by another one, and another one, a carnival macabre of ghouls and ghosts created *by* the stress of trying to exorcise them.

Whatever the solution is, it cannot be found until attention widens, until self softens and until ego dies; then sunlight can enter by which to see the situation and the solution as they actually are, rather than as the little self desperately wants or doesn't want them to be. Then pain can be listened to and the lifelong project of ego to obliterate the secondary suffering caused by it can seen for what it is too, a trick by which ego pushes the primal suffering of *being* an ego from awareness.

§107.

Ego *is* suffering. It is *constant*, primary, emotional suffering, because it is *constantly* menaced by unself. It deals with unself, with the constant threat of *attack*, the only way it can; by ENLARGING SELF and by SUPPRESSING UNSELF. These are the only two approaches to unself that can make noetic, visceral, somatic or thelemic sense to the self-informed self. Reducing self, having less, going slower, losing, giving up, letting go and allowing death, darkness and unconditional quality to penetrate awareness may be formally accepted, as representational advertising—in fact they *must* co-opted in this way—but they cannot ever be allowed into experience.

Self is enlarged, and unself suppressed in three ways; by over-exposure, the usual term for which is ADDICTION, a means of *expanding control* or gaining *power* over experience, by ASSIMILATION, or *co-option* of the existential threat of unself, and by ANNIHILATION, or [violent] *suppression* of unself and unselfish quality.

§108.

Addiction is the self-informed self's innate urge to experience itself more and more intensely, or more and more frequently. This urge we call CRAVING; *by* a 3D slice of the whole 4D self—the self-informed ego—*for* a 3D slice of the 4D whole—the particular thing the self is addicted to. Because the slice is ever-changing, through [*impermanent*] time, anxiety is attendant on all craving, as it is on all possession. It's not that the loved one, the high, or the nice house that my self feeds itself with *might* leave me, it's that they certainly *will*. Every egoic man is Dorian Gray,* but with a painting not just of his face, but of everything he owns, everyone he loves and all his medals and prizes, locked away in the attic while the reality of them turns into something more closely resembling hell.

There are almost as many addictions as there are human beings to have them—particularly as ego likes its addictions to be *special*—but as the growth of ego tends towards itself, so the list, while long, is limited to indulgence in the particular swollen mode of the self that ego is over-focusing on. Thus alienated from anything beyond self, self tends towards crude, cliched forms of 'pleasure'.

i.   The soma-oriented ego tends towards physical indulgence, over-eating, pampering itself and sensory stimulation (particularly the 'near' senses of touch, taste and smell), along with all activities which ensure physical security, such as acquiring property, a large family and secure, worldly power.

ii.   The nous-oriented ego tends towards thinking, thinking, thinking and more thinking. It might be addicted to study, to reading, to 'high-ideals', or to acquiring knowledge. Politics, talking, disputation and debate, gossiping and mindless quizzes, puzzles and crosswords are also addictive 'needs' of the conceptual system.

iii.   The thelema-oriented ego tends towards action for the sake of it, business, constant work (of whatever kind), constant striving and sport. Being at the active pole of the self, it also has a restless need to control, to dominate and to being the centre of attention.

iv.   The viscera-oriented ego, on the other pole, prefers giving up control, being dominated and being completely out of the limelight. It tends towards drama, sentiment, drug addiction, dreaminess, fantasy, and all activities which stimulate the emotions.

---

* Oscar Wilde, *The Picture of Dorian Gray*

The cause *and* corollary of objective or manifest addictions are the subjective emotions that motivate them and, as the pendulum swings from the high back down to the low, that selves are left at the cold turkey mercy of. Somatic types are given to phobic fear, disgust and horror; noetic types are given to stress, anxiety and neurotic fear; thelemic types are given to anger, frustration and boredom; and visceral types are given to depression, sadness, melancholy and madness; all of which are also addictions, in that ego perpetuates and replicates itself through them; even as the self strenuously 'doesn't like' them. People who grow up in emotional households become habituated to stress, fear, sadness and anger and find the absence of this suffering creates unease, the feeling that 'something is missing', which ego will then seek out. This is why the ego, in the absence of stimulation, will whip up negative feelings through thought—things to be angry about, to be melancholic about, to be anxious about. Consciousness is astonished to watch 'my' mind actually *go looking* for reasons to feel atrocious, to dwell on madness, revenge, horror and loss, unaware that it isn't 'my' mind at all doing it, it is the on-board computer which long ago programmed itself to fly into tornadoes if none are around.

The egoic self is made up of a unique medley of addictive forces, feelings and impulses. I might be addicted to thelemic power in the somatic-sensory world of farming or cooking, while given to bizarre intellectual-emotional phobias which, as I age, give way to a pathetic sentimental attachment to the past. I might be a sadist to my employees, a masochist to my wife, a narcissistic exhibitionist at parties, a reclusive coward in business meetings, high status to my cows and low status to my antiques. In addition, some addictions, although *particularly* seized on by noetic, visceral, somatic and thelemic modes, are endemic to all selves, albeit differently flavoured in each case. Selfish sexuality, for example, might be less of an addictive outlet for the very old, or for highly cerebral types, but it is such a fundamental component of self that, one way or another, all selves find themselves addicted to it, albeit with different emphasis; as a means of sensual gratification, or an outlet of conceptual perversity, as a sadistically wilful power play, or as abandonment in a self-indulgent theatre of passive masochism. Money, which stands for anything a self can get, is, by the same token, almost universally addictive, as is idle thinking, worrying, fantasising and so on.

Finally, the forms of addiction are class-specific. Lower-class folk prefer opiates, mass sports, alcohol, video games and noisy, material consumption. Upper-class people prefer travel, elite sports, elite drugs and quiet, tasteful consumption. The latter predictably seize on the more conspicuously destructive nature of the addictions of the former and declare that they are *real* addictions, or are particularly disgusting. This isn't to say that skanks begging for fix-money aren't disgusting, or that anyone with any sensitivity to noise wouldn't prefer to live next door to a *nice*, cold, middle-class couple; but that quiet, friendly, socially-approved addictions are no less self-serving than the grotesque choices of outcasts.

§ 109.

The manifest variations of addiction might be infinite, but the basic principles of addiction are more or less the same in every case. The distinguishing features of any addiction are: craving, preoccupation, impaired control, persistence of 'need', ecstasy, hangover, self-disgust, attempted abstinence, relapse, intolerance of difficulty, of uncertainty, of effort or of any volitional act that does not lead to addictive satisfaction, desensitisation of affect (numbness, crude emotions, boredom) combined with hypersensitive awareness to sources of satisfaction (forever prowling for a score) and to potential sources of frustration, denial and criticism, all of which are violently suppressed. All of this is accompanied by background shame and continued use despite ill-health, creative atrophy, unhappiness, dishonesty, fear of others and impotence.

Addiction, being an egoic process, is founded on picking out and hyper-focus. Addiction provides pleasing stimulation of swells along with atrophy of stunts, which amounts to diminution of genuine alternatives; *different* pleasures and *different* ways of living. The addicted ego attaches itself to that part 'I am best at' or that 'I most like', because it is afraid to relinquish control to *the whole of life*. This leads to a self-reinforcing obsession with *more*. Less—less pleasure, less power, less emotion, less knowledge—is synonymous with death.

This is the foundation of DESPERATION and GREED, the pathetic selfishness of which is invisible when they are mine, but *very* visible when they are yours. The terror of the miser at the prospect of having a few quid less at the end of the month, the dread of the epicure at having to eat dry toast, the anguish of the intellectual without books, or of the ambitious businessman unable to achieve 'excellence', or of the mountaineer unable to get to the top of the tallest isolated mountain that he has set his heart on, the frantic search for used dog-ends that the nicotine addict conducts when her fags have run out, the fury of the wilful driver at being delayed for more than two seconds, the misery of the compulsive gambler or shopper when the money runs out, the abyss of boredom that opens up before a shallow young woman, addicted to positive attention, when forced to rely entirely on her own resources for entertainment, and the violence of the man of habit when asked to sit at a different desk or eat a different breakfast; all this strikes those with *different* addictions as preposterous, laughable. How desperate they are! How greedy! How silly!

Addiction therefore limits consciousness of the whole to the confines of narrow, *marked off* boundaries of experience that, firstly, are sufficiently safe, predictable, and repetitive to serve as a bulwark against consciousness, and, secondly, allow the addict an ever-present opportunity for escape (from pain) and reassurance (that egoic values are 'okay'). This causes further atrophy of stunts, and further limitation of awareness. The addict is no longer able to discern reality with any real discrimination. Reality is what I like and want; the hit, the orgasm, the purchase, the win, whatever—and unreality is what I don't like and don't want; everything else. That's it. The precise character of the hit, its pros and cons, the context in which I get what I'm after, along with the character of everything else, all become levelled into a single crude point of desire obscured by a series of functionally identical hurdles which I spend my *day* overcoming, in order to get back home and play video games, or shoot up, or buy curtains, or that I spend my *life* overcoming, in order to acquire a maximal quantity of orgasms, children, cars, cash-credits, likes or wins.

All this causes further attachment and fear. Leaving the addicted thing behind becomes intensely traumatic; a trauma which is felt as depression, or as a sense of futility or meaninglessness—the experience known as WITHDRAWAL—which is, to the ego, death. This is why addicts hold on so tenaciously to their phones, their cigarettes, their food, their possessions, their money and their dreams of success, fame and importance; and why they react so violently to even the suggestion that they might or should be deprived of them or give them up. Letting go of an addiction is like letting go of a barbed-wire fence leaning over a cliff. Agony to hold on, but better than the void below.

§110.

Although self can be addicted to anything, the paradigmatic addiction is to drugs. Not to *intoxicants*—chemicals used to temporarily soften, suppress or assist self—but to *narcotics*, chemicals (usually the same chemicals as intoxicants) used to enhance, justify and protect self. Addiction to narcotics begins at around the same time as most classic 'mental health' problems, particularly schizophrenia, for much the same reasons; to abdicate responsibility, to defer difficult decision-making, to excuse a refusal to engage with an arduous world outdoors, to enhance feelings of specialness and to alleviate aimlessness or boredom. Narcotics are often given up with maturity, but then other addictions take their place; work, consumption, sex, children, other people, being spiritual and so on.

Drug addicts, like most so-called 'mentally ill' people, fear or hate reality; they fear or hate the world and they fear or hate people. They use narcotics to suppress their feelings of fear and hatred, as a shield against the difficulties of engaging with experience, and as an excuse not to have to. They often like to think they are rebellious, but they are deeply submissive people dependent on friends and family, on professionals, on institutions, on states, and on the system. They have been indoctrinated, at home, as children, into an acceptance of a submissive or dependent role (a role which will help them to fit into the institutional system later). More than anything though, they are dependent on people like them, fellow addicts, who can help them maintain their distorted worldview. The professional symposium, the corps, the bridge association, the gaming team, the fan club, the Sally Army coffee morning, the anarchist demo and the girls' / lads' night out serve the same groupthink function, to reassure members that their hyper-focus is good, healthy, fun.

§ III.

The ultimate sources of addiction are, like those of all suffering, within the self. It is only ego that is addicted and that can create addiction; not genes, not drugs (no matter how powerful), not the environment, no matter how pornographic, and certainly not phantom 'mental illnesses', even as they proliferate, bringing every conceivable fear and desire within the reach of biomedical intervention. Such objective influences may be powerful, and it may be necessary to eliminate them in order to live well—to redesign one's environment for one's own greater good—but, ultimately, it is the self which is the cause of addiction. This is why it is the most egoic people, the most sadistic or the most masochistic, who are the most susceptible to addiction.

The origins of addiction in ego is also why non-egoic people can take the most powerful drugs and not be affected, or give them up with hardly any withdrawal, why they can take placebos and become almost miraculously intoxicated, and why there are dramatic individual, social and cultural variations in responses to narcotics.* It's also why, when ego overcomes addiction, it immediately latches onto another object. Alcohol becomes boring and is replaced by heroin, heroin completely ruins one's life and is replaced by promiscuous sex,

---

* Stanton Peele, *Love and Addiction*

promiscuous sex ruins intimacy and is replaced by being the centre of attention, fame slips away and is replaced by meditating and being 'enlightened'. On and on it goes, through lovers, video games, Instagram, chocolate, aspirin, cocaine, Jesus, yoga, family, furniture, academic knowledge... anything that can bring pleasure to the self can be attached to by the self for existential self-protection and augmentation.

The usual explanations for addiction are, therefore, at best misleading and at worst outright lies. Fatalistic possession of an 'addictive personality', genetics or epigenetics, a traumatic childhood which translates into neurological 'rewiring' and 'bad brain chemicals', having some kind of mental 'illness', or coming into contact with devilish hard-drugs that are 'stronger' than the will of the individual are not just airy conjectures,* but crude falsehoods designed to minimise criticism of the self and the system, and to keep people helplessly dependent on professionals (PSYCHOCRATS) whose prestige is thereby enhanced.†

Psychocrats faced with addiction advocate helplessness ('powerlessness' the AA calls it), total abstinence, reliance on experts (psychotherapists and priests), on comfortingly crude rationales and on more drugs. None of these really work—at best a destructive addiction is replaced with a more benign one—but the point is abnegating personal and social responsibility, not actually dealing with problems. This is why such techniques are so enormously popular amongst therapists and patients, and why furious condemnation greets all talk of the proximal causes of addiction—of the manner in which ego suppresses free consciousness, abnegates responsibility for the suffering it engenders and retroactively generates emotion (anger, despair, fear, etc.) which justifies the actions it desires (hitting your wife, staying in bed all day, shopping in Mayfair, etc.)—along with all talk of the distal causes of addictive misery—an unnatural and inhuman life of confinement, frustration, poverty, hyper-abstraction and meaningless—in short intelligent understanding of *my* responsibility and *our* responsibility for addiction, both of which are reflexively condemned by the users and pushers of psychocracy.

---

* ibid.
† See *33 Myths of the System*

§112.

Addiction, ego's constant endeavour to expand the reach of self in order to gain power *over* experience, is founded on *assimilation*, the absorption of unselfish experience *into* the self. Once something has been reduced to a somatic percept (experiencing it as an isolated thing), noetic concept (thinking about it), visceral affect (wanting or not wanting it) or thelemic action (using it), it can be controlled. Ego doesn't have to *try* to assimilate unself; it doesn't have to *try* to break up a free society into manageable factoids, to fell a forest for profit, to obsessively plan its life, to rigidly force a child to behave, to demand proof when confronted by quality, to buy off sources of potential conflict (children, for example, or the workforce, or one's wife) by providing them with pacifying satisfactions, to rationalise away intelligent criticism, to absorb great art into the market, to manipulate a lover into dependency, to convert a girlfriend into a prostitute, or to attach itself to a team or a nation or a fashion. The innocence, mystery, truth and freedom of unself is *instantly* and *automatically* assimilated into knowable, tractable experience by the act of selfish sensing, feeling, willing and thinking. Self experiences such assimilation as right and natural, while consciousness experiences it as DEFILEMENT, DESECRATION or VIOLATION.

Ego is *compelled* to defile; its existence as an autonomous entity precludes non-interference. *It cannot let be*. Ego cannot let innocence be, it must defile it with excitement or spite, provoking an emotional response from animals, young children and women. It cannot let silence be, it must defile it with mindless chatter, such as gambling, listening to a moronic radio station or playing video games. It cannot let a moment's peace be, it must defile it with wanting and worrying and discursively picking through the trash of the memory—endlessly so. It cannot let a genuine individual into its ambit without defiling him with a generalised label (age, sex, race, profession, nationality, religious and political beliefs) to render him thinkable. Ego cannot even let a blank wall be without writing its own name on it, or photographing it, or knocking it down.

Ego will attempt to deal with the threat of unself by CO-OPTING all forms of its expression. It will seize — *like* — the formal manifestation of all original artistic, spiritual and revolutionary truth. It will isolate secondary elements of the truth and then use them to *dress itself up* in costumes, cliches and tokens. Like a photocopy of a photocopy of a photocopy each successive iteration of the co-option becomes cruder and more ridiculous until it becomes the target of satire, discarded, and then the whole process can start again.

Jesus of Nazareth, to take one example, expressed the truth of unself in staggeringly original parables and profound metaphors of unself. These metaphors were taken out of context by his followers (particularly by the authoritarian nutbag Paul of Tarsus) and embedded in a self-serving narrative upon which an equally self-serving religion was constructed. More and more costumes, cliches and tokens were piled upon the original, simple, message, which became cruder and cruder, more and more absurd, until it was (at least to some small degree) swept away in the north of Europe by the protestant revolution, whereupon a different set of costumes, cliches and empty symbols instantly started building up.

Artistic movements, such as Romanticism, impressionism and reggae, suffer the same fate. First of all they burst into life with all the ultra-vivid originality of unselfish expression — and are, often, widely ignored or derided for that reason. To the extent that ego can perceive original work, it is disturbed by it, bored. Audiences are confused, potential agents, editors and producers aren't interested, only a few are touched, and they might go on to create excellent, if not quite as original, works themselves. Time passes, and the threat of the origin, the character of the moment that the artist expressed, is lost with the moment. The original work may then be 'rediscovered', but the source has been lost. Derivative works appear, indeed the originating artist himself is now creating cliched versions of his *own* earlier material, which is now popular; as popular as all the other copies appearing, each one cruder and shallower than the last. Eventually, the 'cultural armour' around the movement, now widely popular to the armoured mass, is an easily mocked absurdity, the targets of which either adopt the mockery as part of their personality (sweating-headed politicians singing punk rock songs, caricatured office workers adopting the catch-phrases of comedians who are ridiculing them, etc.) or take as a cue to abandon the tottering edifice, which, now without substantial support, collapses under its own [light] weight.

§113.

Ego intellectually assimilates expression through the process known as BELIEF. The believer domesticates the mystery of unselfish expression by taking the form of metaphor literally or by adapting it to literal reasoning. Jesus literally came back from the dead, chaos theory therefore God, Quantum mechanics therefore ESP, we are literally in a dream, or in a VR simulation, or in one of an infinity of alternate realities… and so on. This divests the metaphor of consciousness, making it appear cliched or symbolic; but for the believer this is the point. If belief were a response to consciousness it would be fluid and contextual and would no longer serve as a fixed point around which fixed selves can, conglomerated in groups, orbit. The literalist believer, like all literalists, deals with paradoxical metaphor by appropriating its form and then collectively believing in it. Anyone who offers a non-literal—or merely alternative—interpretation is dismissed as a heretic, blasphemer, infidel, 'suppressive person', or unscientific fool. The metaphor of 'God' for example doesn't really stand for a bearded psychopath on a golden throne, but for the community which believes in a particular presentation of Him, *us*, *we* the chosen people, *we* the special ones, *we* gay Sannyasins, or *we* biddies at the weekly Bring'n'Buy. This is why *we* are menaced by a god which *also* means *them*; the *non*-chosen people, the primitive pagan, the austere puritan, the kafir and the orgiastic cult in the woods.

Theists and atheists alike project their literal selves into the unknown in this way, the former more conspicuously than the latter. That an all-powerful old man was sitting before the beginning of the mud-ball universe, ready to flick it into action, or that a magical cloud of soul gas hovers over the material mind operating it like a flesh puppet, these appear to us to require more 'belief' than that a timeless, spaceless nothingness caused reality, or that mind is an epiphenomenal illusion generated by evolution to help man hunt bigger burgers. That there is more literal, objective evidence for scientific beliefs than religious ones does not make them any less of a belief, any more than the enormous amount of evidence I have that my lunch will be nice is. They are all ideas, projections of the egoic self onto the backdrop of the unknowable thing-in-itself that lies "behind" the cinema screen.

Belief is always of something which is unreal, or at least not verifiably before the conscious senses. You have to *believe* that your lunch will be nice, or that the big bang happened, or that the dictatorship of the proletariat will lead to a stateless utopia, or that the world will end in ten years' time, or that 'God' is sitting up in heaven playing billiards with Jesus, or that the earth is hollow, or that science will one day be able to create a fully-functional brain that acts just as if it was a real brain; you have to *believe* in these things because you're not actually experiencing them. This doesn't invalidate use of the word 'belief' nor does it mean that some beliefs aren't far more justifiable than others; properly speaking, science is the useful practice of trying to find the best possible belief. The fact that the truth always, finally, eludes the self, and that belief is always therefore necessary for it, only becomes problematic when self takes complete charge of itself. Then belief becomes not a permanently provisional projection into the unknown, but, because there can be no unknown for the self-directed self, *existence itself*. Then we say 'I believe in God', but we *mean* 'god exists', or we say 'I believe that death is the end of consciousness', but we *mean* 'life is purely representation'. This is why ego clings so tenaciously to its beliefs, no matter how ridiculous; because they are addictions.

Ego does the same thing with *agreement,* which, rather than being the shared expression of a shared truth—two strings vibrating to the same chord—is used by ego to *dispense* with criticism. A critical idea is accepted, perhaps with much enthusiasm, while life goes on exactly as before, now in a reassuring or trendy new ideological t-shirt. Ego takes its *entertainment* at radical ideas as *understanding*. A variation of agreement is 'oh yes, I've heard that before' — an attempt to label away the truth of an expression by pinning it to a super-ficially similar form. 'Oh, it's basically Taoism'. 'Oh, it's anar-chism, yawn'. 'Oh, you're a conspiracy theorist', and so on.

A common and shifty type of egoic agreement comes in the form of a commitment to change. Ego finds itself confront-ed with its shameful fears, squalid attachments and perpetual dishonesty, and it tells itself 'I'm going to stop lying / stop beating my wife / stop shopping / stop masturbating / stop worrying / stop playing video games / stop eating sugar', in short 'I'm going to be a better person from now on'. Naturally, if the resolve is profound, such a statement might have some truth to it, but nearly always it is an egoic sleight of hand, misdirection to stop consciousness from seeing what it is really doing. By placing an idea of 'the better me' in the future, ego essentially splits itself into three; the self in the present that feels bad and that doesn't want to, the self in the past that has caused this bad feeling, and a future self that is free of it. But no matter how honest the assessment of the past self is, and no matter how noble the future ideal is, *the split itself is egoic*. Focusing on what has happened and what will happen keeps consciousness of what *is* happening out of the picture, and with it, the only time and place a solution can ever be found.

§114.

If unself cannot be assimilated by ego, it will be IGNORED or ANNIHILATED. If there is no way to reduce a nuanced expres-sion of truth into an idea that can be wrangled with, or no way to make a profit from an untouched environment, or no way to *get* a thing or a person of real beauty, or no way to emotionally attach itself to an experience, ego will perceive them as attacks, apply the judgement of 'boring' or 'stupid' or 'childish' or somesuch other low-quality label, and attempt to walk away. If this is impossible, it will attempt to destroy them. This impulse will often arise long before the attack has reached any form of awareness, for ego is hyper-alert to potential threat and can feel out the danger of unselfish quality from the vaguest whiff, detect the approach of criticism from half a mile away. Nebulous feelings of 'not gelling with someone', of feeling uncomfortable in new situations, of 'not liking' a book which puts its finger on a cherished deception, all propel the self-instructed self away from a critical truth long before it reaches full awareness, which reflexively shrinks, narrowing focus onto isolable details which, sooner or later, throw up a 'good reason' to snub someone, leave the group, give the book to charity or invade Nicaragua.

Ego will deal with the somatic, thelemic, visceral and noetic attacks of unself in predictable ways. If egoic will is impeded or if ego begins losing things—particularly money, but also treasured possessions, friends, mobility, acuity—and there is no way that self can ever go where it wants, or get what it wants, or get back what it has lost, it will start persuading itself that the things it can no longer have were actually wrong or harmful and it never really wanted them anyway. Or it might start to hate those who have them—the young, the rich, the beautiful, the successful—using this hatred as a means to avoid facing its reduced condition. Old egos are particularly susceptible to this one; directing annoyance, disgust and merciless censure at those who enjoy pleasures that they no longer have the mobility, energy or influence to enjoy.

§115.

If attack comes from the moral discomfort of conscience, ego will typically deflect the threat with EXCUSES (or justifications) and ACCUSATIONS. Excuses include: I'm depriving you of freedom for your own good ('I am humane'), I'm torturing you because you need to learn ('I am realistic'), I can't be happy in a relationship because of my bad luck ('I am cursed'), I keep failing because of the prejudice of other people ('I am a victim'), I drink because I'm Irish ('I am helpless'), I can't leave him because I'm scared of what he'll do ('I am kind'), I just couldn't ask her out ('I am shy'), I killed her because I'm emotionally disturbed ('I am not responsible') or I destroyed what little is left of society, crippled the poor and vastly inflated the power of the state-corporate system because of a flu-like virus ('I care'). All of these excuses and justifications mean the same thing; 'I am good' or 'It's not really my fault'.

In a world dominated by biocratic and psychocratic institutions, one of the most popular forms of responsibility-shifting justification, used to deflect attention away from ego and justify the oceans of emotional pain it causes, is to declare that one has a 'mental illness'. I am not a coward, or a bastard, or conceited, or bored, or without character, or breaking up with shame and guilt—how can I be!? No, I *have* OCD, schizophrenia, anxiety, depression or I am 'on the spectrum'. It can't be that these 'diseases' have to be voted into existence,* that only their effects or correlations are ever discovered in the body (never a mythical cause) or that self-less people or peoples never have them; it can't be that I am responsible for my life—or that, at one remove, my society is—because if I were, ego would be under threat.

Egoic accusations very often take the form of *table-turning*; ascribing one's own egoic thoughts, feelings and motives to others. Such accusations can appear flagrantly, outrageously hypocritical, as anyone who has been accused of tight-fistedness by a miser, or hostility by someone with a permanent chip on their shoulder, or cruelty by a sadist very well knows. Particularly common is the subtraction of self from an interaction by the ego, which cannot see that other selves are reacting to *it*, and not to life. Egotistical people mistake your attitude to them for your attitude to the universe; because their egos literally fill up the universe. Ergo, if you find them difficult, it can only be that you find *everything* difficult. You are not temporarily bored by them, you are a boring person. You are not temporarily annoyed by them, you are an angry person. You are not temporarily confused by them, you are a strange or stupid person. The prisoner is behaving sullenly and so the warder thinks he is sullen, the student is angry because

---

* Thomas Szasz, *The Myth of Mental Illness*. See also; *33 Myths of the System*

he has 'oppositional defiant disorder', an employee frustrated by the absurd demands of a maniacal boss or an over-bloated institution appears to the manager as madly radical, a wife cheats on an unloving husband and it's all her fault. It can't be me who is making you behave this way; it must be *you*. Your resistance, frustration and boredom first reach ego as a vague feeling of discomfort—*here is a threat*—which it will meet indirectly, through tone (bored, sneering, curt, etc.), body-language (turning away, closing up, etc.), implication (the little hints, the 'subtle' but painful put downs) and so on; or, when cornered, it will openly attack.

Another popular form of egoic accusation is the *conspiracy theory*; a belief that certain groups of people (parents, politicians, shapeshifting aliens) are conspiring to ruin your life. As with many beliefs, this doesn't mean that there *aren't* people who want to ruin your life—there certainly are, and it is useful to expose them—but that ego avoids looking at itself (and its world) by *hyper*-focusing on the plots and plans of others, forever on the *why* of the world, and never the *what*.

§116.

If the strident call from conscience we call physical pain is the source of existential threat, ego will react predictably to suppress it, and the unself it represents. The selfish self will either move to obliterate the source of the physical unease by plunging itself into tranquillising distractions, or it will literally tranquillise itself with narcotics and medical interventions. Clearly, dealing with pain is a priority for any sane self, but ego is pre-programmed to *refuse* to face pain, to refuse to see the cause of it and to refuse to listen to its directions or to respond to them, because facing pain means being conscious, and preventing pain means giving up addiction.

Ego will also attempt to annihilate pain by designing environments in which nothing painful can ever occur. Schools in which students are showered with praise, never losing and never hearing a negative comment, social media echo-chambers in which only those who support one's worldview can be heard, institutions which foster obsessive hypochondrical cleanliness, rituals of purification and hyper-ordered religious taxonomies of what can be touched or eaten, spotless high-tech homes in which every last bacterium is exterminated, relationships in which phobic terror before all kinds of physical risk or uncertainty are pandered to, and 'safe spaces' in which ego may find 'freedom' from all forms of unpleasant experience and criticism. All meet ego's objective of closing its ears to or excusing itself from the demands of pain and the calls of conscience. These boil down to; *courage* (acting despite ego's attachment to a trouble-free, anaesthetised life of unpain; the courage required to release attachment to whatever addiction caused it), *sensitivity* (to pain before it reaches ordinary awareness; it is quite possible, even common, to not realise you've got a constant headache) and *acceptance* (of a dirty, chaotic, uncontrollable, messy natural world, in which pain, like the death it presages, is unavoidable).

Today, the most widespread means of avoiding pain is living virtually. Finding an 'ideal' partner through virtual channels, socialising through 'social' networks, working online, playing online… all painless. The *suffering* that all this entails speaks for itself, but few are really listening. If they were, they would be working to destroy the technological system, or at least giving up their cars, consoles and smartphones. But no. As with the painless mask of personality that man put on at the dawn of time, everyone is playing the same game, and those bizarre characters who aren't can't be heard. There is no emoji for what they have to say.

Ego will also attempt to block pain out from awareness by embracing certain controlled and limited forms of pain. Adolescent girls will cut themselves in order to block out the deeper pain of ennui, loneliness or numbness, nicotine addicts will create the pain of withdrawal in order to feel the pleasure of satisfaction and order-obsessed egos will exalt licentious depravity and condemn 'puritanism' in order to avoid having to face the agony of love; not just self-immolation on the pyre of true romance, but the open invitation, every moment of the living day, to experience unconditional love.

For if the drugs ever ran out, if the satellites fell to earth and the internet went down, if there was no way to access any kind of porn, if, suddenly, there were no more ego-reinforcing hierarchies, such as corporations, and no more ego-reinforcing technologies, such as money; if, in a word, civilisation collapsed, and all our manifest addictions were impossible to satisfy, men and women would see that their ups and downs are, actually, an illusion. For ego, there is only down and a series of fake ups to hide it. When the latter are removed we see the truth, that we are constantly suffocating the peace and pleasure of unself, because we are constantly afraid of it.

Eventually. Between addiction and freedom stands THE GUARDIAN AT THE GATE;* the wasteland between civilisation and the forest, the cold turkey between drug-dependency and being clean, the world of weeds between the monofarm and the permacultural paradise, the boredom between the internet and the earth, the heartbreak between the relationship I have to leave and a better way of life, the don't like between what ego likes and what I love. The guardian at the gate only lets heroes and heroines through, back into the garden. Everyone else is lost, the merest suggestion of difficulty gives ego the willies and has it scuttling back to the world, a world made to protect itself from its own nature revealed, an experience once called NEMESIS.

§117.

Man is continually afraid. He is afraid of what other people think of him, of his colleagues, of his bosses, of his servants, of getting a job, of losing his job, of having sex, of not having sex, of getting sick, of getting well, of getting in debt, of getting out of debt, of nature, of civilisation; on and on and on it goes, only appearing to stop when it flips over to the opposite pole of desire, of wanting to *get* somewhere, *get* something, *get* someone. The objects of fear and desire vary from person to person, from moment to moment, just as the character of the emotion varies, from need to worry, to irritability, to attraction, to shame, to guilt, to excitement, to depression, to

* See *The Apocalypedia*

the permanent base camp of ego's mountain of depression, stress and anxiety; BOREDOM.

Boredom, like irritability, depression and moodiness, is ego without object, but where depression and moodiness have given up on looking for something to want or not want, and where irritability is on the hunt for something to attack, boredom is on the prowl for something to *want*. The bored self restlessly isolates one thing after another from the subjective world of thought or the objective world of things, looking for something that it can want or not want, like or dislike, fear or desire; anything which can augment self and diminish the needling threat of unself which rises up when the tension of self slackens. Needless to say, ego cannot choose anything genuinely fascinating, thrilling, joyous, meaningful, sweet and delightful to suppress the pain of boredom, because quality is precisely what the bored man is running from. This is why people who complain of boredom are so horrendously boring. They have no quality to *bring* to a moment which has stopped giving them things.

Not that the world isn't boring; a more perfectly unadventurous, uninteresting and ugly life than the one we lead at the end of the system's long, equally boring, history, could hardly be imagined. The spontaneity, freedom and love required to make a fascinating, beautiful adventure of one's life are all illegal, or as good as, and not by accident. The world is boring by design. One of the best ways for a society to protect itself against the dangers, pains, ecstasies and absurdities of philosophy, politics, history, theatre, art and even nature is to make them all horrendously boring, which is what it does.

Ego's need to escape the torment of boredom we call *restlessness*. Stopping, and embracing stillness, reaches the ears of ego as the sound of annihilation. Doing nothing, thinking nothing, just *being*, like a cat or a broom, is impossible. Unless dressing up is involved, or guru-club membership, or a sense of specialness, or relief from being sodomised by corporate, or floating around freaky-deaky realms of psyche, ego cannot seriously consider entering such an unconditioned state, any more than a cow can consider working in a post office. Even slowing down provokes egoic anxiety, which is only alleviated by more, and more, and *more*. Attention glides over one article, or email, or pleasure, or idea, or ambition, or partner, or hobby after another, briefly alighting, before it is sidetracked by something else. Sometimes *I* awake, as if out of a trance, and realise, in a moment of stillness, that I've been completely wasting my time, or my life, before again being carried away by the river of distraction.

The hollowness of boredom compels the bored to slap bright, gay, wondrously fascinating adverts over the hole where their heart should be. The bore cannot let his life speak for itself and must speak for it with giddy yawking, facial italics, philosophical haircuts and signposting language, 'Oh my *God* it was *so good / tasty / weird / exciting / beautiful / cool...*' Boring societies, such as businesses, must do the same, covering themselves with adverts for what they have destroyed. Everything in a corporate advert is 'new', 'important', 'excellent', 'powerful', 'stunning', 'unique'; words which spread over the surface of the earth like psoriasis when, in the nineteen eighties, business took control.

§118.

Boredom appears to egoic awareness as unremarkable, ordinary, but, like the frustrated wants and likes which motivate it, it is the visible tip of an iceberg of suffering. The prospect of nothing to want or like opens up to ego a path to annihilation, for ego *is* wanting and liking. As it is also not-wanting and not-liking, it will, if sufficiently bored, stimulate these emotional experiences within itself with worry, inner bitching, complaint, hyperbole, hysterical excess, bizarre violence and shameless volume, which it will then cling to. Constant moaning protects man from the void, as does the constant irritability which expresses itself in violence and the constant restlessness which expresses itself in business. As Blaise Pascal correctly noted at the start of the most boring period of human history—our own: 'All human evil comes from a single cause, man's inability to sit still in a room'.*

---

* Blaise Pascal, *Pensées*

Ego gets restless when nothing is happening, it desires something to happen, expects it to happen, pumps itself up with anticipation, gets tense when it looks like it might not happen, angry when it doesn't happen and then over-excited when it gets the prize; the gold trophy, the orgasm, the promotion, the purchase. The misery of egoic unbeing is obliterated, for a moment, in the big up, before, a few hours or days later, self tumbles down into a slough of infinite despond. All of this is because ego takes, and must take, *joy*—the intense-yet-subtle feeling-infused, context-fused experience of unselfish life, which has nothing to do with *getting* something—to be the same as FUN, the stimulation and over-stimulation of self getting, getting, getting. Joy, unlike fun, is not an 'up', and so is not followed by a down, while narcotic highs, self-fuelled fucksex, masturbation and similar forms of pornographic excitement, such as ultimate fighting, Disneyland, video games and royal weddings, are *always* followed by a slump, a hangover or a tense, brittle feeling of discontent.

To suppress the gathering agonies of boredom, ego can rely on no other resources than its own, which is why, when it finds itself in an unfun wasteland, it relives past victories, or imaginatively wins those it lost, or dreams up fabulous futures, or masturbates to old girlfriends, or twiddles through an infinity of mental junk, or makes a life-size model of Mussolini out of bread rolls; anything to fill dead clocktime, or whip up some emotional slack when the pressures and stresses of institutional unlife (a.k.a. *work*) have ceased. It will even seek pain to keep the void away. A foul itch loves to be scratched*; but only by the bored. In fact, so horrifying is boredom that, no matter how much ego moans about selling its life to someone else and subordinating its instincts to the misery and futility of wage-slavery, it will, if given enough free time, gladly *return* to that slavery in order to avoid being bored. An offer of freedom to a bored man is like a trip down memory lane with an amnesiac. He doesn't know what he's doing, or where he is going, and so he instantly sets about 'having fun' (enjoying his self) in order to relieve the fear. This is why people who are 'having fun' so often look like they're working.

---

* Seneca, *On the Tranquillity of Mind*

§119.

The clearest, most obvious form of attack that comes to the attention of ego is conceptual. We call this CRITICISM. We can say that conscience, pain and frustration are forms of somatic, visceral or thelemic criticism, but we usually reserve the word for explicit, noetic verbalisations; you are wrong, you are blind, you are selfish, you are immoral, you are insane. These can of course—and usually do—originate from self, in which case we are dealing with a false criticism, but to the extent that there is truth, or unselfish quality, behind the critique, ego will instantly marshal its conceptual defences in response. These defence mechanisms are crude and predictable.

i.   Ego will IGNORE THE CRITICISM. It will simply pretend it doesn't exist; indeed it might not even see it in the first place. As it is impossible for ego to look directly at a fundamentally critical truth, it will automatically drift past it like bored gallery-goers sweeping past masterpieces; it knows just where not to look. This is particularly common if the critic is young, strange looking, or some kind of 'nobody' (i.e. insufficiently powerful, or famous, or not 'one of us'). As soon as someone becomes sufficiently famous, or is impossible to ignore, ego brings heavier artillery to the battle.

Ego will also cultivate relationships with people who cannot or will not criticise it. The former group is largely made up of employees, servants, slaves and sycophants, the acquisition of which forms a large part of the appeal of power to the sadistic ego. The latter comprises the mass of friends which ego cultivates; relationships, that is to say, that are built on a tacit agreement to turn a blind eye to each other's fundamental faults, to excuse or even exalt them so that one can get a free pass for one's own.

ii.   Ego will GET PERSONAL. The next tactic ego uses to push unselfish criticism from view is to insult the critic, to laugh at him or make a joke at his expense. It doesn't really matter if the joke is weak, as the purpose is not humour but to belittle the critic or to call on the approval of the likeminded mob. People with an emotional age greater than twelve tend to avoid out-and-out abuse of critics, preferring to focus on secondary attributes, and then damning those. This might be age ('Talk to me again when you've got forty years of misery behind you'), profile ('Sorry, *who* are you?') or appearance ('Freak!'), or it might be moral purity ('Unattributed point? Plagiarist!' 'Cheated on your wife? Unfit to talk about morality!'). Personal attacks more often than not focus on tone and style—you might have a point, but it can't really be the truth because it *sounds* so boring, pompous, pretentious or convoluted—or on technical credentials—if you haven't spent thirty years of specialist study in an institution, you can't possibly meaningfully comment on any matter of importance.

iii.   If ego *has* to address the content of a criticism it will REMOVE CONTEXT from it. This is the foundation for ego's intellectual response to criticism, for it cannot defend itself against what someone is saying until the speech has been broken up into isolated thought-things. Ego doesn't need to try to do this—the self is an isolating machine; it *automatically* removes context from content—but it will, when threatened, narrow its focus tighter and tighter on individual points until it has 'won' one and can exit all this unpleasantness post-haste.

Ego will do everything in its power to not have to address the *primary* or *overall* point of a criticism—that to which all other statements are ancillary. The most common approach is to pick on the *secondary* points used to back it up. This game can go on almost indefinitely as, by zooming into the details, more and more 'holes' start to appear between the branches of an opponent's case. That the solid root of the matter is being ignored, over and over again, is not a casualty of bickering over details, but the whole purpose of it. When individual statements are isolated from the overall context of the conversation, book or argument, they take on a different character. Take the statement (selected more or less at random from this book) that 'there is nothing wrong with what can be *called* masochism'. Remove it from the paragraph, remove the italics (which, in spoken English, would come to us as tone), and it looks very much like I am saying that masochism is okay. Take a second comment out of context, 'masochism is founded on a profound cynicism' and it looks like I am being hypocritical or inconsistent. Isolating individual claims about quality automatically makes them look abstract or suspicious, while isolating factual examples makes them look trivial or, ironically enough, 'cherry-picked'. The accusation, for example, that 'you're untrustworthy' will—no matter how profoundly the critic knows it to be true—strike its target as bizarrely unreal. When pressed for details, all the critic may be able to offer is an instance of passing on some confidential information and of carelessly handling a matter of importance. 'Is *that* all? Just *those* two things...? And anyway, didn't *you* once let someone down...?'

iv.   Ego will also employ FALLACIOUS REASONING to sidestep an arrow of criticism. All fallacies are attempts to remove context by appealing exclusively to a source of truth beyond it; to popular support, to 'nature', to authority, to tradition, to familiarity, to consistency and so on. Not that these things are devoid of *secondary* truth, but that ego will immediately abandon the context for them in order to avoid the *primary* point.

v.   Context is removed through SHIFTING FRAME; by widening or narrowing the context in order to create a new context in which the original point appears in a different light. Let's say I make the general claim that 'life has deteriorated for mankind'. Let's also say that, in the context of this book, this claim makes perfect sense; ego has slowly overtaken self. Ego—particularly the institutionalised ego—threatened by such an idea, will object to it with frame-shifting objections. One such might be that we're so much better off than feudal peasants (narrowing frame to the last thousand years plus narrowing frame to certain improvements in quality of life, such as lifespan and tinned tomatoes, while excluding others, such as access to nature and to free time). Another objection might be 'Deteriorated for whom? Quality is subjective' (widening frame to every human on the planet plus narrowing frame to a literal, factual interpretation of quality). A third objection might be that we didn't start our lives in egoless Eden; our Palaeolithic past is more nuanced than that (widening frame to include various problems with the pre-civilised past or quality events within civilisation). Another, more personal, objection might be that the author is hypocritically anti-progress, when he wrote this very book on a computer (shifting frame to the self of the author plus narrowing frame to the fact that he is forced to participate in a technocratic society).

vi.   Ego will reject expressions of unself with the APPEAL TO OBJECTIVE LITERALISM; hyper-focusing on quantitative, factual-causal meaning. Arguing with someone immune to fundamental criticism, one has the feeling that one's words are being *seized on* rather than listened to. There is no generosity of interpretation, no forgiveness of error, no acceptance that, although ideas referring to unselfish quality have a definable, dictionary-fixable meaning, they are, ultimately, elusive. All conceptual carriers of quality—metaphor, ambiguity, apophacy, vagueness and generalisation—are dealt with by ego in this manner. Metaphor, for example, is taken literally, its frame reduced and a summary conclusion 'you're comparing apples to oranges' or 'I don't get it' used to dispose of it; Osiris, Jesus and Odysseus cannot *literally* have risen from the dead, so the myths are meaningless, we don't *actually* play with Centrifugal Bumble-Puppies, so Huxley was exaggerating, there really *is* a physical, biological cause for 'schizophrenia', 'depression' and 'OCD', so mental illness is not a myth.

Generalisation is also pushed aside by focusing on the literal facts, usually by presenting counterexamples from the 1%, 5% or 45% of cases not covered by the generalisation. When ego is threatened by an expression of quality, such as 'nature is peaceful', 'school is demeaning', 'management doesn't care about us', 'women can't write great songs', or 'humans have ten fingers', the image of a lion hunt, a happy schoolgirl getting a grade A, lovely Steve Jobs, Nina Simone and Anne Boleyn pop into the mind, obliterating the threat.

A further step, for the objective sceptic, beyond taking expressions of unself literally, is to DEMAND PROOF or, conversely, to point out that the identity of consciousness and the thing-in-itself, or the existence of a fourth spatial dimension, or the meaning of god, or the paradoxical nature of reality, along with all ethical statements and aesthetic judgements, are all impossible to disprove ('unfalsifiable') and therefore meaningless or 'metaphysical'. And of course the sceptic is factually correct. No *conceivable* measurement, observation or occurrence can ever prove that something is good, just, moral or metaphorically true (unless the quality is reduced to quantity), or that there is anything beyond facticity and causality that can be found in the thing-in-itself. It is absurd therefore, says the objective physicalist, to make statements about the ineffable. One might as well claim that there are infinite parallel realities or that we're living in a VR simulation designed by Zorp the Archon. Because the physicalist is unable to experience the ineffable, any expression of it is indistinguishable to him from solipsistic nonsense.

The impossibility of penetrating the provable world of the objective physicalist is made total through the ubiquity of a literal world. The physicalist, through complete specialist control of intellectual domain (the fields of enquiry that make up serious study), has not only appropriated metaphorical form but has manifested it everywhere. Objective literalism isn't just the knowledge of the world, it *is* the world. Everything that surrounds us is a product of literalist knowledge; all the buildings, the adverts, the products, the cultural artefacts. A literalist bias is not just built into the armour of our intellectual experience, accumulated over countless generations, compelling us to invest more and more into the system of facts, theories and techniques that gives the intellectual confidence, but into the entire civilised world, which reflects back this safe, dependable, monolithic network of mind-graspable facticity and causality. This is why attempts to generalise feelings, to metaphoricalise 'expert' knowledge and to represent scientific findings as non-literal, are not just taken as unforgivable naivety—amusing perhaps, but not to be taken seriously—but as an insane denial of 'reality'. Hence, the common variant of 'prove it' is *'weird!'* — the response of the normal man on the street, to genuine metaphor, or to any qualitative experience which has its origins beyond the coordinates of the known, both of which are taken as sinister attacks on existence itself, not much different from an alien invasion.

Finally, ego avoids exposure to critical quality by never meaningfully using any quality words, such as 'good', 'bad', 'truth', and 'love' — all of which are trivialised — or investigating what they mean. The self-informed self obsessively, albeit unconsciously, avoids any situation in which it has to speak or think metaphorically, or address any experience which cannot be neatly classified or controlled. Just as egoic 'individuals' will defend themselves against quality in this way, so will egoic societies, which will go to unimaginable lengths to classify, control, outlaw or obliterate ambiguity.

vii.   Ego APPEALS TO SUBJECTIVE LITERALISM. This, the opposame tactic to appealing to objectivity, is the reaction of the subjective solipsist when faced by criticism. In both cases, the metaphor is taken literally, but where the physicalist appeals to the factual pseudo-reality of the *objective* world, which makes the metaphor look *unreal*, the solipsist appeals to the non-factual pseudo-reality of the *subjective* world, which makes the metaphor look *untrue*. The physicalist points out that Juliet cannot really be a sun, the solipsist points out that, well, she might be the sun for *you*, but for *me* she's a rancid apple.

Meaning, self, truth, beauty, love — all these things are, says the subjectivist, invented by individuals and by groups of individuals, and to privilege one meaning over the others is intolerable psychological authoritarianism. Sure, reality is God's transdimensional dream imperfectly glimpsed through a limited dimensional prism; but reality is also Flopsy Bunny, Darth Vader and David Bowie; and reality is also the dread nothing of the suburbs; and reality is also a man in a suit and tie telling you that you haven't filled in the requisite forms; and reality is an immense fibre-glass cock and balls hanging over the edge of the Tate Modern. Everything goes!*

---

* See *33 Myths of the System*

Where egoic physicalists dissect metaphor in the factual lab, egoic solipsists *appropriate* it by claiming personal possession of metaphor and objecting to objectivist interpretations as intolerable incursions into the kingdom of the self. I'm a gay Buddhist neuroscientist working for Google, you're a disabled Muslim artist and dropout, and anyone who points out that either or both of us are clinging to projected illusions must, by claiming sovereignty over other people's experience, be a fascist. It is simply unforgivable for anyone, ever, to claim that the truth is not a matter of opinion; to do so must be a attempt to objectivise quality (beauty, moral truth, gender or what have you) into an intolerant, absolutist, essentialist fact.

Ego defends its right to have an opinion, for the same reason it justifies its likes, wants and beliefs. Without them it is lost. Opinions are like lucky charms and house-insurance; they make you feel safe, but life will crush you anyway. This has been the case since the birth of ego, but relativist opinion reached almost god-like status in the ideological output of the late-capitalist system, in the movement loosely referred to as 'postmodernism'. As the world-system made its final, decisive power-grab, the truth was made, officially, a matter of opinion, allowing the atoms of the mass to cling to whatever little identity, religion or philosophy they pleased, until life crushed them anyway.

viii. Ego will SEPARATE SYNONYMS to suit its purposes. It will alternate between appealing to objective physicalism—to cold, hard, dependable facts—and appealing to subjective solipsism—to warm, cuddly, fuzzy opinion. It will alternate between 'you're being irrational', and 'well, that's just your opinion'; between 'follow the science' and 'follow your heart'; between 'God is dead' and 'oh God, what have I done?' That, *ultimately*, the intellectual truth of nous, the physical beauty of soma, the volitional morality of thelema and the affective quality of viscera, are unselfish, neither fact nor opinion, neither subjective nor objective—*panjective*—this doesn't get a look-in.

Most people spend their lives rewriting their self-justifying life-scripts in self-serving oscillation between self-assertive sadism and self-pitying masochism. In responding to criticism, one has to determine, more or less immediately, if the cause of the problem is me or the situation. The undiscerning self-informed self cannot possibly decide on 'me' (the absolute refusal of the sadist to ever critically inspect himself) and so it settles either on *you*, or on an *idea* of me (the masochist's need to generate and nurture a pathetic, worthless, stupid me which needs other people to take care of it, sympathise with it, take responsibility for it, and so on).

Egoic societies operate in the same way, swinging from moral absolutism to moral relativism, from 'anarchic' chaos to 'law-like' order, from centralised socialism to decentralised capitalism, or from pious pacifism to 'realistic' bellicosity. Egoic authority will abandon one opposame for the other in a hot second in order to justify or perpetuate itself, without ever really being aware of its profound hypocrisy.

ix. Ego will, likewise, CONFLATE FUNDAMENTAL ANTONYMS. Character and personality, love and desire, primal and secondary attractions, and so on, are readily and continually assumed to be the same thing, as the latter can be justified by being described as the former. A love of nature, for example, or fine art, is seen to be a question of personal preference, like an interest in bicycles or wearing blue.

Self, by itself, is unable to distinguish between formally similar but fundamentally different expressions of self and unself. It therefore automatically conflates such opposites into one idea, refusing to acknowledge that there is an essential difference between work and mere activity, or education and mere schooling, or ire and mere anger, or even between being asleep and awake. To do so is to acknowledge the existence of a reality that the quantitative self and its institutions is absolutely unable to perceive, possess or control, and, consequently, must define negatively as 'extremist', 'unnuanced' and, most tellingly, 'black-and-white'. Ego sees all fundamental antonyms as 'shades of grey', just as it judges all fundamental synonyms to be 'black and white', switching between the two as needs must.

x.   Ego will GET EMOTIONAL. This is more fundamental than any intellectual rejection of criticism, as subjective emotion is the cause and consequence of objective egoism. Underneath the egoic argument there is a ball of fear and desire ever ready to throw up barricades, or, if they are breached, to launch a thermonuclear strike. Particularly volatile and unstable egos — which is to say particularly superficial selves — practically live in an emotional state of self-justification, ready to fly off the handle at the merest whiff of a critical idea. They are unconsciously aware that if the eggshell of their persona cracks even a little, the whole thing could shatter. Facts presented to such people just make them more emotional, and more determined to grip onto themselves.

Restless emotional focus on criticism aids the assimilation of unselfish threat by *automatically* picking out details. The emotional ego cannot settle on the flow of meaning, following it through the light and shade of tone and implication, or taking in a carefully reasoned argument; rather it flaps overhead looking for *targets*, isolated prey, no matter how small. The 'adrenaline' effect of emotion, particularly anger, narrows focus, cutting off one or two aspects of the context from everything else. Self finds out more and more about these aspects, literally blowing them out of the context at it becomes more and more 'right', while cutting itself off more and more from the reality, or meaning, in which they exist.

§120.

Ego loves emotional ARGUMENTS; or the sadistic pole does. The masochistic pole will run a hundred miles rather than engage in conflict, while the pure, defined, self-focused self of the sadist would rather die than admit it is wrong; for to do so is death. The sado-ego loves to pick out a thing from the totality of character and then do emotional battle with it. This is the quintessence of futility, like fighting a dragon's fingernail.

The problems we have with other people reach deep into their proximal consciousness and far away into the distal context. Fiddling around with the wrangled facts of a dispute is fine for superficial matters, technical questions or when someone is already close to abandoning some aspect of selfishness, but when it comes to consciousness, and all its qualities, we can get no closer to each other through argument than through flapping our arms and attempting to fly. It is *impossible* to communicate quality to someone who is not conscious enough to experience it, because conscious quality exists in another dimension to selfish quantity. Attempting to explain what is beyond self to self is like explaining wakefulness to the dreamer who has never woken, or Butoh to a Flatlander, or cricket to a shrimp. They might understand the words, sounds, images or movements, but only according to the quality of their own conscious experience. They might say they understand, or enjoy it to some extent, but they don't really *get* it, because it can't be got, and *nothing* you can say can bring them *any* closer to getting it; because what you mean is not at a *distance* from them. Not that ego ever covers consciousness completely—self is born defective, with a rip that lets the light in, which every now and then the sun strikes and passes through—but for the rest of the time truth expressed to ego just bounces off ideas and emotions which agree or disagree, but which *remain* ideas and emotions; which makes someone who experiences conscious quality, trying to explain it to someone who doesn't, feel not just like a sane man in a madhouse, but a sane man in a madhouse in which all the inmates believe they are doctors.

Ego can only agree or disagree, without understanding either way. It exists in an aggressive or defensive emotional state of self-justification, and all its arguments, no matter how sophisticated or elevated, are in service to this. They are a means to justify or conceal the fears and desires—and consequent acts—of ego, to others or to itself. Arguments are subtitles for the emotions. This is why, as experience narrows, and emotions consequently intensify, the ideas of an argument are clung to ever more tenaciously; the smaller the experience, the larger the certainty. In addition, because ego and egoic society are one, the former creating itself from and relying on the power of the latter, man will almost never give his own view or offer his own reasoning, but will hastily grab whatever opinion is shared by the group his self clings to for support, ideally one bolstered by the wondrous authority of expert opinion. Debating with such people is beyond futile; criticise a slave and the master will reply. In the past it was the king, or the priest, today it is the doctor or the scientist.

In the end, if none of the defence mechanisms of ego work, or are going to work, and if ego has sufficient power, it will deal with criticism by destroying the critic. Anyone who embodies or expresses unself must be disciplined or exterminated. Such people include real women, innocent children, the hyper-sensitive, the genuinely independent and the radically original, along with the consciousness of everyone on earth and the earth itself. To the extent they are unselfish, their existence is a standing insult to ego, a dire existential menace. This is why ego built the world we live in, to protect itself against unselfish nature, culture and nothing.

§121.

Self produces manifest CULTURE, and then that culture shapes self. First, self is externalised as an expression—some kind of act or presentation. The expression appears as an object, a thing in the world, which is related to other objects, which are then reappropriated by man back into the self.* A band releases an album, a building company constructs a block of flats, an advertising agency puts up hoardings around town, an individual recounts a few anecdotes. The songs, the dwellings, the signs and the stories become part of a world which then shapes those within that world. If self is unselfish this process ultimately begins "beyond" culture, with consciousness, to which the reappropriated modifications are subject to some kind of evaluation—I can *reject* the bullshit music, the ugly council estate, the advertising lies and the witless jibber-jabber. If, however, self is fundamentally egoic, consciousness is given no freedom to operate, and the caddis case is formed almost entirely from without, walling up inner quality, and with it, genuine individuality.

---

* Peter Berger and Thomas Luckman, *The Social Construction of Reality*

First self speaks, then the words get set in stone, then the stone speaks to the self, writing its words back into the human heart, which speaks again.* If there is freedom to speak, and to be heard, and to walk away, this DIALOGUE (or DIALECTIC) is fruitful and serves man. But just as if one person screws another down and forces words into her head it is no longer a conversation, so if SOCIETY (culture plus self, or selves) fills its schools and lines its streets with messages that all say the same thing, with no way of escape, then we are no longer individuals participating in a society, but stackable storage units for whomever or whatever is filling us with the things we are forced to feel, eat, look at, think about and energetically engage with; in short, build our selves with.

Culture was once built from nature, and, more intimately, from the unselfish origin of that which nature and culture have in common. This is why pre-civilised man considered nature and culture to be identical. The more culture came to be built from itself, the less it served the essence of man, until it came to compel man to accept its objective validity or suffer the consequences. Not in an overt tyrannical sense, but in the unalterable fact of its existence. You can think away culture or pretend it doesn't matter—ignore, say, the rules of language or pretend that they are dispensable, but you will be punished, mocked, excluded, brought back into line or killed. Likewise, if your social self is at odds with your individual self, then all kinds of problems are on their way. This does not mean that I must be something *other* than my social self, but that I am continually compelled to harmonise the two, and if I can't—if I cannot be in the world who I feel I really am—then I will suffer in the world, as everyone who is honest does.

Ego keeps this suffering at bay by endlessly affirming its social self. As that most unreal and egoic of sources, the average Teevee-American has it, 'I *am* a cop, it's *what I do...*' 'I *am* a mother, it's *what I do...*' Or, alternatively, 'This is *my* town, these are *my* people'. Such a 'self' is not something which is invented, it is there, 'inside me'. I look inside and see that I *am* the cop or mother that society takes me to be (or, for the fake outsider, that I wish society to take me to

---

* Ibid.

be). And I have no desire to be anything else. Not that there is anything wrong with inhabiting a role, nor with identifying with a community, nor that there aren't always elements of self that do not fit into what is required by the social world; rather that ego hides from itself in its social representation.

Man may be psychologically and spiritually deformed by his activity within the egoic group or institution, he may work in a mechanical manner, in mediated environments, in order to produce or manage things which have no recognisable human meaning, and he may be forced to conceal his horror and disgust behind an upbeat mask of emotional management, but if there is no truth beyond a self constructed from the group, he will *defend* his deformity, and consequent duplicity and misery, as truth. All criticisms of the group are taken to be criticisms of the self—'I am mortally offended by your prejudice'—and all criticisms of the self are taken to be prejudice against the group—'It's not because you are repulsed by my moral deformity, it's because you are racist / homophobic / anti-white / anti-American / etc'.

The seamless unity of self and society in the egoic mind explains man's *total* blindness to systemic constraints, and to the fundamental paradigms of the system. They are one with his ego, which is why, today for example, man spends so much time thinking and talking about voting, about reforming teaching, about having fairer laws, about creating cleaner motorways and so on and so forth; but not a word on how disabling democracy is, or education, or law, or transport, or the encompassing system, which is as invisible to him as water is to a fish, or anger is to a van driver.

§122.

The social self and its inner component, the personality, are maintained through communication, through constant confirmation (either explicit or implied) of who I am to others. When there is nobody to validate my personality, it dies, which is why solitude is so necessary to people with character—who need to periodically let their personality wither away in winter so that spring life might grow—and so terrifying to people without character, who must exist in a constant stress of forced blooming for the world. Likewise, if a critical avenue of personality-confirming communication is permanently disrupted—if a lover leaves, or a mother dies, or self is forced to live in another country, cut off from its culture—the whole world crumbles. The egoic self, forged through the shared reality created with a partner, a family or a society, is ripped out. This is why people stay in abusive relations and in abusive societies. Leaving the objective world of the known is to be plunged into chaos, a fate worse than death for ego, which may even choose death in preference.

Loss of self-reinforcing dialogue is not just a threat to the individual self, but to the social body, which provides all kinds of ritualised means by which the disrupted self is expected to deal with its disarray and return soothed and placated to the 'normal' world. A spouse torn apart by the death of a partner is fine, we can accept and sympathise; but if the grief is too noisy or outstays its welcome, then the social world will take measures to exclude it, quarantine the infection as it were, and remove conspicuous misery from the scene, so that production and consumption can smoothly proceed.*

For the same reason, madness, bizarre dreams and visions, psychotropic intoxication, spiritual extremism and all other exits from the system—including literally leaving it to gad off into the forest—are to be bricked up, or, if that's not possible, managed by society, which deals with the void by projecting a screen of rationalisations onto it.† Your visionary dream was a message from Satan, or a repressed desire, or a random brain signal, your glorious experience of the fundamental oneness of creation was a message from Allah, or a crazed illusion, or confirmation of your status as our Mystic Cham. All of these validations are gratefully taken up by the ego, which cannot bear to be cut off, alone (or alone with unself), and prefers to masochistically submit itself to The Worldview—or, on behalf of that world, to sadistically control others—rather than have to face any kind of reality beyond the boundaries of the social known.

---

* Ernest Goffman, *The Presentation of Self in Everyday Life*
† Peter Berger, *The Sacred Canopy*

Just as society is threatened by loss of face and loss of reason, so it must also deal with the danger of men and women rebelling against their internalised role;* finding, for example, that being a nice obedient little wife, or the upwardly-mobile manager of a car-rental firm, is something of a burden, and that they'd rather be members of a non-stop erotic cabaret or hunting-and-gathering in Botswana. It's fine for a man to masturbate to high-budget porn, or for a woman to spend a month on safari, but to actually *do* something about their dreams, particularly the genuinely wild ones, is out of the question, and again, if substitutes are not functioning, the machinery of social meaning must step in to make sure such desires are suppressed or channelled into something 'productive', or at least that the dreamer is reminded that if they are not, he can expect to pay an horrendously high price to realise them.

§123.

The most potent and pervasive threat to selfish society is not in this or that criticism, loss or disruption, but in unself itself; which is, as consciousness and the context it is one with, everywhere and at all times. Unself must therefore be *continually* suppressed, and man's relation to it, to ever-present unselfish quality, continually managed. This is largely done, on a social level, through LAWS, LEGITIMATIONS,† TABOOS and TOTEMS. These are the rules of society—the 'walls' of cliched thought, feeling, sensation and activity—which range from everyday non-verbal norms of behaviour (we greet in such and such a way, we react to bad news in such and such a way), through more explicit linguistic formulations of what is right and proper (the shared ethics of society, encoded in its wisdom, its maxims, its proverbs and even its jokes), through the art, myths and folk tales of a culture (by which we learn what is appropriate or tasteful, and what is to be condemned), through the explicit legal codes of a civilisation or of its various institutions, up to, finally, the various sacred justifications or secular theories which explain, in the most abstract sense, why things are as they are. Although all these legitimations

---

* Ibid.

† Ibid.

are constantly in conflict, they work as a whole to order men and women's responses to their own conscious impulses and the context they find themselves in. In a selfless society, these 'orders' are soft GUIDELINES (or, if you prefer, flexible *human* laws)—useful and necessary, but fluid, and at the service of the individual. In an egoic society, the individual must serve the laws, legitimations and taboos. If he breaks them—if he smiles when he should frown, does what the gods say never to do, questions evolution, utters the magical 'n' word or sends a magnet in the post—he'll be punished.

Note that men and women must be *continually* reminded of these justifications and *continually* enjoined to affirm their commitment to them, just as communities of belief must be *continually* reinforced and protected. Human beings are never far away from their original nature, and easily forget what has been programmed into them from without. This is why ritualised laws of defilement, containment of outsiders (physical or ideological), and, above all, walling off experiences of unreality (dream, madness, apostatic transcendence, death and love; even taking a shit puts one outside the bounds of history and religion and must be legitimately dealt with) play such an important, ongoing role in *all* ideological systems. Today, in the West, continual reinforcement takes the form of constant affirmations of the goodness and rightness of a highly invasive, technocratic, global market-economy and of constant reminders that without the various ideological totems required to engage in it—tolerance, respect, pacifistic acceptance, keeping two meters apart from one's fellows and keeping your trousers on in the supermarket—everything would fall apart and we'd all drown in a flood of anarcho-fascism, or die of a medieval lurgy, or be overwhelmed by the Beast. If it looks like these reminders aren't taking hold, then their intensity is stepped up and penalties for contravention escalate and intensify until you get your mind right.

Laws, legitimations, taboos and totems, being self-justifying and self-created, are *entirely* causal. The notion of law is coterminous with the notion of causality; a non-causal law is a contradiction in terms. In reality there are, ultimately, *no* laws in nature, in consciousness or in human affairs, because there is, ultimately, no causality in them; the world today was no more caused by the world yesterday than the morning was caused by the night before. The laws we find in history (e.g. Hegel's or Marx's), or in nature (e.g. Aristotle's or Newton's), or in society (e.g. Confucius' or Comte's), or in consciousness (e.g. Leibniz's or Freud's), are products of self, and therefore only applicable *to* self; occasionally useful, as facts and causes are, but with *zero* qualitative truth. The truth of an individual or society moving through 'time', like that of a tree, like the meaning of an act or the essence of reality, are invisible to causal consideration, which can only perceive a tumult of interrelated bits and pieces, slices and sections, and shrink-wrapped events, never the whole; which means it can never give an appropriate response *to* the whole (except by accident) which becomes impossible as soon as laws are set, and [directly or indirectly] enforced.

This is why people without direct experience of reality, isolated from it by money, power, fame, technology or drugs, rely on laws and legitimations, and give them the same existential status *as* experience. When it comes to right or wrong, for example, they cannot trust their experience, because they do not *have* experience, and so they cleave to factual-casual calculation. Property is inviolable, therefore stealing is wrong; a man steals an apple, therefore he must be punished, no matter how wealthy the supermarket he steals from. Context—the history of the supermarket, the functioning of the market, the state of society—and consciousness—compassion for the man, empathic understanding of his life—*cannot* be allowed into consideration. To do so would disrupt one's entire life. The brutal inflexibility of the law-abider is sometimes seen as a 'lack of imagination', but imagination is part of the abstract schema that the law-maker appeals to, the series of ideas codified as The Law; it is *wrong* to lie, it is *wrong* to kill, it is *wrong* to steal. When these ideas harden into eternal truths—when, in the management phase of civilisation, they are codified or written down, in holy texts or in statute books, or in the consciences of men and women—they serve, *and can only serve,* that which is incapable of abandoning facticity and causality, the inherently dishonest, selfish and violent ego. This is why you can't trust a law-abider.

§124.

Self, on contact with society, appears as the presentation of personality—beliefs, scripts, definitions, choice of clothes, choice of words, haircut, gesture, tone, pause; everything is significant, everything says something, and very little of it is lost on the audience, which is as interested in your performance as you are.* The only thing that really matters, however, is whether there is a conscious character behind the mask of persona. If there is, we can play, if not, if the self is motivated by self (as it must be in egoic societies), all flexibility is lost, all irony, all consciousness of what metaphor indicates and with it all spontaneity.

Ego cannot present itself to society, because it is basically cowardly, boring, masochistically anxious, sadistically angry and selfish. It therefore constructs a social mask to conceal its pain, mediocrity and hatred. This is constructed out of whatever resources ego can find in the self to justify and conceal itself. Rationality, hope and a big smile for the neighbours are all part of ego's PR department, as are the various scripts and games it learns to extract attention, sympathy or compliance from its fellows. The feigned hurt, the veiled threat, the complainy-hint, the shifty boast, the stare of death, the exasperated eye-roll, whatever it takes to maintain face.

As more and more is invested in the social performance, there is less and less to enjoy within it, and then, as the quality of self comes to be imputed, by egoic group members, to the social performance of it, so the unspoken laws which determine how to properly uphold self and how to deal with loss of presentation are rigidly policed, with transgression—an 'inappropriate' laugh, the 'wrong' length skirt, an 'offensive' comment, a 'bizarre' pause—mercilessly punished by ridicule, censure or ostracism. That the performance of self has nothing to do with morality and almost nothing to do with who

---

* Ernest Goffman, *The Presentation of Self in Everyday Life*

one really is, is irrelevant to the group-huddled ego; until, for whatever reason, attachment to the group weakens or it breaks down, and ohmygod I can't believe what a *cow* she really is.

§125.

All egoic groups, of whatever size, are on the constant look-out for signs that *your* social mask, which we all depend on to keep *our* masks in place, is slipping. Society is ready at any moment to step in to patch up the broken machine. On a day-to-day level nothing but a few plasters are necessary, a warm hug, a nice cup of tea, a bit of time to yourself and you'll be fiiine. If the problem is more serious, some form of corrective surgery might be necessary. Today we call this 'therapy'. A multitude of psychologists, psychotherapists, social workers, teachers, counsellors, probation officers and other psychocrats are employed to integrate selves into the system or manage those who cannot be subsumed. In order to do this on a sufficiently large scale, a massive quantity of information must be collected, through surveillance and monitoring, bureaucratic fact-gathering and the documentation of every facet of human life through the science of state; statistics.

All egoic cultures have some form of expiatory or re-medial activity for when gaps open up in the social fabric and a defective unit is in danger of falling through the net. Man needs meaning at such times and the prevailing ideological managers will give it to him, either in cosmic terms or in secular ones, when he starts to wonder what it's all for. What's the point? Why bother? At such times he will call to mind the characters in his favourite dramas, or the advice of the Caring Professionals on television, or the wisdom of The Sages, or one of the ethical cliches of the people around him. He will suppress his confusion and misery, and carry on.

One of the biggest problems for mind managers is when man starts to wonder why *they* have nice houses, or why *I* have to work so sodding hard, or why nature is turning to ash in my hands, or why it is necessary for us all to live cut off from each other in a boring global supermax, or why everything is so abominably, outrageously, horrifyingly fucked up. To be sure, this doesn't pose quite the same kind of danger to the system as an explosion of hyper-dimensional intensity between the eyeballs does, but it's an urgent threat and must be faced head on with some kind of explanatory system-myth.*

§126.

Consciousness "pre-exists" the forms of its social manifestation, but self does not. Self and society are one representation; the latter made by innumerable selves, over countless generations, the former a consequence of the myriad social influences (morality, culture, language, etc.) targeted upon it. How self thinks, the style of its affections, the ways it acts, its physical appearance, all of these things are indissolubly blended with society. But consciousness, the source of *true* individuality, still comes first; until it is squeezed out by representation.

In sane, natural societies, the growth of the individual character and that of the natural-cultural caddis-case personality are one; which is why those who grow up in natural cultures appear both uniquely *out* of the world and uniquely *of* their world. If unself is in charge of the individual self or of the social body, experience is freely directed towards whatever is demanded by consciousness and context, causing the appropriate mode of the individual self, or the appropriate individual self of the social body, to strengthen, supple or sensitise. Because self grows where attention flows, and because conscious attention always flows *freely*, waltzing past the no-entry signs of like-dislike markers, and *naturally*, in infinitely complex, strangely-ordered, self-similar fractal patterns, so I and we both become complete, balanced and fractally beautiful complements. Consciousness swells my individual tastes, but not at the expense of the whole, which also grows, enabling me to noetically communicate and viscerally commune with unlike others. My genius may not inflate my skills as a pianist or baker, it might not drive me down into the deepest depths of psyche, it might not overflow me with thelemic energy or inspire me to read and understand literary masterpieces; but

---

* See *33 Myths of the System*

my corresponding stunts will be sufficiently sensitive to love the sonatas, loaves and poems of others, to help out—and love helping out—with tiling the neighbours' roof, or bringing in the bean harvest, or contributing to the play, even as just a bit part, or behind the scenes, or come harvest time. The natural social body thus grows as the natural individual self does, composed of utterly unique, completely distinct, yet socially blended components, each able instantly, directly and empathically to understand the other.

In a sane society, children grow to be both themselves *and* the society. They learn cultural norms during the sixteen to twenty years in which they are completely dependent on the social group, but, at the same time, they are guided out of their original state of unmediated consciousness, through facing up to the various challenges presented to the developing self entering the human world, towards a form of isolated individuality that, in its uniqueness, shines as a never-to-be-seen-again star, yet one with the universe. The consciousness of the sane adult naturally contributes to the social fruit, yet is ever rooted in the darkness and charm of the unselfish universe it left behind as a child.

An egoic world, on the other hand, is backwards. It begins with the imagined fruit—power, permanence, pleasure, prestige [for those who control it]—then builds the most efficient machine it can to manufacture it. Initially this machine is integrated with nature, but as man isolates himself more and more within his fabricated culture, it separates itself from nature, which then rears up before ego as a radical Other which must be controlled. Over time, the machine, self-informed like the selves that build and maintain it, becomes more and more machine-like, and is eventually composed, like all machines, entirely of unnatural, functional, interrelated, end-directed components—isolated, contextless *parts* of nature; which is to say unnatural, functional, interrelated, end-directed PART-PEOPLE, human ballbearings which are *entirely* subordinated to the mechanism of an unnatural society (and are therefore entirely fake, for anything or anyone that is interchangeable cannot be itself).

The logic of the egoic social order is the logic of ego on a grand, objective, collective scale. It 'understands' only itself, and so all its precepts and injunctions boil down to one imperative... *more*. Where ego only understands what *I* want, so egoic society only understands what *we* want. The objective, social 'knowledge-world' of laws, theories, scientific fact, moral maxim, culture, etc., is to the collective what the personal world-view or philosophy is to the individual. It is only secondarily, and very often trivially, related to any truth beyond what that society *wants* to be true. The man engaged with a fundamentally different truth, a reality which has nothing to do with wanting things, occasionally makes the mistake of believing he has only to show that his truth has more going for it, or at least deserves a place, and it will find that place. In fact, he faces fundamentally different *desires*, which nothing he can ever say will alter. Only when those desires change will what he says get a look-in.

§ 127.

For the socially submerged self, independence and escape, along with any genuine alternative, become impossible to even conceive of. Selves that grow in selfish environments—families motivated by selfish emotions, institutions which exclusively reward hyper-specialised over-focus on a few system-friendly tasks, cities and digital 'social spaces' in which everything is made by and for selves—are like dreamers who have never woken. They have the sense that something is profoundly wrong, but it is so subtle that it is easily smothered by the immense weight of factual evidence, that everything *is* as it *seems*, that life is a question of being a thing here amongst all those other things over there. We call this fundamental acceptance of the laws and legitimations of society CONFORMISM.

There are two kinds of conformist; sadists and masochists. Masochists, who blindly accept authority, worship power and accept whatever norms are most likely to maintain security, if through nothing else than by sheer force of numbers. They seek to deal with the pain of being a self by submitting to the institution, or to the system, or to their representational figureheads—celebrities and leaders—or to their ideological foundations—religion, science, postmodernism, etc. Masochists cannot maintain ego and at the same time consider themselves *as* sheep, which makes them feel a tad embarrassed, so they make much of their superficial opposition to antagonistic forces *within* society; to elites, or blacks, or politicians, or right-wingers, or whoever; really any out-group will do, but naturally those which are *perceived* to be battling for the same resources make better targets, which is why working-class white folk can get more up in arms about working-class black folk than about their monstrous overlords, despite having *much* more in common with the former. Likewise, lefty, middle-class stagversives get themselves into a lather about right-wingers, fascists and the like, despite sharing *precisely* the same basic assumptions about society with them.

Over on the active pole of conformity, sadists also accept authority, but deal with their alienated misery by *inhabiting* it (although always on behalf of something bigger; justice, or God, or the nation) and by attacking threats to the *status quo* which protects them. All threats, any of them, but particular enmity is reserved for anyone (or anything) who represents unself (the uncorrupted and the incorruptible), who is indiscriminately rejected as insane, dirty, disordered or impure, morally reprehensible or downright evil. Such people and ideas loom massive and menacing on the sadist radar, but he will react with astonishing fury at the tiniest threat to his world. The sadist intuitively understands that, just as it is impossible to radically change one fundamental problem with the self without changing the whole, so it is impossible to radically change (i.e. obliterate) one institution in society without a complete revolution. This compels him to react to trivial threats with a fury totally out of proportion to the perceived cause. He seeks to annihilate a weak state, or a non-violent movement, or a lone, subversive author, or comedian whose example threatens to spread the terror of independent thought; all, of course, for morally justifiable reasons. For just as sheep cannot accept their wretched servility, so wolves cannot accept their vicious belligerence without feeling morally compromised, and will go to great lengths to persuade themselves and others that they are noble, justified, realistic and essentially caring. They are doing it for you, for your *health*, for your *well-being*, or, as the Nazis liked to say, for your *security* ('für ihre sicherheit'), words which evoke the terrors of hell for the free man and the free woman.

§128.

In order to submerge selves into conformity to the social machine, egoic society must crush consciousness, sever all rooted connection to unself and then compel man to amputate *himself* to fit into whatever role he can most usefully serve the system by inhabiting. One way this is done is by inflating likes into SPECIALISMS; each person must *play his part* (a telling expression, although the 'game' is a joyless chore) with hyper-focused, psychotic intensity and with no real interest in anything else. Wants are inflated into addictions, into attachment to the machine (and to the role one plays within it), which must be obsessive and needy. Naturally introverted impulses must be directed towards masochistic subservience to the community or to the market, while extroverted impulses must be directed towards sadistic control of others, so that sado-masochists will serve or consume or sacrifice or snitch on or massacre themselves and each other as required; and over all this the upbeat social mask of the persona must be held in place. For without it, the agony and unhappiness of being crippled and forced to behave in a manner which betrays one's inner nature would emerge, like a transient glance of *genuine* disgust in a movie when the star is forced to kiss a leading man she detests, or a squeeze of terror which grips the calm face of the CEO or PM when the wrong question is asked, and the illusion is shattered. This is why an upbeat, can-do, yes-sir! attitude is demanded by all sadistic authorities, particularly from 'client-facing' lackeys at the live end of power-relations (conspicuous misery is permitted in the end links of long bureaucratic chains), and in advanced organs of social control.

In such a society, 'individuals' are almost entirely swollen caricatures of themselves, unable, through the suppression of their stunts, to communicate or commune with anyone else (except through technique) and therefore essentially antagonistic to them. The *game* of society is no longer to learn to play it well, or to have any real fun, but to *win*. The other is reduced to an ally, which I call a 'friend', someone who is wearing a mask just as deformed and caricatured as my own; until she is no longer of any use, in which case she immediately becomes an 'enemy', whom I must defeat by any means necessary; chiefly by manipulating her to make the moves I want her to make. In order to do this, I have to gain as much information about her as possible, which is why institutions spend so much more energy on gathering data about people, and assessing and manipulating their *personality*, than on task *performance*, which is often almost an afterthought.

The consequence of all this is that society, which is supposed to be a game, or series of games, ceases to be a source of enjoyment which we have the power to change, in order to make it more enjoyable, and instead becomes a grim Disneyschwitz which I am *compelled* to 'enjoy' by 'bettering myself' and 'having fun', winning enough points to climb up a neon ladder of swords, to the point where I can compel other people to climb it as cheerfully as I had to.

§129.

Without shared experience of the unselfish context—the never-ending source of unconditional pleasure that sane trees are rooted into and from which sweet fruits of meaningful interaction grow—egos must instead form *alliances* based on shared likes and wants (goals, diversions, etc.) and shared don't wants and don't likes (fears, anxieties, etc.). Essentially antagonistic selves sign a series of temporary peace treaties with each other in order to win whatever battle they are waging against a hostile universe. These treaties are the techniques which all egoic selves must use to keep their groups together—one of a collection of self-reinforcing cliches and tokens we call CULTS.

A cult is an enforced set of cliches and empty symbols adopted by a group of people upon whom, through the size and technical strength of the group, power is conferred in increasingly large quanta; a power that, through the many years served in acquiring it—learning in-group facts, rituals, dialects and procedures—and the pleasurable sense of specialness and security felt in wielding it, serves to bind the individual to the cult, ally the individual to its values, motivate the individual to further its aims and *subsume* the individual within his or her cultic personality or 'identity'.

Cults maintain and augment their power through four kinds of EGOIC CONTROL, or BRAINWASHING:

i.   EGOIC CONTROL OF CONTEXT. The context comes to *you* through *us*, through the world we design, a world *which* we design so that no interruptions from beyond the controlling system may enter. Control of context entails our exclusive use of technology and equally exclusive access to the environmental resources upon which such machinery can be used, until you have proved, through a long period of training, that you can be trusted to *always* put the needs of the cult first, then you may be given the correct password and allowed to think, speak and act 'freely'.

ii.   EGOIC CONTROL OF QUALITY. Quality is what we say it is, and only those who manifest such quality—goodness, cleanliness, beauty and purity—are admitted into or permitted to rise within the controlling system. Deviance from legitimating standards, particularly in the carrying out of non-approved rituals, is *ipso facto* impure, unclean, ugly and evil.

iii.   EGOIC CONTROL OF MEANING. The power to write and enforce laws, the ability to impose the 'correct' definition of words relating to quality. Deviance from expert or official definition is deviance from meaning, and therefore from truth, and therefore from reality itself. If you say anything, directly or indirectly, which contradicts the truth as officially presented, you will be ignored, ridiculed, reshaped or destroyed.

iv.   EGOIC CONTROL OF SELF. Your self belongs to us. It is, like the objects around you, just temporarily on loan to you. We can take it back whenever we like. Everything that happens in your self, including your thoughts and feelings, must be public (confessed, measured, recorded, etc.) so that we can take possession of it. Failure to reveal your self is illegal in all egoic systems.

Total control gives the impression of total normality to those who inhabit the cult. The tribal cult, the religious cult, the state cult, the professional cult, the institutional cult, the personality cult, the cult-of-two and the overarching system cult all endeavour to cover every point at which self meets reality, making the cult appear to *be* reality. From the outside, the ritualised subservience of cult members—the masks, dialects, customs and costumes—appears freakish, ridiculous or creepy, without purpose (although, *nota bene*, 'the outside' is often a larger cult of its own, and therefore disposed to see the ecstatic genius and loving scenius of a genuinely living culture, with its non-egoic forms of authority, as cult-like).

Any incursion into cultic authority, any insight or even any style of thought that originates from beyond egoic cult power, is met with incomprehension or ridicule, and in a world dominated by cults—the massively powerful cults that today we call INSTITUTIONS—any genuinely independent non-institutional group or society is completely, or at least effectively, banned from managing itself, regulating itself, feeding itself, entertaining itself, educating itself, healing itself, communicating with itself or even thinking for itself. The idea that such things are even possible is eradicated from the mind of man, who must conclude that, outside of the institutional cult, the single man or woman is the largest viable building block for human society, and that one's inbuilt need for society can only be fulfilled by merging with the painted surface of the world. Unless, of course, you are at the top of the institutional tree; then you can have a real, physical social life, albeit one from which human warmth and fellow-feeling has been scooped out, leaving a glittery image. Rich and famous people don't need to watch cheap soap operas because they are living in one; which is why commissioning editors are so eager to put their lives on television.

§130.

Cults—clans, teams, cliques, classes, religions, faculties, professional institutions and nations—are distinguished from fluid selfless groups or societies by the fact that they are *egoic*, which means that their form and function correspond to the self, but are degraded by being cut off from consciousness and context into thelemic cliche, somatic symbol, visceral GROUPFEEL, and noetic GROUPTHINK.

Groupthink is a set of self-reinforcing ideas, attitudes and actions that bind egos together. Groupthink reinforces and reassures 'who I am' by stigmatising 'who I am not' and glorifying 'who *we* are'. It can be seen and felt in fascist rallies, monotheistic sermons, menopausal tea breaks, gentleman's after-dinner clubs, anarcho-co-ops, teeny cliques, gay-rights marches, football clubs, small town back gardens, professional symposia, corp-journo twitter feeds, wankers' bars, riotous mobs, entire nations and entire social classes; in short anywhere and everywhere that domesticated egos, anxious of unself, congregate.

Groupthink comprises excessive generalisation and stereotyping, ever more extreme views (as members obtain the favour of the others by expressing extreme attitudes in the favoured direction), an illusion of invulnerability, unquestioned belief in the morality of the group, blindness towards inconvenient facts, pressure to conform on dissenting voices, self-censorship (creating an illusion of unanimity), disregard for empathy towards out-groups (whose faults are exaggerated), unconscious urges to help those who are perceived to be similar (who look the same, share the same values or have the same origins), to reject the outsider, no matter how affable, and accept the insider, no matter how obnoxious, exclusion of anyone who does not display competent use of in-group vocabulary (i.e. JARGON), emotional blindness to nuance, a crude, collective taste-matrix (rejection of which produces censure), exaggerated outrage at criticism (which is then used as justification for savage condemnation of threats to group cohesion), and, most subtly but powerfully of all, a reassuring collective vibe, or atmosphere, which 'feels good' to be part of.

If the glue and fuel of cults is groupthink, the actual structure is cliche, or an enormous number of cliches; self-reinforcing feedback loops of empty routines made up of empty symbols and gestures hurtling back and forth across empty space to serve an empty representation of ego. Empty in that inside the Soviet party conference, or the corporate boardroom, or the lefty 'safe-space', or the nationalist Facebook group, or the Scientology Clearing Congress, or the Oscar ceremony, there must be no quality, no context and no consciousness (unless by accident); at best fear and desire, or like and don't like, more often than not nothing at all, which is why cult members seem robotic, and why, in the greatest cult of all, *our world*, they can be replaced by robots without anyone noticing the difference. All there is to a robot is the series of cliches we call programmes. In fact cults can be considered as massive cliches (just as cliches can be thought of as microscopic cult-fragments).*

All groups demand cliches, but the largest, formally established institutions require the most profound and rigid conformity to 'how it's done'—the right attitude, dress, jargon and algorithm. It is true that *innovation*—the development of new formal techniques which can enhance the power and reach of the institution—is encouraged for the professional part-people inserted in the management node, who have been rigidly trained in how to innovate in the right direction, but foundational *originality*—a radically playful approach to cliche (to conversation, dress, attitude, time-keeping, speed and style of work, etc.)—is taboo or illegal for everyone. What this tends to mean is that activity within groups becomes, firstly, more and more *mechanical*, as consciousness is not only not *required* to speak, think, feel and act in a cliched manner, but actually *disrupts* cliche; and, secondly, more and more [hyper] *specialised*, as cliche can only conceive of quantitative

---

* Anton C. Zijderveld, *On Cliches*

improvement in one direction, and one direction only; that which I am 'best at' or which I like the most.

The inherently uni-directional, mechanical nature of cults is why the egoic system responds to all problems by massively augmenting whatever institutional structure is already in place. It can only conceive of mechanical expansion. 'Better' does not actually exist in the cult dictionary; it can only ever mean *more*. Thus, to solve crime we need more prisons, more surveillance and more laws, to solve sickness we need more doctors, more drugs and more medical interventions, to solve stupidity we need more teachers, more 'learning apps' and more study time, to solve boredom we need more toys, more leisure centres and more video games, and to solve death we need more 'life', meaning more healthy momentum. If nobody stops, nobody will realise they're going nowhere.

§ 131.

A sane human society comprises selves that are wide enough to *generalise*—to do many things as well as necessary to survive and thrive—and focused enough to *specialise*—to do a few things better than anyone. If the width of great generalisation, free to wander at will, is absent, self-informed institutional HY-PER-SPECIALISATION takes over the group, forcing fractal selves down rigid paths of digital cliche, annihilating everything that I am not best at, and creating isolated, functional units which can be slotted into the machine.

There are several consequences, for the self, of living in a hyper-specialised world:

i.   Crossing disciplines becomes difficult or impossible. The funnels of education might cross here and there but, as with all digital taxonomies, they are discrete and bounded. You can be a specialist in dynamical systems and differential equations, or in tropical diseases, or in tyres, or in any other part of the social mechanism, but to be a generalist, to study widely—or, even worse, to *live* widely—is useless to the social machine and automatically punished by it.

ii.　　Criticism in compartmentalised societies is difficult or impossible. Everyone is—*officially*—nice to each other and polite and supportive and friendly; until they get home, or leave the conference call, take off their masks and scheme and bitch like mad. When criticism does appear, it always seems to *matter*, because the part the personality is cheerlessly playing is under threat. In sane societies, or sane relationships, criticism is constant and it doesn't matter at all.

Because the selfish thinker confuses what he knows about reality for reality itself (technically speaking, he confuses ontology for epistemology) a world constructed by such people necessarily takes criticism of ideas as threats to existence; because their world is not merely built *from* ideas, it *is* an idea, or collection of ideas. This 'body of knowledge' is not consciously invented, but builds up over generations of people doing little more than considering or describing their experience. Descriptions of how things *are* become inseparable from how they *should be*, deviance from which automatically becoming an act of rebellion. Again, not for any intellectual reason, but because, to the extent that ego runs the show, reality itself is being threatened.

iii.　　Everyone becomes just as you would expect them to be. All are standard, cliched, methodical; never unexpected. The teacher looks and behaves like a teacher, the shop-assistant looks and behaves like a shop-assistant, likewise the doctor, the engineer, the rebel, the reactionary, the manual labourer, the writer of serious fiction, the tabloid journalist, the pianist and the palm-reader. This is why the first question people want to know of each other is what they do, because there is a very high probability that the answer will reveal something substantive—what their cliche is and, crucially, how much they appear to be departing from it into one of the two threatening exceptions to the Standard Man; the exceptionally bad and the exceptionally good, the former having not the minutest interest in being able to do anything other than satisfy the crudest of desires, the latter having pulled himself free of the cliche that society demanded of him.

The confinement of consciousness that inhabiting a hyper-specialised part entails is why the people most enthusiastic about engaging with reality through specialised roles—the teacherly teacher, the doctorish doctor, the professional this or that—are the most boring, the most ridiculous, the most selfish and the most hated.

Hyper-specialisation degrades (digitises) cooperative societies into mere groups. These EGO-GROUPS are composed of separate, specialised part-people who are unable to experience what they are not (for example, *each other*) and so must rely on their adherence to what they know or feel they have in common; their shared fears and desires. Such a group must compel members who do not share these fears and desires to co-operate *through* fear (of guilt, punishment, deprivation, etc.) and desire (for acceptance, money, power, etc.). The ego-group *appears* to end up being made up of members who are overwhelmed with existential terror and psychotic appetite, an ocean of suffering raging underneath the parquet flooring of the ordinary world; although the appearance is deceptive. It is a grievous mistake to suppose that the misery *of* the world is caused *by* the world, which merely amplifies, reinforces and proliferates it. In truth the world is caused by misery.

§132.

Forms of cultural expression exist on an apparent continuum between self-oriented technical work and unself-oriented character or quality work. We usually call the latter ART and the former CRAFT. These refer to our expressive work in the world, although we can also speak of the art and craft of everyday activities; conversation, dating, walking, even glancing and gesturing. Both art and craft require technique *and* character, with—at least in high quality work—the former subordinate to the latter, for quality is "closer" to unself than technique. This is why a poorly executed work of charm is preferable to a perfectly executed work without it, and why genuine mastery is obsessed with technique, but is *more* obsessed with letting go of it. The master knows that he needs to know, but he also knows that his knowledge imprisons him.

All art-work and craft-work demand an alternation or fluctuation between the quantity of tight-focus thought and perception—clench—and the quality of wide-focus awareness of character—release. The mechanic and the mathematician isolate, analyse, experiment, fix and then, when they get stuck, pull out, relax, soften and look. The author and the painter and the sempstress and the cook and the ordinary man and woman in mutually-enjoyable conversation all do the same; focus, focus, tight focus, then release, take in the whole.

The absence of either craft / technique or art / character, through being unable to clench-focus or being unable to release-relax, leads to work we call 'low-quality', of which there are, very roughly, four kinds:

i.   Technical work without character. For example; dull or pretentious food, clothes with clashing colours and patterns, tasteless decor and design, plodding scholarship, boring (but effective) play, and photography, journalism and research.

ii.   Technical work without technique. For example; clumsy sport, lazy scholarship, confusing technical writing, gimcrack building and shoddy manufacture ('cheap', 'crappy', 'inept'), inedible food, dangerous driving and incompetent medicine.

iii.   Character work without character. For example; pre-dictable fiction, realist and hyper-realist art, boring music (spiritless cover versions, passionless classical performances, self-absorbed MOR guitar solos), abstract academic philosophy, self-help, yoga, spiritualist guru-fakery, psychoanalysis and spiteful, crude or superficially surreal comedy.

iv.   Character work without technique. For example; mod-ern art, award-winning fiction, low-effort music (techno, hip-hop, ragga, grime, modern R&B and pop, most experimental music), agonising impro and all forms of postmodern and poststructural philosophy.

Where the physicalist ego is threatened by non-factual subjectivity and so is over-attracted to technique, deriding character as mystical, subjective, pretentious and so on, the solipsist ego is threatened by factual objectivity, and so *it* is over-attracted to character, or its idea of character, deriding technique as boring, conformist, repressive and so on.

§133.

If technical work is predominantly a means of satisfying the needs of the literal, measurable self, while quality work is predominantly a means of expressing the quality or character of non-literal, ineffable unself as it manifests, it follows that:

i.   Technical work can be rated; and ratings can be trusted. If a thousand people (actual people of course, rather than bots or corporate employees) give a pair of scissors five stars, or a burger, you can be certain that it's a good pair of scissors and a tasty burger. If a thousand people give a comedy show five stars, or a work of philosophy, you can be equally certain it is excrement. It's not for nothing that Jesus of Nazareth chose to deliver his message through speech and not through carpentry, and why, if he had been born in the twentieth century, it wouldn't have been as a photographer or pastry chef

ii.   Many are the books and courses on improving craft, on becoming better at *doing* something, but few are those on improving character, on becoming better at *being* someone (or doing nothing). And many are the beautifully designed books, houses, films and clothes with nothing living inside them, but few are the beautiful creators who seek emptiness, who embrace obscurity, who pursue activities which will not lead to getting something, who welcome pain.

iii.   Great books are not about interesting *things*, but are written by interesting *people*. While the answer to the question 'what is it about?' may be interesting, it can never tell you if a film or book is going to be any good; any more than 'what does he do?' can tell you if someone is worth spending time with. Unless you hope to *get* something from him.

iv.   The funniest comedy and the most disturbing horror strike ego as meaningless, because they formally present an hilarious and disturbing reality which ego is unable to view intrinsically. This is why ego cannot *get* them, any more than it can *get* the genuine paradox that spiritual masterpieces express and experiments in quantum physics measure. Great comedy is not in being superior to *things*, but in being lost in *no* thing. Great horror is not in *losing* this or that thing, but in being *lost* in things.

v.   Comparing feelings of sorrow at the death of a friend to the effect of, say, Beethoven's 15th string quartet (or vice versa) would be understandable (if possibly pretentious), whilst giving your grief a score or comparing it to a bad experience in a restaurant would be monstrous.

vi.   Many are the [literalist] masters of technique with nothing to say, who can teach a subject, but make no original or lasting contribution to it and are baffled by the brilliance of those far less 'able'. Many, too, are the great artists who continue to be technically adept but are frustrated that they can no longer create anything as beautiful as they did before they were so skilled; or, of course, before they were so famous.

vii.   Many are the [solipsist] artists and craftsmen with poor technique, no recognisable tradition, limited intellectual or cultural experience and even general stupidity, all of which are not merely excused on the grounds that quality cannot be proven, but are actually celebrated. Many too are the photographers, hairdressers, journalists, designers, DJs and VJs who consider themselves to be avatars of creative immortality.

viii.   Machines can do technical work. Not necessarily *well*, as quality is necessarily as absent from completely mechanical activities as consciousness is, but well *enough* to satisfy the self-bound self. It would be possible, if horribly *unsatisfying*, to live in a world in which all our clothes, food and buildings were made by machines, provided that all our arts were made by conscious humans. But machines cannot produce character work. To live in a world in which the greatest craftsmen provided everyone with the finest crafted things to live with, while we could only receive 'high' culture from or communicate with machines wouldn't be quantitatively uncomfortable, it would be a qualitative nightmare. In fact, it *is* a nightmare.

ix.   Ego is completely satisfied in a world of technique. Somehow people know that *something is missing*, but they spend their lives suppressing such knowledge. They might live very comfortably in a world of breakfast-television interviews, steamy period pieces, thrilling football tournaments, Paris catwalks, light lunch at *great* restaurants, massively multiplayer online role-playing games, smart-talking, sufficiently neurotic, New York comedians, private views at the Serpentine, Glasto, unspoilt Croatia, well-bred, symmetrically faced, actors with a talent for mimicry, nice shoes, office chat, German shoes, Swiss clocks, amusing cat videos, PVC, Batman and amateur Asian porn. But *something is missing*.

x.   An unconscious society, composed of unconscious people, uses a functional language that is, essentially, drained of quality. Quality words, like 'love' and 'beauty' come to be used more often than masking tape and in the same manner as technical words, such as 'spanner' and 'carpet', as *things* we 'all know the meaning of' or as operational markers, symbols requiring a standard response. When someone says 'beautiful', it means the kind of women who are called 'beautiful', the kind of scenery which is called 'beautiful', the kind of accommodation which is called 'beautiful' (although not necessarily officially, because superficially antagonistic subgroups with their own sub-definitions are part of the system), all conceived as literal things, as the known, as that which can be measured ('she's an eight'), got ('she's a keeper') and lost ('she broke my heart'), all eliciting one of a handful of Standard Reactions.

xi.   Ego is satisfied with this kind of conversation. A: What did you do on Sunday? (request for fact). B: I had some friends over for a barbecue. (fact). A: How was it? (request for rating). B: Oh it was great (positive rating), but it rained (negative rating) and John got drunk and started acting up (negative rating). A: Oh no, that's annoying (negative rating confirmed). I love him to bits (positive rating), but he can be a real pillock (negative rating). B: Yeah, I don't understand how he's so popular with women (negative rating). His last girlfriend was well fit (positive rating). A: Well, he's good-looking and confident (positive rating). B: I wish I was a bit more confident (negative rating), but I just feel awkward imposing myself (positive self-rating). A: Yeah, I know what you mean (positive rating). Anyway, fancy a drink (request for positive excitement)?*

xii.   People without initiative, meaningful experience, sensitivity or other unselfish qualities require grades and other forms of extrinsic motivation in order to learn. This doesn't just include students, but teachers also who are dependent on shuffling facts around, who have nothing to say and so must depend on method. This makes them mechanical, and easy to mock. It is more difficult to satirise the selfless.

xiii.   Technical work without quality is necessarily isolated from consciousness and context. Consequently, it necessarily results in outputs which can be integrated into neither. We call these outputs WASTE, that which cannot be harmlessly reintegrated into self. A society constructed by and for ego is necessarily wasteful, a world so built suffocates itself in short order.

xiv.   It is impossible to literally prove that character work is low-quality. A contemporary drama, novel or song may be devoid of character, but there is no *comprehensible* or even, for ego, *instinctive* way to tell it is so. Character, to the extent that it is understood at all, is experienced by ego as an irritant, at best incomprehensible or naive silliness, at worst horrific nihilism and existential terrorism. We *can* speak of 'useful'

---

* Barry Long, *Only Fear Dies*

paintings or stories, we *do* need to master objective elements of craft to produce high-art, and to some extent an ugly song *will* affect, even torture, the body; but, *ultimately*, there is nothing *materially obvious* about the benefits that quality work confers.

xv.   With the technical arts on the other hand—design, fashion, architecture, joinery, cookery, sport, etc.—there *is* an objective standard by which quality can be known; utility. It is the importance of utility—the nourishment of a meal, the sturdiness of a wall, the readability of a block of text—that separates quality work from technical work. The technical arts *do*, at their rare heights, contain elements of the ineffable (the astonishing beauty of a masterful carpet, the animal grace of a master tennis player and the presence, dignity and authority of a master shoemaker knocks that of, say, an average musician into a cocked hat) just as quality arts contain objective technical elements (the long, punishing craft of great drawing and writing). As with most such distinctions the dividing line is fuzzy and scattered; but the reason why I can clearly and correctly show you that you are a dreadful sempstress or smith (or that, *technically*, your songs and stories are second-rate) and the reason why there is no way to prove that your melody lacks the beauty of life, or your tragedy the truth of it, is that there is a difference between technical work, which is *essentially* comprehensible, as subjectivity and objectivity are, and quality work, which is essentially incomprehensible, as panjectivity is.

§134.

Character work, or art, is composed of four modal elements; [noetic] metaphor, [somatic] fractality, [thelemic] transdimensionality and [visceral] aura.

i.   The *noetic* METAPHORICAL ELEMENT in art comes from the unselfish and therefore paradoxical source of all modal experience. In "preceding" the isolated modal elements of self, unself generates SYNAESTHETIC experience, in which a single, unselfish, root experience appears as one mode (one

265

perception, conception, affection or volition) but is sensed echoing in other modes. I hear, for example, a D-major chord struck on a piano and somehow feel the colour yellow or the taste of apple. The chord is not *causing* the colour or the taste, any more than standing under causes understanding; rather they are both emerging from a common "root". If man, as the modes of his self differentiate and acquire experience, grows connected to this root, his consciousness will feel or do or think about *one thing*, but the experience will 'echo' through the selfish self as *other things*. The letter A will appear as red, Juliet as the sun and the Kingdom as the leaven in bread, the expression of which we call metaphor, and the experience of which, as we the reader or audience feel the *actual* connection between apparently separate elements, we call art.

The prototypical metaphorical art is poetry, although metaphor is also fundamental to prose and to meaningful symbolic imagery, and there is a metaphorical element to music too in that the mechanics of metaphor—omission, violation of expectation and sharing a common root with apparently unlike modes—apply, albeit in a direct and non-representational manner, to great melodies.

ii.   The *somatic* FRACTAL ELEMENT of art is not a copy of the external beauty of nature, but an expression of the inner beauty of the natural self "animated" by unself, which appears as the infinite paradox scientists clumsily express as 'chaos theory'. It can be said that consciousness "has" a fractal "shape", which expresses itself as a *taste* for interconnectedness, interdimensionality, immeasurability, unpredictability, constant iteration, self-similarity and self-organisation. The great artist writing a television series or painting a triptych or composing a symphony need not bring this taste to explicit notice, he feels out what, in the form of his art, is betraying his innate sense, and eradicates it. This is how men and women who live in cities can, occasionally, speak the strange language of bees; because you can't get closer to nature than your own body. As urban life sucks men and women out of their senses, so fractality degrades to mere chaos and order.

The prototypical example of fractal art is painting, in which the majestic *principle* of nature is expressed in two static dimensions. Sculpture and architecture can express fractality in three dimensions, song, dance and story in four dimensions.

iii.   The *thelemic* TRANSDIMENSIONAL ELEMENT of art is the presentation in three dimensions of a four-dimensional whole. The 'shape' of the human psyche is mirrored in the path of characters through stories and of tones through songs, from which, although we enjoy them *in* time, we receive, from the sense of the *whole* story or symphony, a glow of pleasure from *beyond* time, for we have experienced a timeless *whole* which stretches beyond all the *parts* we've just experienced piece-meal. In being a whole, the formal parts of a transdimensional artistic event relate to each other as the parts of any other natural object do; just as the roots, trunk, branches and leaves of a tree are ultimately one object, so the call to action, the training, the world-turned-upside-down, the battle with the beast and the return-with-the-chalice of the hero's journey are, each reflecting the other.

The prototypical example of transdimensional art is myth, or story (in prose, speech, theatre, etc.) which express-es four-dimensional objects in three dimensions, by relating events, through time, to each other. Music does the same with sounds and philosophy with concepts.

iv.   The *visceral* AURIC ELEMENT of art is the sniffing out of flavour, atmosphere, quality or vibe in objects, actions, words and colours, in order to express that which is pre-selfishly sensed as more truthful than the immediate, material fact or abstract idea of the thing. Aura and transdimensionality go hand-in-non-representational-hand, as sensitivity to the affective quality life of the oak tree, of the discarded ballet shoe, of the babushka's face, is not sensitivity to a represented idea or perception of the 3D thing, but to a *feeling* which also encompasses the acorn, the ballerina and the devochka, thus expressing the non-formal *reality* of them, outside of what we call time. Ultimately the life of the tree, the Russian nation, the entire human race, even nature herself are single 'objects', the feeling-quality of which the artist endeavours to represent in his painting or his song. None of this reaches the literalist ego, which, seeing only the fact, finds no aura *in* objects, nor does it reach the solipsist ego, which can only sense its own atmospheres and vibes, which it then *imputes* to objects.

The prototypical example of aura in art is music, which, as it contains (lyrics notwithstanding) nothing representational, directly expresses viscera and energy (and so directly expresses destiny), hence its status as the queen of the arts; although all art forms have aura, notably acting.

These forms of art correspond to forms of meaning; the manifestation of character in the life's work of the artist. Thus we can say, schematically, that there are four kinds of genius (or, in the system, OUTSIDER); the thelemic genius, with a miraculous will, burning with the fire of the gods, the somatic genius, 'like an animal with a sixth sense',* the visceral genius, able to feel the living quality of experience and give artistic form to it, and the noetic genius, the inspired thinker, who turns the clay of matter into mythic or mathematical jewels.

§135.

The greatest art of all, expressing the genius that all partake of, is life itself, particularly as it manifests in conversation and communion with each other. Collectively, the most intense expression of life is in FESTIVAL, which, through choral song, synchronised dance, imitative ritual and impro, combines metaphorical, fractal, transdimensional and auric elements into a unified empathic experience. The asphyxiation of the nature and culture that festival depends on, and its slow corruption into forms of centrally organised fun, saw the rise of its degraded (although still potent) reflection, *film*, which also combines all forms of art, but with zero participation. Reading, theatre and sport are also passive experiences; also potent, but nowhere near as powerful as active jamming, live speech, improvised theatre and their union in participatory festival.

---

* Aldous Huxley on D.H.Lawrence

Although festival requires the individual genius of consciousness, it is more deeply rooted in the collective SCENIUS (a.k.a. community spirit, or *communitas*) of the context. Scenius emerges from sensitivity to the atmosphere of the situation, which manifests in the collective self of a living society. The various expressions of culture have various relations to each other, many of them causal, but they are themselves expressions of the time-in-itself, which is why there is a shared atmosphere amongst the cultural products of a time. Just as the shape of a conscious woman's hands, the tone of her voice, her dress, the activities she is drawn to and the dreams she has are all somehow consistent, drawing from the same well of character, so the traits and characteristics *of* an era (or a *people*), its mathematics, its fashion, its philosophy, its attitude to nature, its art and its attitude to children, are all related *to* the era / people (and why only historians who are sensitive to such things really have anything to say). The common root of genius, manifesting as various artistic branches, also explains why ideas produced by great writers are gladly taken up by other great artists of the same era, who find the same ideas on the tips of their own tongues. It's also why many people can have together, in various degrees of coherence, the same original idea or feeling come to them, which they then recognise and enjoy in the cultural productions of the greats.

The nature of scenius is particularly evident in its music, which is impossible to consciously listen to or consciously create without feeling a connection between what it says and the time, the weather, the atmosphere of the collective and the union between the listeners' hearts and what is happening around them. On an immediate level, people make and enjoy quite different kinds of song when dancing on the beach after having made love to those which they make and listen to when sexually frustrated and surrounded by breeze-blocks. To move beyond the immediate situation into the 'atmosphere' of one's people, of humanity, or of conscious life itself, and then express it *collectively* in music—by singing and playing and dancing together—is the supreme art of man. Nothing we can do together is more beautiful.

§136.

Festival is a means of connecting the past, the present and the future into a transdimensional whole. Experience in a festival is simultaneously dissolved into unselfish collective consciousness and modified or shaped into a symbolic form that the self can take away and use. This is also evident in RITUALS, which are solemn festivals in miniature, a set sequence of words and actions, scattered throughout the year or the day, used to modify or affirm the represented self. The hunter dancing around the fire and calling on the goddess of the hunt to bless his arrows is neither calling on a factual personality, who will literally guide him to his prize, nor is he engaged in a fanciful exercise of wishful imagination; he is *actually* changing the world, the only world that he can ever know—that of representation—in order to fully participate in the living quality of it. Gods don't literally exist, but the spirit of the hunt, the aura of readiness for it, the character of focus and resilience during it, and the need to release tension and effort into the calm certainty of being guided by a higher-dimensional intelligence; these are all real qualities, which can and must come to man non-literally, or mythically, or, once again, he is left with nothing but method, which is all he *was* left with when mythic sensibilities departed from culture.

Now that we no longer consciously participate in representation, we find we have no need for festival (or rites of passage), while the festivals we do have are perfectly idiotic. New Year's Eve, The Olympics, Bonfire Night, The Oscars—what is the point? really? Even graduation ceremonies, weddings and funerals bring with them, at least to those paying attention, the powerful sense that something fundamental is missing here, that we are not being *nourished* by this feast. Modern rituals, where they exist, are even more absurd and grotesque, not to mention dependent on the mechanised system; taking a selfie in front of a famous landmark, watching a weekly soap opera, reading a morning paper with a cup of coffee. We cling to the granules of comfort they give us in order not to see how unbearably pathetic it all is.

§137.

Just as everyone participates in life, so everyone participates in festival; because everyone can potentially be, in the foundational unselfish sense, a GENIUS.

There are two fundamentally different meanings of the word genius. One, the original meaning, is as a synonym for unself. In this sense of the word there is no such thing as a 'genius' person, only a *host* to genius, a self sufficiently soft-edged to let the miraculous quality of life suffuse into it and sufficiently sharp-edged to slice away something beautiful from the represented world.

And so any self which is conscious can 'be' a genius. Such a self directly announces itself in its unselfish quality or presence, a subtle sense of power, or of innocence, or of inner beauty. This is the self-blended genius of love, the genius of madness, the genius of fools, the genius of woman and the genius of nature, burning permanently in the bellymind or, as if from nowhere, flaring up in a rare and glorious 'moment of genius', when an ordinary man unexpectedly flings himself above himself, all of which appear in great stories. It also sometimes emerges in the wild, when we let go of ourselves and meld for once with something not made by mind, or it can emerge when in the company of someone who is profoundly conscious, and a sense of enigmatic otherness and relief wells up inside, which we might call love.

There is a common thread that connects a two-year old girl playing innocently on the beach, a great comic actress brilliantly improvising, a sensitive and competent forty-year-old gardener, two people in love, a wise old man fully facing death, the pre-conquest San people of southern Africa, an ecstatic ritual of insane praise for the unspeakable, and Frédéric Chopin composing. They all have the quality of unself about them, which is why there is something brilliantly creative in an infant, and something infantile in the brilliantly creative; why there is profound wisdom in the belly of the female and profound femininity in the heart of the wise; why there is something of death in love, and something of love in death.

§138.

We commonly (and misleadingly) use the word 'genius' to describe individuals who strive to create, with the blade of a self sharpened to a razor's edge, the finest metaphorical-fractal-transdimensional-auric forms. These are our great artists and masters. They are geniuses in the same sense as a self-soft young lover, a self-blasted madman and a self-blended collective are, but they dedicate their entire, individual lives to the truth of consciousness, and so present to us not just *a* record of unself, but the finest one an individual is capable of. We can live with two-year olds, we can learn about pre-civilised people, we can touch true love, we can weep purifying tears of sorrow in a dying choir and we can know one or two people who live above themselves; and then, drawing the threads between them, we can understand genius. But it is in the work of the person we *traditionally* call genius (the *Romantic* genius) that, *at least today*, we discover what that means:

i.   Genius is synonymous with courage. It is impossible to know unself if self censors itself. Consciousness must be anarchically free to go where it wills; a freedom which the genius knows he must sacrifice his self-life for. There is nothing more courageous than letting go of what self *must have* in favour of what it cannot even *know* it doesn't have; a courage we love to see in myth, but which we very rarely encounter in 'the real world'. Occasionally, we speak with someone who takes such risks on a moment-to-moment scale and is prepared to look a fool knowing that, if a wrong step is made—an unnecessarily 'outrageous' comment, a cheeky dance that doesn't quite 'work'—he will be conscious enough to pick up on it, admit it and, *through being conscious*, be forgiven.

ii.   The genius reveals his innermost life by exposing his freedom. He has no need to selfishly *confess* the cowardice and depravity of his ego *to* the world (for confession, in the sense of displaying one's faults for entertainment and relief, *is* self, and as such is one of the lower forms of narrative art), but he is prepared to *risk* displaying the sewage in his heart, because he knows that psychological freedom can only lie in such risk, in the possibility that spontaneity will illuminate a terrifying or shameful unknown. Consciousness admires such risk in the actor, the musician and the essayist who expose their hearts, even when they fall, while ego *waits* for them to fall, ready to stick the boot in. Lesser lights—'creatives', with 'talent'—protect themselves from the inevitable blows of ego. They do not take such risks, they stick to where they know there is something to display that will be approved of. They are cowards and whores, and they will be forgotten.

The terrifying exposure of genius is why anxiety needles the second-rate artist. He is able to convince himself that he is showing a beautiful body to the world—because those with ugly bodies applaud it—but he can't escape the voice of his conscience whispering to him the reality, that he is exhibiting a corpse. The exposure of genius also explains why it is feared. Ego knows, in the company of someone who allows the light to go where it pleases, that it is in danger of being seen for what it is, which is why ordinary egoic people always find something *off* in the company great minds, something uncomfortable. In fact, because ego knows that it is unable to create that which the psychologically free can, it often finds it feels hatred for them, 'for no reason', just as it hates those who can unconditionally love, or who are truly innocent.

iii.   Genius, in its essence, has never done anything for the world of practical method, and it never will. Its ultimate uselessness is its stamp of authenticity, its perfection.* Although he cannot be immune to material needs, the genius does not, first of all, work to *get* anything or to materially benefit himself or anyone else. He *has* to work, to write or to sing, or the only thing he values in his heart will die, and he *has* to present his work to the world, even though he knows that the world will not see it for what it is; for if the nice and necessary people of the world could see genius for what it is, they would *instantly* set about striving to create it themselves, and not squandering their lives in nice and necessary pursuits.

---

* Arthur Schopenhauer, *The World as Will and Representation*

Those who love and seek to express their love, simply or super-excellently, have been ignored, ridiculed and repressed since the beginning of the world; because they do nothing *for* the world. Campaigns against 'geniusism' aren't quite as popular as those against racism though, or homophobia. The prejudice can't even be conceived of, let alone dealt with.

iv.   Unselfish genius, being somehow "outside" the boundary of facticity and causality, reaches us as *timeless*. This manifests in symbols which are, in their unselfish essence, both intimately recognisable, yet genuinely enigmatic, representing primal but perennial realities long buried in the life of our species. We don't have to learn to be afraid of snakes, nor do we have to learn to be mesmerised by paradox, fractality and intimations of eternity in images of strange, characterful faces, or serene, full bodied women dancing with skeletons, or red rooms and dwarves, or anything else the genius pulls up from beyond the depths of his species-memory.

The timelessness of genius explains its profound *indifference* to ordinary pleasures and values. The self which once sustained such things has left the cinema. It has found something infinitely more valuable than the represented world, and the ordinary fears and desires which play over its surface, which is why he seems aloof or insensitive to those attached to such fears and desires. It is also how he is able to bring qualities to light that nobody ever could have imagined existing and yet, at the same time, which are so *recognisable*, so 'of course it is so', for he sees the thing-in-itself hidden in plain view. The man of talent can hit a target nobody else can hit, but the man of genius can hit one that nobody can even *see*,[*] which, again, is why the genius is so often ignored or resented by the people around him, as 'the seen' is given by the culture, by the coordinates of the time which ordinary egos are forced to cling to, but which the genius sees through, and beyond. This is what makes the genius, in *this* world, an OUTSIDER.[†]

v.   The timelessness of genius also explains a fundamental quality, or capacity, that sets it apart from talent; *timing*. The

[*] Ibid.
[†] Colin Wilson, *The Outsider*

genius feels out the whole of a timeless 4D object, thelemical-ly 'building' it from a series of actions in time. This is most evident in music, dance and speech, where we recognise the fractal balance of the art, through timing, or rhythm, although a large number of skilled crafts also operate through embodying natural rhythms which are, in themselves, as beautiful as the products which arise from them. This is why we love to watch great chefs, tailors and potters at work. It's not what you know, it's when you know it.

vi.   The timelessness of genius also explains why it endures beyond its time; in fact why it takes so much time for others to see genius *as* genius. Each step down from the originating void is a copy, then a copy of a copy, then a copy of a copy of a copy, each more palatable to the time, until you reach the Hollywood blockbuster, the stadium-rock pop-band, the Booker Prize winner. This is why the most popular artistic forms are usually the most degraded, and why the genius only requires (and in fact can only really expect) the next step down to recognise him. By the time everyone does, he's long dead.

Mass appreciation of genius is often possible with music, because there is nothing verbal in music, and with certain kinds of painting, poem and myth, which slip their truths through the back door so to speak. The 'message' of music is pure vibe, or pure atmosphere, while that of great myth and portrait-painting is, in an inherently non-threatening sense, beyond the boundaries of the literal self; although even superb music and myth are almost always missed by those welded to the egoic form of their society or sub-society. Bach, Beethoven and Mozart all had problems being recognised by their time, fell out of fashion and were derided for it, as did William Shakespeare, William Blake, D.H. Lawrence and many others.

vii.   The timelessness of genius is not in the endlessness of time, but in the absence of it; a cessation of the mental-emotional momentum that keeps alive the previous moment and the next one. This is why deep experience of unselfish art (again, particularly in festival), like deep experience of love, returns us to a world made new, because we are seeing what is before us for the first time, unfiltered by what we know of it or feel about it. Immersion in mediocre art or in one of the many, many substitutes for love, leaves us instead with the dreary sense that everything is as it always was.

viii.   It is impossible to know and express the thing-in-itself of consciousness, or genius, without knowing and expressing the thing-in-itself of the context, or scenius, which is as inimitable as that of the person. Logically, it should be possible to produce an Inuit ivory carving, an Etruscan tomb painting, a Gothic church, a Victorian light opera, or a nineteen-seventies funk epic. Actually it is *completely* impossible, for each art form rises from the time, flourishes for a moment in time, and then dies, never to be seen again. So unique is each style or genre, there can hardly be said to *be* a single category of 'art' that they belong to. It is certainly futile to talk of how they are formally connected, to tell a nice, neat 'story of art'. That said, an enigmatic panjective thread *does* run through all of the truly beautiful creations of mankind, which we can, with sufficient poise, and perhaps a little learning, dip into when we read the Ramayana or stand in Winchester Cathedral.

Scenius begins with the mood of the room, the taste of the particular now. Beyond that, on a wider level, the greatest art is informed by the culture, by the genre of the time, its quality and cadence, and by the state of society, which rarely features in second-rate novels, poems, films and so on, unless as graceless realism. It is notable, for example, that worldly *power* is as rare in art as it is in psychology. Not that addressing it is a necessary precondition for creating great art, but that class, wealth and the secret world of power-relations play a significant role in every civilised context, and therefore in scenius, which is conspicuously absent in the second-rate art of those *with* power; the professional and owning classes.

Beyond the particular situation and society of the artist lies the context of humanity and beyond that, reality itself, which the greatest of artists (and the loveliest of festivals) give voice to. This is why they sometimes declare that their work is for humanity, or even for the glory of God, or, even if they don't, we get the powerful sense that, despite the mystifying particularities of an artistic or spiritual message, which is always directed to the people of the time, it is in some profound sense universal; although 'universal' does not mean 'for everyone' — in fact timeless artistic universality only ever applies to a numerically tiny proportion of people — and it certainly does not mean 'improving the world' — the pathetic, futile, largely socialist project of attempting to kindle a more enlightened state in the immense, sodden, mass of man — rather, the universal is the noble ideal, or [*non*-abstract] principle of *mankind*, the 4D tree of humanity that the genius, like the celebrant of scenius, feels out, underneath the character of the world.

ix.   At the heart of genius is sensitivity, or femininity if you will. Sensitivity to the fractal majesty of nature, to the inner pulses of the human heart, to the mood of the room, to an animal, or tree, or unique, lovely thing in front of you, without any preconceived idea as to what it is, just a selfless bond. Another word for this sensitivity, which can only be achieved by surrendering the insensitive self, inured to the context by cliche, is love. Not that those we call geniuses are necessarily paragons of fellow-feeling — many have been afraid of love, slaves to manic insensitivity or, as they aged, slowly buried under layers of self — but that such love is at the heart of their genius. As Mozart wrote, 'Neither a lofty degree of intelligence, nor imagination, nor both together go into the making of genius. Love, love, love; that is the soul of genius'.* It is love we hear in the best of his music, and that of all the greats; profound, sacred and serious love, or pretty, profane and playful love; and the reason we cannot create such lovely things, is because we do not love enough. Not just each other, but nature, the good things around us, the ineffable and the unconsidered; the bricks, the hot water, the way people say the word 'hello', the posture of the people on the number 16 to Purley, the precise plummy taste of *this* plum, the scent of a lover's thigh and, around any thing, the all-containing yet borderless frame; the present-moment, the never-to-be-repeated

---

* Entry in Mozart's souvenir album. Quoted in Maynard Solomon, *Mozart: A Life*

flavour of the situation. It is true that we have not acquired the mind-bending technique of the masters, acquired from decades of dedication, but the reason we did not try, and the reason we do not wish to invite genius into the bridle chamber even now, is because we do not say *yes* to what is before us.

x.   Although the source and soul of genius reaches beyond self, it manifests as the unique taste-matrix of the individual self. Generally speaking, all conscious selves can appreciate, say, quality music, be it baroque, disco, blues, glam or jazz, or quality comedy, be it slapstick, bawdy, schadenfreude, verbal wit or surreal absurdity, just as they can appreciate fresh, home-cooked Indian, Chinese, Japanese or Mexican cuisine; while at the same being attracted to their particular swells and sensitivities, which evolve over time and place.

Although the genius makes the finest of distinctions in his craft—between this and that tone-shade, between too much, too little and just right—in the means by which he brings his genius to the world, he makes no such distinction in the quality that animates it. Education and recreation are one, seriousness and leisure, labour and levity, religion and play. However hard he works to manifest his art in form—and the artistic genius works his bollocks off—he remains grounded in the universal art of living, in which every moment is a cause to experience and to express the unnameable.

§139.

We call the spontaneous freedom of the artist's and crafts-man's consciousness—which freely crosses markers, thresh-olds and boundaries, freely wanders through the swells and stunts of self, freely acts, feels, thinks and perceives, without egoic constriction—PLAY, the same free spirit that motivates the splendid rituals of our pre-civilised forebears. This quality of playfulness, in great art and craft, alternates with the qual-ity of super-intense SERIOUSNESS. Because both are qualities, they can no more be described literally than masculinity and femininity can; which is why we require art.

In music, seriousness is expressed in minor keys, and playfulness in major keys. In painting, seriousness comes to us as images of the sublime—that which threatens the self (desolate spaces, storms, deadly animals) and playfulness as images of the beautiful—that which nourishes the self (woodlands, glorious sunrises, pretty flowers). In myth, seriousness is represented in tragedy, and playfulness in comedy. Naturally though, great art is not either-or, but both-and, the tension between the two creating the paradoxical sense of mystery that we detect in romance with a sense of the tragic and horror with a sense of the farce. Non-Western and sacred music, not to mention many enigmatic hits of modern times, often inhabit an atmosphere that is neither gay nor sombre. Likewise, the greatest comedians always have something tragic about them, and the most profoundly dark thinkers have, at the depth of their purest sentiments, 'un peu de testicule'.* Children also, in their egoless innocence, are capable of almost as much seriousness as silliness. Although the composition and quality of such 'poles of levity' shifts over time (towards seriousness) and although it is different from one gender to another (men are more serious) and one culture and person to another, it is always true that, being qualitative, the depth of seriousness one is capable of is, if not equal to, at least consonant with, the depth of playfulness, and vice versa, which is why those with a shallow sense of humour have an equally shallow sense of sadness, and vice versa.

The essential unity of playfulness and seriousness is particularly evident in the literary poles of comedy and horror, which are formally similar, sometimes identical. A slight tweak of context, mood music and delivery turns the funniest sketch instantly into an horrendously disturbing nightmare, and vice versa. Imagine, say, Charlie Chaplin repeatedly getting hit in the head to a major-key piano piece, then imagine Jack Nicholson (c. 1978) getting beaten up in precisely the same way to sombre music, or imagine Monty Python played at half-speed with backwards music. With great horror we are feeling the warped world-upside down as a threat to ego, which we must unselfishly rise to the challenge of, overcoming the

---

* Denis Diderot, *Letter to Étienne Noël Damilaville*

illusory fear. With great comedy we are seeing it as a friend of unself, which we laughingly surrender to. Switch perspectives and suddenly the joke isn't very funny any more.

§ 140.

Low quality art is either objectivist or subjectivist, because reality, to the self, is either objective or subjective. The more a society takes reality to be objective, and therefore rationally knowable, the more artists assume their function is to accurately (or 'realistically') represent what is 'out there'. The more a society takes reality to be subjective, the more artists assume their task is to 'imaginatively' express themselves. In the first case, 'artistic truth' is largely a measure of how well the artist has 'captured' the world of space and time. In the second case, fidelity is irrelevant; either I like it or 'agree' with it (for reasons I need not, perhaps cannot, express), or I don't, and that's all there is to it; there is no question of my enjoyment of a work of art being related to anything 'real' or 'true'.

Objectivism and subjectivism in art are a consequence of having no character, a common problem in the art world. Where there is no consciousness, there is nothing but self; tricks and techniques employed to reach—which mostly means manipulate—other selves (in this case, the audience). Without consciousness, the artist is incapable of pure contemplation, and so has nothing to say. He therefore turns to his self for material—his subjective feelings, fears, desires, theories and imaginative thoughts (subjectivism, or hollow art), or his objective perceptions and techniques (objectivism, or hollow craft). Both of these poles are therefore, ultimately, opposames. Extreme 'objective' realism and extreme 'subjective' imagination appear to be radically different, but they both occur in and as the represented, representing self, and so both, like science and religion, are just as unreal, empty and tediously predictable as each other.

While it may seem that art has 'progressed' from Mesopotamian frescoes to postmodern installations, this is at best an illusion, at worst the opposite of what has actually

happened. There have been important technical develop-
ments, and art always expresses and addresses itself to the
unique context or milieu of the artist, but truth in art, as
in philosophy, does not get or go anywhere—because it has
nothing to do with objective facticity and causality, or with
subjective thought and emotion. Artistic truth is neither objective nor subjective—it is panjective.

§141.

PANJECTIVIST (or simply 'great') ART takes its legitimacy from,
first of all, consciousness, and secondly, from the conscious
self-in-the-world, which is to say both from the context, which
all great artists honour, and from organic tradition, which all
great artists study and master. Panjective creations are entirely
unique, but they have common features:

i.   The basic experiential effect of great art is stillness.
Where second-rate art, unable to touch the centre of the self,
compensates with tricks and techniques to *move* it, great art
silences emotion, discursive thought and concentrated self-led
perception and action, leaving a taste of eternity. This is why,
when we leave the cinema after a great film, or stop reading a
masterpiece, or stroll off into the forest after a mind-cracking
choral groove, everything around us seems that much *more*;
because the *less* of the self has faded. As Gurdjieff memorably
replied, when asked what the difference is between unconsciousness and consciousness; 'everything more vivid'.*

ii.   The greatest artistic experiences elicit astonishment,
perplexity and delighted confusion, the kind that real mystery
evokes. These declare more intelligence to the world than
any solution to such mystery can ever provide, not because
mystery is betrayed by explanation—we clearly need to know
why things are as they are—but because explanations are a
completely different kind of experience to astonishment; as
different as recognising a photograph of the sea is to swimming
in it. The man who presents answers is to be respected, but if

---

* Quoted in William Patrick Patterson, *Struggle of the Magicians*

his answers are not embedded in a wider context of laughing bafflement, he is not to be trusted.

iii.   With the *bona fide* work of genius we sense that there is no way, ever, we could get anywhere *near* to creating such a masterpiece. With the art of the merely talented we feel that, if we put in the hours, we could produce *something* like it. It tastes of the essentially knowable, just as the artist does. Not so with The Tale of the Princess Kaguya, St. Matthew Passion, The Brothers Karamazov or the sleight-of-hand of Ricky Jay. Even the genius *himself*, looking back on the heights of his creative odyssey, wonders how he ever could have scaled them. The vast technique of great art is welded to, and the unself-ish sacrifice of the artist's self is open to, the perfect selfless individuality of the artist's life in the *moment* of creation. I recognise this individuality as me, but not as mine.

iv.   With great works we sometimes feel some degree of shame, the sense that here is a man or woman that is living as I should have, saying things which I too could have pulled from my own soil, were it not so grievously barren. The silent clench of anguish, when he reads the words of the masters, is because the average man knows that he has betrayed his own genius. He could have lived as they did, touched eternity and brought it down to the body of the earth. But no.

v.   The finest art is perfectly self-contained; not in the sense that it doesn't lead from or onto other works, but that it is not really *telling* us anything. The consciousness and context "behind" the art is not causing it, there is no *message* which I can *take away* from it, but a quality, impossibly "melded" to it, which takes *me* away, from my self. Great art is merely showing us itself, and that self *is* consciousness. This is why great artists are irritated by questions about what their work 'means'. If I could sum up the meaning in a few words to you, do you think I would have gone to the trouble to devote my entire life to expressing it in the work you are now asking me to betray with a capsule summary?

Panjective works of art are their own 'proof' that the miracle of existence is as the artist presents it; neither objective nor subjective. Just as a gigantic oak 'proves' the indescribable beauty and intelligence of nature, so the songs of The Beatles and The Velvet Underground, the art of Mark Rothko and Vincent Van Gogh, the novels of Leo Tolstoy and Fyodor Dostoevsky, the cello sonatas of J.S. Bach and the late violin quartets of Beethoven, the great tragedies of Shakespeare and Thomas Hardy, the films of Akira Kurosawa and Stanley Kubrick, the Gospels and the Tao Te Ching; all speak *for* that which they speak *of*.

§142.

Genius comes to ego as existential threat. As Goethe wrote, 'we prefer to be surrounded by mediocrity because it leaves us in peace'.* It flatters us. It is easily digestible. It is, unlike genius—which attacks us, insults us, unsettles us—*painless*. The total psychological exposure of genius, its freedom of consciousness, disregard for fashionable attitudes, worldly uselessness, immersion in unselfish eternity, acceptance of the context, and unconditional love are all to be resisted, with a predictable palette of responses.

First of all, just as ego continually endeavours to bring love down to its level (it's a subjective myth, an objective chemical, an intriguing meme), so it never stops trying to degrade genius; by reducing it to technique (The Beatles were 'really' clever plagiarists), by 'explaining' it in crude evolutionary terms (Shakespeare was 'really' just trying to get laid), or as a biochemical side-effect (Van Gogh was 'really' bipolar), or by 'humanising' the transcendent character of genius (Bach was 'really' a beery brawler), or by trivialising it as 'mere' imagination (the gospels are 'nice stories' about a guy who didn't really exist). Scenius is similarly disposed of (mammalian group-bonding, mass psychosis, self-satisfaction, etc.).

The most common means by which ego protects itself against genius, however, is in celebrating modesty and exalting talent. In order to avoid having to be reminded of

---

* Johann Wolfgang Von Goethe, *Maxims and Reflections*

what is absent from its life, and to justify its own second-rate creations, ego holds to the idea that greatness never declares itself, that the wise do not know they are wise. It is true that, essentially, genius is unselfconscious, but it is impossible to reach the pinnacle of human expression without doing so knowingly, which is why all great artists and teachers either frankly announce their genius, or, in their private correspondence, show that they are fully aware of it. This certainty irritates second-rate minds, because they are always unsure of themselves, which is why mediocrity demands that greatness slip in modestly and leave unnoticed by the tradesman's exit. Alternatively, it puts uniqueness on a distant pedestal labelled 'talent', which of course 'I' do not have.

The word talent is used by most people to dispose of something which they do not understand. They vaguely situate it in the machinery of the self, a kind of technical capacity,* which little old me, unlucky that I am, was not born with. It is *they*, the *special* and *talented* ones, who are capable of greatness. That genius *always* repudiates this 'talent', that the great man shows that the conscious essence of genius is available to anyone who can see, that he continually points out that the manifest technique of mastery is available to anyone who works hard enough, and that genius makes us *forget* talent (and, in fact, when genius departs the bedchamber, man is left holding the garment, called talent, where she used to be); none of this is of interest to the average man.

§ 143.

The great panjective artist and craftsman uses his unfocused senses to integrate an immense range of experience into focal judgements. He calls on a combination of noetic-knowledge, thelemic-skill, somatic-discernment and visceral-sensibility to judge what is before him. This is his taste; a series of minute ['end of the blind man's stick'] judgements, originating *from* a fully incarnate sensitivity to the context, used to fit the piece of music, or suit, or story, or theatrical judgement, or piece of furniture, *to* the context.

---

* Leo Tolstoy, *Anna Karenina*

Taste however, which comes through the subjective and objective elements of self, does not provide the artist with insight into quality, for it is an "effect" of consciousness. Subjective feelings and thoughts, like objective perceptions and actions—the so-called inner form and the so-called outer form—have a common origin. It is only by looking *through* the form of a thing, *to* that common origin, that consciousness can freely operate in it. What we understand as 'natural' or 'graceful' timing and tempo, or a 'creative flow' of new ideas, is disrupted by excessive focus on form, which cuts consciousness off from the context.

This is why when the artist is *stuck* he must give up what he knows—put everything aside, or delete everything, or go and gaze at the ocean—in order to feel out living quality; where he ought to go, how he ought to move. This is the *care* of the great artist or master—his dedication to the source of self before him, and a desire to reach it and do justice to it—and his *humility*—the continual self-mortification required to do so. Carelessness and self-absorption are impossible in any kind of genuine creative work. Great artists and superb craftsmen might appear to be slapdash or arrogant, but these surface forms vanish the moment they set about their work.*

Self-soft sensitivity to unself is the means by which interiority, the subject of art, is accessed, the means by which I can leap the fence and cross empathy's membrane into what is. Just as it is only through my sensitivity to the presence of a football, say, that I can connect sweetly with it, so it is only through my sensitivity to sound, that I can *participate* in its meaning, rather than merely assess or measure it, or physically access it. Similarly, it is only through my sensitivity to *you* that I can take part in your situation, judge your actions from *your* point of view. This might not lead to any kind of Christian forgiveness—indeed many times taking another's part is an extremely unpleasant experience, like suddenly being locked into a badly fitting suit of armour—but it does lead to discernment, understanding, and through that, at least *some* measure of forgiveness, all of which form the essence of characterisation in great stories.

---

* Robert M. Pirsig, *Zen and the Art of Motorcycle Maintenance*

We call sensitivity to *what is* 'being with it', 'being in the zone', 'mojo' and so on. In this state of *release*, there is no subject or object, no looking *for* things, ideas, feelings and actions; just looking, or just being, so that whatever things, ideas, feelings and actions are required will emerge (whereupon they can be *clenched* into form). Such a state of faith borders on the mystical, which is why great mystics have something of the artist about them, and great artists have something of the mystic about them; they both know they must surrender to an enigmatic nothingness in order to bring up the solution, or idea, or gesture they need. Needless to say, the low-quality artist or scientist—the subjectivist and the objectivist—knows absolutely nothing of all this, and scoffs at the suggestion of it.

§ 144.

SUBJECTIVISM, also known as modernism, POSTMODERNISM and relativism, is the reduction of consciousness and context to a system of signs and symbols with, first of all, no objective referent. Objective truth, tradition, craft, facticity and causality are rejected in favour of what the self likes or wants. This means that subjectivism is only possible in character work such as music, film, literature and fine art. Technical work has an objective element and so *must* be useful, which is why you don't see subjectivist trousers (made of rice paper, perhaps, with one leg), or relativist handbags (cemented to the floor), or postmodern restaurants (selling postcards of food).

Because the likes and wants of subjective art are not "backed" by any kind of conscious reality, there is no felt quality to them; but neither is there any way of demonstrating that quality is lacking, which is the entire point. A novel about writing a novel about writing a novel, a mile long copper rod in an art gallery, and a three-hour film about a woman who eats a pie are all immune to criticism. When objectivity is rejected and consciousness is conflated with whatever I happen to feel like writing a story about, or exhibiting, or putting onto celluloid, there is no possible way to articulate outrage except to grunt in disgust, as many people do.

The consequence of a work of art that says nothing at all is that we have to be *told* what the artist intends. The work cannot 'convey just itself', because itself is excrement, so it must be sprinkled with the glitter of advertising or boxed up with verbose explanations. This is why language is of inordinate importance to postmodern artists and theorists. What they create is not to be looked at, but to be trafficked by the tradesmen who comprise the art world who must add value to it through the production of deep-seeming verbiage.

Artists once expected to get very little material benefit from their work. You don't need to be cold and hungry to make great art—poverty is almost as much a barrier to creativity as wealth—but anyone who knows quality knows that there is small chance he will be materially rewarded for it, or least for a long time. Now, anyone going into art in order to serve art, or truth, or humanity, is hopelessly behind the times and anyone doing an art degree without the expectation of making it big is a fool. Being totally subservient to the established order, unable to do anything with any degree of expertise, and either completely ignorant of artistic truth or openly disdainful of it; these are all *virtues* in the modern art world.

The virtues of the modern artist are complemented by the virtues of modern art, the criteria that any novel, painting or film must meet if it is to get five star reviews in the trendies and a look-in for a big prize or fat commission. These are:

i.   IRONY—the *sine qua non* of modern art. Without the modern artist's religious commitment to the idea that 'It's not supposed to be taken seriously', (itself based on the foundational philosophy of extreme relativism—that quality does not really exist) his or her total lack of skill, or sensitivity, or even dignity, would be exposed to ridicule.

ii.   ARBITRARINESS (known to the Romantics as 'fancy') is *mere* imagination, the hollow, associative play of abstract images and ideas, the inferior shadow of *creative* imagination. Just as the irrelevance of third-rate art is in its isolation from the context, so its arbitrariness is through being cut off from consciousness, leading to mad, surreal strangeness with no felt reality "behind" it, or to symbols with conventional or cliched referents, or to completely arbitrary metaphors in which the pleasure of an *actual* connection between two remote modes is replaced by the pseudo-pleasure of one selfish, solipsistic feeling validated by another.

iii.   FORMALITY, or lack of practical function. It is absolutely forbidden for postmodern art to have any kind of use (unless it's ironic). A chair you can comfortably sit on? Fail. A teacup cut in half? Pass. A picture that would add serenity to your bedroom? Fail. A close-up of a bleeding vagina, ideally your own (or perhaps Tilda Swinton's)? Pass with merit.

The formality of subjectivism explains its tendency to low technical quality; or rather, cack-handedness, laziness and isolation from the meaning and beauty of nature and culture tends to excuse itself with subjectivism. No contact with consciousness and context means no felt experience of quality, therefore no felt care for one's productions, therefore no desire to master one's tools, therefore an appeal to a 'philosophy' which justifies third-rate paintings, clumsy plotting, half-dimensional characters and a knowledge of music which barely extends beyond three chords.

iv.   TITILLATION is the one component of modern art that is part of a tradition—that of pornography. The naked women and sumptuous feasts of yore have now become gusts of strawberry-smelling air, high-tec blobs of latex that feel oooh, slightly odd to the touch and piercing screams from vents in the floor that make you feel interestingly sick; although these feelings, like all feelings stimulated by pomo-titillation, are somatic phenomena. The vast mass of armoured selves that plod through art-galleries aren't able to, properly speaking, feel anything, so a surprising squelchy sensation underfoot is a welcome reminder that they are still alive.

v.   BLEAKNESS; a commitment to reflect the repellent brutalism of the modern world through an absence of fractality or natural atmosphere. Bleakness is popular in the pseudo-art of photography, and in trendy middle-class 'art' films, where it appears as long, long, long silent takes in which nothing happens, but oh the cinematography.

vi.   IRRELEVANCE, intimately connected to extreme formality, is the need for all modern art to have no meaningful bearing whatsoever on what is actually happening in the world, or to the felt character of the moment. Formality and irrelevance can be seen as the self's appropriation of uselessness; there is no objective point, but neither is there the slightest conscious reality to it; no genius or scenius.

Absence of scenius doesn't just mean that modern and postmodern works of art all seem or feel the same, but that the artists themselves all look and sound the same. Listen to an interview with a famous painter, sculptor or architect today and you'll be struck by how banal they all look and sound; the same characterless faces mouthing the same characterless platitudes. They look like management; because they are.

§ 145.

The opposite pole in art to subjectivism is OBJECTIVISM, or technique without consciousness or context. Objectivism in technical work is the norm, as absence of quality, being secondary anyway, is not felt so acutely; we prefer antiques to flatpack furniture, home-cooked cuisine to chain-restaurant food and tailor-made suits to off-the-peg jeans, but we can and do live without them. Objectivism in character work is also the norm, but a big-budget Hollywood hit, a best-selling novel, a number-one album, or any other technically competent artistic trash feels, at least to someone with taste, like a migraine.

In the fine arts, objectivism, or realism, is (again, unless somehow ironic) hopelessly gauche. Replicating 'material reality' precisely (extra points if the medium is rabbit droppings, Monster Munch or Queen Victoria's eyebrow hairs, or if it provokes the response 'oh my God, that must have taken *ages* to do!') is fine for the masses, but a risky tactic for the ambitious artist, because it smacks of the measurable and the objective, and so is unlikely to win you a Turner Prize or a round of applause from the New York Times.

Objectivism, being essentially uncreative and empty, has a tendency to *embellish*, to over-emphasise in an attempt to seem more committed, passionate or profound, with the advertisement we call 'style'. This is common amongst artists whose creative flame has been extinguished by fame. Older musicians, very often, when covering their own earlier masterpieces, add emphatic decoration and melisma.

Another consequence of objectivism is a tendency towards cliche and copy. Although originality must, to some extent, build its caddis-case from the material of what came before it—the various influences and echoes which resentful egos seize on as evidence of non-existent 'plagiarism'—its "source", ultimately, is that of the self; unself. This is why it strikes the self as original, fresh, familiar yet enigmatic, shining with a mix of the unique character of the creator and the unique character of the life around him. Substandard artists are unable to get beyond their selves, and so, unable to get "underneath" their influences, they fill their work with the lightly modified ideas, styles, melodies and insights of their greater forebears—sometimes not even greater, very often from substandard antecedents and contemporaries. This is true plagiarism; an essential lack of meaningful content, artistic truth or genuine insight. In their place, second-rate creators present the life of others; teevee shows, books, films, tweets, newspaper articles and the minds of those around them, also second-hand, filtered through their own thin, denatured experience, then mashed up into the bland pabulum we call 'culture', all of which greets ego, which can *only* recognise cliche and copy, as 'quality'.

§146.

Because subjective and objective anti-art are without any kind of meaningful quality, they must use substitute *effects* in order to gain approval, and, therefore, success. These substitutes are *entirely* directed towards satisfying and stimulating self; presentations of sex (either suggested or explicit), propagation ('Ahh, cute!'), consumption (food, technology, luxury), power ('ooh, how the other half live!'), violence and groupthink bonding ('Up the Arsenal!' '#metoo!' *'Dulce et decorum est pro patria mori'*), physical invulnerability (burglar alarms, insurance, surgical masks), comfort (soft fabrics, heated blankets) and sensory titillation; all compensate for lack of quality. Self is not stilled by the experience, but *moved* by it.* Ego then registers the experience as 'good', as 'quality', while consciousness experiences it for what it is; PORNOGRAPHY.

Pornography is the cliched *form* of addiction. As with all addiction, it offers one predictable experience, repeated with minor variations, over and over again, in order to produce a *quantitative* high. This desensitises the self, which is then forced to experience more and more extreme highs—weirder sex, sweeter chocolate, faster cuts, greater factual realism and so on. The egoic urge for *more* is incompatible with the selfless love of *better*—of a greater range and depth of experience— which strikes the self-informed-self as boring or annoying. This is why those addicted to aural and visual junk complain that great music and myth 'sound the same', while those who love great art make the *same* complaint of porn. 'The same' for the former means quantitatively indistinguishable while for the latter it means impossible to qualitatively tell apart.

Just as we can speak of cliched conversation, pathognomy, nutrition and technology, so we can speak of pornographic conversation, pathognomy, nutrition and technology—but the word 'pornography' is ill-suited to such somatic-thelemic forms. Porn, here, is noetic-visceral addiction to quantitatively addictive ideas and feelings; to exciting violence (including an overdose of swearing), nostalgia ('ooh! I remember those!'), curiosity (whodunnit?), empty surrealism (suddenly, and for no reason, a marmot starts playing cards), aggressive rhythms (grime, ragga, thrash), sentimental or self-exciting melodies (the pop hit, the cheesy ballad), mawkishly reassuring endings ('Yes, the holocaust was terrible, but, ahh, at least our wondrous hero was victorious.'), group-bonding comedy ('ha-ha-ha

---

* James Joyce, *Portrait of the Artist as a Young Man*

look at *that* guy!'), empty horror (exciting gore, cheap jumps) and so on and so forth. All stimulate the mono-compulsive mental-emotional personality.

The system completely depends on such stimulation. It is built on the egoic fear and desire of the hollow outer self, which—because a society of non-addicted lovers of quality is ungovernable—it must *continually*, pornographically, stimulate. In HUXLEYAN systems subjectivist porn predominates, in ORWELLIAN systems,* objectivist porn, although, in the perfect system, both complement each other in much the same way that postmodernism and scientism do, or sadism and masochism, neither capable of experiencing, and therefore expressing or considering, reality.

§ 147.

We metaphorically, or artistically, consider manifest reality, or the UNIVERSE, as a self. It does not feel, think, will or perceive, certainly not as human selves do, but it contains objectively, scientifically, observable soma (MATTER) and thelema (ENERGY) and subjectively, unscientifically, 'subservable' viscera (PSYCHE; subtle atmosphere or vibe) and 'proto-conceptual' nous (or TECHNE; that within reality which is amenable to thought, is tool-like and creates, or appears to create, conceivable order, complexity, and, finally, intelligence).

We have a word for the 'proto-self' of the universe; we call it NATURE. Nature is not merely the objective things and outer activities of the non-human world, but its quality and principle, neither of which can be literally defined. We can say that the principle of nature tends towards qualities such as cooperation, balance, sensitivity and fractality—which is why when we say someone is behaving 'naturally' we normally mean that she is somehow benefiting her fellow creatures, is in tune with her environment or is expressing subtle qualities of intelligence, presence and beauty; and why, conversely, when we say someone is behaving 'unnaturally' we normally mean that he is rigidly self-serving, closed off from the context, hyper-ordered or a total, ugly mess.

---

* See *33 Myths of the System*

Ultimately though, the meaning of the word 'nature' is enigmatic, because what self can know or experience of nature represents unself, the thing-in-itself. This is why all of the parts of nature work so astonishingly well together. Not because they have *evolved* to harmonise with each other. Natural forms *do* evolve, of course, just as 3D life-forms learn or change through time; but the harmony of nature "originates" in the 4D whole of life-in-itself, appearing in self as time and space. I don't need to learn about nature to 'know' it, for I *am* it. The thing-in-itself that I am is the same thing-in-itself that nature is. Similarly, I don't need to control nature to benefit from it, just guide it here and there to bring its apples within reach. Only ego needs to control nature, because only ego feels unnatural.

§148.

The main reason people—particularly abstract philosophers and scientists—rarely use the word 'natural' to refer to the actual principle of nature, is that very few people are acquainted with it. This is why the parts of their lives do not harmonise; why they are as disordered and mutually antagonistic as the parts of an unnatural society, and require the same despotic control to keep together. Humans now have very little contact with nature-in-itself, including with their own natural bodies, and so, although they may enjoy walks on the beach, study insects, or hike the Hindu Kush, they can only experience the *form* of nature through them, which is why the metaphors they choose for nature are formal—not to mention grim, superficial or sentimental—and why they cannot recognise the glory of natural harmony and grace in great art, any more than they could recognise Sanskrit dropped into a pop song. Nature, for those living in the social machine, is *also* a machine, a war in which only the fittest survive, a *re*-source; when, in reality, it is an organism, an experience of unending peace, a *source*. Nature only appears as a cross between a battleground and a warehouse when it is sliced up by the mind into useful things and violent moments.

Formally, it seems that, over time, the natural universe becomes more ordered, more complex and, finally, more intelligent; which means more freedom—to see, think, move and feel—which, in turn, entails greater subtlety and sensitivity. In reality, however, in the thing-in-itself, there is no 'becoming', for causality and facticity are a function of representation. This is how it appears to us that life has, through the process called 'natural selection', evolved in time; as indeed it has, but only in the representation our selves present to us. The reality of the thing-in-itself—of the context "beyond" the object, and its power to epigenetically affect evolution—and of consciousness "behind" the subject, and the impossibility of it being caused by non-consciousness—vanishes in the cinema screen that self presents to us of reality, leaving a handful of genes (around 30,000 in the human body; fewer than a rice plant, which has between 40 and 60,000) which somehow tell 37,000,000,000,000,000 cells what to turn into and where to go to fulfil their function. Nobody really knows how this happens, for the simple reason that it doesn't happen; it's just all we can seem to see that happens.

When scientists study brains, and genes, and dinosaur bones, and redshift, they think they are looking into the past *of* reality, whereas, *in* reality, they are looking into the past of our shared *representation* of reality. This representation is not an illusion any more than Flatland is; it *is* real and it "*represents*" something that is real—only a solipsist denies this—but it is not reality-in-itself, nor can it be, and so it is impotent to explain how representation came to be, or, ultimately, how it operates. This is the function of MYTH.

§ 149.

One of the first meaningful questions human beings ask is 'Where did I come from before I was born?' Conscious children sometimes ask adults this, often around the same time they ask 'where will I go after I die?', although they soon stop asking, because intelligent answers are not forthcoming. Prior to the rise of science, all cultures of the world answered this question in the same way, mythologically. Man—and particularly woman—has always understood that unself, that which can be said to be the cause of existence, is literally unthinkable. No causal relation to representation is possible, and so the story of how unself "gave birth" to the universe, or to the self, can only be told non-literally, through the mythic personification of quality. Myth directly expresses consciousness and its manifestation as a living, growing and dying self, which is why conscious selves love truthful myths and stories.

The locus of myth appears to be in the subjective self, in the mind and emotions, not in anything which 'really' exists out there, in the world. But the world comes to us in and as the self. That we call 'world' objective and 'self' subjective is more than just convention, or there would be no difference between dreaming and wakefulness, but *both* subjectivity *and* objectivity ultimately occur as representation. The colour blue, for example, while being a literal, formal, perceptive experience, denoted as scientific knowledge, contains just as much non-literal, informal, affective experience, connoted as artistic expression. The literal, *quantitative* colour blue and its *qualities* of vastness, serenity, coldness and so on are ultimately as inseparable as objectivity and subjectivity are. Thus, when we tell ourselves stories about dragons or conduct rituals of exorcism or immerse ourselves in hymns to the glory of God, we are not, as literalist scientists like to believe (and *love* to ridicule), attempting to change the facts of the objective world, but are *actually* changing our experience of its quality.

Although such myths are not to be taken literally, no myth on earth prior to those of modern times, has ever warned the listener that they aren't *real*, that God didn't *really* create the universe out of Himself, that gods didn't *really* walk the earth, that heroes didn't or don't *really* exist, or that magic and magical beings aren't *really* real; because all these things *are* real, just as love is, and beauty, and truth, just not literally so. Thus, as Erich Neumann, Joseph Campbell and other comparative mythologists remind us, primal peoples and religions have presented primordial reality as some kind of unifying, ineffable darkness—unself—which split itself into dark and light, or heaven and earth, or sky and land, and then, into this realm of nascent qualities, came the life of consciousness; because this is what, *metaphorically speaking*, actually happened. Consciousness, as psyche, then "manifests" as men and women who must somehow learn, over the course of their lives, to become selves, to separate themselves from unself, while yet remaining always in contact with it. Because unself cannot be literally expressed, the ground of creation—variously understood as god, gods or impersonal divine forces—along with men and women's adventures "from" and "through" and "back" to it—is presented metaphorically, in that elusive but inexhaustibly rich waking dream we call myth.

§150.

The source of creation might be presented as an egg, or as a lake, or as a serpent, but all these symbols, and many like them expressive of fecundity, completeness or generative power, are representations of the common mythological symbol of unself, the archetypal Great Mother.* She appears to the self as the source of the terrors of the world; of its sickness, loss, death and disaster, ever louring on the horizon, of its 3 AM fears, that even atheists are prey to. But she also appears as the inexhaustible *bounty* of life, the sense of benediction that life brings to us after chaotic storms, the unconditional *goodness* of being, and all the consolations of a good, sunny, existence. In both cases, or aspects, the strange mother, the primal female, was not worshipped *as* a female—as the personality of a 'goddess'—but as a natural, FEMININE PRINCIPLE, the thing-in-itself "*from*" which the masculine hero-self emerges, *as* which he must battle with his self and *to* which he must selflessly return. In some primal cultures, this principle is so immeasurably immense and yet elusive, so awesomely powerful and yet subtle, it is barely characterised at all. There are no sacrifices or prayers directed towards it, and no myths explaining its fabulous deeds. The people themselves hardly know of it in fact, and yet it is known to "inform" all things, an enigmatic, ineluctable force which directs all lives, mythic or otherwise.

---

* Erich Neumann, *The Origins and History of Consciousness*

It can be said, then, that the universe was born from the mother's egg, and—from the perspective of time—grew into more and more differentiated forms, or selves. Today we understand this as the widely misunderstood and much-ridiculed metaphor that 'God created the world'.

§151.

Just as three mind-knowable dimensions of space appear to us, so it can be said that there are three mind-knowable kinds of spatial self, which, it can further be said, appeared 'one after the other' in what we call 'time'. These were NON-LIVING SELVES, LIVING SELVES and, finally, HUMAN SELVES.

As these selves appear to evolve, so they become more conscious, or manifest more consciousness. Non-living selves, such as rocks and pencils, are conscious *in* two dimensions *of* one dimension, which we call 'mere' BEING or brute existence. Living selves, such as nematodes and bats, are conscious *in* three dimensions *of* two dimensions, which we call ANIMAL AWARENESS. Finally, human selves are intuitively conscious "*in*" four dimensions *of* three somatic dimensions, which we call HUMAN CONSCIOUSNESS (*noetic* three-dimensional Cartesian space, unknown to primal man, is a separate matter).

Consciousness "*in*" means intuitively existing in, or as, one dimension 'higher' than that which can be experienced *by* the manifest self. Dogs intuit three dimensions, but they only know two dimensions. They cannot know a solid object as a thing, much less an abstract thing; there is no such thing as a three-dimensional 'house' for a dog, only this house and that house, which appears as a shifting surface, not as what we understand to be a solid object. Likewise, you and I intuit four dimensions, but our somatic selves only experience three-dimensional things and bodies.

§152.

Although there is no hierarchy of consciousness—for it is, ultimately, the 4D thing-in-itself of all consciousness everywhere and at all times—there is a *dimensional* hierarchy of selves. Human selves are more conscious than gorilla selves, gorilla selves are more conscious than mollusc selves, mollusc selves are more conscious than poppy selves, and poppy selves are more conscious than pebble selves. This does *not* mean that human beings are *separate* from or *outside* of nature (and so forced to contend with and dominate it), and it certainly does not mean that it is our much vaunted noetic, abstract 'intelligence' that puts us in a position of superiority. The power to think in three abstract dimensions, is a *consequence* of human consciousness. Male thinkers have preferred to believe that consciousness is a consequence of rationality, so as to justify an unconscious, and wicked, rational dominance of nature, which, *in* their unconsciousness, they cannot participate in; for much the same reason they cannot immerse themselves daily in the ocean of love inside their wives' petticoats.

Humans and animals are 'equal' to each other in that every animal (or species) has its own 'superiority', something it does better than any other animal. If we use agility as a measure of superiority, then humans are far below squirrels, if somatic sensitivity is the scale, we're smashed by catfish, when it comes to courage, we can be at least equalled by the little wren. Humans are also equal to animals in that we evidently *are* animals. Although the unnatural world prevents us from getting good at apeishness in the wild—at spontaneity, physical sensitivity, hardiness, animal beauty, group intimacy and connection to our home—apes we are, and, difficult as it is for most of us to believe, wild as well. Humans are also 'equal' to animals in that all animals are conscious to some degree. They all feel some kind of joy, delight, love and pain, including what we would call acute visceral pain. It's dreadful for anyone with any sensitivity to watch an animal suffer, it's heartbreaking to see the extraordinary grief of higher animals, it's inspiring to see the lengths that they will go to avoid this pain and to protect their own, and it's depressing to hear a scientist anthropomorphically 'explain' a bird singing as 'a declaration of territory' or somesuch; as if there can't be two or three reasons, as if birds don't feel pleasure in their song.

Ultimately, animals, humans, plants and rocks all have the same qualitative 'interiority'—the thing-in-itself, about which primal cultures have a range of attitudes that dispense of any kind of distinction between nature and culture, founded on the assumption that, when we are not looking at them, magpies are playing cellos and jaguars racing go-carts. This is why we love stories in which animals speak and think as we do.

Modern, civilised thinking attempts to eradicate the 4D singularity of nature and culture, the staggering oneness of the whole of nature, by reducing nature to a system of cultural tokens, or by reducing culture to a consequence of genetic-environmental determinants, but this doesn't mean that the *manifestation* of the thing-in-itself, the 3D self, doesn't exist in hierarchical gradation, that the capacity of the self to experience the thing-in-itself did not and does not evolve, with human beings at the pinnacle of conscious manifestation in the natural world. It's not a popular idea amongst modern solipsists, postmodernists and masochists, but it remains true that human beings are more conscious than animals. That:

i.   No animal feels wonder at its own existence, wets itself laughing or weeps tears of complete psychological rupture. We know this by attending to animals, which express their inner life just as clearly—if not more clearly—than humans do, and by attending to our own conscious experience, the source of the intense wonder, hilarity and sorrow that are denied animals, along with the fears, desires, frustrations and physical pleasures we evidently do have in common.

ii.   Cats, apes and elephants do not suffer as much as humans. Cats with two legs don't give a toss. Worms don't suffer as much as rats—have you ever seen a worm grieve? Courgettes do not suffer as much as worms, and bacteria can hardly be said to suffer at all. The Spider Wasp, which paralyses spiders and lays its eggs in them, which then hatch out and eat it from the inside, is often given as an example of the pitiless cruelty of nature; but the spider does not suffer as much as 'caring' people like to anthropomorphically think it does.

iii.   Humans can feel more than any other animal. In fact some humans can feel more than other *humans*. Unfeeling humans we rightly disparage *as* animals; perhaps not as unfeeling, say, as baby orangutans, but at least as 'brutish' as snakes or beetles or worms, all of which are, quite naturally, terms of insult for us (although the use of the word 'pig' to insult someone's intelligence or honour can only be made by someone who has not spent quality time with a pig). This doesn't mean that beetles and worms are hateful, stupid, disgusting; it means they are less conscious than we are. Just as there is a scale of conscious sensitivity in the animal world, so there is in the human world, at the bottom of which are those people who do not really feel wonder (everything around them strikes them as unremarkable; only the valuable and the threatening worthy of note) or joy (excitement at getting and winning takes its place, although the basest humans don't feel much excitement either) or sorrow (mere depression and anxiety, or numbed nothingness), who don't laugh very often (certainly not as much as they did when they were children, and even then not very much) or cry very deeply (if at all, perhaps every now and then when a few crude drama-buttons are pushed) or react to loud noise, harsh light and clashing colours. Actually, this could be most people, but there's still a scale, the existence of which translates, at least analogously, into animal experience, which is why those towards the bottom of the scale say, or would say if they considered such things, that 'animals and humans feel the same' (because they can feel nothing deeper than an animal can) and why those capable of genuine empathy feel gutted if they run over a deer, troubled, perhaps upset, if they kill a mouse, momentarily sickened if they step on a snail and completely unconcerned about pulling up a dandelion plant to make way for some carrots. Because in our *actual* lives we recognise, despite what we like to tell ourselves, a hierarchy in nature.

iv.   Animals, less free than humans, are more susceptible to addiction. Caged animals are particularly prone. Children, also less conscious (and less able to see a qualitative difference

SELF AND UNSELF

between humans and animals) are also more prone to addiction, as are caged humans. *Men* in cages—in the things that we call 'houses'—spend as much time masturbating as caged apes. Wild animals, like wild humans, rarely self-pleasure.

v.   Humans are, or at least potentially are, more individual than animals, which are more individual than plants, which are, in turn, more individual than minerals. This is because, as Schopenhauer observed, each has successively more freedom of will; minerals are governed by cause and effect, plants by stimulus and response, animals by awareness and motive (an awareness which, incidentally, puts the lie to Kant's idiotic conflation of awareness with abstract thought) and humans by conscious feeling and conceptual thought, projected far into the past and future, all of which leads to finer and finer degrees of individuality, manifest in the gloriously individual human face. This is why, again as the animal-loving Schopenhauer realised, where animals exercise barely any discrimination between mates, this discrimination in human beings is 'instinctively and unreflectively pursued to the point of violent passion'.* It's also why character in animals—although unquestionably there, and loveable with it—is fainter than in humans and gets fainter and fainter the further *down* you travel, from the reasonably distinct character of apes, cats, elephants and cockatoos, down to the much vaguer individuality of pigeons, lizards and fish (which is, as anyone who lives with such creatures is well aware, also there), down to the practically non-existent character-distinction between one bee and another, or one aspidistra and another.

vi.   We don't feel too guilty about domesticating animals, which is essentially slavery. To domesticate a dog you have to force the wildness out of him. That this is not a particularly difficult job—dogs have been so trained for forty-odd thousand years—doesn't alter the fact that dogs are trained to be our slaves, and nobody cares, as, of course, they shouldn't. Imagine treating a human being that way though. That human beings *are* often considered in need of domestication

* Arthur Schopenhauer, *The World as Will and Representation*

and that we have the wild beaten out of us, often literally so, doesn't change the fact that having a child at your *complete* beck and call, pulling it around on a string and delighting in its ability to do demeaning tricks for you would be considered monstrous—because we all understand that animals have less psychological independence than human beings, are less conscious, less free and suffer less.

vii.   It's okay to eat animals. It is not morally wrong. If we assume that the animal has lived a good life, ideally in the wild, and is killed humanely (i.e. as a *human being* is capable of doing, not tearing it apart with our teeth), there is *nothing* immoral in killing and eating it. *Every* animal on earth eats something which is beneath it. Again, that animals do *not* live happily in the human world, that keeping them for our food in the industrial system is as cruel as it is ecologically destructive, that people who treat animals as walking kebabs are monsters, that a *mostly* vegan diet is both healthy and natural, that there *is* something repulsive about putting flesh in your mouth (try eating bacon when you're in a state of radically self-softened sensitivity); none of this alters the fact that, firstly, the most ecologically balanced societies that have ever lived, or that ever could, namely small primal bands, are all omnivorous (a vegan diet is, for the most part, a *civilised* diet) *as the human body is*; and, secondly, that a slaughtered animal does *not* suffer as we anthropomorphically take it to suffer.

Thus, intimacy and love are possible between humans and non-humans. Humans can gaze in trust into gorilla's eyes, share jokes with crows and receive loving reassurance from horses, but the most conscious will always seek the company of conscious human beings before they seek the company of animals. The reason why many consider their love for their pets to be equal to that for their friends, family and lovers, and why some people (often appallingly cynical) practically worship them, is not because animals are as loveable as humans—they are not—but because humans can no longer love each other. If they could, they would love animals *more*.

§153.

Mythically, or metaphorically, speaking, the semi-animal self of human beings was once one with the void. Men and women felt pain, but there was no transdimensionally conscious 'I' *to* whom it was felt, or no 'you' that I hurt. Subjectivity and objectivity were panjectively one, as they are for those most animal-like of humans, babies and very young children. Then a moment came when the explosive light of human consciousness struck man with the realisation that *I am I*. I exist. I do not know who or *what* I am—there is as yet no separateness—but I know, before all knowledge, *that* I am.

The DAWN OF MAN (or, if you prefer, the DAWN OF HUMAN CONSCIOUSNESS) can be metaphorically understood as an event of transcendent magic, as a ray of light piercing the film of unawareness over man's eyes, or even as God reaching down from above and firing the clay of animality with divine, conscious life; but however it is artistically understood and expressed, what 'really' happened, and when, is and always will be an enigma. All we know is that something *did* 'happen' to "create" consciousness as we know it, and that that 'happening' cannot possibly have been something that can be literally expressed; only myth and metaphor can give it to us.

After the dawn of human consciousness, primal man remained one with unself, with its immediate representation in nature and human nature (manifest as the tribe), for many millennia, unable to develop himself as an individual for very long or for very much. The solid, literal, bounded, fully externalised, objective universe that we live in was a reality for early, 'pre-historic' man, but it was softer, more fluid. Unself shone through the collective psyche, mythically 'animating' it. This is why Australian aborigines call this bygone epoch the 'dream-time'. Not because life was unreal, but because the collective representation of life was 'seen through', just as it still can be. Just about.

To us this time appears as PARADISE, for there was no suffering, for there was no ego to sustain suffering. There was pain—although nowhere near as much as we like to imagine, for we were unbelievably fit, our diets, our immune systems, our gut-microbiota and our skin microbiomes were as powerful as they were diverse, there were no zoonotic diseases, no tooth-eroding sugars (and no crooked teeth, which appeared with weaker modern jaws), no chemicals or hyper-refined carbs, and we were far more aware of what we were doing, and more skilled at doing it (our brains were much larger), and so far less susceptible to stupid accidents. The earth was also abundant to a degree now almost impossible to imagine. And when there *was* pain, there was no ego, and so it was not magnified by a super-aware 'I' not liking it. There was savagery, but again far less than we suppose, for without ego there is no fear of death, no hostility to the body, no desire to lord it over others or to control children. There was also greater sensitivity to the inner life of others, and so to hurt them was to hurt one's *own* sense of self. Many of those hunter-gatherer tribes who, until recently, were *relatively* unscathed by civilisation (although of course, after ten thousand years of history, ego, and its corrupting effects, is everywhere) regarded domination and killing—even of animals and plants—as an outrage.

Proximal consciousness and quality, medial self and society, distal world and universe, all were once intuitively understood to be the same thing. Because man consciously participated in his projection, he saw through it to the ineffable unself "behind" it all, an experience which naturally appeared to him as a mysterious 'super-nature', a hovering suchness "behind" the manifest nature before his attention. Everything struck him as *God*, or *pon*, or *shango*, or *kwoth*, or *fufaka*, or *pepo*, or *maasauu*, or whatever other word he gave to the immeasurable, unspeakable power. The willow tree there, nodding over the bubbling stream, the shoulder of warm rock rising out of the mud, the magic cloud of tiny blue butterflies twinkling in the sun, the monkey-alien and the rabbit-alien, all God, or gods, or aspects of God, an ongoing invitation into mystery that we call ANIMISM.

Just as God, for primal man, was both unutterably vague and strange, while, at the same time, a concrete experience before his senses, so the 'soul' was seen *metaphorically* as a common spiritual essence, both one with, yet distinct from, the body, while the 'body' was conceived of as a form of "clothing" through which alterity was apprehended as such; although more often no clear division existed in the animist universe between body and soul at all, or between appearance and essence, or outer and inner. This was how man could, just by looking at a plant, know whether it was good to eat, or would soothe his sore throat, or could induce an abortion; he could perceive the non-literal transdimensional reality or 'idea' of the thing, the meaning of it "behind" its manifest objective form, just as sensitive people can today, much to the condescending perplexity of literal minds.

§154.

With the new consciousness of reality came a new technical power, that of abstraction, systematisation and language. Initially this was a faint echo over the music of the direct experience and communication which preceded it, but over time it hardened into concepts, relating to techne, each differentiated one *from* the other and related *to* each other into systems. The earliest 'science' of man, manifest in his tools (including his extraordinary powers of navigation, his vast botanical knowledge and his capacity to study and learn from the heavens) originates at this point, long before the first scientific revolution of the classical age.

The separate self—the emergent, isolated 'me'—was, in the early days of mankind, a fleetingly felt reality. There was individuality and self-consciousness, far more than in even the highest animals, but it only appeared briefly above the surface of the groupmind, into which it gladly—for there was no social compulsion, alienation or victimisation to unnaturally sustain it—re-submerged. With the hardening of self came the hardening of taboos and moral imperatives to keep reckless impulses from disrupting the collective will too violently, and to strengthen the self, such as it was, against other selves, now understood to be, at least potentially, a source of danger. But still there was no exploitation, no war (no evidence has ever been found of any), because the self still blended seamlessly with the mythic universe, which centred man and his fellows in nature, gracefully ordering their progress through it.

From the dawn of human consciousness, hundreds of thousands of years ago, to the beginning of history and civilisation, around 12,000 years ago, man slowly, very, *very* slowly, pulled himself from the void, into self-conscious awareness. In the early days of mankind, those who became individuals were practically god-like. They may even, in their capacity to live both in the amorphous world of the collective psyche and the objective world of manifest form, have come to men and women *as* gods, much as a highly conscious psychonaut might do so to a group of naive, egoic trippers. This is what Barry Long tells us,* although the qualitative life of early peoples is impossible to completely, or accurately, penetrate. From the observation of primal groups today, from the analysis of tribes that existed before civilisation, from their bones, burial practices and middens, and from the echoes of those of their myths which made their way into writing, we can learn much about our earliest ancestors. We can, however, learn more about primal experience from the art of remote cultures than from evidence of what people merely *did*. It is in how people physiognomically expressed themselves that the conscious observer can feel from within how literal they were and what quality of consciousness they brought to experience.

Ultimately, however, our knowledge of early man reaches a wall which cannot be surmounted; by the self. We can put together the earliest chapters of the human story through assembling facts and impressions, but the meaning of it, the quality of genuinely primal peoples far away in time and space, can only ever exist in one place, the only place where I can ever know what it means to be human; *my* primal, panjective consciousness. Facts can never be ignored, but they can make no sense unless subordinated to consciousness. Nowhere is this truer than in the study of man, which is why the most astute observers of distant cultures, such as D.H. Lawrence, Carl Jung, Joseph Campbell, and Barry Long, demonstrably possess the most *self*-knowledge.

---

* Barry Long, *The Origins of Man and the Universe*

§155.

It goes without saying that it is impossible to completely or accurately summarise the cultural and psychological life of countless cultures, spread across the entire globe. The diversity of human societies before civilisation was as great as that of non-human, animal 'societies', changing, not just over tens, but over hundreds of thousands of years. Nevertheless, just about all societies everywhere share a huge number of 'human universals', such as, to name but a small number (and, naturally, with a few exceptions here and there); abstraction, aesthetics, baby talk, childcare, classification of age, of flora, of fauna, of space and of tools, containers, dance, diurnality, facial expressions for happiness, for anger, for fear and for surprise, fire, gift-giving, hospitality, jokes, leaders, basic logical notions, some form of marriage, medicine, use of mood-altering substances, mourning, onomatopoeia, phonemes, private inner lives, proverbs, risk-taking, awareness of self-image, semantics, sexual attraction, tickling and disapproval of stinginess.* What concerns us here, however, are those commonalities which pertain to the essentially non-egoic quality of being. All primal people and primal societies were, to a lesser or greater extent:

i.   EGOLESS. Men and women experienced the thing-in-itself here—I or consciousness—and, through that experience, knew the thing-in-itself there—reality or nature—which was not merely known to be good, beautiful, divine and so on, but was fundamentally I. *I am that.* In primal cultures there was no autonomous egoic self, separated from consciousness and context. Man was a unique individual, but his manifest *specialness* hardly existed and was rarely referred to. Names—of people, places and things— were fluid, adapting to circumstance. Self-consciousness, self-awareness, self-determination, self-respect and narrow focus didn't play any significant part at all in primal society, which means that disagreements were not backed by strong negative emotions; anxiety and agitation vanished almost the instant they appeared, and the constant

---

* Donald E. Brown, *Human Universals*

sense of being surrounded by hostile, alien forces was un-known, as was, consequently, the desperate need to escape into thinking, wanting, worrying and other addictions.

We are accustomed to viewing primal folk as bound by more beliefs than us, but in reality they believed *less*, which is why the thinking of pre-civilised tribes fluidly binds experiences together in a way we find incredibly strange, including experiences which seem to us to come from within, but which to primal man come from without, and vice versa. Subject and object were considered from the same panjective perspective, and so gods and worldly facts mingled; not because men and women were too childish or unsophisticated to tell them apart, but because self and world formed a whole. Through having a relatively undifferentiated self, without a front-and-centre 'I' taking on the task of identity, voices and visions could come to man that expressed the mystery of reality as it panjectively is, rather than as it merely objectively or subjectively appears to be; just as, echoing up from the primal depths, it still does today, in the subtle hearts of great artists and innocent children and in all of us in moments of radical astonishment. In other words, man was a genius, and lived in a community of geniuses, as evidenced by his strange and beautiful art.

ii.   PLAYFUL. Their productive 'work' was playful—so much so that primal cultures make no distinction between work and play—as were their religious beliefs and practices, as were their relationships and their social rituals. Even the way they punished selfish and cruel behaviour was playful, through the use of humour and ridicule, which was also used to pull down ego where it arose, promoting equality and companionship. Even their *battles* had an element of play. All visitors to ancient cultures reported buoyant light-heartedness, good-humoured optimism and outright silliness as the norm.

The playfulness of the unegoic mind, living in nature, is a collective joy of free but meaningful metaphorical communication (alternating with practical literality), blended empathy with the other, with whom one effortlessly 'plays off', and the mad, slapstick, improvised silliness of innocence. E. Richard

Sorenson, who lived amongst 'hunter-gatherer-gardeners' of New Guinea, described the intuitive rapport of primal minds as 'synchronous cooperation punctuated by playful surprise triggering ecstasy... each constantly enlivening the others by a ceaseless, spirited, individualistic input into a unified at-one-ness... alien to my Western consciousness, and so beyond the English language that there are no good words for it...'* Panjective consciousness is rarely noted by anthropologists for much the same reason that unripe tomatoes are not noticed by the colour-blind.

iii.   REWARDING. It has been, for millennia, something of an irritating fact to more civilised leaders that hunter-gather-ers, with no rigid hierarchies, no money and no possessions, and with only the simplest tools, lead lives that are far more satisfying, far *richer*, than those led by citizens of civilised societies, either agricultural or industrial. Anybody who has spent any serious time in the wilderness—even in the marginal and unproductive habitats which remain today—understands how good it is to provision oneself from the wild and to feel the pleasure of natural peace.

The high level of [craft] skill and extraordinary intelli-gence of primal peoples matches and carries their awareness and, again, has been noted by all Western observers. It is not, as it is for us, that one or two hyper-specialised people are able to do one or two things very well, but that *everyone* can do *everything* well (or everything they have to do), each meaningfully contributing to a vast range of physical and cultural activities the products of which stand before them as their own. ALIENATION, the sense that one's culture and its products have been made by another's hand (with the atten-dant sense that everything you do within it goes against your better judgement), and ANOMIE, the sense that culture cannot speak to one's lived experience (and so nothing you encounter within it seems to really make sense), were both unknown.

iv.   FEARLESS. Non-egoic man feared death as animals do, in the moment. When he sensed danger, adrenaline flooded

* E. Richard Sorenson, *Pre-Conquest Consciousness*

through his body, his senses became more alert and he prepared to fight or fly. He avoided that which he did not like or want and held to that which he did, but with consciousness at the helm, he did not *cling*, because there was, ultimately, nothing that could possibly be lost. This is why the earliest conceptions of death appear to be identical to life (and a good life at that). Death can only appear to that which creates an idea of itself coming into and passing out of time; the self.

Man was not afraid of death because death was constantly present to him; both literally, in that he was constantly faced with the reality of dead bodies, and non-literally, in that he used ecstatic rituals and joyous festivals to let go of his self and peer into the void, not least of which the ecstatic ritual of love-making, which, with no egoic fuckself to degrade into self-pleasuring porn, was a constant festival of super-intense joy. There was little or no masturbation, no pornography, no sexual frustration, no attempt to control each other's sex lives, and although androgyny occasionally appeared (and, in representing paradox, was honoured), there was little or no *consistent and persistent* homosexuality.

v.   NON-COERCIVE. Primal children are, as anthropologists have observed time and time again, universally well-behaved. They are rarely punished and are at liberty to live, essentially, as they please. There were no social classes in primal societies, no fixed royalty with the power to order other people around, and, again as numerous anthropologists have observed, gender relations were egalitarian, with men and women free to decide their own movements, activities and relationships. If there was a difference between the sex-roles, it was not one of power but of *domain*, with men typically taking the manifest lead in public decision-making, then ratifying the decisions privately or informally with women.

Primal economies, such as they were, were also non-coercive, meaning there was no such thing as money or fixed debt. What today we might call 'economic arrangements' were conducted informally and organically, through gift-economies, in which surplus was carefully shared out, or just given away, and the innate human drive for fairness allowed to arrange matters to everyone's mutual benefit, punishing stinginess and pride with disapproval, ridicule and censure.

Primal societies were therefore anarchist. This does not mean there was no leadership—there has to be in human societies—or no restraint—of those who seek to control others or who have no control over themselves—but that there was no *domination*. No primal leader ever forced anyone to do anything, and, if he did, he would be ignored. Just as the body of society grew anarchistically, with swells and stunts fractally balanced, each person able to experience the other from within, so each individual body grew selflessly, with the likes and dislikes of personality adapting fluidly to the needs of consciousness and context, creating an unaddicted fractally balanced character.

vi. MIRACULOUS. The selfless, panjective, four-dimensional unity of the thing-in-itself "behind" both the experiencer and the experienced was registered, by self, as an intimate sense of intense *wonder*. With the factual-causal self soft or secondary—and therefore with no great interest in factual-causal *whys*—there was and can only have been, by self, a sense of ongoing astonishment at the primary, uncaused, *what*.

Knowledge for primal man and woman did not primarily come from an intellectual investigation into the causes of phenomena, although naturally this happened, but from consciousness of their *significance*. Man became conscious of the representations of self as *signs* for something which was intuited both "before" and "beyond" phenomena, but which, paradoxically, only appeared *in* or *as* phenomena. He thus became *fascinated* with things in a way which animals cannot be. Animals are interested, sometimes *extremely* interested, but the interest reflects back on their selves, on something which is related *to* their selves. You never see cats looking up at the stars (although, to be fair, if ever an animal did, it *would* be a cat), or swans weeping at sunsets, or macaws gazing in awe at their own claws (although, in empathic appreciation of our shared interiority, we love to metaphorically think they do).

For man, the possibility of seeing beyond self opens up a new world in objects, an experience which fills his heart first with wonder, and then, later, with dread.

The—to self—miraculous nature of existence, its selfless, panjective transdimensionality, was reflected in PRIMAL LANGUAGE, which was very different from modern, Western, languages. Primal language had no 'I', or an 'I' which changed over the course of a lifetime, or even day (as it does in Japanese). Judgements of quality were semantically panjective (again, as in Japanese, where 'samishii' means simultaneously 'I feel sad' and 'It is sad'), there was no copula, such as our 'is, am, are', and so no automatic conversion of opinion into fact (as with many languages today, where the statement 'Darren *is* upset' is impossible; only 'Darren upset', which retains a level of interpretative, panjective subtlety that the copula hands over to an eternal fact), and descriptive terms were purely metaphorical (such as in Yélî Dnye, where one cannot say 'the snow is white' but only 'the snow is white like the cockatoo'). There were no tense markers in primal languages (as in many languages today, such as Chinese), and no words for time (as in Hopi), or time meant the same as the weather (as in Tagalog, Spanish and Irish today) or the passing of the sun (as in Kuuk Thaayorre). Language flowed in and out of music, with words and phrases being interchangeable with clicking, whistling, humming and singing (as in Pirahã). Finally, language was inherently and fundamentally metaphorical, in that the metaphorical, the musical and the literal were *all* "expressions" of the thing-in-itself.

None of this means that primal people could not distinguish, in thought or speech, between today and yesterday, between subjective me and objective thee, or between a literal thing and its metaphorical qualities; but that such distinctions were entirely secondary to panjective awareness, and so they were not *rigidly* encoded in language.

vii.   IMPERFECT. Despite this time in human history being regarded by all the cultures which followed as paradise, as, at the very least in comparison with what followed, it unquestionably was, it wasn't *completely* free of violence, shame, pain and exploitation. Ego appeared, and caused suffering, but its presence in nature-culture-nothing was as that of viruses, bacteria and cancerous cells in a healthy body; instantly squashed.

The imperfection of primal people doesn't just relate to their occasional outbursts and manias, their sometimes silly or even harmful beliefs, but to the fact that their selves were not developed. In being completely one with a collective mind, itself one with nature, they were in a paradise analogous to the one we enjoy in early childhood, or even in the womb. There was, contrary to the arrogant distortions of some anthropologists, no lack of consciousness in early man, no naive stupidity nor even lack of individuality—quite the opposite—but in order to fully realise consciousness, the individual self had to separate itself from the group, and this had to mean catastrophe.

The evidence for the above is overwhelming, but the essence of it, relating as it does to human nature, is only accessible through consciousness. Egoic anthropologists and historians cannot access their own human nature and so obscure or explain away that of mankind by focusing on a limited selection of facts—a lavishly provisioned grave here, a violent death there—grouped towards the civilised end of pre-history.

§156.

What we can say of how early people perceived nature, of what they experienced, and of how they loved, can only be expressed non-factually; metaphorically, or in myth. To speak intelligently of the psyche of unegoic man we must speak of gods and auras and souls and magic, not because these things were literally real, but because what was real was non-literal. We can say, for example, that primal man lived in paradise, that he had a golden egg-like aura surrounding him which intensified when he made love, that his soul merged with the soul of the forest, which, when disaster struck, he saw was also sad and needed to be cheered up with song, that the gods and goddesses spoke to him and appeared to him, that he lived in a world permeated with magic; until the fairies and trolls departed, driven out by TECHNOLOGY.

Technology is the cultural manifestation of techne, the proto-conceptual component of reality itself. There are four modes of technology, corresponding to the modes of the self. There is THELEMIC TECH, such as the axe and the pneumatic drill, which extends our power to act, SOMATIC TECH, such as the telescope and geiger counter, which extends the power of our senses, VISCERAL TECH, such as narcotics and GM plants, which enables us to extend our desires and limit our fears and NOETIC TECH, such as the alphabet and the clock, which enables us to extend the power of our mind to know. There are also approximately three scales of technological complexity. At the smallest, most concrete scale is the simple HAND TOOL (bags, boxes, axes, pencils, bricks). This is followed by the larger-scale MACHINE TOOL (ball-bearings, bucket-wheel excavators, printing presses and computers), and then, finally, at the largest or most abstract scale, is the SYSTEM TOOL (institutions, networks, money and, ultimately, the civilised system itself).

When a tool, any tool, reaches a certain level of autonomous power—meaning brute concentration, coverage and complexity—it starts to demand more energy from the user than it provides in return,* an energy which, moreover, necessarily diffuses across users, increasing their individual dependency while reducing their individual autonomy. The point at which tools or habits stop serving their users and start subordinating them to cliche is the UTILITY TIPPING POINT. A stone axe, to take an example of a simple hand tool, demands a reasonably high level of energy (effort, activity, intelligence, skill, etc.) from the individual to make, maintain and use, but its low level of complexity and potency means that the individual and his community maintain control over the axe and its effects. As axes developed, they became more and more powerful, and required more input of energy from society to make. The most developed 'axe' today is a petrol chainsaw, which requires a small level of energy from the

---

* Ivan Illich, *Tools for Conviviality* and *Energy and Equity*

individual to use, but demands a vast, almost unimaginable, investment, from a colossal interlocking network of industrial, political and administrative institutions, all of which completely subordinate individuals and communities. The individual cannot make a chainsaw, or take care of it, must deal with the destructive outputs of the corporations, states, refineries, factories, roads and shops required to manufacture, market and transport chainsaws, and must live in a world in which forests of trees can be—*must* be—cut down, using colossally powerful machines. Likewise, when a system tool, such as a transport network, becomes too concentrated, extensive and complex, we must spend more time and energy taking care of it than we gain in time and energy saved travelling. Result: roads become more inflexible, cars slow down and nobody can use their feet to get to where they need to go.

Tools, as Marshall McLuhan famously taught, are not separate things used by separate selves—selves extend into the tool, so that the hand becomes the axe, the mind becomes the text. What's more, the tool *numbs* whatever part of the self it amplifies; so the axe numbs the hand, degrades its skill and power, the text numbs the mind, makes it dependent on written knowledge.* Such relatively simple tools can and did corrupt consciousness and conscious society, but, as tools developed, the numbness, degradation and dependency increased. The printing press, the map, the loom, the computer; each saw an increase in output at the expense of the subtlety, sensitivity and skill of the man or woman at the input end, until man became, next to his tools, useless.

§157.

There is a tool which is at a subtler and far more intimate scale than hand, machine or system tools while, at the same time, being more powerful than any tool on earth. This is the conceptual-visceral component of the self, the thinking-emoting mind, which was and is the first autonomous tool of man, and the first to disastrously cross a utility tipping point, enslaving and numbing him. Initially, thoughts and desires 'emerged'

---

* Marshall McLuhan, *Understanding Media*

from the self and then, when the job was done, returned to it, as a hammer is returned to the shelf, leaving simple, incarnate, consciousness. When it became too powerful, however, the mental-visceral self began to take charge of consciousness. Its habits became cliches, its signs drained of significance and the source of meaning faded from experience. This happened some time between ten and fifteen thousand years ago, a few thousand years before civilisation began. Precisely where, when and how is impossible to say, but at some point in our collective history—as in each individual history—the mental-emotional self took on a kind of autonomous existence, wanting and not-wanting, liking and not-liking, and manifesting these fears and desires as ideas, beliefs and opinions. It is not simply that I became consciously aware of being someone, but that this 'someone' took charge of my self, and, trapped by its empty symbols and cliched operations, I came to think and feel that *I am it*. Or rather I continued to *believe* that 'I am I', but the throne of consciousness had been usurped without me realising it; because the me realising was now self. The mask of the egoic personality had taken over the character of man. The usual expression for this cataclysmic event in human history is THE FALL, the birth of ego and its reflection in the world, THE SYSTEM.

When the mystery of the thing-in-itself which "produces" both culture and nature is overtaken by the self, it begins to seem, to late palaeolithic people, just as it does to children emerging from the undifferentiated oneness of infancy, as if there is nothing else in existence but its representation of self. Representation becomes therefore 'God', and its existential status changes from being "of" the thing-in-itself, to *being* the thing-in-itself; which can thereby only influence itself, not be influenced from "within" or "without", for there is no longer either. Soma, nous, viscera and thelema then become a constellation of images, or IDOLS,* which command total attention; a series of separate, alien things, whose interiority becomes fundamentally unknown and has to therefore be SU-PERSTITIOUSLY believed in, a factual-causal-associative method which exists solely in order to control, acquire or placate—in

---

* Owen Barfield, *Saving the Appearances*

a word *manage*—the idols that reality now comprises. These idols, although animated by superstitious assumptions, were creations of the noetic-somatic mind, and so were understood literally. Like the physicalist scientists who followed, fallen man applied literalist assumptions to unself. Where we, free of the subjective, myth-saturated guesswork of superstition, have literal particles, literal forces, literal consciousness and literal 'mental illnesses', fallen man had literal souls, literal ghosts, literal gods and literal demons. In both cases, anything which threatens the literal representation, that appears to come from beyond it, is an existential threat which must be rejected or annihilated.

§158.

It is obvious—at least to anyone with any real experience of men and women—that the first sex to fall was man. His self was naturally tilted towards tight-focused conceptualisation, and so it was he who, overcome and overblown with thought and desire, first became egoic. The consequences, which slowly spread through society, were disastrous:

i.   Time appeared. Man was greeted with the existence, in the unconscious, of a terrible new entity, THE PAST*; the suffering of the ego, pushed out of awareness, into the darkness of the visceral system, where it fused with the mechanical self, effectively operating it by remote control. Much later the *idea* of time (as a measurable *thing*, divided up into various tenses) appeared.

ii.   Existential fear appeared. Everything which directly expresses unself became a source of fear, hatred and, in order to control that fear, violence. Women, children, unfallen others, the human body, and beyond that, the natural universe, including consciousness itself, became alien entities which had to be disciplined and controlled. Rituals and festivals, which had freely expressed unself, became formalised into propitiatory cliches; spiritual begging, essentially.

---

* Barry Long, *The Origins of Man and the Universe*

iii.   Wisdom was degraded. Conscious intelligence came to be encoded in cliche, in set expressions, handed-down revelations and bizarre associative reasoning. Such patterns had existed before, but they were light paths through the mind, from which the speaker or thinker could wander at will. As ego took hold, these came to become *set* into culture, such that they could be consistently written back into man and 'handed down'. After ego usurped consciousness, egoic (and therefore cliched) culture appeared to reflect reality itself. Transgression of 'how we do things' (or say things or think things) thereby came to be seen as a transgression against the cosmic order. This was the beginning of TABOO; feelings, ideas, actions and images which threaten the cliche and groupthink that egoic society is composed of, and TOTEM; feelings, ideas, actions and images which reinforce cliche and groupthink.

iv.   Love-making became sex.* The tight focus of ego placed a corrupt filter over experience, channelling the sado-masochistic urges of the self-informed self towards a desperately exciting idea of what was happening, or what could happen. Man left his incarnate body, which consciously enjoyed the complete experience of being inside a woman, and began getting off on the arousing thought of it. The pleasure of sex began to feel almost identical to the thrill of victory, as woman became, literally, booty.

v.   Myth was degraded. When consciousness departed from the universe, the fears and desires of self took its place. No longer did self and society both express the same unselfish origin. Instead, they were understood to somehow *represent* a higher order, or to be positioned within a divine chain of being, stretching back through one's ancestral lineage. Gods no longer reflected the inexpressible reality of unself, but the expressible *needs* of self, and started to behave like egoic men and women, with the same kinds of fears and desires. Heaven, like earth, became divided into antagonistic factions, a hierarchy of deities and ancestors upon which, with man now living in a terribly uncertain universe, security now depended.

* Barry Long, *Making Love*

vi.   Inequality appeared. Ego's fearful attempt to annihilate the uncertainty, loss and death of unself manifested as personal and collective power-grabs. Chiefs began to arrogate to themselves the ability to divine the tribe's true interests, and to make binding declarations of how to meet them. Spiritual authority also degraded into decadent forms of shamanism, which relied on the charisma of individuals and ever more elaborate rituals, rites and ordeals in order to confirm and maintain their power over the minds of their fellows. Those who could command others, through charisma, manipulation or naked force, did so. This didn't create power-relations or stratify society—power, authority and even 'shallow' hierarchies are natural—but created more and more massive and, crucially, more and more rigid pyramids of inequality, with those at the bottom now in a new state, or 'STATUS', called *low*.

vii.   Social-esteem and self-esteem, always closely and naturally connected, became fused with status. Low status, and everything attached to or associated with it, became unpleasant, not just because of discomfort, which humans can well tolerate, but because of the existential threat of unbeing that it represented to egos forced to inhabit rigidly hierarchical social structures. This is how manual labour, bodily participation in nature and even the body itself became *distasteful*. Official taste could not, as it still cannot, accept genuine physicality into its sphere; only from a distance can the soma of the world be enjoyed, through the prism of value, or *appreciation*. The middle and upper classes do not live by using their bodies, or live in their own bodies, or live in nature, or even live in anything like a meaningful society; they just *appreciate* these things, just as they *appreciate* the art that comes from them. They have to, because, without being in the body, or actually living in an incarnate world, they have no real experience, no real character and no source of real pleasure in their lives, and so they acquire tokens for pleasure, character and experience. They resemble a teenage boy who compensates for never having known physical love by acquiring a museum of expensive erotica.

viii.   Art was degraded. The organic quality of the earliest art forms became schematised. Instead of expressing life, art began to *symbolise* it, not in symbols that man could participate in by 'seeing through' them to the enigmatic experience of unself that he and the artist shared, but rather in tokens (or *cyphers*) that represented the literal fact, or literal elements of it. Images of women, plants and animals gave way to images of men and man-made objects, particularly weaponry.

ix.   Language was degraded. Before the dawn of human consciousness, language was indistinguishable from song, full of direct meaning but, like song, without a directly literal or indirectly metaphorical component (referring to the past or the future). When man acquired the power of literal expression, explicit ideas referring to the new dimension of time could 'emerge' from the music of speech to serve explicit and literal needs. 'You left your axe next to the river' must have a non-literal, implied, tonal meaning underneath it, for it can only occur between two living people in a living context, but the phrase itself must be literal and must be understood as such—if it weren't, I would not be able to find my axe. As self took charge of self, the literal component of language took over the music and poetry of it and it started to become *entirely* explicit. Tenses, pronouns, subjective-objective distinctions, nominalisations and copular equivalents 'hardened'. The tonal content of communication—the music of it—began to wither, and its subordination to the conscious context was detached, opening up a new hyper-abstract realm of detached thinking. Names—for people, place and things—then became binding, and were then used in emotionally-charged disputes over meanings, rights and possessions.

x.   Intuitive rapport disintegrated. Literal language had to be relied on more and more as empathy started to sink under the weight of the mental-emotional ego. No longer would consciousness and context instantly shape the collective activity of the group in a miraculously synchronised whole. Instead, people had to be coordinated and managed.

xi.   The body became *distasteful*. Prior to ego, 'I' was—if any-where—centred in the solar plexus. Now that 'I' was different, a separate thing, it stopped being located in the natural body, and was instead located in the increasingly unnatural head; in the vanishing point of isolated thought, which narrowed more and more tightly onto the things of the world. Consequently, the somatic ground of the self, the body, became an enemy to man, a source of shame and guilt, and even fear, to be disciplined, concealed and controlled.

xii.   Man was numbed. As the tool of the mental-emotional ego took over the body, so the body lost its acuity and sensitivity. Senses started to dim, particularly those "closest" to undifferentiated consciousness, the immediate senses of smell, taste and sensate feeling. Awareness was sucked by concentrated egoic thought out of the eyeballs and into a focal point the width of a target, creating a quantitatively noetic-somatic world *of* isolated things, and isolated ideas *for* things, all at arm's length. These things and ideas began to be related to each other in a proto-scientific attitude to nature, the necessary precondition for the technical organisation which was to come later.

xiii.   Man became afraid of death. Self, looking at itself, saw that it was limited in time and space, vulnerable and certain to die. This didn't just come to mind as an explicit idea, but also as a far deeper existential anxiety which appeared as night-terrors, nameless dread and fear of the other, of what is radically different. Uncertainty crept into human awareness and with it a need to protect and guard the boundaries of the known, of the self. Man's fear of attack—of noetic criticism, somatic loss, thelemic impediment and visceral pain—manifested as an urge to build a world to protect his ego from it.

xiv.   Just as the self of man, once soft and free, hardened into ego, so the culture of man, once liquid and available to man and woman, dried up too, and hardened into the Leviathan we call CIVILISATION.

§159.

The incipient effects of the fall initially appeared only here and there and in most cases hardly at all; existing in potential only. A society's fall into ego can be almost unbelievably rapid—a primal tribe coming into full contact with modern civilisation can go through millennia of suffering in a few weeks—but we must assume that initially it did take millennia for the cancer of ego to get a hold on collective life. Around 10,000 years ago we begin to see evidence of 'Big Men', violent deaths, lifeless art and so on, but the full horror of ego would take thousands of years to fully realise itself, with much 'falling back' into primal consciousness en route. When agriculture began, around 9000 BC in the area around modern Syria, Israel, Jordan and Iraq, society remained largely unegoic (egalitarian, playful and non-coercive) for around four thousand years.

Nevertheless, with the uniquely bountiful conditions that obtained around the appropriately named 'fertile crescent', that most pernicious of influences—an easy life—began to feed the human ego. As populations grew, as some groups of people became more powerful than other groups, as they began to depend on, and then tax, easily stored and quantified grains, as the wild moved beyond man's experience and reach, so his thinking-emoting self started to became more powerful. Warfare began, the subjugation of women and children, the despoliation of nature, the appearance of coercive cults, the rise of literalist [proto] science as a technique of governance, the violent repression of minorities and the ponderous cause-and-effect record of the misery of the world we call HISTORY.

Truthful histories do not present to us a series of events related to each other, via 'laws', along a string of time, because, unless metaphorically reimagined, there is no truth in literal facts, which is why purely factual accounts are, to any but purely factual minds, so boring. There is no truth in history, no consciousness, only a lie—albeit an instructive one. History, as we know it, is the story of the false, the long invasion of the unreal, (an unreality deified in our time those by arch-prophets of turgid historicising, Hegel and Marx).

§160.

The most powerful egos on the planet desecrate people and nature on a grand scale, but the activity of the most mega-lomaniacal king or billionaire on earth is trivial compared to the violations of the egoic addiction-assimilation-annihilation machine, or the vast collection of cults, we call THE CIVILISED SYSTEM. As the power of ego increases, so it begins to mould both the nature and the society around it into its own image, until it becomes reality for the people who live within it, who are then also formed in its image. We call this pseudo-reality the SPECTACLE, which is to representation what ego is to self. When egoic society only informs itself, a spectacular self-rein-forcing vicious circle begins, generating more and more ego as men and women are forced to conform more and more rigidly to the tokens and cliches of what appears to be reality. The nightmare of the self and the nightmare of society thus reflect each other, until one or the other collapses or is destroyed.

The representation of self and the representation of civilised society can never be completely one, as each self comprises individual experience that can never be fully con-tained by the symbols and legitimations of the system. In order to prevent this experience deviating too much beyond the legitimising boundaries of society, the official spectacle must be presented as 'given from above', not made by the hands of men. Thus, when you do something 'wrong' — when you sleep with the wrong woman, when you eat the wrong food, when you use the wrong form of address with a superior — you are not merely contravening an expedient invention of man, but are disrupting the entire cosmos.* This is one of the chief pur-poses of the system of civilised legitimations we call RELIGION.

Religion is a complex affair, all kinds of influences go into making it up and all kinds of meaning are taken from it, but one of its chief purposes for civilisation, and for those who own and manage civilised resources, is as a means to obscure the origin and nature of the cultic or institutional order, which must be presented to the people as somehow having existed since the birth of time. This is as true for the

---

* Peter Berger, *The Sacred Canopy*

secular 'religions' of modern times (physicalism, professional-ism, statism, capitalism, socialism, etc.) as it was for those of ancient Mesopotamia and Egypt. The belief that reality can be symbolically reproduced is a religious belief—whether the believer is theist or atheist is completely, almost laughably, immaterial. All religions begin with an unspoken, idolatrous faith that representation is, ultimately, reality (which is why fanatical religious believers take words as things, and criticism of ideas as a kind of *physical* violence), and all religions must induce a sense in man that in his day-to-day life of service to that representation—to the world—he is realising the deepest aspirations of his own being (his 'calling', his 'dharma'), in harmony with the fundamental nature of existence; and not pointlessly slaving away in a machine made by other minds.

Religion, from the very beginning of the system, went hand in hand with science, or rather the proto-science that had emerged during the fall, in which reality was conceived as a series of desacralised bits related to each other. This ab-stracted view of the universe developed during the early stages of civilisation into a more exact series of measurements used to transform land and labour, input and output, into the fun-damental unit of civilisation we call the CITY; huge numbers of people harnessed to the externalised ego, or world, rationally working in a coordinated manner in order to produce more such world. Initially, the city was a relatively pleasant place to live—more of a *hub* than a *state*—but with self in charge it slowly became, over the centuries and millennia that followed, an egoic machine, the prosperity of which was founded on plunder, the pleasure of which was founded on addiction, the growth of which was founded on waste and the freedom of which was founded on manipulation.

The two principal technologies of the new city-machine were LITERACY and MONEY, both of which transformed man's attitude to reality. No longer was life a *story*, a sensate three-di-mensional journey through a mysterious four-dimensional landscape which came to man as creative inspiration; it was now a *process*, an ongoing project to manipulate, memorise or possess causally related facts encoded in a series of marks on a two-dimensional page or a two-dimensional coin. Just as ideas and values could now be stored and controlled, so could those *things* for which ideas and values stood for, the totality of which was now man's world, a place where creative truth was no longer welcome. The rise of literacy saw the fall of genius and scenius, or individual and collective inspiration, as reality and social reality no longer came to man directly, through the senses, but through the text. The rise of money saw the fall of the unselfish sense that reality was a totality of integrated, heterogeneous qualities, as the price of things depended on them being discrete, quantitative atoms.

Henceforth, all atomising civilisations would depend on—and therefore attach *moral* value to—a high degree of literacy and numeracy. This meant that they were also dependent on a greater economic surplus for the new class of literate and numerate intellectuals to live on, a surplus that was impossible without a complex technocratic social organisation extracting that surplus from people who didn't want to give it away. Thus the appearance of the intellectual necessitated the appearance of the soldier and the slave.

§ 161.

The history of each civilisation (along with eras or ages within it) follows the same general path. Initially, internal conflict is kept under control, as a central power-group works to subjugate first its own populace, and then that of its neighbours, so as to build and then consolidate the power of the state. This is the ENTREPRENEURIAL PHASE,* in which—for the elite group—restraint, foresight and manly courage are promoted and rewarded. Free culture (through adaptive guidelines) can flourish, as it did in the early days of Greek civilisation, but as it grows and becomes established, it starts to harden into legitimating dogma, into 'how we do things'. Heroic qualities start to become useful only to peripheral security forces—in fact they become something of an embarrassment, as the real task of civilisation is now *management* of the area under control. Here, in the MANAGEMENT PHASE of civilisation, it is not

---

* Arial and Will Durant, *The Lessons of History,* Oswald Spengler, *Decline of the West*

courage and creativity which are rewarded, but bureaucratic *intellect*, at least amongst the management class; princely elites and owners can now shut themselves off in their pleasure palaces without really having to do any work at all, while the new class of clever men, which would eventually engulf the world, could direct their existential fear and violence into ten thousand tomorrows of endless wanting and planning.

It's at this point that the society becomes divided into the rigid power-groupings, or CLASSES, we are familiar with today: the owners (or UPPER CLASS), the managers (the MIDDLE CLASS), the producers (the WORKING CLASS) and the excluded (the UNDER CLASS, or POOR), each of which are glued together by groupthink and structured by cliche into more and more caricatured versions of themselves. At the top of society we now find the typically unempathic, cruel, arrogant, dull, courteous, superficially 'nice', cultured and cowardly people we call aristocrats and professionals, and at the lower end the crude, sick, miserable, violent, undisciplined, stupid, warm-hearted and realistic people we call workers and servants; the whole system representing a body, in which, by the division of hyper-specialised class-based labour, the superior head does the thinking, praying and playing and the most despised parts carry away waste matter. Each sub-caste community in a local region is aware of its relative standing in the scale of order or purity, with the complete outsider, the barbarian, as disgusting as the nature that she is still part of.

The management phase of civilisation sees technocrats and bureaucrats take the place of artists and heroes. The laws and legitimations they manage harden into unchanging concrete. Without character—the genius of the natural whole and the scenius of the social whole—professionals have no option but to use instrumental control to organise society, to curate culture rather than to create it and to scientifically isolate human and natural units (things and people) and then slot them into the civilised mechanism, the elementary working unit of which is the *man-as-instrument*; the thing-man we call SOLDIER, the means by which, after expansion has ceased, foreign things and people can be ripped from context and transported back, as now manageable plunder, to the home city; and the thing-man we call SLAVE, the means by which standard, cliched activity can be carried out, a living tool, which, through repeating the same movements over and over again in a coordinated whole, can produce more output; more crops, more gold, longer roads, bigger moai and so on.

§162.

The management phase of a developed and established civilisation comprises large numbers of people who have, for two or more generations, been separated from the natural context and from individual consciousness. The process of having one's self formed by an unnatural attitude (complete passivity) to an unnatural environment (a non-paradoxical, non-fractal spectacle) we call DOMESTICATION, which, in both animals and humans, leads to a series of predictable features and outcomes:

i.   Increased egotism, which means increased masochism and sadism, increased anxiety and boredom, increased fear and desire; and with these, all the addictive outlets civilisation produces to pacify the restless mental-emotional momentum of its members, namely sado-masochistic spectacles, pornographic art, loveless fucking (with casual mates, same-sex partners and, a new category of civilised human, PROSTITUTES), pointless rituals, decadent feasts, senseless festivals and other sordid forms of egoic 'fun'.

ii.   Plumper, softer and blander physiognomy. The stiff, hyper-cliched physiognomy of the early pioneers of civilisation—the heroes and the conquerors—gives way to the soppy, puppyish, punchable jelly-head of the typical manager. Hard, monstrously ugly atavistic throwbacks continue to be found, largely in the excluded under class, the sometimes unbelievably ugly peasant and, later, prole head, but the main body of the civilised mass, particularly its middle class, eventually comes to resemble human marshmallow.

iii.   Increased docility, submissiveness and infantilisation. Man becomes unable to do anything apart from his specialised machine-task. In the early days of civilisation, total speciali- sation, and therefore total dependency on the machine, was impossible, but even there (and again, particularly in the upper levels of the urban core) man became pathetically dependent on the social machine for what he could once do on his own; namely feed, house, clothe, entertain, heal and defend himself.

iv.   Simplification of complex behaviours (such as court- ship) and a chronic decrease in empathy, loyalty and generosity (except to power). Domesticated man, like domesticated cattle, closes in on himself, confining his life to the predictable, ever deepening ruts that civilised 'life' lays down for him, becoming more and more anxious about or resistant to change. The cul- tural output of domesticated man is also chronically reduced. As 'civilised' history progressed, so the sweet, stirring strange- ness of nature, innocence, mystery, femininity and life-loving art declined. Artists were now cut off from the darkness of life and portrayed death not as they had previously—as a splendid continuance of the subtle mystery of life—but as suffering, loss and torturous obscurity. The purpose of art became to impress, frighten and conspicuously display power and wealth. Violent clashes between large, aggressive animals became a common theme, along with terrible scenes of punishment and warfare, and of enemies being tortured and slain. The mythos, poetry and drama of intensely domesticated societies, such as Imperial Rome, seventeenth and eighteenth-century England, Nazi Germany and contemporary America, is almost unbearably dull, empty, lugubrious and matter-of-fact, little more than 'creative technology', for, as cultural rigor mortis sets in, only mechanical culture can move the rigid body.

v.   Massive reduction in life expectancy, height, strength and general health, reduced hardiness, greater susceptibility to disease and atrophy of the senses—first smell and touch, then taste, then hearing—impoverishing reality and, consequently, speculation about and expressive articulation of that reality, resulting in the degraded art and mythos of civilised man. As sensitivity to the context wastes away and the machine takes over the entire functioning of the self, a complete numbness takes hold of man, an inner deadness reflected in his dull, dead, fixed and staring eyes—the permanent pornstare of civilised man, ever on the prowl for something that can never satisfy him.

§163.

As the machine takes over the entire functioning of society, it comes to comprise a crowd of feeble, dejected, half-alive automatons, occasionally sparked into a reflex-reaction of emotional fear or excitement, before slumping back into the quotidian dread-state it calls 'living', but which is, in truth, a living nightmare, a core of constant fear and guilt which surfaces in the dreamlife of the enslaved world, a place where zombies, ghouls, shades and human shadows live, preyed upon by blood-sucking devils and menaced by frenzied beasts; all of which are folded into the ever-darkening mythos.

Finally, a civilisation over-extended beyond its powers of management, over-burdened by the self-replicating bureaucracy of the self-replicating management class, and pointlessly 'led' by inept figureheads with no power to either comprehend or influence the vast, bloated, hyper-complexity that society has become, enters a DECADENT PHASE of decline and fall, in which the social body begins to fall apart, its cults and institutions break down and various diseases—the civil unrest, madness and warfare that come from exploiting culture, and the fires, floods and famines that come from exploiting nature—attack the weakening system and destroy it.

Each civilisation has a different history, with those of the earliest systems being a mere outline of what followed. The rule of the earliest egoic systems over unself—over the natural context that surrounded them and the natural consciousness that animated them—was tenuous and unstable, never maintaining very profound or very widespread control for very long, leading to civilisations continually fragmenting and breaking back down into their uncivilised or semi-civilised constituent parts. The fundamental egoic drive to create civilisation did not die however. It lived on in weaker neighbouring polities until they were powerful enough to deal a death blow to the declining empire, take over its machinery—without the enervating institutional baggage that had built up—and, in a new entrepreneurial phase of energy and enthusiasm, use it to expand and develop a new form of the system. This is how the various civilisations and sub-civilisations of Mesopotamia, India, Egypt, Greece, China, Rome, Arabia, Mongolia, Europe and America proceeded (or PROGRESSED), handing the blinding, life-annihilating torch of control—of civilisation-building techniques and legitimations—from one to the next, until the final civilisation, our own, appeared.

§164.

The spread of ego can be traced through the increasingly violent and abstract mythologies, or MYTHOI, of the fallen world. Civilised legitimations and egoic techniques were encoded in an official canon of tales about the gods which embodied the civilised ego and its civilised institutions. The values of the gods were both produced by and filtered down to the idioms, folk wisdom and even the individual conscience of 'the man in the street' where they were felt and expressed as 'reality'. Early religious tales featuring the now demonic forces of chaos, nature and femininity, for example, justified the domination of unself, a domination that the system was founded on. The dark, the wild and the female were to be the objective *other* to the bright, ordered, male subject at the centre of civilised life.

This isn't to say that there was one monolithic mythos in each civilisation. While society as a whole pushes towards totalisation, its constituent groupminds battle over the form, both physical and mythical, that this totalisation is to take, leading to a variety of competing sub-universes of meaning from competing sub-cults; a constant, tedious ideological warfare that makes it nearly impossible to rope everyone under a single system of legitimations, not least because powerful groups also have to manipulate outsiders and discipline insiders. Outsiders have to be manipulated to acknowledge the authority of the cult and insiders have to be disciplined to stay within it. If the layman rejects authority, the heavies will be called in to get his mind right, if the professional strays, the men in white coats will be called in to guide him back in.

Despite the various mythoi that make up the various components of civilisation, the myths and legitimations of the dominant group—the upper class and its priestly elites—predominate, largely determining the form that others have to adapt to. In the ancient world, this appeared as a pantheon of egoic gods, headed by an increasingly powerful male Boss-God who battled and defeated the dark forces of natural chaos, symbolised by monsters, snakes and women, before handing down a load of rules which men and women had to obey (although compulsion and even indoctrination were usually unnecessary, as pre-domesticated minds, then as now, gladly upheld and even contributed to the mythoi that enslaved them). These masculine MONO-GODS all appeared in civilisations in which large populations had to be centrally controlled by rulers with some kind of 'mandate from heaven' (in the East, 'karma', an ethical system in which the evil get their comeuppance *elsewhere*, fulfilled a similar or complementary function). Boss-Gods began to gain prominence and power towards the end of first phase of civilisation, or BRONZE AGE, which culminated in the great civilised collapse of the twelfth century BC, from the rubble of which rose two foundational legitimations and techniques, the twin pillars upon which our world was to be built; objectivist, atheistic Greek RATIONALITY and subjectivist, monotheistic Hebrew THEOLOGY.

§165.

Atheistic rationality began when nous was completely separated *from* consciousness and context, and completely separated *into* isolated, abstract representations, or ideas, causally related to each other. These representations were, for thousands of years, a series of semi-mythological, *ad hoc* theories with very little relation to each other until, after the invention of money had ruptured them catastrophically from the context, the classical-era Greeks came to the conclusion that mind and matter, subject and object, form and substance could be separated from each other; in fact *had* to be in order to convert them into financialised values. By so doing they created a purely formal idea of 'nature', which for the Greeks meant the objective universe (somatic representation) minus consciousness and context (and therefore meaningful culture). For Homer, speaking nearly half a millennium before Plato, in the distant 'irrational' dawn of Greek civilisation, there was no such 'nature', because the divided conceptual system which creates it had not yet been developed. Rather, there was a unified experience of reality as a unified living totality, along with an unhesitating acceptance of foreign gods, of conflicting myths existing side-by-side, and of a playful and pleasant attitude towards mere opinion. All of this hardened as what we call the classical age drew in. For an aggressively disputatious emerging intelligentsia in classical Greece, gods ceased to be metaphorical symbols reflective of psyche or of nature, but became embodiments of literal *ideas*; ideas which *created* the universe and which *compelled* humans, by violence, by fear and, crucially, by an internally coherent *law*, to understand and obey them.* Eventually, the gods were dispensed with, leaving just the violence, the fear and the rational law.

Knowledge and intelligence thus went from a question of consciously *fitting into* the contextual environment, to knowledge of rules and laws that are independent of it. Reality was now split into a cacophony of radically separate domains, separate from each other and from the context, which required expert understanding to grasp. Laws floated above the surface of the earth, pristine and pure of dirty circumstance. Language became more abstract, more general, emptier of poetic spontaneity and tonal variety. Humans ceased being 'a playground of partly internal and partly external elements of consciousness'† and instead became the 'autonomous subjects' of today, an aggregate of rational constructs, separate from an environment, which became an essentially alien object to be

---

* Max Horkheimer and Theodor W. Adorno. *Dialectic of Enlightenment*
† Paul Feyerabend, *Against Method*

studied, controlled and conquered. Time stopped being an animate, fateful stream that carries our lives to us and instead became synonymous with objective action, our own or that of others. Things stopped having qualities which they beamed outwards and became instead mute, characterless forms which the quarantined I had to breathe rational life into.

For the Greeks of the later classical period, the factual-causal-conceptual faculty could arrive at the truth of being, because being was essentially knowable, and it could penetrate through the mere seeming of outer appearance, into a newly abstracted mind-knowable 'truth'. Because one *had* to act on this 'truth', they concluded that rational knowledge must be the foundation of a just society. To put this in technical terms the ancient Greeks saw epistemology, ontology and morality as being essentially one. This meant that those who must work for the leisure of others—who were therefore unable to know, because they don't have time to study—must be unpeople, evil by virtue of their stupidity. Although the upper and middle class do not consciously think this through, it is this reasoning which has governed their condescending attitude towards *lower sorts* ever since. Aristotle also—quite rationally—included women and children in the category of unpeople as they, like slaves, were unable to *know*.

The rise of the objective 'natural world' which lay before the equally objective 'rational mind' saw, as a consequence, the parallel rise of a solipsistic, subjective world of imaginative—but unreal—fancy. With no rational truth to ground them, subjective events vanished into a shifting, unreliable dreamworld of appearances which poets, dreamers and children could idly gad about in, but which had nothing to do with the serious business of dealing with 'the real world', which now had to be unpicked by a mind made sufficiently uniform, not to mention sufficiently narrowed, to grasp it. The application of the abstract mind to this 'real world' inspired THE FIRST SCIENTIFIC REVOLUTION of Pythagoras, Anaximander, Xenophanes, Zeno, Euclid, Archimedes and Aristotle. Egoic art in Greece, which had hitherto been subordinated to the selfish *subjective* emotions of fear and desire, now focused on equally egoic *objective* ideas of perfection and accuracy, the purpose of art no longer being to subordinate people to the might and majesty of the legitimating mythos but to habituate them to a rational-symbolic 'reality'. Bodies, for example, were no longer represented as they *essentially* are, in their ineffable particularity and sensuality, but as they *merely objectively* are, perfectly accurate scooped-out shells; no more truthful, fundamentally, than a *mere* photograph. We call this CLASSICISM.

Although gods remained in Greek society, particularly for the superstitious, irrational masses and the silly, unserious and happy poets, it became, essentially, one of the first atheistic societies on earth. Physicalist ATHEISM is the natural consequence of living in a universe presented as nothing but a configuration of objective, quantitative particles, in which human existence is understood to be aimless, and in which morality is nothing but a tool to control the masses and to serve a society subordinated to the accumulation of money. Such a universe—such a civilisation—may permit religion, may permit all kinds of personal, local or 'free-time' beliefs, but these play no part, whatsoever, in the meaningful business of ownership and management—which is to say, of *work*.

§166.

At roughly the same time as atheism was being developed in Greece, a thousand miles away a group of people called the Jews were developing precisely the same ideology under a different, but complementary form, MONOTHEISM. For both Jews and Greeks the thing-in-itself could be *known*, for the former through the 'creator of nature' or *the* idea of God, for the latter through 'ideas of nature', or *ideas* of gods. The Jews commanded the faithful not to worship the sun, while the Greeks turned it into a bright rock; in both cases the actual miracle of life-giving light, the living window through which joy itself poured out into the body of the world—the sun, the happy sun—was a *thing* rolling over a morbid wasteland of *other things*. In other words, both the Jews and the classical Greeks were IDOLATERS. *They worshipped representation.** They

---

* Owen Barfield, *Saving the Appearances*

were hostile to reality; to actuality, to nature, to the unspeakable, to the other, and to woman, all sources of chronic unease, bordering on dread, which explains the stupendous misogyny of Greek and Jewish philosophy (as the Jewish Testament of Reuben frankly states; 'women are evil'), the poverty of metaphor in Greek philosophy and in the Hebrew Bible (with some notable, beautiful exceptions), their tedious 'spelling out' of how it is, their essential joylessness, and the conspicuous absence of playful innocence.

Monotheistic Jews were as ruthlessly rationalising as atheistic Greeks, fanatical in their desire to purge their religion of all magical elements, to purify their totalising devotion to the singular Idea, Word or Law, all of which assumed cosmos-filling importance; had to, because God was now away on business, having completely departed the universe to sit in a singular position of detached, never to be reached, remoteness. His actions no longer directly affected man or woman, but appeared in *time*. Festival, once a celebration of immediacy, and through it eternity—in which time couldn't possibly play any part—was brought down by the Hebrews to collective chanting in gratitude for a *way marker* on a one-way ticket to nowhere; not unlike our pathetic 'New Year's Eve'.

The Hebrew religion was also the first consecration of sado-masochism on a universal scale. Judaism demanded total, solipsistic submission to an immortal sadist, an absolute Other which could neither be reached, challenged or questioned. Participation is completely out of the question with absolutist monotheism, as a single God stands utterly apart and utterly alone, both in His theoretical position as well as in His absolute ethical authority, one which brooks not the slightest dissent. The masochistic follower must submit utterly, detest all somatic engagement with the context, and love his bodiless submission, or be sadistically obliterated, like the hapless Amalekites whose total annihilation Yahweh sanctioned.

The Jews were the first group of people to wage total war on what they hypocritically called 'idolatry'. As the first hyper-literal religion, they hated, as all literalists do, images of god-in-itself; because they are unable to see them as such.

For the literalist, representation is all there is, the *known*; either causal scientific ideas or the causal religious idea. The literalist cannot therefore see their own idols *as* idols, because there is nothing really "beyond" which the idol can represent, just an idea, albeit a terribly sacred one. This is why playful and metaphorical images of an ineffable other seem so threatening to idolaters, because they cannot experience anything other *than* images. Symbols or teachings which refer to an actual experience of unself, here and now, "*in*" the flesh, appear, to the man or woman who cannot *escape* flesh, evil. It's not then so much that such religions brand old gods as devils, rather that by the time monotheistic religions cover reality with the screen of literalism, these gods have become diabolical.* The literalist *must* therefore destroy what *he* calls idols and replace them with his own literal symbols, which *he* calls truth; and this is what the Hebrews did, just as the miserable monotheistic and atheistic literalists who followed them did.

Yahweh was handed down to monotheistic *Islam*, which was—if this could be possible—even more cheerlessly monotonous (taking the smashing of 'idols' to a new level), hysterically sadistic (constantly recommending that unbelievers be slaughtered) and fanatically masochistic (the word 'Islam' essentially means masochism) than the Judaism it rehashed; and to *Christianity*, which accidentally opened a back door to magic and mystery by introducing the idea of 'incarnation', a return of God to the flesh. This permitted a parade of heavenly creatures to march down to earth, at the head of which, the thoroughly un-Jewish, practically pagan notion of 'the mother of God'. Despite this, Christianity was, like Judaism and Islam, fused with Greek rationality, obsessed with textual law, uncompromisingly authoritarian and rigidly historical (and therefore obsessed with a 'coming saviour'), so when the Protestants dispensed with the Catholic carnival, stripping their religion back to its 'essence', and began taking on the lessons of the proto-capitalist Islamic mercantilism which inspired the Renaissance, the ground was prepared for the final onslaught of egoic ideation and the logical end-point of monotheism; atheistic modern science.

---

* Ludwig Wittgenstein, *Culture and Value*

§167.

The dismal adventures of ego spread far beyond its birthplace. By the time the first egoic super-power, Rome, took to the world stage—fusing Greek atheism and Jewish monotheism into the most cheerless, boring, matter-of-fact, profane and profoundly uncreative society the world had yet known—fallen man and his ego-justifying legitimations and ego-enhancing technologies had spread across much of the globe, indirectly influencing even remote cultures. As Greek civilisation was flourishing, for example, Mohism and the aptly named 'School of Forms' were busy in China purging the senses of mystery and exalting the semi-monotheistic principles of function, logic and causality. Nevertheless, the egoic vanguard remained to a large extent in the near-East, from whence, via a brief Eurasian interregnum, it found a home in Renaissance Europe. We call the area of its progress THE WEST, in distinction to the region vaguely beyond or outside of it, designated by THE EAST, which either lagged behind the spearhead of egoic progress, or lived in a subtler state of 'psycho-social' egotism— the mass mind has always been, for introverted good and for masochistic ill, more important in the East—or, with varying degrees of success, avoided it altogether.

Generally speaking, when looking into the past, it is not history that we find in the East, or in those areas of the world which escaped ego's expanding wasteland, but its opposite. The West, focused on linear progress through linear time (and infinite space), regarded that which cannot be grasped, which is beyond the pool of light thrown by the self, as an unpleasant or at best dreamy mystery. The West has always considered this enigma or (the modern term) 'unconscious' to be a *consequence* of a physical consciousness situated in a physical world. The opposite has always been the case in the East, where dreams are "caused" by 'the unconscious', *and so is waking life*; both with the same common origin as literal and metaphorical language. This is why, *generally* speaking, the East understands qualitative gradations of consciousness which are invisible to the Western mind, why its mythic art has tended towards the heroine's wandering tale—less concerned with individuality of character and, consequently, of change—rather than the hero's one-pointed quest to know and overcome his self, why soteriological techniques for *experiencing*† reality are more important in Eastern philosophies than ideas *about* that reality, why these philosophies have been less interested in picking over such ideas and more interested in exploring where they come from, and consequently, why celebrated Eastern teachers would have treated Aristotle, Descartes, Leibniz, Chomsky and Žižek as in need of help.

As the egoic world grew, fell, regrouped, grew again, collapsed, formed somewhere else, developed more powerful tools, extended even further, fragmented once again and reformed once again, the original truth of unself remained untroubled, untouched, out of time and, in large part—despite their own slow suffocation under the weight of ego—buried in the Eastern soils of India, China and Japan. Although the thing-in-itself that I am may appear to have been paved over by the concrete of civilisation, being out of time it was and is inextinguishable, and although, as unself "entered" the changing times, its form appeared *in* time and adapted to it, the root or ground remained the same. This is why, despite differences in style and emphasis, there is fundamentally no difference between the message of Lao Tzu, Chuang Tzu, Jesus of Nazareth (and the great mystics inspired by him), the message of the Upanishads, the Puranas and the Bhagavad Gita. As Henry David Thoreau vividly put it, 'the oldest... Hindoo philosopher raised a corner of the veil from the statue of the divinity; and still the trembling robe remains raised, and I gaze upon as fresh a glory as he did, since it was I in him that was then so bold, and it is he in me that now reviews the vision'.* The 'fresh glory' of Thoreau and the 'Hindoo' philosopher was the same as that which the earliest pre-fallen men and women gazed upon, and which countless geniuses ever since have experienced and expressed in essentially the same way, and which is available now, even now, to the selfless. This is why Aldous Huxley termed the various expressions of the glory 'the PERENNIAL PHILOSOPHY'.†

---

* Henry David Thoreau, *Walden*
† A. Huxley, *The Perennial Philosophy*

SELF AND UNSELF

§168.

All perennial, panjective and contemplative (as opposed to merely abstract) philosophies relate truth to a consciousness and context that can neither be literally expressed, nor solipsistically imagined by the egoic self. Where atheism, Judaism, Pauline Christianity (which redacted the message of Jesus of Nazareth, overlaying it with the comprehensible concerns of the Christian church cult) and Islam place all hope in a conditioned future, perennial philosophies direct attention to the unconditional present moment (the Gospel of Thomas: 'It will not come by waiting for it... the Kingdom of the Father is spread out upon the earth, and men do not see it'), to the 4D unity of phenomena (the Chuang Tzu: 'The ten thousand things are all one') and to that which is transdimensionally conscious of now (the Upanishads: 'Thou couldst not see the true seer of sight, thou couldst not hear the true hearer of hearing, nor perceive the perceiver of perception, nor know the knower of knowledge. This is thy [un]Self, who is within all'*). Correspondingly, fears *of* the self are mocked, ignored or thwarted in perennial philosophies, while that which the self is afraid of—hell, death and the devil—is, like the fleeting excitements the self is addicted to, transferred *to* the self (the Bhagavad Gita: 'The non-permanent appearance of happiness and distress, and their disappearance in due course, are like the appearance and disappearance of winter and summer seasons. They arise from [selfish] sense perception, and one must learn to tolerate them without being disturbed'†). The comprehensible ideas and laws of egoic ideologies are confounded in perennial philosophies with morally-paradoxical stories (the extraordinary parable of the vineyard workers in The Gospel of Matthew, Arjuna's destruction of his own people in the Bhagavad Gita and the constant attack on conventional values in the Chuang Tzu), intellectually elusive paradoxes (the Tao Te Ching: 'Do when there is nothing to do, manage affairs when there are none to manage, know by not knowing. Regard the great as small, the much as little') and a vast number of surprising and memorable metaphors.

* The Upanishads (tr. Roebuck; parenthesis mine)
† The Baghavad Gita (parenthesis mine)

As with all expressions of truth, perennial philosophies were instantly intermingled with or co-opted by conservative egoic elements, which suppressed their politically subversive elements (the only time Jesus is angry in the gospels, apart from a baffling episode with a fig tree, is a public denunciation of money changers; and yet his recorded words are eerily quiet on the subject of resisting worldly power, even suggesting that we *repay* debts), converted the introversion demanded by conceptions of the ineffable into affirmation of egoic legitimation (the transcendental concepts of 'dharma' and 'Tao' for example were put to work justifying the brutally iniquitous class systems of India and China) and promoted masochistic acceptance of spectacular representation; a masochism which continues to be the chief characteristic of middle-class spiritualists today. The result is that the perennial philosophy needs to be picked out of scripture like blackberries from a forest of thorns and continually rescued from the cheeseball cliches of priests, psychonauts, crystal-healers and promised godmen.

§169.

Originating wisdom wasn't just injected from afar into the cracks of empire while it stood, but was found among the rubble when it collapsed. When Rome, that vast empire of sadists, slaves and servile epicures, fell, and the glare of egoic power shifted east, Europe gladly embarked on a thousand years of *relatively* pleasant darkness. The medieval period could be horrendously unpleasant, lives could be nasty, brutish and short, and, incarnate magic notwithstanding, the all too familiar psychological monstrosities of the Catholic church, combined with an obsessive hatred of soma, made a horror of human life. Contemporary qualities, such as a sense of irony and an interest in the viewpoints of remote others, however skin-deep in our society, do not seem to have been common in the medieval period. Ego and its world reigned over the medieval world; but its grip was not as tight as it was during the miserable reign of Rome nor as it would be during the far more miserable reign of capitalism.

The medieval world was one of immense hardship, but the human end of the blind man's stick was still alive; there was still a natural, contextual, gendered 'background' to human affairs, to home baking and shoe making and ocean sailing and horse riding and even to map, palm and book reading, a background oneness with consciousness, making the world, for all its torturous pains and discomforts, *home*. The mysteries of death and madness and the wild were welcomed; they were understood to *accompany* man through his life. Once again, we know this not so much from the facts, but from the expressed quality of the early and high-medieval period—from how the almost impossibly beautiful cathedrals were built, from how paintings presented reality as a bizarre non-literal whole, from cute characterful carvings in little churches, and from the various letters and poems we have from the medieval period (across both Europe and Asia). Panjective, pre-modern medieval art of the East and West may (like the pre-civilised masks of the Inuits or the pre-Roman tomb-art of Etruria) seem naive and 'childish', but it is often grounded in sensate experience of the balance and character of the natural world, overflowing with vivid uniqueness, sweetness and an intimate sense of the actual living quality of 'inanimate' matter. There is a felt sensitivity to the character of nature, which, as objectivity returned to art in the Renaissance, began once again to fade.

Before THE SECOND SCIENTIFIC REVOLUTION of the sixteenth and seventeenth centuries, reality was understood much as it was before the first scientific revolution of ancient Greece, as a constellation of resemblances, sympathies and emulations brought to consciousness as metaphors, signs or signatures; manifestations of quality. Rational man is quick to laugh at astrology, at the four humours, at the complicated clockwork of alchemy, and in many cases he is right to—many medieval resemblances and sympathies were nothing but insane solipsistic associations—but, quite apart from the fact that modern 'educated' folk almost never actually investigate the 'superstitious' systems they scoff at, they miss the fact that the point of these so-called 'pseudo-sciences' was *not* to fix a factual system onto the represented world of the ego, but to express a fundamentally *non-causal* attitude to it, one in which a common quality physiognomically animates one's eyes, the shape of one's hands, the stars in the sky and the shape of the entrails you've just pulled from a dead crow.

§170.

In fifteenth century Europe everything came together for ego. There was initially a great outpouring of joy at the beginning of 'the Renaissance', as the male principle, suffocating in the weird spirit of the now decadent medieval groupmind, pulled itself into independent light; but, almost immediately, his knowledge overwhelmed his joy and began rendering reality as the *merely knowable*. The modern mono-man was born; placeless, timeless and genderless, no longer consciously existing in self-transcendent complementarity with selves that are different, but unconsciously *cohabiting* with selves that are the same, everywhere. Depictions of women and animals no longer expressed the inexpressible, focusing instead on the representable end of character, a new 'individuality' which, despite its liberating accuracy, suffocated the spirit, of nature and of life, which appeared less and less truthfully in the machine world that the Renaissance rediscovered and began to rebuild, now in a radically new secular, 'humanist' manner, betraying even the sacred elements of the Greek philosophy they claimed to have rediscovered, but had actually *appropriated*.

The Greeks and Chinese had put barriers on the development of the machine, so that it wouldn't dominate society. They declined to develop certain technologies, and—amazing as this might sound to us today—refused to 'progress'. With the Renaissance and Reformation, all such barriers were removed. The partly desacralised universe of Judaism and Greek philosophy was fused into the new software of Protestantism, clearing northern Europe of superstitious Catholic magic, encouraging the domination of nature—through constant work—and providing the tools by which to do so. The hardware of technology had also continued to progress, leading to the development of three world-changing inventions: *maps*,

which shaped man's perception of space into an artificial series of bounded isolates, *clocks*, which did the same for time,
turning the whole of the four dimensional object we flow
through into a series of separate moments, each related to the
last or the next in 'an independent world of mathematically
measurable sequences',* and the *printing press*, an intellectual
nuclear weapon which laid waste to vernacular orality, creating
a literate world in which truth and justice were to emerge not
from the live flow of embodied speech, but from a critical
relationship with manageable tokens.

The abstract self wasn't just focusing more and more
upon the subject, splitting up its immediate experience into
factual-causal chunks, but also extending its reach outwardly,
laying its thinking matrix over distant lands and distant worlds.
Thelemic and somatic tech, such as gunpowder, the plough
and the lens further extended the reach and power of the
self into more and more remote realms, now viewed almost
entirely through the screen of the rational ego. As more and
more facts built up about the world, so ego's power to possess
those facts increased, leading to more social stratification, and,
as the social head detached itself from the social body, various
techniques to control the latter from afar, including bureaucratic accounting and a new emphasis on *self*-control. Public
manners were to become orderly, odourless and pacifistic—in
a word, *bourgeois*—and unmanageable spontaneous behaviour,
which had been freely accepted in medieval society, was to
be progressively hidden from sight, invested with shame and
made to submit to self-scrutiny, self-judgement and self-con-
fession, all of which could be added to the chart of accounts.†

§171.

The new representation of the new world was expressed by
four key thinkers of the seventeenth century; Francis Bacon,
Thomas Hobbes, René Descartes, and Isaac Newton.

Francis Bacon was the first modern, scientific *manager*. He realised that, for ego to fulfil its mission, the individual had to be effaced, and, in its place, a mass system

---

* Lewis Mumford, *Technics and Civilisation*
† Norbert Elias, *The Civilizing Process*

of knowledge-gathering initiated, one available to anyone who could follow *method*. This method would not require consciousness or sensitivity to the context, genius certainly wasn't required, or love, or independence of spirit, or any other quality, only hyper-concentrated focus on an external collection of specific, objective facts revealed *by* that focus, which could then be added to the collective, literate, mind. Henceforth, MASS MAN was to be the genius, a mass composed of innumerable little PARTICLE MEN, each working by himself on his granule of practical knowledge, or granule of wealth-gathering, or granule of world-building, that he could then add to the abstract mass. *By* himself, said Bacon, the individual is nothing, he can understand 'only as much as he has observed, by fact or mental activity',* but, as he beetles away at his little research project, or administrative task, or industrial-technical manoeuvre, he masochistically merges with the scientific world brain, and quantitatively surpasses the geniuses which he can never understand and, despite lip service to the contrary, despises.

All of this demanded a massively augmented system of centralised control; the modern institution (or in its most complete form, STATE), along with the modern INSTITUTIONAL MAN, attuned not to truth (which, as Bacon taught us, does not exist apart from utility) but to *information*; committed to doing nothing but gather it, control it and then *use* it to control things and people now reduced *to* information. The birth of modern science thus coincided with the birth of the modern institutional state, because they are the same thing. It also coincided with a new emphasis on DEMOCRACY, governance by particle man, which, like culture by particle man, *automatically* excluded unself and *automatically* necessitated technical management to realise.

Thomas Hobbes was the first modern, scientific *statesman*. He described truth as 'the right ordering of names', which depended on 'precise definitions',† which must then be learnt and built up, via an orderly method of combination and recombination, into an edifice of scientific knowledge. Metaphor had no place; reasoning upon it being nothing but

---

* Francis Bacon, *Novum Organum*
† Thomas Hobbes, *Leviathan*

an 'absurdity' which leads to 'contempt'. Love also was suspect, if not dangerous, and even God had to defer to a central authority which must have absolute power over every aspect of man's life. Hobbes' work, like that of all the philosophical technicians who were to follow him, reads like an instruction manual for a machine that nobody needs.

No quality was to be admitted into the new universe but that which benefits the machine, and, in Hobbes' appalling worldview, no society was possible but that which organises man in such a way that his *innate* self-interest—the solitary, poor, nasty, brutish and short state of continual warfare Hobbes called 'nature' (even time and the weather were seen as battlegrounds)—cannot disrupt the operation of the *super*-machine; the state, 'Leviathan' or 'common-power' we require 'to keep [us] all in awe'.*

René Descartes was the first modern, scientific *philosopher*. He inaugurated a new age of completely bodiless thought, in which classical mathematics, based on material things and sensuous limits—and therefore unwilling to accept such notions as negative numbers, irrational numbers, infinite series and so on—was relegated to day-to-day sums and subordinated to a system of purely relational points and functions spiralling away into a realm of perfect abstraction; a 'perfection' reflected in Descartes' strange and horrific image of consciousness, a singular point of computational thought operating a mute, mechanical body. His infamous formulation of our essence, 'I think therefore I am'—an exact reversal of the truth, 'I am, therefore I think'—became the foundation upon which the modern ego was to build itself.†

For Isaac Newton, the first modern scientific *theorist*, standing on Descartes' bodiless shoulders, reality—now sliced up into factual-casual 'time and space'—was no longer a real somatic *thing*, as it had been in classical thought, but entirely, or ultimately, an *idea*, or idea-like. Henceforth, the universe was to be a machine, and (despite the bizarre idea of the clock-winding God who set it all in motion) nothing *but* a machine, with nothing prior to the literal thoughts of the mind and nothing beyond the mental objects of the world.

---

* Ibid.
† René Descartes, *Meditations*

§172.

Since the fall of man, it had been understood that man's individual consciousness—his qualitative sense of justice or dignity or love—must have no freedom to meaningfully build his world, that this should be taken over by elite control; but the new machine mind being built by Bacon, Hobbes, Descartes, Newton and the newly powerful bourgeoisie [instinctively] understood that, firstly, elite princes and priests were often disastrously human and secondly, that their vestigial responsibility to their people was a liability. Democracy could solve both problems, removing irrational power and responsibility at a stroke, replacing them with the rationally aggregated and mechanically managed 'will' of the particle people.

Democratic particle man became fundamentally, functionally, identical to every other democratic social participant. His vote mattered, his purchase, his role and his manufacturing manoeuvre; but *he* didn't. He was completely dispensable, interchangeable, and so, because he was deprived of his unique consciousness and consequent character, he was nothing but a personality, or mask. A mass of such masks, sufficiently educated—trained to be a productive particle—could be predicted to do the right thing, which is to say, fit their activity into the scientifically managed mechanism. At home, in private, the mask could be removed, but at work, at least insofar as that work had even the slightest practical effect on the world, it had to stay on. Individuality, character, consciousness, conscience, creativity, spontaneity, honesty, generosity and love—in a word *humanity*—were erratic, dangerous, unproductive and weird. As society increasingly reflected the mask, and as the mask then adapted itself to the mask-world, so people became more and more mask-like and mask-*a*like; with what trivial mask-differences there were between them subordinated to the requirements of separate, self-reinforcing, mask-based institutions. Finally, at the end of the day, the mask could be taken off, and the exhausted worker could go home in order to consume a world made by masks. There, he sometimes found that he felt insane.

§173.

The creation of a scientific-democractic-institutional world of rational masks would eventually lead to the decline of monotheistic religion. Just as the atheism of the Greeks and the monotheism of the Jews sprang from the same desacralised ego-world, so the new science was initially identical in all important respects to the monotheistic religion it lived with. 'Command over things natural', Bacon wrote, 'is the one proper and ultimate end of true natural philosophy',* just as it was the 'one proper and ultimate end' of unnatural religion. In addition, science and monotheistic religion were based on exactly the same idolatrous focus on a hollow universe of things. But religion, like the priests and princes it relied on, was not up to the task of managing vast rational systems. Its God (or, in solipsistic polytheistic religions, gods) was an unnecessary burden, as were the direct ethical laws that He kept His people in line with, as were the objectively ludicrous 'explanations' that religion gave for natural phenomena. These were a burden not just to academic science but, crucially, to bureaucratic worldly management.

The 'skill-set' institutional man required to succeed—an intensity of literalness, and, consequently, a *non*-intensity, or numbness, of consciousness—did not include knowledge of sacred texts and could not include religious virtues such as piety and charity. Religion had to be banished to a private world. You could be religious at home and in your yoga or prayer break—*that* was the place for virtue or transcendence, not at work, where religion—including new-age religions—was only supposed to serve a rhetorical function. When the modern institutional system spreads into a religious society, such as post-dictatorship Spain or modern Saudi Arabia, the business of running the country becomes, while retaining an outwardly advertised display of religiosity, *functionally* secular, not because science has somehow proved itself to be a superior explanation for the mysteries of existence—it is worse—but because science is what the system needs, and what those who own and manage it need; and *it is need that determines belief.*

---

* Francis Bacon, *De Sapientia Veterum*

The final consequence of scientific management taking over from religious management was PLURALISM, the appearance, in the modern world, of a supermarket of religious and philosophical products which have to compete with each other the same way that all products have to compete with each other,* by standardising themselves to the lowest common denominator and plastering themselves with exhortative adverts. Eventually, the difference between modern, Western Islam, Judeo-Christianity, Hinduism and atheism became negligible, a matter of packaging. Religious 'truth', once 'obvious' and 'known' to all, because it was reflected everywhere in society's symbols and legitimations, became even more questionable, necessitating even more emotionally-motivated 'faith'. Finally, unrooted, the 'truth' of religion floated up into the clouds of mere opinion, where it remains today, while the real, practical *business* of the world is carried out in the church of scientism, with periodic breaks taken in the solipsist playground of postmodernism, the two manifesting in the social or political world as the modern religions of socialism and capitalism.

§174.

Socialism and capitalism, are, despite much noise from their adherents about their immensely important differences, functionally identical; domesticating, workist, statist, technocratic, rational, literalist, functional and obsessed with progress into an imaginary future. They share their hollow, matter-of-fact and *functional* tyranny with their literalist religious progenitors; monotheistic Judaism, 'mainstream' Pauline Christianity and Islam, and atheistic Confucianism, Buddhism, late classical Greek rationalism and Stoicism. All of these worldviews are *essentially*—despite their various surface differences, despite various creative reinterpretations (such as Sufism, medieval Christian mysticism and Zen) and despite much fine-sounding flannel about compassion, peace, equality and whatnot— identical. They are all religions of the urban merchant and professional, alike in their arid, humourless abstraction, their systematic, causal reasoning and in their *basic* lack of interest

---

* Peter Berger, *The Sacred Canopy*

in nature, in place, in the peasantry, in bottom-up rule, and in the incarnate, bodily reality of the present moment. Instead of a paradise spread over the earth *here and now*, it is a *future* heaven which holds their attention, a time when Jesus will throw his ladder down through the dome of the sky and carry up the elect, or when nirvana has been reached, or when the working class will take charge of the machinery of society, or when that machinery will allow the Great and the Good to sit around drinking Dom Perignon in perfect safety. Instead of free physicality, there is fastidiousness about digestion and hygiene, taboo and totem, or there is anti-puritan licentiousness. Instead of truth, there is causal reasoning, fact-gathering and, of course, endless, boring pontification.

Buddhism for example (again, *original* Buddhism, not its strange and wonderful florescences in foreign lands) largely comprises lists of values and moral exhortations; be wise, be peaceful, be compassionate, say nice things, think right, do right, etc, etc, etc.; along with long passages of causal reasoning and tidy systematising; ten grounds for resentment, four noble truths, five dangers in impatience, four kinds of vipers, three marks of indigestion, etc, etc. All *believably* boring. Essentially, it is a dry, pragmatic, solipsistic, socially-submissive religion of tradesmen and managers, like Judaism, Paulism, Islam, Stoicism, Confucianism, socialism and capitalism.

Compare all this, the general tone and approach of urban religion and worldly man, with that of primal animism, Taoism, Orphism, the more exuberant texts of Hinduism, Nazarene Christianity and the wilder (and *entirely* non-socialist) outer reaches of anarchism, which are directed to, or honour, the simplest people, take inspiration from love of nature—which pervades their metaphorical expressions—have an unserious acceptance of the body, are unconcerned with laws and legitimations, are not particularly concerned with history, society or literate, learned, rational 'intelligence', address the physiognomic-panjective *whole* of phenomena, are contemptuous of authority and direct their conscious attention to the present moment. None of this appeals to the modern merchant or priest—the landowner and professional—for obvious reasons. Merchants and priests might devoutly 'worship God', or they might live in a vegan ashram and prostrate themselves before an Indian master, or they might be aggressive atheists, pouring scorn over every myth and fairy tale they can put their literalist paws on, or they might be fanatically hedonistic capitalists, bobbing about on a sea of stimulating excess, or they might be dedicated socialists, ceaselessly campaigning for 'the people', or they might co-opt the form of Nazarene Christianity, Taoism, Advaita or Anarchism; but they are *not* interested in abandoning what they have, or who they think and feel they are. This is why it is almost impossible to find a socialist who thinks for himself, a democrat who agrees with the will of the people, a Taoist immersed in the anarchic paradox of life, an enlightened Buddhist, a Christian who owns nothing, a pious Muslim or Jew with a silly and subtle sense of humour or an anarchist who rejects *all* unjustified domination; monarchies, democracies, states, corporations, post-industrial technologies, the egoic worldly and the worldly ego. This is not a question of sectarian purity. It is the simple truth; the vast majority of people on earth are unconscious, and so they either believe in ideologies which justify unconsciousness, or they co-opt those which do not.

§ 175.

We can see ego's colonisation of the world 'outwardly', in the events of history, but also—and more clearly—'inwardly', in its art. Just as the first scientific revolution scooped meaning out of form, so the second scientific revolution hollowed out space, subordinating it to the witnessing ego. Up to the medieval era, space was considered to be a living, continuous extension of consciousness. When science sucked it empty of significance, perspective entered, subordinating sensate space to the tightly-focused witnessing ego, so that an unnaturally definite mind-made world could appear. This appeared in the technique of PERSPECTIVE, invented by renaissance man.

Lines of perspective force the viewer to subordinate the whole of the image to the concentrated [vanishing] point of it. The lines of walls, roads and tiles are not to be viewed in themselves, or as *equal* parts of a whole, but as *symbolic* markers for the perspectival idea of the isolated, yet central, viewer.* The schematised form of perspectival images is a *subservient* signifier of uniform, mind-made, space, used to emphasise the illusion of solidity and homogeneity, and to de-emphasise both the role that consciousness has in creating and perceiving experience and that the self has in forming space, distance, size and so on. We are, in effect, tricked into thinking we are viewing an accurate representation of objective reality, when we are actually viewing a highly abstract matrix of interlocking symbols representing, at best, a partially-real egoic illusion. Newton's physics creates much the same illusion.

This isn't to say that artistic truth cannot be expressed in perspectival images, or that perspective is an arbitrary invention, or that Newton's mechanical time and space doesn't correspond to *something* which exists; but, rather, that we are presented with *a realistic form of noetic interpretation*, which through its dominance came to devalue 'unrealistic' natural qualities; alternative, intimate experiences of time and space, along with that which is "behind" and "beyond" the factual-causal universe; consciousness and context.

The same devaluation of consciousness and context was also evident in a new form of myth or literature, which began to express a view of reality whereby 'realism' was not merely one approach to reality, but was, in principle, reality itself. As with perspectival images, artistic truth was certainly able to appear, but the move to truthful realism in literature began to devalue *truthful non-realism* (particularly that of vernacular orality) which became an oxymoron. Henceforth, the only non-realism allowed, the fanciful productions of 'imaginative writers', was 'mere fiction'. Again, in the hands of the masters, novelistic fidelity to the objective world could be used to expose that world, see through it, but the *overall* movement towards mythic literalism was one that made the mystery of existence appear unserious. The *serious* business of real fiction, like all serious business, must be left to the professional, literate, educated, institutionalised expert. Only he

---

* Erwin Panofsky, *Perspective as Symbolic Form*

can be trusted with the power to disseminate his views, which is why the independent, unprofessional poet, storyteller and craftsman migrated upwards to the middle class, creating a new set of professional skills, a *standard*, which then shaped artistic output. Anyone who had not learnt those skills in the correct manner and in the correct institution was, by that very fact, unable to create art.

§ 176.

The beginning of the nineteenth century saw a collective cultural rejection of formality, and of objective, rational mentation, which gave way to instinctive, subjective emotion. Haydn gave way to Beethoven, Gainsborough ceded to Turner and Kant yielded to Schopenhauer in the movement which came to be known as ROMANTICISM.

The barrier between self and unself was initially permeable, it hardened with the Greeks and Hebrews, who could barely conceive of unself, let alone speculate on it, calcified into concrete with the Romans, softened again in the middle ages, when literal conceptions of unself swam into consciousness in countless bizarre forms, hardened again with the second scientific revolution, then softened again when the West colonised India and became reacquainted with the East, the unselfish philosophy of which filtered back into Western consciousness, via Friedrich Schiller, along with the collective realisation that, despite the misery and toil and sickness of the medieval period, it allowed for *something else*, now rapidly draining from life. In philosophy, the thing-in-itself returned to serious reflection via Immanuel 'the all-destroyer' Kant, who, almost despite himself, made the most important discovery of Western philosophical thought, that the primary properties of time and space are not outside of us but brought to a reality which mind cannot penetrate. Despite only showing us to the door—not having the gumption to step through it himself—and despite his horrendously dry and complicated noetic system, Kant's 'transcendental idealism' formed a kind of distant star round which the genius of

Goethe, Wordsworth, Coleridge, Stendhal, Schopenhauer and even the largely non-Romantic Tolstoy, orbited, throwing the sterile certainties of classicism—that all genuine questions can be answered, that these answers are knowable, and that all the answers must be compatible with one another—into doubt. The result of questioning these falsehoods was an outflowing of magisterial music philosophy and art, some of which—the novels of Tolstoy, the music of Beethoven, the paintings of Van Gogh—are still, to anyone with unselfish taste, unequalled.

The maggot in the Romantic apple was subjectivity (visceral emotion, thelemic will, noetic imagination), which they conflated, disastrously, with consciousness. They returned to nature, sometimes to the source of nature, but they brought emotion, will and imagination with them, and so, on the subtlest but most powerful level, ego lived on. Instead of breaking down the barrier between self and unself, Romanticism conflated the *unselfish* source of genius, something which comes from "beyond" the self, with the subjective *self* of the artistic genius (which is why Haydn—incorrectly—considered Beethoven to be an atheist), directly puffing up that self to cosmic importance and indirectly supporting solipsism, creating the division we are familiar with today between its complementary opposame, literalist science, which is dull but truthful, and art (or religion), which is interesting but full of lies.

Finally, the membrane between self and unself hardened once again, leaving consciousness and context incapable of penetrating the world. Today, we know that there is 'an unconscious', we know that there is something mysterious 'on the other side' of our instruments, and we know that the foundational assumption of scientism, that the non-phenomenal is non-existent, leads to an endless series of perplexing absurdities, but we can find no way to cross over, to get out of ourselves without falling into a solipsistic, navel-gazing dreamworld. In order to cross the threshold, we must overcome the rule of the chimerical subject *and* the useful object, which, given that both have fully colonised consciousness and context—or, in manifest form, self and world—is not just difficult to do, but impossible to know it needs to be done.

§ 177.

European civilisation reached its peak in the nineteenth century. As it began to fall, the next empire, waiting in the wings to
take over, was ostensibly the United States of America, but in
reality the machine *itself* was preparing to take charge, the first
global system managed by transnational financial and corporate institutions, with nation states taking the executive role
of policing the people and extracting taxes from them. This
final phase of human civilisation, which we call MODERNITY,
was initiated at the culmination of the industrial revolution
by Frederick Winslow Taylor, the grandfather of the modern
world, and his system of scientific OBJECTIVE MANAGEMENT.*

Objective management was not the first attempt to sys-
tematise productive life, but it was by far the most thorough.
As with creating any system, the first step was the isolation of
facts, in this case, of every microscopic motion made in a factory, the second step was measurement and documentation of
facts, and the third step was control of the facts. Subordinated
to the facts (*compliance*), the things of the factory could then be
organised or planned (*orderliness*) to produce the greatest output (*productivity*) in the shortest time (*efficiency*). The 'things'
of the factory comprised the raw materials, machinery, power
systems and man; *all* now tools. 'In the past the man has been
first', said Taylor, 'In the future the system must be first'.

For scientific management, the only goal of human life
was increased compliance, orderliness, productivity and efficiency. Technique therefore (TECHNOCRATIC expertise or, today, digital algorithms) was superior to conscious judgement,
the measurable was superior to the elusive, greater output was
superior to greater pleasure and speeding up was better than
slowing down. What this meant was that human beings were
a *liability* and had to be mechanised or annihilated, their creative consciousness parcelled up into a series of discrete steps
that could be optimised to produce more and more, faster
and faster. After Taylor, the worker followed a script written
by someone else, and then, in late modernity, when artificial
intelligence, or AI was able to take over, by some*thing* else.

---

* Frederick Winslow Taylor, *The Principles of Scientific Management*

§178.

Taylorism soon spread far beyond the factory. In the new world, a vast number of people were to be rigidly coordinated into centrally managed productive and regulatory activities. In order to do this, the natural, the spontaneous, the chaotic, the local—in a word the VERNACULAR—had to be exterminated. Society was to be broken down into particles. First the tribe had to be broken up, then the village and the local community, then, finally, the family. Mostly this could happen automatically, through assimilation into a technocratic system, which, firstly, compelled those who could work towards places where work was available, leaving the very old and very young back in the village, and, secondly, which separated young people from their cultural traditions, forcing them into peer-oriented relations with their equally rootless coevals, further opening them up to market exploitation. Ideological support for this destabilising process came from the capitalist, technocratic, progress-worshipping right, which painted the past and everything associated with it as moronic, superstitious ignorance, and from the equally technocratic, progress-worshipping socialist left, which painted the family as an exploitative prison for women (which, in many respects, it was) and the labour-market as a paradise of independence and self-improvement (which women, at least those still in touch with their feminine hearts, would soon discover was far worse).

Vernacular social practices, integrated into an ungoverned natural context, also had to be destroyed. They had always been a threat to the civilised system, but the totalising demands of objective management massively expanded the category of NON-COMPLIANT. Local languages, local land practices, unplanned community living, fluid informal naming conventions, local traditions, fractal landscapes, chaotic living arrangements and unique cultures are disorderly, unproductive and inefficient.* They cannot fit into a complete, rational mechanism, and so they had to be replaced with standardised knowledge, standardised institutions, standardised cities, standardised landscapes and standardised people. Travel the

---

* James C. Scott, *Two Cheers for Anarchism*

world today and you can see the outcome of what was to become a global project of industrial STANDARDISATION; everywhere the same schools, the same airports, the same music, the same cars, the same hospitals, the same farms, the same parliaments, the same banks, the same roads and, underneath their 'diverse' personalities, the same people.

Henceforth, competence in the world was to come from being *instructed*, productivity from being *managed*, orderliness from being *planned* and happiness from being *satisfied*. The principal consequence of this, of the destruction of the vernacular artisan and the structuring of vernacular production, and, beyond that, of vernacular society itself, into a rational mechanism, was that it became impossible for an individual to learn how to do anything useful. After twenty years of gathering knowledge stuff, followed by ten years making cars, or handling tax returns, what does a man know? Nothing, or next to, which is exactly what the world wants; highly specialised infants who can do nothing but suckle at the tit of the machine. As Alex de Tocqueville asked* of Adam Smith's model of the newly hyper-specialised man, 'What can be expected of a man who has spent twenty years of his life making heads for pins?' The answer to this question can be found in any staffroom, factory floor, laboratory, shop or office you care to walk into.

More crippling than an inability to really do anything in a scientifically managed system, is a disinclination to *try* to do anything. The system-integrated self is not just compelled to inhabit a specialised role but, constantly reinforced by its specialised integration, becomes addicted to the security the role provides and terrified of the very real negative consequences of crossing institutional barriers into radically different fields of enquiry, radically different fields of activity, radically different fields of social intercourse, or even into radically different *fields*, which become a source of anxiety, leading to the self becoming pathologically inflexible and unadaptable. This is why, in a highly developed world, conscious people, able to respond to changing circumstances, find themselves at continual war with both those who are *not* able to, and with the rigidly restrictive world they plan, design and develop.

* Quoted in ibid.

§179.

The external physical compulsion of the pre-modern king was, and would continue to be, necessary to exterminate the vernacular, as would the use of systemic force to eradicate or eject collective and individual quality which did not fit into the system, but increasingly as a last resort, when subtler techniques of manipulation had broken down. An efficiently regimented mass is compelled not by the authorities, nor even by the functioning of the system, but unconsciously, from *within*. This was the beginning, and the result, of the final phase of the system; SUBJECTIVE MANAGEMENT.

Subjective management was achieved by shaping the self into a systemic component. This superficially necessitated indoctrination through advertising, government propaganda, explicit instruction and so on, but to be really effective it required that the experience of man be *completely* mediated; everything he felt, saw, did and thought had to be a product of self. Then nothing in objective 'reality' could reflect unself—and the subversive qualities which arose from unself would cease to appear real. Man acted in a way which appeared to be right, rational and meaningful; he avoided the foolish, the crazy, the weird, but in so doing he screwed himself deeper and deeper into the machine. He did not act consciously, any more than those who shaped the world for him did, for consciousness was the unreality he was now trying to avoid.

Just as factories could not be objectively managed without isolating exposure and measurement, so the inner world of the new machine-self, to operate optimally, had to be exposed to scrutiny and forced into the light of literal attention, where it could be distilled into manageable abstractions. Experts in business and in occupational, motivational, organisational and vocational psychology opened up new fields of 'human engineering', by which to measure and then regulate 'attitudes' and 'sentiments', so that companies could commandeer the factory of the self,* and then manage it 'for excellence'. The crude objective adjustments of Taylorism—the specialisation of work and rationalisation of activity—were supplemented by

---

* Nikolas Rose, *Governing the Soul*

minute interventions into motivation, enthusiasm and belief. The *whole being* of the worker was to be engaged in work or in consuming the products of work, and if he couldn't do it, if he was not sufficiently enthusiastic about being a ball-bearing in a reality-eating machine, well then there must be something wrong with him; it was *his fault*. He had a 'mental illness' and required *care*.

§ 180.

There was, in the wondrous new world of total management, to be nothing that did not come from the machine; buildings, furniture, clothing and other tools, all kinds of work-activity, financing, accreditation and procedures of motivation, along with all forms of education, recreation and even, eventually, communication were to come to us from the hands of hyper-specialised mindselves, serving an egoic system, serving *itself*. The end point of this process was total dependence upon the state, the corporation and the technocratic system, through total subordination of social and individual life to the manager, or professional EXPERT. Life became a question of learning skills from professional authorities and following their plans. Taking an independent course—home-schooling, self-medication, refusal of bureaucracy, working outside of the market, disregarding professional advice—led to the uncomprehending disapproval of 'public opinion' or, if that didn't work, legal sanction and punishment. If you did not listen to experts you were, at best, a reckless fool, bad parent or threatening eccentric, at worst, a murderer, criminal or fiend. Just as the Greek slave was an unperson by virtue of his inability to acquire rational truth, so were those, in the fully developed system, who refused technical expertise. They were not merely turning their back on knowledge, but on reality itself.

While the objective world was being designed and managed by an army of technical experts and managers, another army—practically a nation—of managers arose in order to direct the functioning of the subjective self.* These were called THERAPISTS. They had three basic functions:

---

* Ibid.

i. To deflect the cause of misery away from its *distal* origins in the functioning of the system. Power was omitted from therapy—the power of the system and its owners and managers over the individual—which held as much interest to the professional therapist as it did to the professional script-writer, journalist, doctor and teacher. The horrors of poverty, of pointless schooling, of wage slavery and meaningless work, of living *as* a manufactured good *in* a warehouse world, none of this made its way into the therapy room. Therapists weren't interested in curing the system; they *were* the system. Not that there is anything wrong with power, even in anarchist accounts of the world; the question is how it is distributed, how it is used, and how much freedom those who are subject to power have to disobey orders or to question their subordinate position. In the world presented by modern therapy it was to be *zero*, because there *was* no power to refuse. Machine man was, when he inevitably broke down, to be persuaded that *he* was the cause of his misery, and not the fact that he spent his life squirming under the thumb of the Leviathan.

ii. To produce a series of comforting ideas that could be used to avoid addressing the *proximal* cause of man's now meaningless, futile, stagnating life. Therapists never meaningfully spoke of SANITY. The word was unintelligible to them. They had no real "relationship" with contextual reality or with any conscious experience "preceding" such reality, and so were unable to see through the veil of representation to the source of meaning, and therefore to sanity. Not that this troubled them overly, as there was no actual, physical society in which to realise anything but the trivial, system-friendly values they were paid to manufacture. The result was that all the modern ideas of self-respect, self-belief, self-actualisation, autonomy, inclusion, 'mental health' and all the other stand-ins for sanity, were just words. They might sometimes appear to have meaning for a cosy hour with a *nice* therapist, or for a comfortable upper-class columnist, but as soon as the reader or client re-entered his actual life he was once again rudderless on an ocean of futility and meaninglessness.

iii.   To manage the inner world. Psychologists and psycho-therapists were paid to collect psyche-data, so that human subjectivity could be more easily controlled, compliant particles could be more easily identified and disruptive particles more easily tranquillised. In order to do this, the inner world of man had to be sliced up into the academic categories of psyche professionals. Just as objective life was to be understood solely by the rational manager and by his rational, managing machines, so subjective life was to be understood through the rational categories, assessments and diagnoses of psychological expertise.* How men and women thought about the troubles of children, interpersonal problems, creative frustrations, fear and despair, was all meaningless unless translated into the machine code of the psychocrat. Particularly naive was the use of words that express truth, such as 'love', 'beauty' and 'sanity', which had no place in the lexicon of psychology unless reduced to fact or technique. Character gave way entirely to personality; a series of manipulable bits that could be adjusted and reassembled to fit the needs of the system. Because managed reality had entirely hollowed out the caddis-fly case of man, the psychological scientist, when he went looking for an inner world, found nothing but fragments of personality, the impulses, phobias, drives, faculties and complexes of an alien-ated mind-machine, which he then poked around in trying to manipulate to some normative end. Man no longer needed to empathically experience others from the inside, which from a modern, behaviourist perspective was impossible anyway. All he had to do was recognise the signs by which human beings revealed themselves, and then adjust these signs accordingly. This is how man learnt to *manage* his self, *manage* his fears, *manage* his desires, *manage* his life in society and *manage* his relationships,† and how the manager, in turn, managed *him*; through analysis, repetition, rehearsal, manipulation of body language and various psychotherapeutic techniques.

Psychology as a 'scientific' discipline is shallow, barren and almost completely pointless. Because it directs itself entirely to the measurable in man, its only use is in controlling

---

* David Smail, *The Origin of Unhappiness*
† Nikolas Rose, *Governing the Soul*

him, which is why it exists at all. Those writers in the field with
genuinely artistic sensibilities—sensitive, empathic, truthful—
are excluded from syllabuses everywhere, as is all intelligent
reflection into quality, consciousness, physiognomy, the thing-
in-itself, destiny, the context, or anything else which cannot
be spatially mapped, technically systematised, or *used*.

§181.

The worker had never been imagined as an individual genius,
yearning to see through the self and realise its vision in society,
and since the industrial revolution he had not been considered as a social creature either, with powers and obligations
derived from being part of a communal whole. Now, however,
he wasn't even to be understood as the servant of productive
forces, rationally pursuing wealth. Assisted by the psychocrat,
particle man was now searching for what he called '*meaning*';*
which was actually a search for a *self-improvement* which could
only end in subjectively 'meaningful' work *for* the system and
equally 'meaningful' consumption (of excitement, knowledge,
identity, citizenship, etc.) *in* the system. By completely allying
the self *to* the system, the option of discovering freedom *from*
the system became effectively unthinkable. Compliance, orderliness, productivity and efficiency in the factory, the office,
the school and the home thus arose automatically from the
'natural' desires of the 'ordinary' self.

There was no need for this to be a difficult, violent
or painful process. It was all, by now, easy, straightforward,
obvious. It was clearly an act of *compassion* to help human
beings 'get out of poverty', 'live together', 'progress' and 'succeed' in 'life', be 'healthy', 'happy' and 'resilient'. The swarms
of educational and medico-hygienic technicians let loose to
register, observe, teach and intervene in the lives of families
were very often, for example, made up of Very Nice People
who Only Wanted to Help. They may have felt the demand
for record-keeping was an onerous irrelevance, they may have
complained about the impersonal demands of management,
but they were perfectly unaware that they existed to define and

* Ibid.

sort the components of the social machine into 'cases', that the viruses and bacteria they were teaching people to ward off had taken the place of terrorists and devils as a means to keep them in line, or that techniques for dealing with the problems of childhood, which ordinary people were quite capable of learning for themselves, were being taken out of their hands and, through becoming a matter of technical expertise, being integrated into an inhuman programme of social control.

None of this would have been possible unless experience had not been converted, by abstract, egoic philosophy, into knowledge. This enabled the body to be considered as a [genderless] *knowledge thing*, along with the mind, language and society; all knowledge things (or, insofar as they related to quality, VALUES), inserted into man by knowledge-owners and managers — GNOSOCRATS — who taught him to see his self as a *thing*, as a mechanism, composed of *bits* — interchangeable components — which required the correct inputs to produce the correct outputs; health, intelligence, meaning and culture. Man thus became an abstract thing to himself, and, crucially, an abstract thing to the systemic experts who managed his life.

As this expertise was disseminated through society, people could no longer think of raising children unless through a technical lens, or education unless as something handed down from system-approved middle man, or health unless as a product of management. They could no longer think of *any* kind of life unless it happened through an institution or was sanctioned by it. Human life in its entirety, along with all quality and meaning, was slowly becoming obsolete.

§182.

Each step literalism made, took it further away from meaning. Late-literalist society simply had no use for it. Since Freud had transformed all moral impulses into rationalised desires, it played no part in psychology. Marx didn't need it, and all forms of socialism paid nothing but lip-service to it. Institutional scientism rejected it — you could not advance anywhere in the sciences by seriously suggesting that what you were investigating was *meaningful*. Literary criticism, journalism, academic output of all kinds, none of it talked about life or any phenomenon within it as meaningful. In [post] modernist texts the notion of meaning was simply laughed at, in educated discussion it was synonymous with the most barbaric forms of superstition. Moral neutrality reigned in discussions of history, anthropology, politics, literature, art and social affairs; unless the subject was official enemies ('bad') or friends ('good'), or as a pluralist frill. Almost any attempt to inject meaning, truth or quality into serious discussion of a serious topic was met with, at best, bemused perplexity.

Literalism built a world which, in its totality, presented itself as reality. No alternative was conceivable because the whole world was conceptualisation made objective flesh, ideology made reality. Ego created the world and made escape impossible; which *made the real egoic*. Escape from egoic rationality and emotion was, *ipso facto*, insanity; a radical launch into the unknowable, indistinguishable to the physicalist, in its rejection of the primacy of objectivity, from the most extreme—*yet equally literal*—forms of schizoid solipsism.

This has been the case since the dawn of civilisation, when man first projected his ego into his legitimising cults, but as the world manifested ego completely, it became its own perfect police and propaganda. Ego *automatically* reproduced itself in and as the world. Provided that man could fit into the world, and wasn't allowed to escape from it, the world automatically shaped his self (without overt coercion, indoctrination or propaganda, which were used to shape the *form* of belief, not to generate the *need* for it) into a machine, which then *automatically* produced the right actions, opinions, emotions and perceptions. Man was brainwashed by his own life. There was no longer any need to instil system-subservient values into people, because the system *was* reality, no need to force experience into an isolating hyper-rational emotionality, because there was no other way to experience. Working in the [home] office, or in the factory, buying sandwiches, moving through space powered by a motor, playing video games, consuming fun, exercising in a gym; all of these activities made the mind and the body machine-like, separating the consciousness welded to the machine into a series of mental-emotional bits called 'I'. The psychological horror of this was literally unspeakable, and so, on the level of literal speech, man could never literally put his finger on what was wrong.

It became *literally* impossible to leap the fence into a new dimension of thought or feeling because there was nothing, anywhere in experience, to encourage or validate such a leap. In the literal machine world, sensitivity was a burden (unfeeling ugliness in all directions tore the heart to tatters), fractality was painful (moving, eating and acting naturally, all felt *un*natural) and spontaneity was impossible (all impulses had to pass through a system-installed mind-bouncer). Freedom, love, truth—all forms of quality became meaningless beyond their capacity to satisfy ego within the system. There was an infinite range of options, all kinds of good things, lovely people and truthful utterances; but they all sustained the system, so much so that the difference between the system and the self came to seem theoretical.* People recognised themselves in their clubs and teams, in their theories and beliefs, in their kinks and fetishes, unaware that, ultimately, all these things were *imposed upon them*, not consciously, but through the activity of the egoic system-mechanism, which automatically liquidated reality, not just from without, but from within. It was not just that 'the world' represented unself as the known, as the cliche, as the *thing* which self, with nothing else to guide it, then took to *be* reality; it was one's *own* self, at work and at play, that produced nothing but lies, meaninglessness, ugliness, suppression and death. It was not that everyone was walking around experiencing a copy of reality, as this is all that the self can present, but that, in their unconsciousness, they were experiencing nothing *but* a copy. They were imprisoned within themselves, within representation, with no possible access to anything which could not be grasped by self.

Ego does not know, does not know it does not know and, worst of all, it *cannot* know it does not know. This is why we find stories in which people are trapped in photographs, films and virtual realities—*trapped in masks*—so terrifying.

---

* Herbert Marcuse, *One Dimensional Man*

§183.

One of the clearest manifestations of the literalist's constant war on unself took the form of the so-called 'SMART system' of systemic management, in which all activity within an institution had to be Specific, Measurable, Achievable, Realistic and Time-bound; which is to say isolable and isolated by egoic perception (specific), assimilable to the conceptual self through an abstract number (measurable) and through an abstract goal (achievable) within the coordinates of the rational system (realistic) and the literal self (time-bound). The SMART approach to reality was to take a problem that in its vagueness and generality—its non-literality—expressed a qualitative whole, of which an approximate, metaphorical or weird expression could be the only possible accurate manifestation, and then reduce it, or him, or her, to a quantitative CASE, which could be managed and 'solved' 'satisfactorily', which is to say; on paper. This did not just leave the actual problem as it was, but pushed it entirely out of conscious awareness, into the unconscious, where, like all repressed problems, it festered, incubating; before breaking out as a plague.

Everything, but everything, came under the hammer of the *smart* objective (or some version of it). All kinds of traditional methods of assessing competence, or later of determining the rights and obligations of workers, all kinds of informal means of communicating and of working around problems, all kinds of subtle but powerful instincts for quality in work and, needless to say, all kinds of vernacular attitudes or practices; all of them had to be, by the literalist, replaced by *smart* definitions of competence and appraisal, *smart* restrictions on information and communication, *smart* hierarchies of accountability, *smart* plans, *smart* objectives and *smart* outcomes. All planned and managed by very *smart* people.

This smart software was to run on the most powerful tool yet devised by the literal mind; the smart computer—built into the smart phone, smart home, smart city and smart body—the hardware of the VIRTUAL WORLD, the complete replacement of life with an entirely artificial, egoic simulacrum.

§184.

In the final stage of the system, man's life went completely online. There was to be, particularly for the mass, no society beyond the limits of the screen, no nature and no culture, not just because man was compelled to live online, but because a high-tech automated world structured to support *virtual* reality inevitably destroys *actual* reality. As our images of rare animals became perfect, high-definition reproductions, so those animals went extinct; as our towns became covered in tokens representing nature, so nature itself vanished; as the world *appeared* neater and neater in bright, artificially organised bureaucracies, so chaos grew in the darkness beyond them; and as we relied more and more on our virtual 'social' networks, so actual society dried up and died, not as a direct consequence, but as a consequence nonetheless.

Instead of bodily participating in a natural, fractal, embodied representation, provided by a self unified with consciousness and context, men and women were to engage with the world by hyper-focusing on an unnatural, automatically generated and managed, representation of a representation, beamed into the tightly concentrated mind through a small square of light, an experience something like a cross between *hypnotism* (sense-dimmed isolating focus on a hyper-desirable object severed from the context) and *lobotomy* (an initiative-rupturing separation of frontal focus from a fully conscious experience of sensate life).

Only a small group of elites could afford to live without screens, could afford to have physical friends, and use their senses, and enjoy privacy, and spend free time in nature; but just as the financially wealthy of all ages can only acquire wealth by proving themselves unable to creatively spend it, so the new elites of the end of the world could only gain or maintain power by being insensitive, insensate and unnatural. Their friendships were therefore indistinguishable from their allies, their senses did not reveal reality but divided them from it, their privacy hid nothing worth knowing and their freedom maintained their confinement, and ours.

§ 185.

Artificial reality and intelligence, built on the back of a planet-wide industrial machine, eventually took over mass life completely, its remit, or PROGRAMME, being to maintain the egoic system, and further addict users to it. Virtual addiction, the means by which *users* were hooked to the system, was achieved by, first of all, making it impossible to live offline, without a computer or a smart phone—the stick—and second of all—the carrot—by constantly feeding ego, its likes and its wants, and by constantly reflecting back to ego its own image; provided that image was compliant. Anything essentially non-egoic was automatically excluded by AI, which was programmed to recognise and reject any non-standard expressions of desire; a need to love and be loved, for example, or a need to surrender to the wild, or a need to be still.

What ego wants, most of all, is to have godlike powers, to be able to walk through walls, to be able to perfectly and instantly duplicate itself, to be able to 'undo' its mistakes, to be able to have sex with anyone or anything it can imagine, to engage in solipsistic flights of rootless fantasy, to be the centre of everyone's attention and to have unlimited power over other men. All of these desires were, in one way or another, available online. VIRTUAL MAN could view life and the universe with total cold detachment. He could receive prayers and other upvotes. He could know everything and be everywhere instantly. He could create and destroy worlds. Man had become a god, but an insane and lonely god.

The perfect system was maintained by forcing people (now cases, or instances of categories) into subservience to virtual systems, apps and algorithms designed to marshal human life down automatically managed system-friendly routes, or cliches. In the case of the tourist, the warehouse worker and the road user, these were literal routes; in the case of the social media user, the online student and the call-centre operative, they were virtual paths of attention. Computers cannot measure spontaneity, empathy or originality, and so these qualities were punished or obliterated by automated management and marking schemes. This meant that only rule-followers, those who were themselves functional computers, were rewarded, promoted or allowed to survive. They were comfortable in virtual worlds, talking to digital masks through their own digital armour, and uncomfortable in their bodies, unable to have anything like a natural human interaction with another.

§186.

First management was split from actual production. Then it was replaced by AI, and man was forced to serve algorithms and applications. Waste treatment, logistics, recruitment, security and surveillance, financial services and trading, education, medical diagnosis and treatment; *every* act of social decision-making was handed over to machines, ensuring that quality, in any form, could never intrude in human affairs. Not just human virtues such as sensitivity, empathy, wisdom, generosity and love—these had already been stamped out by (and out of) the manager—but even human *failings*, such as irrationality, exhaustion, confusion and self-interest were obliterated. Running 'perfectly', without a trace of life, became the 'moral imperative' of tech companies such as the satanic cults of Google, Apple, Amazon and Microsoft.

The 'perfect' virtual existence—total immersion in a virtual reality embedded in an AI-run government—answered every literal like and want of man, while the only thing that he *actually* needed was missing. Because he could not *literally* describe this need, he was unable to communicate it, to others or to himself, and either seized on ridiculous, random attempts to meet it, or just assumed he was going mad, living in a frightening, unreal dream. In reality, it was virtual reality that was unreal, and virtual man who was insane:

i.   Virtual man had the attention span of a gnat on acid. With non-literate conversation the entire reality of another could enter consciousness immediately. With a book, ideas could slowly enter long-term memory, one by one, building themselves up into an edifice of knowledge. With social media and the internet—with the constant decision-making and restless emotional excitation of scrolling away through link-infested text with multiple tabs open—egoic likes and desires all threw themselves, at once, at the same tiny door of attention, with only the most aggressive, or perhaps the luckiest, making their way through, whereupon they found themselves alone in the mind, with nothing to connect to. Computer games, hypertext-laden text and social media posts all involved rapid decision-making and tight focus. The former excluded consciousness, the latter context. Calm, connected thought was the loser, while the ability to rapidly sift through a large quantity of abstract data, assess it and sort it, was enhanced. This was precisely what computers did; and so the more we used computers, the more we became like computers.

ii. Virtual man was a loser. He was playing against an opponent with *zero* playfulness and which was *only* out to win. In order to manipulate behaviour and attention, AI set out to know every literal, *definable* thing about its users, and it succeeded (or succeeded well enough to successfully manipulate man; bizarre or even monstrous errors occurred, but he remained entangled). Man's literal self was allowed to win online battle after online battle after online battle as, in *being* online, *he* continually lost the war; to freely exist. He was allowed to get pellets of social or intellectual nourishment by hammering away on virtual levers, but he was never allowed to be anything other than a rat. This is why people who spent a great deal of time online seemed like 'losers'—they had lost their actual lives, about which they had nothing interesting to say, nor, even if they did, any particularly engaging way to say it, for numbed to life meant numbed to each other. Highly virtual people were notoriously poor at picking up social signals, reading physiognomic cues or gracefully uniting with sensate fellows. When the soft-selved contemplation that communion demands became impossible, so did awareness of the other from the inside, leaving man in a world of androids who could only communicate to each other with the brash digital symbols they spent their unlives analysing and manipulating.

iii.   Virtual man was dead. Deadness, numbness, lack of vivid feeling, was, in the 'perfect' system, everywhere, in everyone, *nearly* all the time. Moments of hyper-stimulated excitement and horrified panic were what was left of the human soul, spasming to electrodes of fear and desire. Genuine aliveness, delight, depth and consciousness were very, *very* rare. Virtual man had merged his self with the screen and the screen had anaesthetised that same self; his nervous system had melded with the digital information system at his fingertips, stifling his memory, suffocating his awareness and numbing his will.

The deadness of virtual man, as the profundity of his soul was filled in tight-focused, isolated streams of information and rapid decision-making, became evident everywhere. He was unable to react to nature, to culture or to his fellows. He was, when confronted with anything new or unexpected, or subtle, or fractal, immune to reaction. He did not have strong feelings, rather he oscillated rapidly between excitement, anger and depression, before returning to a base state of bored numbness or agitated confusion. Everything moved too fast for him, there were never enough hours in the day, yet nothing ever seemed to be happening (a paradox called KINERTIA*), he was mentally tired for no reason, a dull fog enveloped his consciousness, muffling him from life, which he perceived but dimly, as if from very far away. In the end, human beings became nothing but (to paraphrase McLuhan) the numbed sex-organs of the digital system† and, as such, completely dispensable. This was one reason why many 'people'—flesh-appendages to the virtual system—committed suicide. They felt they were surplus to requirements; and they were (although virtual man was usually too bored to kill himself).

No computer can create a qualitatively new metaphor. It cannot be anything other than its own knowable self, which means that it can never be conscious, never be aware of the context; just like the self-informed selves which created and managed it. Society had progressed to the point where the only people who could verify whether a computer was conscious were themselves unconscious.

---

* See *The Apocalypedia*
† Marshall McLuhan, *Understanding Media*

§187.

The arrival of virtual reality signalled, for the *literalist* pole of ego, the arrival of paradise, the perfect world, or rather a perfect *solipsist* representation *of* the world, the two finally becoming one, for finally, nothing now appeared to virtual man but appearance, nothing spoke to him but speech, nothing came to mind but mind. He could not leap the fence beyond the ordered norm, because he was that norm, made flesh.

This was the state presaged and justified by the philosophy of POSTMODERNISM, the fully developed theory that nothing exists beyond representation. Postmodern thinkers told us that there was nothing beyond the mask of personality, beyond the parodic surface, and so anyone could be anything by adopting whatever external sign or series of spectacular images, they pleased. The waking [gendered] body, like the body of nature, was no longer a biological given, but an arbitrary, self-informed *choice*. The solid, waking representation we all share had been dissolved, not just into a sleeping dream, because the metaphors of dream reach beyond themselves, but into a dream which only dreamt itself; a NIGHTMARE.

Such ideas were initially a means for academic theorists to excuse and celebrate the hi-tech, hyper-capitalist society being introduced to the world in the nineteen eighties, which they did by denying both unself, the only source of quality, *and* by denying self, its literal form, its literal facts and its literal history. But just as everyone came to live the dystopian hell of Franz Kafka, George Orwell, Aldous Huxley and Philip K. Dick,* so we all came to live the dystopian heaven of postmodern thinkers such as Jacques Lacan, Jean-François Lyotard, Richard Rorty, Roland Barthes, Jacques Derrida and other intellectual frauds for whom only the symbol existed, only language spoke, and therefore anything beyond symbolic language, including the entire natural universe, was essentially an illusion. Only spectacular, symbolic eidola were real for pomotrons, and anyone unable to access the hi-tech symbolic universe was, like the slaves of ancient Greeks, living a lie, because only lies—self-referential symbols—were truth.

---

* See *33 Myths of the System*

A common-or-garden postmodern belief, shared by many people who would not think of allying themselves with postmodern thought, was TECHNOLOGICAL RELATIVISM, the idea that technology, at any stage in its development, is, like the truth of a 'text', somehow 'neutral' or value-free. This was a *most* convenient egoic fiction for modern man. When you transform nature and human nature into a reflection of ego, that transformation, that technology, can then *only* serve itself. It is only possible to maintain the illusion that (at least when it has passed a critical utility tipping point, as all technologies had) a technology is not *inherently* coercive or destructive by splitting cause from effect and then declaring that because the effect is or can be 'neutral' so must its cause be. Thus, a pair of scissors, a laptop and a nuclear bomb were 'neutral', just as the felling of a rainforest was 'nobody's fault'. Connect them to their totalities—which is to say, to the entire egoic system—and you find a multi-national system of invasive exploitation, a state-corporate military-industrial-entertainment complex and ten thousand years of suffering, along with a range of apparently neutral tools which we *seemed* to be free to make and use as we please, but which *actually* demanded *the entire system* to be made or used; just as the end of a blind man's stick requires his entire consciousness to use. In truth, a teevee, a tractor and a torch are only neutral in the same sense as schools are neutral—in the isolated specifics of how they are used, what shows are on, what I look at with the torch and what is on the syllabus. That man *had* to sit sense-dimmed in a state of uncritical hyper-focus to watch television, that he *had* to ruin his sensitivity to the entire dark-world to use a torch, that he *had* to see and feel and understand like a tractor (i.e. *not* see and feel and understand) to use it, that he *had* to submit to the operational demands of school and syllabus; all this was glossed over by hyper-focus on the measurable effects, just as conscious experience was glossed over in physicalist over-emphasis on facts and evidence.

Where consciousness accepts form, fact and history as actual components of the noetic-somatic self, while looking through them to non-literal quality, postmodernism rejected form, fact, truth and history in order to create, from and for itself, an *advertisement*, which is why the poverty of postmodern thought was not unlike that *of* advertising* (or, for that matter, of pornography and super-hero films) which all had to continually combine and recombine the same essential and self-defeating meaning—that there is no meaning—in order to make a sale. While advertising, porn, big budget movies, world cup matches and the like had to rely on emotionally potent simplifications dressed up in highly stimulating imagery to do this, postmodern thought had to rely on prose so obscure, dense and unreal that, after an hour of decoding a single paragraph, the reader was left very much with the same feeling as he had after spending an hour in a business meeting.

§188.

In the first few decades of the twenty-first century, mankind reached the decadent phase of the final, perfect, postmodern empire of the self, a WORLD SYSTEM, over which sat in command the reified self of humanity entire, a bewildering network of hyper-literal expert judgements and AI algorithms, plugged into, and ultimately powered by, the selfish feeling of every ego, conglomerated into a huge ignorant mass. The fully-developed system had total *managerial* control over nature, human nature and human culture, with horrific consequences:

i.   Freedoms became juridical rights, which became violently enforced obligations. Control eventually became total, or TOTALITARIAN. Where you could stand and sit, who you could talk to and when, what you could say, what you were allowed or not allowed to wear; everything came under the control of the system, forcing the world into two easily identified groups, one composed entirely of submissive cowards, constantly consuming pornography and propaganda in order to validate and fuel their constant emotionality, the other composed of people who refused to submit to authority and had therefore to be cleared away. It didn't matter to the system if this latter group was just as insane, desperate and essentially

---

* David Smail, *The Origin of Unhappiness*

selfish as the former group—they often were—or if it was made up of revolutionary heroes and spiritual ronin; any more than it did that most of the plants cleared by a logging company might have been of use. They were just in the way.

What was once freedom to be healthy became a *right* to health services (the horror of health and safety), which then became, based on fictional scenarios of apocalyptic doom, a violently enforced *obligation* to health (the nightmare of biosecurity), punishable by death. As Illich taught us, traditional health and hygiene, far more effective than paranoid moderns liked to believe, meant a total programme of sociability, cheer, good eating and sleeping, loving, making art, fighting and surrendering.* Thus was man equipped for his inevitable confrontation with pain and death, neither of which the modern mind could face without going *out* of its mind.

What was once freedom to learn, or rather to acquire culture naturally, as humans had done for millennia, became a *right* to schooled education, which was entirely a means to divide people into functional parts (and experience into commodified knowledge) and habituate them to an *obligatory* domesticated existence, to the *obligatory* authority of managers, to the *obligatory* rhythms of the factory or, finally, to an *obligatory* virtual shadow-life. 'Literacy', the great chalice of civilised goodness, had, for most postmodern people, no real purpose, as nobody read anything worth reading. The *actual* reason everyone was forced to learn to read and write was so that they could consume journalism, fill in tax returns and write product reviews. In a sane society, many (or even most) people are illiterate and 'ignorant', and more intelligent for it.

ii.   All selves became the same. Different in their memories and beliefs, but all remembering and believing; different in their likes and dislikes, but all liking and disliking; different in their hopes and fears, but all hopeful and fearful; different in their personalities and masks, but all agitated and numb; different in the quantitative content of their lives, but all viewing life instrumentally, *as* quantity, as a collection of things which must be manipulated to 'achieve optimal results'. They

---

* Ivan Illich, *Medical Nemesis*

found great art boring and wise speech unintelligible; both of which passed through them like a gourmet meal slides down a plastic pipe. Silence did little for them also, and nature, and character, none of which postmodern people could perceive. The voice of those with character and experience reaches the ears of the self-informed self as the voice of a Solidlander reaches those of a Flatlander—incomprehensible, terrifying or useless—no matter how radical or groovy the Flatlander is, no matter what marvellously 'unique' personality he has. In each case, the substance varies but the alienated essence remains the same, which is why left and right will team up to obliterate the threat of a position which cannot be plotted on the spectrum—the only time the goodies and the baddies stop fighting is to team up to defeat the paradoxies—and why the vast majority of people are so predictable and so eager to conform. They come pre-subjugated.

iii. Human beings became totally helpless, totally dependent on the mechanism for all their needs; totally domesticated. In fact, because these needs were met by the system, particle man did not really know what his own needs were. Just as self views itself as reality, with nothing beyond its limits by which to judge its limitations, so those within a completely egoic system view the state of being completely dominated as a form of freedom. They do not, therefore, *need* freedom, just as they do not need parties that are joyous, or work that is meaningful, or love. In fact these things irritate them and they do their best to make sure they don't or can't happen.

iv. Masochism and sadism massively augmented. The masochistic ego reacted to total alienation by regressing into a consoling sense of subjective, solipsistic specialness, combined with a desire to cling to whatever validating group was closest at hand, ideally one with sufficient moral high-ground from which to piss on threatening others. The sadistic ego reacted to total alienation by obsessive work in the world, motivated by an ambitious drive to suppress its anxiety by acquiring and then wielding power over others.

v.　　Adverts were everywhere, which is to say that lies were everywhere, not just in the exhortations to satisfy the self on every flat surface of the world, but in the friendly explanations, the cosy meetings, the chatty pamphlets and the constant reassurances—I understand, I sympathise—all of which were carefully managed appropriations of lost humanity.

vi.　　The most egoic people—liars, thieves, murderers, gangsters, frauds and *total* mediocrities—were those most favoured by the egoic system, and ended up ruling it, openly so. They were not just recognised by the egos beneath them, but admired. Not that, in 'ruling' an advanced totalitarian system, such people had any real power—and what little they did have was useless to them as they had to prove themselves to be insensitive, uncreative and submissive in order to gain power.

vii.　　Man became appallingly lonely. Not so much through being cut-off from society, which all conscious people must do, but through being isolated from reality, from nature, and from the *love* of their fellows. The wisest and most competent group of people on earth, the very old, were locked up in prisons overseen by warders of unbelievable insensitivity and cruelty who reduced their 'clients' to helpless infants, while the freest and most beautiful, the very young, were strapped into their seats with only parents and professionals able to get within touching distance.

viii.　　Children took leave of their senses. Plugged, their every waking hour, into the hyper-addictive self-reinforcing spectacle of the digital world, with nothing but fleeting encounters with their own bodies, they became agitated, depressed, pathetically weak, denatured, decultured automatons, bizarrely passive and terrified of reality. Even in dreams they lived in digital landscapes. Domesticated adults corrupted their response to every crisis they faced; of primal awareness, bodily awareness, symbolic awareness, social awareness, awareness of pain, awareness of death and sexual awareness, each of which was stifled by the world, coerced, co-opted. Unable to step beyond themselves into the other, into the body, into symbol, society, pain, death and sex, they went insane, unreachably so.

Each generation is born into a newly constructed world it finds normal and defends as such. Previous generations try to explain what has been lost, but their words come from *outside reality* and sound like a foreign language echoing through a boiler pipe. This is why critical descriptions of childhood, like those of culture, are dismissed as being motivated by nostalgia for 'the good old days'. At the end of the egoic world however, when *everything* had been lost, this began to change. Even [a few] children knew that something was horrifically wrong with their experience, although nobody *really* knew what.

ix.　　Games of all kinds lost their purpose, which was once pleasure, to be replaced by scores and prizes, which became more important than having real fun, with massive, absurd significance attached to winning and losing; unless you were in a postmodern Western school, where, in order to protect ego from the lightest brush of criticism, 'everyone is a winner'.

x.　　Abundance, in the West, partially overcame the early industrial problem of immense misery, and replaced it with endless, appalling ennui and a permanent nameless dread. In the factories and warehouses of the world, where old-school misery still reigned—and therefore with it the danger of revolutionary pain—the non-compliant worker was automatically disciplined or automatically exterminated.

Work is hell; both entail eternal, futile meaninglessness and pain, although for the Western mind-worker the pain was muffled by cosy offices and classrooms which were either indistinguishable from cosy homes, or *were* the home, which became also the cinema, the nightclub, the art gallery, the gym and the shop. Just as all postmodern work was admin, moving units of data from one microchip to another, while an electronic brain watched and judged man's every move, so all postmodern fun was. There was a *slight* difference between being a professional and a client, or being a cashier and a customer, or being a programmer and a player, in that the former entailed suppressing the torment of egoic existence and the latter entailed giving it license; but both caused brain damage.

xi.   The earth was exterminated. There was as much wild life left at the end of the world as there was in human hearts. Those few patches still existing were far apart, usually inaccessible, and impossible to live in. Where there was once mind-blowing abundance, everywhere—seas thick with fish, skies black with birds, forests carpeted in flowers, life, everywhere life—there was now a wasteland. Our old-growth forests had all but gone, our top-soil had been almost completely eroded, our waterways were poisoned, and of fauna there was little more than a few fat seagulls and the occasional rat.

xii.   Culture was also dead, and for the same reasons that nature was. Everything that could be said about the death of nature, everything we know about why it was happening— the insensitivity, cowardice and greed that led to its destruction—along with everything we know about the effects of an unnatural life on human beings—the confusion, misery and corruption that result from being estranged from the wild; all this applied to culture also. Culture is supposed, like nature, to produce true human beings. That is its purpose—or can be said to be. Really nature and culture have no purpose, they are ends to themselves—there is no 'why' to them—yet this is the inevitable result of their 'what'—the genius of mankind, which, because nature and culture were dead, was dead also.

Postmodern man was stunted, like a diseased tree. He may have been a 'good person', even brimming with potential, but so drastically *reduced*; limited, cut off from life, half-dead and, in many cases, insane. The genius was as easy to find as the eagle and tiger, and for much the same reason. There was no habitat for them, no sustenance, no society that recognised them, no ecosystem for them to fit into. The entire point of education, work, law, politics and the propaganda of the world was to destroy—or at best ignore—them. When they did appear, they *seemed* like eagles and tigers—terrifying, freakishly out of place or a cause for titillating excitement.

§ 189.

What, in egoic societies, is called 'culture', is not culture — the wild, filtered through self — but CULTIVATION — domestication; the covering of the unnatural, inner life of man with super-ficially stimulating effects, dead knowledge divested of its living core and the economically and socially profitable *form* of quality art and craft. 'To be cultivated', Nietzsche remarked, 'means to hide from oneself how wretched and base one is, how rapacious in going for what one wants, how insatiable in heaping it all up, how shameless and selfish in enjoying it',* all of which lay just under the surface of the [high, middle or low-brow] culture-manufacturer and the culture-consumer.

Instead of *immaterial* culture, the expression of quality, scenius or character, there was, at the end of the final empire, a madman's nightmare of news, fun, porn and packaging, all becoming more and more alike, just as decaying corpses do. This was not a culture, but a heavily advertised hypnotic mechanism masquerading as a culture. And instead of *material* culture, the product of quality craft, there was a shoddy prison. Inflexible highways made cliched connections between equally cliched — entirely functional — units of consumption and production. The cupboards that human beings stored their bodies in, called 'homes', were made from cinderblock, plasterboard and flakeboard, papered over with cladding. Furniture, food and faces — the qualitative element of every material object had to be stripped from it, leaving the purely functional — and therefore shoddy and ugly — *thing*.

The meaning or spirit of culture was allowed to die because ego *cannot* discern the difference between it and the form, the representation. Everything, at the end, *appeared* to be the same — the external forms were there, all untouched, all normal, all reassuring — but man's existence was now full of hate, and fear, and madness. He wondered to himself how he could have let this happen, how he wasn't able to *see* that the good in the world was sliding, bit by bit, into the pit; how, only now that it had gone, did he realise that he loved it. The spirit of the world, like all unloved women, had left him.

---

* Friedrich Nietzsche, *Untimely Meditations*

§190.

It was the wealthy who ran the show, but they served the theatre, just as the poor did. There certainly *were* inhuman maniacs with immense power over the world, who conspired together to absorb more *of* the world into the machine, so that more and more power could clunk into their pockets from the output end, and they *were* assisted by professional whores, who enjoyed their lovely middle-class homes and super-comfortable lifestyles, thanks to the constant, lavishly funded programme of management, research and planning that world elites demanded to keep the machine advancing. But the conscious influence of the powerful upon the history of the world was secondary. We reached the final, horrific endgame of civilisation because humanity had, for millennia, acted *un*consciously, building a perfect, monstrous dystopia, piecemeal, bit by bit, with innumerable rational or even accidental acts, which eventually formed, like dead shells creating a limestone mountain, the earth-crushing Leviathan.

There is no need to posit conscious agents behind the growth and expansion of the system. The system itself is far too vast and complex for any Caesar to control. Its relentless, invasive progress into every last corner of the natural world and the human psyche was not and could never be planned or managed—it was, rather, the result of countless expediencies, innumerable innovations employed to cope with temporary problems, or to get a headstart on a competitor, or to flow with a tide of opinion carrying everyone to who knows where, or to advance the interests of a given group; not necessarily connected with the state or with centralised corporate control, in fact very often antagonistic to it. Parents, clergymen, small businesses, charities, tradesmen, trade unions, doctors, radicals, ordinary workers and drop outs all contributed to the effort, just as Bacon predicted they would. This is why, for all the value there is in identifying, resisting and exposing the beasts and androids who crawl over the levers of power, deposing them does nothing to change the reality-eating mechanism that feeds and annihilates us.

§191.

The world was created by ego, which means it was created unconsciously. Consciousness, or unself, has from the very beginning been a threat to ego, *the* threat. Everything ego did at the beginning of the world, and has done ever since then, has been, firstly, to deal with its *fear* of unself, its fear of death, loss, spontaneity, genius, femininity, innocence, love, love-making, wild nature, darkness, vernacular chaos and scenius; to deal with its fear of what it doesn't want and doesn't like, by building a world which is perfectly *safe*. The complementary motivating drive of ego has been to deal with its *desire* for self, its desire for mental and emotional stimulation, security order, sex, porn, progress, technology, masculinity, victory, satisfaction and fun; to deal with its desire for what it likes and wants, by building a world which is perfectly *addictive*.

A perfectly safe and perfectly addictive world is one in which the self cannot be attacked. No noetic criticism, no somatic loss, no thelemic impediment and no visceral pain can reach awareness. Everything beyond the self is automatically defiled, desecrated and violated, but the self, imprisoned in its own symbolic, cliched production, does not notice, for there is nothing conscious within to notice and nothing without to validate consciousness if it were to appear. The world and the self have become one, each a perfect prison *for* and *within* the other, perfectly self-informed and so perfectly secure. Man is not merely imprisoned, but he has hypnotised himself into believing that *he is the prison*.* All talk of absolute freedom sounds utterly unreal to him. The only problem, constantly nagging away in the far-distant background, is that 'reality' is perfectly horrifying.

This horror cannot be dispensed with. It is an essential prerequisite for the functioning of an egoic world. In order to be disciplined and domesticated, man must be kept in a *permanent* state of addiction, which generates fear, and in a *permanent* state of fear, which generates addiction; a permanent state of egoism, or isolation from the ocean of unself under the tiny island of awareness on which ego operates.

---

* Colin Wilson, *The Outsider*

This is how the law works, how elite institutions and elite functionaries wield power, how everyone is reduced to submissive chattel; by separating ego from unself (or 'the unconscious') through constant, *demoralising*, stimulation of fear. When you are conscious you are intelligent, confident, sensitive and spontaneous, and well able to deal with just about any situation, any opponent. When you are conscious you know when you are being lied to, or when you are being hypnotised, coerced or confined, and you are intelligent, courageous and fast enough to find your way out. That won't do. The egoic world demands stupidity, anxiety, insensitivity and blundering deliberation, and so you must be, on the one hand, *bought*—with the apparent security of possessions, power, status, stimulation and the institutional machinery of an immensely powerful system—and on the other, *cowed*—by the fear of losing these things. You must be continually reminded that you are pathetically alone, frail, unable to manage your life without institutional support, and surrounded by a biblical horde of demons; communists, terrorists, drug-pushers, extremists, deadly diseases, perhaps even literal devils. You must constantly feel that, at any moment, a humongous monolith could flatten you, which means you must constantly be *shown* this monolith. Vast inhuman architecture must rise above you, as you scuttle along man-made cracks in the sterile earth. Terrifying, towering, robed priests speaking an incomprehensible tongue, must loom over you as you kneel at their feet in a church, or as you plead before them in a little courtroom cage. When you are a child, incomprehensible monsters must stride around the little desk you are tethered to, forcing you to engage in bizarre and unpleasant activities. When you are sick, you must submit yourself to every indignity imaginable at the hands of men and women who, despite a few wondrous exceptions, treat you like meat or like an infant. When you go shopping, you must be surrounded on all sides by masked faces, all individuality erased, and huge, forceful images of what you don't have, what you could lose, what is coming to get you, and when you go to work, or sign on for your benefits, you must all but grovel at the feet of the boss, advisor or customer.

All of this cuts you off from your selfless essence, makes you forget what you know, fractures your good sense and puts you in an *unconscious* trance state of tractable docility. Not, logically enough, as a result of conscious policy—although, as the chilling planning documents of elites demonstrates, there is a great deal of diabolic planning that goes into building a perfect prison—but because a world made by ego *can only* work this way. It *automatically and inevitably* coerces and cows, which is how the unconscious cyborgs who run the world can tell themselves that they have no choice. Indeed they do not. If they did have a choice, they would have no power.

§192.

Liberation is almost impossible. Only heroes and heroines have a hope in hell. Not just because virtual man *is* in hell, trapped forever in a video screen, but because, by virtue of being *completely* trapped, anything but complete liberation is doomed to failure. When ego's power over the world is complete, *anything* which cannot fit into self—any instinct, any sensation, any quality—cannot fit into the totalising system it has created, and so starves, withers, suffocates or, if it gets a foothold in collective life, is actively suppressed. Any movement towards freedom—a glimpse of profundity at the weekend, a conversation at work which is threatening to make sense, a joyous party, a self-rupturing ritual—all such escape attempts get instantly crushed, from every direction—from the opinions of family friends, from the trivial demands of another exhausting day, from the profit imperative or from just the sheer weight of habitual momentum—making them seem almost instantly unrealistic or unreal.

    The less an individual conforms to the system, the less he is able to fit into it, the less he intuitively feels like 'one of us', the more he feels the fingers of death around his throat. It is not a question of proving that he is irrational or insane. It is obvious; the entire world, *his* entire world, stands as incontrovertible evidence that he does not belong and must be rejected. This is why, when self tries to escape ego's world, it cannot reject it in toto, because self *is* the world. In his own image is the world made, and so man dare not smash the golden calf. The fearful self instead focuses on one local, unpleasant, isolated idol; capitalism being popular in the trendy West, but it could be socialism, or white privilege, or Muslims, or Jews, or the government, or the patriarchy, or the internet, or this or that shady supra-national organisation. Such pseudo-radicalism is not just tolerated but *encouraged*. Stagversive acts of revolt, religious practices, political and artistic rebellions, various kinds of extreme lifestyles and narcotic overindulgence are all integrated into the system as pressure valves, as acts of contrition, and as emotionally satisfying generators of the pseudo-meaning required by the advertising arm of the egoic system. Expressions of genuine revolt, including entire artistic and religious movements, are thereby rendered into cliches, as illusory and meaningless *as* adverts. The totalising world absorbs expressed quality, rebellion and originality instantly, automatically and seamlessly. There really is no *actual* escape, and so formal expressions of discontent (griping, sarcasm, satire*) and 'rebellion' are tolerated, even encouraged. Tread on the wrong taboo though, one held sacred by managers of the power structure you are in, and it will blow up in your face.

What's more, the perfectly egoic world is *perfectly* addictive and thus requires *perfect* courage to overcome. There's something for everyone, and so *every* self must face a personal nightmare of cold turkey in order to escape. It's not enough to drop out, or get a better job, or kick a few conspicuous fixes, or learn the violin; freedom demands doing dread battle with the guardian at the gate, of putting the entire self on the line.

§ 193.

When there is no escape, mind turns in on itself, but without escape, without unifying consciousness, the only thing mind can find is a pseudo-reality of bits, the 'many selves' of Hume and his successors—thoughts, impressions, memories, fragments. Ego, also being a bit, is unable to coherently bring them together, and so struggles instead to *control* the multitude of

---

* Laurie Taylor and Stanley Cohen, *Escape Attempts*

unconnected ideas, urges, feelings, needs, beliefs, fears and desires that surround it. If a billion such fragmented egos then build a world, that world becomes the reflection of a broken mirror, an endless shifting nightmare in which nothing connects up and nothing has any relation to anything else, an inferno perfectly depicted by the greatest prophet of the modern age, Hieronymus Bosch. Today we call this world, and this ego, SCHIZOPHRENIC (or, in milder form, AUTISTIC, or, more simply and directly, INSANE).

The *metaphor* of schizophrenia, like that of all 'mental illnesses', describes a series of egoic, self-directed emotions, thoughts, behaviours and perceptions. As self is taken further and further away from consciousness, and its reflection in nature and culture, it becomes more and more focused *on* self. This focus, which manifests in the *stare* of the schizoid man, finds nothing but objects—including its own 'subjective' thoughts and emotions—which, because they are without their originating, unifying, unselfish source, become, firstly, further derealised and fragmented (specialised, you might say) and fixed in a freakishly hyper-real, hyper-awake, blindingly bright but completely flat, cis-dimensional present. Second-ly, schizoid thoughts are experienced as having come either from elsewhere (a.k.a. *paranoia*; 'the president controls my thoughts') or *solely* from me (a.k.a. *grandiosity*; 'My thoughts control the moon!').* A world which obliterates nature and culture, which relentlessly augments self, and which demands staring, all the time, at everything, is a world of schizoid or semi-schizoid people, not mentally ill, but completely insane.

Schizophrenia was once identified with *regression*, with *childlike* perception, with a *primitive* consciousness unable to successfully 'test reality', or to perceive the difference between the subjective creations of the mind and objective 'reality'. *In* reality, the schizoid state is the most *advanced* and *adulterated* progression—experienced by modern, urban, male (or en-maled) minds—*into* an abstract mind which is as far from reality as consciousness can possibly get.† Schizophrenia along with its solipsistic modernist cognates—autism, OCD, anxiety and depression—is focused, detached and abstract, where

---

* Louis A. Sass, *Madness and Modernism*
† Ibid.

childish primitivism is relaxed, engaged and incarnate. The latter is typified by a kaleidoscope of qualities and feelings, the former is affectless, anhedonic, deadened or terrified, given to: *numbness,* or unresponsiveness, unusual *anxiety,* or terror for no reason and *paranoia,* or intense self-consciousness; also to meaningless *private metaphor, disorganised speech* or cheerless *irony;* to *detachment, disengagement* and *de-realisation,* a sense that nothing is real, a conviction of *literally* living in a dream, a film or a shoddy virtual copy of the world; or to *fragmentation,* the sense that everything is blasted, divided up, in bits, nothing really connecting here, nothing really making sense; or to an *obsessive focus* on things and an *obsessive interest* in details; or to intensely *selfish rationalism,* in which the premises are bizarre and so, therefore, are the conclusions, but the route from the former to the latter is worked out with impeccable logic.

These are the symptoms of the *metaphorical* condition called schizophrenia, the symptoms of being a mass-man, a particle man, a virtual man; of living in a world of constant panoptical surveillance, of constant demands for hyper-rationalism and in a constant state of intense, sense-dimmed over-focus; in a world of total mediation and separation from selfless experience; in a rational machine-world of cheerless, joyless, commitment to total, unending meaninglessness, in which man has two functions and two functions only; to *produce* and to *consume.* There was no schizophrenia in primal groups, no autism, no psychosis, no eating disorders, no 'mental illnesses' of any kind, which were also rare in traditional societies. Mass madness is not an illness, it is the result of a world out of joint and an ego which now perfectly fits within it.

§194.

The collapse of Western civilisation can be traced through the artistic dreamlife of the people who slept within it. This dreamlife comprised two new kinds of myth, the technocratic dream-world—or SCIENCE FICTION—and the technocratic dream-man—or the SUPERHERO. These were, initially, happy, bright, optimistic and gaily coloured, reflecting an uncritical acceptance of industrial and then digital technology. Early sci-fi men and women lived in antiseptic capsules, ministered by friendly, almost-human, machines and cheerful, powerful godmen—while humans, either corporate functionaries or technicians in a strict martial hierarchy, became more machine-like. As the civilised party wore on, and the wine soured, the dreamworld became darker, literally so. The costumes of superheroes became more muted, their personalities more world-weary and flawed, their futuristic worlds more miserable and authoritarian. If anyone smiled, it was grimly, cynically, with effort. Finally, there were no positive visions of the future any more, no world saviours, no happy endings. The dreamer, trapped in an entirely egoic representation, was now desperate to wake up, but, hermetically sealed within the dream, he was unable to imagine waking, and so he projected his horror *into* the dream, creating a mythic nightmare in which the only goodies were those who wished to destroy the nightmare; *baddies*. The final stage of the mythos of the world was one in which the baddies were loved, in which they won, in which the world was *not* saved; it ended, and there was peace.

In the serious novel or art-house film, the kind that educated middle-class selves preferred, decadent man found that every tiny fragment of his experience deserved to be in-spected, divided, further inspected and further divided until nothing remained but the vaguest hint of the vaguest tones and qualities, minute odours wafting from a body that no longer existed. Or he found there was no self *at all*, no meaning, no consciousness, no world, nothing but chaos, covered over with nice alliterative sentences or computer generated effects, or flesh, always flesh. These and like myths were those that postmodern man enjoyed, that, when he experienced them, something in him felt 'yes, this is me'. But what kind of me? What kind of self was it that man discovered reflected back at him in the dreamlife at the world's end? It was that of a child or, more specifically, a teenager; special, but an unearnt specialness, afraid, but *of* what? a self obsessed, but *with* what? There were plenty of answers, plenty of opinions, but never the solution, for there was nothing *but* the self looking for it.

§195.

The end of civilisation was the end of mankind's insane adolescence; that stage in the myth of humanity in which indi-
vidualisation first becomes complete, when the singular self
finds itself alone in the world and resistant to its representation in the world; to society. With no consciousness of its
essential identity with either the distal context or proximal
consciousness, the postmodern, adolescent, schizoid self was
both selfish, yet hell-bent on self-destruction. It didn't realise
that its urge to tear everything down was an urge to pull *itself*
apart, and so it resisted, resisted, resisted, clinging *on* to its
mind, all the while going *out* of its mind.

Eventually, the pressure was too much. From without,
as the natural world which civilisation depended on collapsed,
and from within, as the cultural world which self depended
on fell apart also, the brittle ego and its brittle system cracked
up, revealing the ugly horror of both. When the theatre starts
to collapse, the actors lose confidence in their parts, then they
forget their lines, then, finally, they are forced to remove their
masks and we see who they are.

When civilisation collapses, and ego's hold over the
earth, is released, everyone must face the music. There is no
escape from perfect, insane suffering. The poor face the flames
first, but the fire soon covers the earth. There is no hiding
place. Just as every man and woman *is* the entire dystopian
world, carrying the perfect prison in and as their selves, so
the collapse has its centre in every single human self, which
comes tumbling down, which is the necessity and the justice
of it. Not in the collapsing outer world, which is nothing but
ruin and anguish, but in consciousness, where, in the desert
of charred stubs that man calls his soul, in the rubble of the
little world he built there, which nature has crushed like a
rock-fall crushes a doll's house, life again is free to grow. Just
as only suffering changes man, so only complete suffering can
change the complete non-man. Only total loss, perfect horror
and the presence of a world of death can blast the world from
him, leaving, finally, an adult.

§196.

In a sense there is no such thing as history, rather a field of organic social-cultural forms which are born, grow, mature, senesce and die, as plants and animals do, with their own unique life, their own unique character, and their own unique *limit*.* This is the natural state of cultural or social man, living and dying through what appears to be history, but which is to consciousness a transdimensional whole. There are, however, two important caveats. The first is that there is one cultural thread, the civilised one we have traced here, which is *not* natural, which does *not* live as natural things do, and which is, as a whole, as self-informed, and therefore as cancerous, as the cells it creates. The culture of ego is *anti*-culture; self-informed technique where social life should be. But although it was born with civilisation, lay in the midst of it, and comprised the rotten core that has finally consumed the social body, and although it spread ever further outwards from its various seeds, reaching into more and more remote social worlds; despite all this, for many thousands of years ego never really got the upper hand. Human society always managed to live more or less organically and therefore, to a greater or lesser extent, beyond the miserable history of the little mind. Mesopotamian society, Greek society, Jewish society, Roman society, Muslim society and medieval European society; these too, despite the growth of ego, were organic, unique, beyond any kind of comparison to our own world, and, like all cultures in history, as alive and as beautiful, in their own way, as anything else in nature. Even in our own wasteland, life lives, independence, scenius and genius. The sensate, physiognomic science of Goethe, the glorious flower of Romanticism, William Morris' Arts and Crafts movement, the bizarre freedoms that opened up for a quarter of an hour in revolutionary Russia and Spain, the realisation of the immortal truths of the East in the form of Western teachers such as Gurdjieff and Krishnamurti, individual creative bonfires, such as Henry Miller and Lawrence, and the great last gasp of culture, in the music and literature of the sixties and seventies.

---

* Oswald Spengler, *Decline of the West*

But still the parasite of ego grew along with its progressive reflection in the world, egoic culture and technique, which made the societies and civilisations which led to our own, to the extent that they let the worm live, *the same*, part of the same horrific story. Although the parasite did spread to the East, indeed across the world, we can chart its growth most clearly in the route it took through our civilisation, the dead culture of the West, which is now *entirely parasitic*, entirely egoic.

Ego was born somewhere around the fertile crescent, it grew in the area we now call the near-East, spreading west into the Mediterranean and east into Eurasia and China, taking hold in the Mongol and Muslim empires, seeding itself more or less everywhere in the process, before passing into Western Europe, and from there, via the United States, across the world. All the time, it melded itself with living nature and living culture, just as all parasites do, until the host—humanity and the natural world—died.

This death is the second exception to the culture-as-nature picture of history (first proposed by Oswald Spengler*); for, just as the dead skin of a snake must be shed for a new natural form to grow, so must the dead worm of ego-as-world die so that a more conscious natural, social self can grow on the earth. Not a 'true' civilisation, not the latest and greatest stage of the dreadful 'story of civilisation', in fact not a civilisation at all; but a forest *cleared* of civilisation, cleared of the invasive parasite of an ossified self-informed society, and made stronger and healthier for its battle with it; a forest in which all kinds of cultural life-forms can grow again, each perfectly unique, but each rooted in and limited by a common soil.

In a world free of ego and its dominating institutions, each cultural world, along with each individual cultural form within it (art, craft, science, language, etc.), is *natural*. Like nature it is a "manifestation" of the thing-in-itself, and forms thereby a whole, each element beautifully (fractally) integrated with every other. Natural cultures and their constitutive components are integrated *with* each other, because the parts-in-themselves are integrated *in* the whole-in-itself, rather than cut off, floating through space in a plastic capsule. Natural

---

* Ibid.

cultures then live like all natural things; they are born, they grow into unique never-to-be-seen-again forms, they fruit, and then, without chaos, without anguish, they naturally die, so that another culture can be born from its seeds. Contrast this with the technical and cultural components of egoic history, in which nothing manifests reality-in-itself, and so, because nothing really fits together, all the mutually antagonistic parts must be kept together through coercive *control*. This control, exercised by the ego, hardens culture into a civilised super-order at constant war with a nature become chaos, a chaos which must be, with ever more effort, suppressed. But the more it is suppressed, the more it grows, until the pressure of it shatters civilisation like the 'chaos' of fermentation shatters a wine bottle, leaving a heap of broken shards which the next unnatural culture can build itself from. Only when man stops building culture, stops 'creating value', stops ordering the world to a selfish, technical plan, will the hell of progress cease.

§197.

We are coming to the end of the world. There is no way to say, to literally say, what comes next. We *can* say that sane future societies will function much as primal societies did, with the same fearless, egoless, egalitarian playfulness, and with the same pre-superstitious immersion in the ocean of unself, but they will also be different to our Arcadian origins, because *we* will be different, no longer living on an abundant planet, no longer naively innocent, and no longer immersed completely in the groupmind. The omni-self of society will be there, the soil of man's individuality *from* which he grows, and *into* which he unclenches his individuality, but he will be an individual, one in the self *and* one with the perfectly synchronised dance of humanity, enjoying his complete, independent uniqueness *and* enjoying the glory of walking out on deck with his team, all our individualities harnessed to a single, meaningful unit.

We can also say that the path from here to there will require the unimaginable pain of WORLD-BREAK, which will teach us never again to let our tools take charge, or to let the mask make our decisions, or to lose touch with wakefulness, by falling into the dream of ego. We can also describe certain literal features that sane societies will have; namely a complete absence of civilised and egoic [and therefore professional, royal, democratic, corporate, state and technological] domination. There will be no advanced technology, for example, which is inherently self-destructive (which is why spaceships don't exist; because any society advanced enough to build one would have already destroyed itself), or rigid hierarchies, or inflexible, coercive laws, or inflexible, coercive roads (either subjective or objective), or specialised 'wisdom', or *any* kind of privilege, or even the possibility of it. No temple, no priest. No engine, no expert. Individual possession, beyond what can be individually used, will be impossible, and no *particular* value will be given to any thing, least of all money. Gold will be used to make toilets and if the Houses of Parliament are still standing they'll be used to store manure,* as it is already clear they can fulfil this task very well.

The world to come will also be without our art. Art is not meant to last anyway; like the life it comes from, it dies when it is preserved for too long. In fact, art as we know it will be unnecessary, as will the Romantic genius. When man is an adult he will no longer need paintings, sculptures, symphonies, films and novels, any more than he needs toys. He might make and play with them—why not?—but these activities will be casual blossoms on the improvised tree of the moment, not, as it is for us, a substitute for the life we have lost, just as the great people we call geniuses are a substitute for our own miraculous individuality and creativity. This is why the man of tomorrow will not grieve the loss of the art of today, which he will have as much need for as a man in love has for the services of a prostitute. Culture and nature will again be one, as they are in the consciousness of the reader of these words.

We can give a metaphorical image of the good life to come, but we cannot give literal details of how to get from here to there, and if we could, 'there' wouldn't be worth the price of admission. Anyone who prefers a *road-map* over a *vision* doesn't deserve to get home. All literal descriptions of a free,

---

* William Morris, *News from Nowhere*

conscious world, like all literal pictures of natural beauty, reach us as ridiculously improbable or as sentimental cliche. To say that the world to come will be one of self-regulating federations comprising *perfectly ordinary geniuses* one with each other, one with the wild and one with the unremarkable miracle of mankind-in-itself, true as it is, strikes us as cheesy, dreamy; because it is a literal description of an experience that begins, and must begin, with the elusive quality of consciousness here and now, and always here and now. It is because so few are conscious, that so few can value a conscious life, one *actually* worth living, why they seek instead trivial reforms to the world we have, and why we do not need a revolutionary programme, or theory or manifesto, but a revolutionary *experience*. Which is what is coming, whether we like it or not.

§ 198.

The unacceptable truth is that you are going to die, the unbelievable truth is that you are already dead. This is the meaning of life; the acceptance of DEATH, and the experience of it. When death finds self, self realises it is going to die. This is unacceptable. When *I* find death, there is no self to realise anything. This is unbelievable.

　　When life was good for man, the afterlife was perceived as good. When life was suffering, the afterlife was perceived as suffering, or as an ethical purging (by God or by Karma). When life is without meaning, the afterlife is perceived as without meaning. Self can do nothing but project itself into that which it cannot know. What it does not and cannot realise, by itself, is that the unknowable is not an event in time. The unknowable *is* man, and man *is* the unknowable, in the profundity of his conscious experience. It was when he lost contact with this conscious experience that he first felt fear of death, and it is when there is no conscious experience at all, that there is a worldwide denial of death; which means a worldwide denial of love.

　　Love and death are only experienced through letting go of the self, which is why each 'feels like' the other. When something dies, its self is taken from you; when you love, your self is taken from it; but the experience is the same; the experience of unself. Anything else, anything in the represented world of self, all the things and people that appear to die, are self-generated sections of transdimensional experience, frozen hypermnesiac slices across a single 4D object before us, whose movement out of our dimensional self-plane we call death, but which is no more the end of it, or him, or her, than the leaving of childhood causes that to vanish. If something doesn't move in four dimensions it cannot be alive; it can only be a self-generated 3D thing, which means it cannot be loved, because love is only possible by abandoning the section—the thing, or animal, or person that I love—and experiencing, together, that which it, or he, or she, is part of; a timeless experience which, to us, is death. As most people are imprisoned in themselves, they are unable to experience death, which is why they are so astonished when anything dies, and why, when the truth of mortality finally strikes them, they—those of them with a spark of immortality—rise above themselves. Death brings out the best in people—which is why there must be so much of it—but precisely because it does, it is effectively banned.

§199.

Death does not exist for us. We do not talk of death; we solemnly perform a conversation about it, we do not handle dead bodies; we rarely even see one, and nothing is allowed to fester and rot, before being swiftly carried away. Not just death itself, but all signs of death are removed from direct experience; old people are bricked up, graveyards are pushed further and further from active life, and all signs of organic decay are hidden from view. The mortal body, with its squelching, oozing and shitting, becomes 'disgusting' while sleek, odourless, antiseptic objects and dwellings of plastic, chrome, steel and glass become 'sexy'. Even our worship of youthfulness, power, money, fame and 'health' (and our pathological fear of [viral] 'risk')—even our worship of knowledge—can, at least in part, be seen as a headlong, hurtling sprint away from the void.

Everyone simply proceeds as if they, and everyone they know—not to mention our moribund civilisation—will live forever. The whole world is terrified of death because the whole world is selfish. And because it *is* only and can *be* only the self that dies, it follows that the most selfish people—the most powerful sadists and the most pathetic masochists—are those most afraid of dying. And this is what we find; a world run by and for the existentially terrified, in order to suppress their permanent death-terror.

The modern atheist, looking at the factual evidence, declares that after I die, there is nothing. The pre-modern theist, anxious to legitimate responses to this most threateningly liminal of experiences, declares that after I die, there is, fear not, *something*. How, though, can you correctly answer the question, 'What happens when I die?' unless you know what 'I' is? How can you know that 'love isn't eternal' unless you know what time is? How can you know that 'God doesn't exist' unless you know what *does* exist? Consciousness, time and space have been, to all minds of all cultures, throughout history, as enigmatic as they are today and as they will always be, because they are utterly and inherently opaque to mind. This leaves two options, guesswork—which is to say belief-non-belief, founded on the selfish emotions of fear and desire—or another mode of experience, one that is not of self.

§ 200.

Man loves stories of resurrection because he knows, *somehow*, that, despite objective evidence and subjective wishful thinking, his experience stretches "into" the thing-in-itself, that it touches eternity. Even atheists enjoy seeing the ordinary man transformed into the hero, or the hero [appear to, or metaphorically] die and be reborn, or even the arrival of snowdrops and daffodils in spring. We all love to see transformation, rebirth and resurrection because they represent the fundamentally timeless experience of the conscious I. Self alone doesn't know it, and cannot know it—or can only merely believe in it—but I, I *am* it. I don't just *know* that the sun doesn't set, that winter is already summer or that the unwinnable battle has already been won. I *am* that; provided, of course, that I am not my self.

As I lose my self, I lose everything; and gain that which cannot be lost; as the quantitative self reaches the winter of old age, so the qualitative character of man enters glorious summer; as the world becomes death, so life stirs in the underworld, and spring is not far away. Even in the cold, mute objects around us something sleeps, as it does in all our solitudes, to awaken in time. This is not a question of hope, for a 'life' after 'death', or for a coming golden age, or for a saviour, or for anything else that can be proven or disproven. Ultimately, there is no 'life' and there is no 'death' and so there is nothing to come because there is nothing that went away. The resurrection of man and of mankind is an *ongoing experience*. This is why Franz Kafka remarked that the last judgement is not an *event*, that comes at the end of life, but is a standing court-martial,* a continual reckoning of the three-dimensional mind before the four-dimensional court of eternity.

The fact and truth of the matter is that death is a dead body. It is impossible to see death; the only thing that can objectively appear is the manifest effect or appearance of death, the corpse, from which life has departed. The life hasn't gone anywhere, because it never came in the first place. Self creates what *appears* to be appearance—the birth of the body—and it creates what *appears* to be disappearance—the death of the body, but it can *never* witness the cause of the body, any more than it can witness the cause of the universe, of life or of consciousness; because there is no cause. The objective self of time and space cannot be caused by anything, because *self itself creates causality*. The only way the "cause" or the "meaning" of life can be known is through *experience*, either through the reflection of it in metaphor, or through some form of self-stilling or self-softening action, or practice, or conscious being. The former we call art, wisdom and philosophy, the latter has two names depending on whether it refers to overcoming the subjective self—in SELF-MASTERY—or overcoming the objective world—in REVOLUTION.

---

* Franz Kafka, *Aphorisms*

§ 201.

It is impossible to master self while that self is dependent on and owned by a system built upon and continually feeding from it. Self and world are one, and so *both* must be overcome. This has always been true, to some extent, but when the world perfectly represents the ego, as it does in a fully developed egoic society, when the two are fully one, there is no hope, no exit, unless both are overthrown together. Not that the individual can overthrow the world, but she can free herself from its control over her, from the fear and desire it provokes in her, from the undead numbness it spreads over her body.

Which aspect of ego must be faced in any one moment however — objective world or subjective self — is impossible to say; only I can know it. The individual must learn to discern whether it is her train that is in suffering motion, or whether it is still and the one next to her is bound to hell; whether the source of suffering here is the proximal me or the distal situation. Ego is predisposed to either masochistically blame itself and over-focus on self-help, or to sadistically blame the world and over-focus on revolt. Unself correctly perceives the two as spinning poles of the same egoic source and aptly addresses now one, now the other, to overcome the whole.

This means that self-mastery is a public matter and revolution a private matter. The world is completely addictive (and appears completely safe, reassuring or normal) to every kind of self, and so only complete rejection *of* the world can free consciousness *from* it. Consciousness then freely acts *in* the world; not *in order to* change it — the futile, selfish, ambition of the reformer — but simply in order to be conscious; which then *does* change the world, naturally and profoundly; to the terror of the unnatural, superficial self. Anyone who markets himself as a sage and is not getting in trouble with the boss, or, through the spirit of scenius, facing, transcending and re-newing his social self, is lying. Anyone who calls for revolution in the world without first bringing down the bourgeoisie of the belly, or causing a riot in the parliament of the mind, has nothing to say.

§ 202.

Revolution is the *complete* rejection of the system. This doesn't mean living naked in a field drinking rain-water. It is impossible to completely refuse the *form* of the world, but it is possible to completely reject its *essence*, to disengage from the spectacle, to exit the represented universe of self, to free one's self from institutional indoctrination and the authority of professors, doctors, experts, sages and gurus, to give the self over to creative absorption, to creative revolt and even, here and there, to touch the wild, at least within. This is far from easy, because the world has not just closed off every escape route, but has insinuated itself into every last recess of the individual self, making a complete break *appear* to be impossible; for to do so is to reject what appears to be *my* personality, *my* morality, even *my* life. I will be imprisoned until I can discover, in my own *experience*, that they are not 'mine' at all; they belong to ego, and so to the egoic world.

Only *I* can ever know what is good, or true or right in a particular context, for only *I* am conscious of it. This is why, when consciousness compels me to go against the group—or, as now, to go against the whole world—the ego, one with selfish society, is terrified, for it is facing death. It knows that it must join the egoic machine or live excluded, rejected, dying from the exposure of solitude, exterminated by the community which it has rejected, or *bored*, deprived of the social addictions that self has formed itself from, or appallingly *insecure*, without anything known to cling to, including money. It requires courage to face such suffering, to let the self snap and *something else* emerge, and few are really courageous.

Most people, alas, are not equipped to live in a social void where they must create their own values, meanings and cultures, to face reality naked, without the armour of the world-made caddis-case. They do not seek a new life, not really. They might sometimes say they want new symbols, new metaphors, new rituals, new freedoms, but when the moment comes to *actually* sacrifice their likes and wants, to actually put *something else* first, they chicken out.

§203.

The only truth remaining in a society which has destroyed truth, is to destroy society. This is impossible; right up to the point that it is easy. Just as the mask of the self becomes harder and more shallow the more self-informed it is, so the mask of the world becomes more brittle. When the body of the world is dying, a thousand *natural* infections assail it; floods, droughts, riots, wars, plagues and famines. Eventually a point comes when one sharp stab cracks the mirror into shivers. Until that grim, chaotic time, the *individual* must resist and refuse.

To free oneself from egoic society means resisting subjugation and refusing constraint, which is to say, continually revolting against the technologies and legitimations of the world, and continually breaking its laws. This is impossible while self informs itself. Fear and desire, sadism and masochism, defile, desecrate, violate and co-opt every bid for freedom. This is why, without self-mastery, there can be no lasting revolution, only stagversive reform; changing the pilot while the ship sinks. Socialist, democratic, communist and anarcho-communist fantasies of living in a 'fairer' technocratic civilisation are like calls to a sleeper to vote his way out of a dream.

Attempts to reform cults and institutions; states, corporations, schools, churches and what-have-you are even more absurd. The industrial world required *everything* to be changed in order to revolutionise one thing—industrial cotton factories—which required industrial mines, industrial trains, industrial states, industrial schools, industrial space, industrial time, industrial bodies and industrial minds (*long live Ned Ludd!*). And when one country—England—had industrialised, every other country had to immediately follow suit or be destroyed. The civilised system which preceded it was the same, only slower and looser; the digital world which followed it, which progressed far more rapidly, was even more tightly integrated with everything else, even more totalising. Everything at the end of empire is completely integrated with everything else, which is why it all had to rise together, and just as it all had to rise together, so it all must, and will, fall together.

§204.

Society can only be free when there are no inherently dominating—*cliched*—techniques enforcing order from without.
Money is such a technique, as is specialised power and knowledge, as are machine tools and system tools, rigid laws and
legitimations, institutions and social classes, kings and princes,
taboos and totems, even the rigidly encoded authority of great
art, science and the wisdom of the sages; all of these things
automatically punish or restrict conscious reverie and spontaneous response to the context, which is why they must fall.
The entire egoic world must—and will—fall, or it will keep
ego alive to use the world to gain power over others. As the
Chuang Tzu reminds us, 'Fashion scales and balances for
people to weigh by and they will steal by scale and balance...
Fashion benevolence and righteousness to reform people and
they will steal with benevolence and righteousness'.*

Nobody needs to be persuaded of this. It's impossible
anyway. All that needs to be done, all that can be done, is to
see or to show the world as it is; a metaphor for the self, just
as the self is a metaphor for the world. If I am conscious I
see self and world are they are, as an egoic mask, unliving,
grinning back at me as the frozen face of the devil, as my own
devilish self. When the devil *is* seen, there is no need to be
told what to do. I put everything into tearing it off. To do so
is the ultimate heartbreak, the self-break of the world, killing
not just the false image of the beloved, but of all that can *be*
loved, represented reality entire. To see the mask of the egoic
world, and the mask of the worldly ego, as they are, is to put a
sword through the throat of God, the idol of the Leviathan, the
demiurge we have worshipped since time and the world began.

This is the hardest thing *in* the world to do; for He and I
are one. Self-and-world are all that can be said to exist, and so
there can be no sayable—definable—motive for killing them,
just as there can be no definable reason for wanting to leave
the perfect dream or virtual reality. *Nobody* can be turned to
for support. You die alone; and you kill alone also.

And then what? What lives when self dies?

---

* *The Complete Works of Chuang Tzu* (tr. Burton)

§205.

When I let go of self, represented reality becomes translucent and even, *in extremis*, disappears. This experience has, to self, the appearance of total solipsistic insanity. The solipsist, however, only abandons the *objective* self, the shared factual-causal waking world; the self-informed subjective (Romantic) self of will, emotion and imagination remains. The experience of sacrificing self entirely to I, by contrast, may be profoundly unsettling, nauseating, even terrifying, but something else remains, something entirely and radically beyond self, *which I am*. I, therefore, remain grounded in a reconciling certainty and confidence unknown to the schizoid solipsist.

By experiencing the present moment fully, melting into the dark, living in the wild, facing death, accepting pain (even as I move to rid myself of it) and consciously allowing attention to freely inhabit the body, there is relief from the insane mental-emotional momentum of the self, which cannot feed on such thoughtless fodder. Likewise, in 'stepping back' from the world that feeds the self, in accessing the unselfish origin of self and world, something other than selfish thinking, emoting, willing and perceiving is allowed to breathe, to operate.

In such experience there is freedom from ego, from the control *of* the self *over* the self. There is intuitive knowledge of the "cause" of self, and therefore of its 4D destiny, and with it, relief from worry. There is the thing-in-itself here and with it the thing-in-itself there; empathic experience of the other, from within, and thus, communion. There is originality, the genius of the new, along with spontaneity and apt response to the context. There is character, my unique, original being, buried under millennia of personality. There is natural quality, and with it the source of startlingly apt metaphor. There is no death, and so there is no fear, even at the doorway of doom.

Self-mastered experience is not mere *self-control* (using some parts of self—some thoughts, emotions, auric feelings, actions, acquisitions or perceptions—to control or suppress other parts), nor is it belief in a system, or in a way of life, or in the legitimating blather of religion, rather, it is actually, practically, *doing* something about the rule of ego, *practising* being that which is deeper, more intelligent or more fundamentally true than the thinking-emoting mechanism I normally call 'me', the source of all my problems.

§ 206.

The problem is not the problem. The egoic mind, disturbed by something wrong—a worldly disaster, a broken heart, a bad mood or a catastrophe of personality—will flutter off on a peripatetic quest for *why*. As soon as it has found a satisfactory reason, it can relax, or, rather, return to fretting about less existentially terrifying matters. And yet, strange to say, the problem persists, or it returns in another form; because it is not caused by a thing or event in the world, but by the emotions and thoughts of the mechanical ego.

All suffering, everything we normally call 'unhappiness' (i.e. the negative pole of the got-lost see-saw), is caused by thought and emotion, which means that the truth, the horrendous truth, is, as Barry Long taught us, that you have no right to *ever* be unhappy.* Ego is not too keen on this idea. Ask an unhappy person to give up their emotions and their thoughts, and he or she will react with predictable sophistry. 'I can't give them up. I've got a good *reason* to be unhappy. Look at all these terrible *events* in my life, look at *why* I am unhappy!' Directing unhappy people away from the *why* and into the *what* is likely to provoke a tantrum, for *why* is the ultimate drug. Take away people's pleasures and they get angry, but if you really want to enrage someone, take away their reason to be unhappy. 'But it *hurts!*' Yes, pain is awful, but there's no reason to suffer. 'But if I think about it...' So stop thinking. 'But I *can't*. This person is hurting me, this institution, this system, this life...' So do something about them. 'But I don't know *what* to do!' So do nothing. 'But there's nothing I *can* do! If I leave work, I might lose my stuff, if I oppose my oppressor, I might get hurt, if I rock the boat, I might die'. So lose your stuff, get hurt and die. Better that than live in fear. 'Okay, you win, I agree; so *tell me what to do!*'

---

* Barry Long, *Only Fear Dies*

Telling ego what to do, or what the truth is, achieves nothing. Ego is a mechanism, with its *own* intelligence, so it cannot be mastered by simply *knowing* what to do, *deciding* what to do or *believing* it can be done, any more than the piano can be mastered through a firm decision, self-belief and an upbeat, can-do attitude. It is impossible (despite what middle-class Americans might say) to *positively think* one's way to being a great pianist, or *believe* until it happens—such an approach leads to frustrating effort and the idiotic conclusion that 'I'm just no good at this'. Although, with playful composure, it is possible to learn and have fun on the piano surprisingly quickly, mastery demands practice; constant practice.

Because the self is also unlike a piano; it goes everywhere, even into dream. It must therefore be mastered *everywhere*. What's more, the self is alive; it *intelligently* resists being mastered, and will use every trick in the book to subvert attempts to overcome it. And the book it uses, is *me*. The intelligence of ego is *my* intelligence, its memory is *my* memory, its fears and desires are *my* fears and desires. Ego uses me to perpetuate itself, and so I can only possibly defeat it—just as I can only possibly defeat the perfect egoic world—by *not being my self*, which means being conscious *of* my self, which means leaving behind the *why* (and the *what if*) and keeping solely, and permanently, to the *what*. The what *produces* the why, just as works that address what also explain why, just as, in truth, unself "produces" the entire universe. Going *looking* for why without being able to see what, may solve *a* problem, but it cannot solve *the* problem, because it cannot even see it.

§ 207.

There are traditional techniques that can be used to gain power over the self, such as sitting upright, taking some long, deep, diaphragmatic breaths, slowly placing the attention in the body (far more intelligent and present than the mind), watching whatever thoughts that appear as I would do a cinema screen and experiencing the physical sensation of emotion in the guts, across the chest, in the gullet or across the back of the head;* in short, slipping into the *totality* of the self-representation, a totality that can only be experienced unselfishly.

Such practice, occasionally called MEDITATION, releases self's hold on itself, lifting the stiff mask of causality and allowing *something else* to take the reins; but *by itself* it is useless and even harmful. The first reason for this is that most techniques of meditation are allied with Eastern philosophies which can no longer penetrate the intensely alienated and egoic modern self. The perennial philosophy as a whole remains, as Thoreau said, ever fresh, but ancient teachings do not and cannot speak to *this* context we are in—the hyper-modern Western world—which is one reason why there is a curiously artificial superficiality about the 'presence' and 'wisdom' of modern Buddhists, Advaitists and Taoists. Only a *living* teacher or teaching (or, more commonly, the painful intelligence of life) can break through the carapace of the personality. Consequently, the only kind of meditation which can work is extremely simple and virtually secular in its practical application. The problem with *that* is that it can be, and is, co-opted by a system which demands a passively blissful attitude to its plundering iniquity, half an hour of yoga in the Zen room before returning rejuvenated to the task of sucking up to the system; all of particular interest to the professional class, in which ORTHOPHILIA†—compulsive avoidance of consciousness and context by over-focus on one's emotional life, health or 'spirituality'—comes pre-installed. Orthophilia is built into Buddhism, which was originally a placeless, bodiless system that could be carried anywhere, and therefore especially attractive to tradesmen and merchants, as it is now to UI designers and lifestyle columnists.

Another reason why meditation in itself can be harmful, or at best useless, is that self does not exist merely on the level of thinking, or of surface fear and desire, but also in the subtler realm of psyche. Floating around in the subconscious plasma underneath the superficial me is one of the subtlest tricks that ego can play to keep itself in charge of the self. Self—particularly the masochistic self—will immerse itself in a semi-solipsistic dreamland of weirdness—of archetypes,

---

* Barry Long, *Meditation; A Foundation Course*
† See *The Apocalypedia*

angels, ascended masters and mystic mangos—and call this truth. People who habitually use hallucinogens are prone to this kind of schizoid egotism, which manifests as a curiously self-absorbed beatific abstraction, a sense that character is floating away and, despite wondrous niceness and spiritual activism, no *actual* interest in anyone else. Fake gurus, false prophets and spiritual flimflammers also use experience of psyche—often combined with the corrupted form of character called CHARISMA—to fool masses of spiritual masochists.

Spending a great deal of time meditating, being mindful, jingo-jangling to DMT or swimming through esoteric oceans, often ends up being an extended psyche-wank which severs one's participation to the represented world as it is—the shared canvas upon which the social self paints—which slowly becomes less interesting and less real, leaving 'mystic', meditating man, hovering round his magic, Romantic mind-realm, feeling tremendously wise and enlightened, while, in reality— the reality we share—he is well and truly up himself.

§208.

Meditation must be a small and dispensable element in a far wider project of self-mastery, or BEING; a word which has also been co-opted by promised godmen and beatific robe-wearers, but which means being conscious, without ego. All the time. It has to be all the time, or time will, in time, slip back in. If a gap remains in the day, or year, the pushed-aside past, and its wanting, worrying projection into the future, will creep in and again take control. Being is therefore unavailable to the half-hearted, to the emotionally *curious* and the intellectually *interested*. Only the man who *sees* that his house is on fire, and whose passionate intensity is up to the job of escaping, can get out and, *far* more difficult, stay out.

Conscious being is *found* in the world by refusing to get *lost* within it; by keeping consciousness in the body and not letting it get sucked out of the ears into gossip, or sucked out of the eyes into adverts. It is not necessary—indeed it is positively counterproductive—to *resist* the world, and its constant,

405

hypnotic pornography. To be in the body, to walk, to breathe, to see without looking *for*, diminishes interest in the sordid addictions of egoic society. Being seeks its own reflection in skies, even the polluted ones; space, even in the midst of warfare; and silence, even in the midst of the omnipresent compulsive prattle of the world attempting to draw consciousness onto the conveyor belt of its tedious likes and dislikes.

It is not easy to eat when I eat, shower when I shower, kiss when I kiss, to fully experience what I am doing, to watch the urge to leave what is, and to let go of the urge to focus on something, think about it, think about that, and then about that... and be lost again. It is not easy to give up fidgeting, thinking, picking, twiddling, checking, thinking, dropping things, losing things, thinking, worrying, jiggling, thinking, hoping, thinking, thinking, always *thinking*. It's not easy to give up constant, idle, unconscious mental-emotional masturbation and *be*, or, when necessary, *act*; but effort is not required. Consciously seeing, or feeling, is enough and, when the mind says 'I can't do this! I've failed!' seeing that too.

Being in this way answers every meaningful question containing the word 'I'; 'Why do I suffer?' 'Why am I here?' 'What should I do?' 'How do I deal with other people?' 'Do I love him / her?' 'What happens after I die?' and 'Why should I bloody well even *bother*?' All *answers* to these questions are meaningless unless I know what 'I' is; and nobody does know, because nobody *can* know, at least with the self. I can only be experienced, which *solves* the problem of 'Who am I?' and makes sense of every question with the word 'I' in it. Just as the question 'does God exist?' is meaningless without understanding what 'god' means, so if by 'I' I mean self, then there is clearly no reason why 'I' suffer, or why 'I' am here, and 'I' should obviously do whatever it takes to make sure 'I' get maximum fun, security or power out of any given situation, including my own life, for 'I' am soon going to wink out of existence never to be seen again. *Seriously* go looking for this 'I' however, in the *experience of being I now*, and I find something quite different, unimaginably different, to the person 'I' imagine or believe exists.

§ 209.

An egoic 'I' that has its limits in space, that is bounded by the factual-causal 'me' and 'mine', must always be afraid of the loss *of* 'me' and 'mine'. An egoic 'I' that has its limits in time, that is mortal, that comes to an end, must always be afraid *of* that end, of death. Such an 'I' *has* to spend its time in perpetual self-perpetuation—in constant noetic thinking, thelemic activity, visceral emoting and somatic sensuality—and constant self-preservation, in defending its thoughts, its actions, its emotions and its sensual pleasures from perceived attack or criticism. This project of endless self-perpetuation and self-preservation means, first of all, that 'I' am always blind to the moment, the situation—to life—which means that every single judgement 'I' makes *about* life, or about its life, is wrong (or right at the wrong time), and leads to misery, boredom or calamity. Secondly, building an impregnable armour for 'I' with the quantitative self, can only ever end when every *thing*, the entire universe, is imprisoned within it, forever; which is what 'I' has been doing since it first came on the scene, ten or twelve millennia ago. Living in such a universe, a perfect prison, the self-informed 'I' calls 'freedom', while *actual* freedom, the same 'I' calls 'imprisonment'.

The 'freedom' of 'I' therefore conceals complete FEAR, a constant restless tension which converts into anger, craving, guilt, self-indulgent misery, neediness and violence to conceal itself, and to suit the situation, but underneath remains the same basic, anxious, self-oriented COWARDLINESS. The violently angry man is a coward, the desperately needy man is a coward and the constantly depressed man is a coward.

Cowardliness is rarely seen for what it is, as civilisation offers so many ways to armour, or mask it—all of the shallow stimulants and tinpot offices and accolades of world, not to mention all the opportunities it affords us for having an indirect relation with our fellows; all serve to suppress, redirect and mask self's underlying terror of unselfish life. Self can hide its fear behind money, power, technology, bureaucratic formality, insignia and rank, racial or sexual bigotry, professional power, aimless thinking, intoxication or fun; it can and it does—until it can't any more, and then existential, egoic fear reveals itself as naked violence and perfect insanity.

To overcome fear, I must seek out experience which self can make no use of, that it fears or 'doesn't like'—aloneness, poverty, nature, extreme boredom, innocence, death, madness and love. For self, this is *pain*. The conscious man and woman not only faces pain, but actually goes looking for it; not in masochistic self-abasement, enjoying pain, or enjoying the reassuring sense of martyrdom it confers to ego; but in learning to be guided by it into painlessness. The pain—of embarrassment before others, confusion in a new situation, frustration at not really getting anywhere, hanging on to my self—is not tranquillised, but, like all authority, *obeyed*. Again, not masochistically, but with conscious intelligence. I do what the pain tells me to do; I accept the *discipline* (of self-mastery and tool-mastery), or the *abandonment* (of my thoughts perhaps, or of my silly dreams, or of my stupid lifestyle), or the *humility* (before the truth, before my craft, before my woman) it demands. I twitch to the impulses of 'this feels wrong', step *over* the trap of self-pity and self-judgement ('I'm such a loser, I'll never learn') and step *into* the right, into love, into the moment, or into a life lived without the scripts self writes to navigate uncertainty, without the armoured masks it builds around itself, without the techniques it employs to protect itself and without the emotions it consoles and justifies itself with. These scripts, masks, techniques and emotions all bring more pain, more suffering, but self knows of no other way, which is why it takes its fear to be 'freedom'.

Self thinks it is not free when it cannot [modally] be or get what it wants to; but everything that self can be or get occurs in, and as, a *representation* of reality, which, being entirely factual and causal, is already and always conditioned—by fear of *not* being and getting—and so *without* freedom. Unconscious man does not realise that *actual* FREEDOM only exists *out* of the world, in the thing-in-itself of consciousness. This means the more *intensely conscious* you are, the freer—the more *fearless*—you feel, which is why, although the self of the conscious man must be free, he attacks limitations on intensity with far greater ferocity than he does limitations on mere activity. It's also why ordinary people can never be *persuaded* of their lack of freedom, why lack of true freedom is experienced as perverse, nauseating*, *devitalised* unreality, and why the first and last step out of the world prison is not in what self does, but in what I am. If I don't free myself *before* escaping, I will carry the prison out with me.

§ 210.

Some people are lucky enough to lose everything. Not things, or not necessarily things, but the thing-making self that the world has bestowed upon them, made up of laws and legitimations, idols and beliefs, and all the other spectacular representations their selves are born into and formed by. Some are sensitive enough to never really have had much of a grip on this representation in the first place, or for it to never really to have had much of a grip on them. For such rare and remarkable people the blow of collapse, when it comes, is softened. They never fully departed from nothing, and so, when the world of things falls, they do not fall fully with it.

A man who has built his self entirely from the spectacle, by contrast, is, when the hammer falls, plunged into disorienting futility and nihilism, an appalling realisation that, in all honesty, nothing—no thing—can nourish him, no religious doctrine, no rational ideology, no worldly pleasure or power—all is, ultimately, purposeless vanity, and all men, comfortable in this wasteland, are hollow shadows.† More contemptible yet, far more repulsive than the selves of others, is one's *own* self. It is *self*-contempt that marks the beginning of the journey to the outside of the given coordinates of the social spectacle; but the end is not certain. Liberation and genius are possible, but madness and defeat are more likely. What's more, both paths look, to the self, the same; which is why the self refuses to tread either. The ordinary man sees genius, liberation, truth, all the things his heart yearns for; but that way madness lies, better to rot in safety.

---

* Jean-Paul-Sartre, *Nausea*
† T.S. Eliot, *The Hollow Men*

Love, pain or rapture have broken both the genius and the madman, and enabled both to see through the veil of representation—which is how they can speak such unearthly truths. They both pursue their vision through the same rent, with the same passion, knowing that *there* is the truth, and, running into the unknown, they both *appear* to be in radical free-fall, their minds having metaphysically caved in; the ground of ordinary life—objective facticity and causality—having collapsed from underneath them. But appearance is deceptive. The schizoid man has lost the objective world, but subjective nous, thelema and viscera live on. His self is suspended in mid-air, buffeted by random gusts of emotion, strange and terrifying thoughts and bizarre volitional instincts; still subject to the suffering of the past and the misery of the world. The conscious man, by contrast, has surrendered his *full being* to unself. He holds to a certainty, an affirmation, a yes—*at all [modal] costs*—which is denied the madman. The world crumbles around and within the man alive, but he has released his attachment to its foundations, and so he doesn't fall with it, but remains standing; on a new earth, watered with tears of joy, of gratitude. He is not, after all mad and sick and dead; it was just winter, and now it is spring. Life—not mere living, but *life*—will go on.

§211.

Self, facing the end, indulges in WORLD DESPAIR, analogous to the ghastly mask of grim woe that stares back in the bathroom mirror when splitting up with a lover, or in the middle of a deep self-pity wank. It goes without saying that the death of loved ones, agonising loss and the destruction of all that is good on earth are cause for heart-splitting sorrow; but sorrow is not despair. Sorrow breaks self open, stills me to my core and lets in the awful, glorious truth of life—even as (indeed *because*) all forms of life are lost. Despair is epic self-indulgence, not listening to pain, or accepting it, but giving in to it.

The conscious man knows that *dread is a substitute for destiny*; that pain is not just a part of life, to be unliked in despair, but the voice of the whole. He welcomes pain. Not happily (for shit does, indeed, stink), or fatalistically (for life is not, in reality, a painful business) and not passively either (for there is almost certainly, sooner or later, conscious action to be taken) but in an essential surrender to the fact of pain; to *face up*—without detours into addiction—to what is; 'facing it, always facing it, that's the way to get through. Face it'.* This reveals the transdimensional truth of pain, the whole of it, the cause of it and the destiny of it; what *must* be done. Such revelation might be a minor change of direction (coming clean or taking it on the chin) or it might be a major realisation (that I am a cell in my own body, or that I have no right to be unhappy) or it might be a complete experience of heartbreak, which is actually self-break, the split that lets the darkness in; the dark that is the last thing self dares face.

So it is with death. Ego runs from it, dares not look at it, dares not talk of it (unless following a sombre script), dares not touch it, in mind or in body, unless as a joke, to relieve the tension of it, or as horror and gore, to feed on the excitement of it. Conscious man lives with death, as medieval man did, and knows it as a friend, as primal man did. He speaks of it with his loved ones, and with his children. As civilisation collapses he holds to it, because he knows beyond knowing that death, like his own consciousness, cannot be touched by the horror, the horror, of the world; as D.H.Lawrence cried, 'What a joy! What gladness to think that whatever humanity does, it cannot seize hold of the kingdom of death'.†

§212.

What does the body do when I enter the kingdom of death? What does self do when it realises that self is not here? What happens when I *recognise* a truth I already knew? What is my unfailing reaction to character in a man or woman? What happens when consciousness witnesses self warped truthfully and absurdly by unself? How does the conscious mind react to release from the frame through which it was filtering reality, when what is actually happening is seen from a larger or

---

* Joseph Conrad, *The Inheritors*
† D.H.Lawrence, *Women in Love*

altogether different perspective, when I realise I'm dreaming, or realise I am waking, or when I abandon the likes and dislikes through which my reality is filtered, and see something as it really is? How does the conscious self react to sacrifice, to seeing someone put their entire self on the line for quality; for unselfish love or for unselfish truth? What happens when primal genius makes an anarchic mess of conscious awareness, or when I jam with liquid scenius? What happens when I fall *fully* into the abyss, or when I cuddle the void?

Self breaks. When I witness innocence, when sudden, astonishing beauty opens into the moment, when I see an old friend after a long absence, when I feel profound, parachuting relief, when taboos and totems are broken, when masks and cliches crack, when expectation is thwarted and *hanging on* lets go, when my heart fills with joy as I give what I want to *take* over to what I have to *give*, or when mad, mad absurdity turns the world upside down, then self is broken by the quality of unself; and the sound of self-break is laughter.

Great laughter comes from great COMEDY, the comedy of life; one with unself, one, therefore, with character and, through tone and timing, one with the timeless, ineffable now. This is why great comedians are miraculously present (and therefore miraculously attractive) and tragic misfits, (and therefore tragically out of time). It's also why comedy *explained*, like the metaphor that so much comedy is based on, instantly becomes unfunny. Great comedy is also one with the self, and so, because selves change over time and space, so does comedy, or sense of humour, which is always unique and hyper-specific (gendered, cultured). This is why a brilliant witticism is so rarely funny when recycled, why time-immune comic cliches (such as Dad jokes) provoke groans of pain and why Shakespeare's comedies are only funny when a brilliant comedian reinterprets them (and then not very). It's also why comedy and horror (or disgust, or schizophrenic madness) are formally the same; break of self is hilarious in one context, and dreadful or even terrifying in another. Break of wind also.

For self alone, there is no laughter, just approval and satisfaction; along with a total inability to separate comedy from horror. Just as ego's tears are self-pity over its sad, sad story, so its laughter is diffusion of danger, showing deference, demonstrating status, reinforcing egoic group-boundaries, correcting non-compliant attitudes with punitive, sniggering mockery or relieving anxiety with naughty guffaws. Selfless laughter cannot be heard in courts or in classrooms, in monotonous philosophy or in monotheistic bibles, in important meetings or in important news reports, in civilised homes or in civilised orgasms; only the grim, shameless or giddy laugh of ego, protecting itself. There is a strangely declarative quality to egoic laughter, as if we are being *told* that something is funny, or a cheerless ugliness to it; the crude laughter of the sadist, eating another, or of the masochist, being eaten.

If self is in charge of self, free laughter is a threat. Self, faced with ridicule, absurdity and joy reacts with confusion, anxiety and anger; or, more often than not, it does not react at all. Ego is unable to look at a critical truth that lies over its own fence and cannot bear to try; it gets annoyed when comedy directs it outward (or inward), while character, unless it is safely entertaining, does nothing but provoke unease. Ego finds comic images of distorted representation horrifying, because ego *lives* in representation. It becomes anxious when it is playfully invited to release the frames it depends on to filter reality into manageable forms, when delight demands self-forgetting, when cheer greets its moods; and it becomes terrified—a terror which instantly converts to fury—if its status is threatened by mockery, or any of the masks or taboos, with which that status is protected, are taken lightly. Lightness of touch, an unserious attitude to the 'sacred' and all kinds of wild playfulness vex it. The self-informed self detests sacrifice, unless as weepy sentiment and is deeply uneasy in the presence of anyone capable of sacrifice. It clings onto itself, onto what it *has* and what it *knows* and what it *does* and how it *feels*, because it *is* clinging, and release is unthinkable oblivion.

Unself, consciousness, does not react in this way, because it is not self. The ordinary conscious reaction to the release of self, to the break of self, or to plunging through the transparency of it, is laughter. Or tears. Or both.

Afterword

The traditional word for 'unself' is 'God', but, thanks to thousands of years of literalist thought, it is now virtually meaningless. When the word is uttered we think of an *unknown fact* with a causal relation to the *known facts* of the world. We do not think of an *unknowable* quality, with a non-causal presence in the world, because this cannot be thought of, only experienced, which is why anyone who has ever said anything meaningful about God has spoken non-literally, through metaphor and myth, through art and craft, through practice and being, and through reasoning to the limits of the knowable.

This speaking is not to *give* an experience of God, or unself, because it is not a thing, and so cannot be given. We can metaphorically speak of an artist giving us a truth, allowing us to *participate* in it, but anyone who thinks or presents truth as something that can be given, has turned it into mere *fact*; a thing amongst things. A shoddy, mercenary attitude if ever there was one*; for what can be given can be *given back*, and in rational fact, *must* be given back, or 'repaid'. This is the attitude of the resentful giver or worker,† of the 'misunderstood artist' ('history will prove *me* right'), of secular utilitarianism and of sacred religion; the universe of debt that priests force upon their subjects—you are given your life by God (or by the state), and so you *owe* Him and, as his representatives on earth, us—and that those same subjects console their powerless selves with, reasoning that '*I* shall be rewarded, and *they* shall be punished' in hell, or in a future incarnation.

---

* Søren Kierkegaard, *Concluding Unscientific Postscript*
† The Baghavad Gita (tr. Brodbeck)

If the truth could be given, or taught, or slotted into the head of the listener like a floppy disk, then the world, saturated with knowledge, would be enlightened a billion times over. In fact, our worldbrain, the omniscient, omnipresent and omnipotent internet, would, by this reckoning, *be* God, and, because we love and obey it, we would be God's chosen people (a belief which few people consciously hold to—it's too sick— but which most people unconsciously live by). But the truth cannot be given, because it is not a thing. The truth is and can only be in *letting go* of things, of *all* things, which means letting go of the self in which and as which all things exist.

Naturally, this is impossible while I take that which lets go—I—to also be a thing; but this, the source of all futile therapy and self-help (self cannot let go of itself any more than a hand can), is all the self, by itself, can do. The self is a thing-making machine. If it is self-informed—if there is noth- ing in my experience but self—it will continually reproduce itself by continually looking for things it can be, things it can grasp, or things that it can get. If it is presented with no-thing, it will just get annoyed; and then start looking for *why* it is or should get annoyed. It spends its life doing this, until it dies.

There are two ways to die. The first is to have self taken away, by the death of the body. The second is to let the *domi- nance* of self over my experience be given up to *something else*. The words we usually use for such giving up are 'surrender', 'sacrifice', 'passion' and 'love'. This is what it means to 'love God, with all your heart, and with all your soul, and with all your mind'.* Not to be a subject-thing, here, loving an ob- ject-thing there—which is *idolatry*—nor even to give up self itself—the thinking, emoting, willing, perceiving mechanism which generates such separation—but to give up the dominat- ing force which generates such separation *for* itself; the ego. The traditional term for this egoic force is 'the devil'—and the traditional term for that which generates or sustains the ego, the world which ego has built—is 'the devil's works'.

To conclude. Love God, with all your heart, and with all your will, and with all your mind, and with all your body, and renounce the devil, and all his works. Now and forever.

So be it.

* Matthew 22:36-40

Index

A

D

dog 61, 97, 98-100, 297, 301

domestication 301, **327-329**, 379

total 375

Dostoevsky, Fyodor 283

dread 100, 312, 329, 335, 377, 410; *See also* **despair**

dream 34, 59, 71, **97-101**, 169, 184, 217, 241, 243, 249, 296, 303, 368, 371, 386, 392, 399-400, 403

dreamlife of the world **101**, 329, 386-387

lucid **97**

E

East, the 129, 331, **337-338**, 341, 352, 390

co-opted 404

egg 73, 296, 313

chicken or 73, 96

ego 28, **50**, 56, 63, 77-78, 100-101, 116-121, 142-143, 158-160, 166-173, 177-207, 226, 245, 248, 253, 313, 316, 320, 323, 330, 337-338, 347, 367, 373, 375-376, 384, 397-398, 402-404, 408-411; *See also* **self**

birth of 110, 162, 313, 316-319, 321

fear / suffering of 207-217, 225-227, 378, 409, 411-412

lack of discernment of 59-60, 80, 84, 148-151, 181-182, 185-195, 205-206, 262-265, 268, 275, 290-291; *See also* **discernment, discrimination**

male 128-130, 132, 136-137

no 66, 163, 303-304, 313, 339, 390, 391, 400-404

under attack 151-152, 186, 217-224, 228-238, 239-242, 245, 248, 250, 258, 261, 272-274, 283-284

world / society / system of 35, 78, 90, 132, 139, 150, 159, 168, 176, 243, 245-246, 249, 251, 253-257, **259-261**, 317-324, 329, 340-343, 345, 350, 353-355, 358, 363-365, 371-372, 375,

381-391, 397, 398, 400, 403, 405; *See also* **system**

worldviews of **22**, 31, 75-76

Egypt 176, 324, 330

Einstein, Albert 26, 87

emotion 44, 72, 105, 125, 131, 139, 141, 159, 172, 184, **191-195**, 198, 211, 214, 221, 224, **236-238**, 255, 275, 281, 329, 352-353, 369, 373, 401-403; *See also* **feeling**

love is not 141

management 240

'mental-emotional' 275, 316, 321, 327, 363, 385, 401

empathy 70, 78, 106, 124, 150, **157**, **170-171**, 182, 187, 201, 244, 255, 268, 285, 300, 308, 311, 320, 328, 360, 367-368, 401

enhancement See **self-mastery**

foundation of ethics 186

foundation of morality 157

England 328, 399

eternity **33**, 40, 57, 85-86, 165, 274, 335, 377, 395

artistic 281

Euclid 87, 333

evil, the problem of 199

evolution 89, 294

excuse 220

existential threat / primal fear **51**, 105, 110, 115, 134, 161, **172**, 177, 198, 207, 222, 283, 319, 321

first appearance of 317

expectation 60, 173, 183, 266; *See also* **hope**

experience 25, 42, 44, **54**, 58, 83, 92, 115, 165, 266, 338, 398

expert 71, 106, 232, 238, 253, 332, 351, **358**, 373

exposure 102, 136, 140, 189, 207, 233, 273

adolescent **116-117**

in impro 407-408

of genius 273, 283

extroversion 111, **118-121**, 132, 182, 205, 251

F

G

H

Q

U

ugliness 60, **166-169**, 253, 273, 327
unconscious 32, 50, 78-79, 95, 105, 108, 173, **177-179**, 193, 236, 263, 337, 353, 365, 370, 382, 383
universe 22-24, **24**, 27-32, 38-39, 51-52, 64, 66, 82-86, 95-96, 107, 145, 177, 180, 186, 190, 199, 218, 221, 248, 252, **292**, 295, 303-305, 317-318, 332, 334-335, 342-343, 347, 351, 367, 371, 396-397, 403
unreal 28
unself 15-430
    existential threat of 46, 51, 172-173, 231-236, 242, 250, 255, 319, 329-330, 336, 344, 357, 365, 381
    expression of 65-66, 102
    genius and 271-272
    primal 303-304
    primal pain of 198-199
    woman is 128, 130
unthinkable 33
Upanishads, the 338, 339
utilitarianism 64, 73, 187; *See also* **technique**
utility tipping point 314, 372

V

vagina 100, 132, 145, 288
Van Gogh, Vincent 59, 100, 163, 283
value 362
vernacular 343, 351, **355-357**, 365, 381
violation 215
virtual 53, 169, 171, 365, **367-370**
    addiction 367
viscera 15, 34, 52, 54, 78, 96, 99, 101, 105, 110, 123, 131, 144, 149, 170, 173, 177, 194, 199, 207-209, 215, 220, 228, 234, 247, 255, 267, 284, 291-292, 298, 321, 381, 395
    as quality 55
    as representation 316
    technology 314

W

wanting 106-107, 120, 134, 141, 167, 172-173, 191, 196, 198, **206**, 211, 249, 251-252, 308, 316, 398; *See also* **like and dislike**
weird 98-99, 365
West, the 112-113, 129, 133, 243, **337-338**, 341, 352, 377, 384, 386, 390, 404
will; *See* **thelema**
Wittgenstein, Ludwig 41, 44, 65, 74, 336
woman, female, feminine 121-149, 189, 196, 271, 277, 295-296, 328, 330, 335, 355, 381
    primal 310
    real **139**
Wordsworth, William 353
work 147, 184, 227, 235, 256, 259, 334, 357-358, 364, 375, 377, 382, 393, 410; *See also* **play**
    man's noble 124, 127
world-break 391
worry 183, 192, 198, 204, **206**, 224, 226
wren, the little 47, 298

X

Xanadu 175
Xenophanes 333

Y

Yahweh 94, 118, 119, 335-336
yes, saying 278, 410

Z

Zen 348, 404
Zeno of Elea 40, 74, 333
Zeus 28, 94
Žižek, Slavoj 43, 338
zombie 51, 329
zone, being in the 286
Zorp, the Archon 232